25-A-3

ESSAYS ON ARMS CONTROL AND NATIONAL SECURITY

ALMA COLLEGE

APR 2 0 1987

DOCUMENTS COLL.

For sale by the Superintendent of Documents, U.S. Government Printing Office
Washington, D.C. 20402

ESSAYS ON ARMS CONTROL AND NATIONAL SECURITY

Edited by
Bernard F. Halloran

U.S. ARMS CONTROL AND DISARMAMENT AGENCY
WASHINGTON, D.C.

U.S. Arms Control and Disarmament Agency
Publication 123

Individual essays in this collection are protected under International and Pan-American Copyright Conventions.

Library of Congress Cataloging in Publication Data
Main entry under title:

Essays on Arms Control and National Security.

Includes bibliographical references.

1. Nuclear arms control—United States.
2. Nuclear arms control—Soviet Union.
3. Nuclear warfare.
4. Deterrence (Strategy).
5. United States—National Security.
6. Soviet Union—National Security.

I. Halloran, Bernard
JX 1974.7.E84   1986   327.1'74   86–25932

LIBRARY
ALMA COLLEGE
ALMA, MICHIGAN

CONTENTS

PREFACE

When President Kennedy signed the bill creating the Arms Control and Disarmament Agency in September 1961, he described the attempt to achieve disarmament and arms control agreements as "a complex and difficult task." After a quarter-century of arduous effort—and prolonged, often intense debate on the problems posed by modern weapons and Soviet policy—President Kennedy's verdict remains one on which all sides can doubtless still agree.

The essays in this volume, collected to commemorate ACDA's twenty-fifth anniversary, span not only ACDA's lifetime, but the four decades of the nuclear era. The articles were chosen to provide a healthy sampling of the arms-control-related speculation and controversy that have occupied us in those years.

Some of the essays, like Fred C. Iklé's prescient "After Detection—What?" have long been classics in their own right. Others, like Paul Nitze's "Assuring Strategic Stability in a Era of Détente," have, apart from their contemporary interest, a historical significance, as important markers along the road we have traveled. All are cogent expressions of their varying points of view.

Two broad features of the collection stand out. First, we observe the persistence of certain questions and dilemmas. Writing in our own decade, for example, Robert S. McNamara and Albert Wohlstetter address—and offer sharply contrasting answers to—questions not unlike those which occupied Bernard Brodie and William W. Kaufmann thirty and more years ago.

Secondly, a number of the essays reflect the lessons we have learned over the past twenty-five years. Clearly, we have come a long distance in the past quarter-century. There have been discoveries. There have been many disappointments. Thomas C. Schelling's "What Went Wrong with Arms Control," Robert W. Tucker's "The Nuclear Debate," and James R. Schlesinger's "Maintaining Global Stability," among other essays, reflect these experiences.

The greatest significance of this collection may lie in its energy and variety. As these writings attest, over the last four decades, Americans have poured enormous intellectual energy and creativity into the task of controlling nuclear weapons and building a more stable peace. We have found ourselves face-to-face with a very difficult situation: a weapon capable of causing human annihilation, side by side with an adversary deeply at odds with freedom and heavily dependent upon military instruments to maintain his legitimacy at home and his prestige abroad.

This has been a hard reality, shot through with dilemmas for the democratic nations. It should not surprise us that the opinions of these writers frequently clash head on. Such disagreement is the outward sign of the very freedom we cherish and defend.

In the long history of mankind, twenty-five years is a short time. If it seems long to us, it is not only because it is our own time, but also because the stakes have been exceptionally high. Our fundamental goals—in President Kennedy's words, "the survival and the success of liberty" and the prevention of nuclear war—have thus far been served. But our work is by no means over.

Dogmatism has been defined as "the tendency to identify the goal of thinking with the point at which we become tired of thinking." In this perilous age, we cannot afford to become tired of thinking.

More clash of opinion on arms control will be necessary, and more sober reflection—to gain a clearer-eyed vision of the dangers we face, and to preserve in our national spirit the delicate balance between realism and hope.

September 26, 1986   *Kenneth L. Adelman*

1948

THE ATOM BOMB AS POLICY MAKER

Bernard Brodie

Bernard Brodie was Professor of Political Science at U.C.L.A. until his death in 1978. His pioneering works include *The Absolute Weapon*, 1946; *Strategy in the Missile Age*, 1959; *Escalation and the Nuclear Option*, 1966; and *War and Politics*, 1973.

It is now three years since an explosion over Hiroshima revealed to the world that man had been given the means of destroying himself. Eight atomic bombs have now been detonated—assuming that the three "atomic weapons" tested at Eniwetok were in fact bombs—and each was in itself a sufficient warning that the promise of eventual benefits resulting from the peacetime use of atomic energy must count as nothing compared to the awful menace of the bomb itself. The good things of earth cannot be enjoyed by dead men, nor can societies which have lost the entire material fabric of their civilization survive as integrated organisms.

Yet the dilemma nevertheless faces us that the enforcement of tolerable behavior among nations will continue for an indefinite time in the future to depend at least occasionally upon coercion or the threat of it, that the instruments of coercion against Great Powers will most likely be found only in the hands of other Great Powers (who can dispense with them only by acknowledging their readiness to forfeit whatever liberties they may happen

Reprinted with permission of *Foreign Affairs*. Copyright © 1948 by *Foreign Affairs*.

blessedly to possess), and that those instruments appear fated, largely because of those same imperfections of our society which make power necessary, to include the atomic bomb and perhaps other comparable instruments of mass destruction.

Individuals may retreat from this dilemma behind a barrage of high moral protestation, usually combined with glowing predictions of a better world to be. Such retreat is rendered doubly sweet because it is more often than not accompanied by applause, especially from the intellectual wing of our society. But the nation as a whole cannot retreat from the problem, and those who desert simply leave the others to think it through as best they can.

The impact of the atomic bomb on United States policy has thus far been evidenced most clearly in the almost frantic effort to secure the adoption of a system of international control of atomic energy. It is difficult if not impossible to find an historical precedent for the eagerness with which this nation has pursued an endeavor which, if successful, would deprive it of the advantages of monopoly possession of a decisive military weapon. To be sure, the monopoly is bound to be temporary, but that has always been true of new weapons, the monopoly possession of which has usually been jealously guarded for as long as possible. The United States is even now behaving in the customary manner concerning all new weapons other than those based on the explosive release of atomic energy, a fact which in itself sufficiently demonstrates that the exceptional American position on atomic energy control is based on something other than national generosity. That "something other" is of course a well-warranted fear of living in a world which morally and politically is little different from the one we have known but which in addition is characterized by multilateral possession of atomic weapons.

But the fear which engendered the pursuit of international control also provoked the resolve that any control scheme must contain within itself practically watertight guarantees against evasion or violation. That was and remains a wholly reasonable resolve, but its inevitable consequence is that it greatly reduces the chance of securing the requisite agreement. Two years of work by the United Nations Atomic Energy Commission have resulted in some illumination of the problem but almost no progress towards a solution. American initiative in securing formal suspension of the activities of the Commission is a plain acknowledgment of that fact.

But where does that leave us? It leaves us, for one thing, with the unwanted bomb still in our hands, and, so far as we know, still exclusively in our hands. It leaves us also under the compulsion to go on building more bombs, and better ones if possible. We must continue our search for a workable *and secure* international control system by any corridor which reflects even a glimmer of hope of success, but we must also begin to consider somewhat more earnestly and responsibly than we have thus far what it will mean for the nation to adjust to an atomic age devoid of international controls.

The ramifications of that adjustment process are legion, but certainly they involve above all a continuing reconsideration of the effects of the bomb upon our plans for the national security. For those to whom "national security" appears too narrow a concept for an atomic age, there are at least three observations that might be made.

In the first place, as the world is now organized, and as it now operates, American security is for all practical purposes synonymous with world security. It is no longer a question whether our political leaders understand that to be the case, though there is much evidence that in the main they do so understand. It is simply that we have reached a stage where large-scale war without American participation borders on the inconceivable. Secondly, national policy, which is perforce concerned primarily with national security, is the only policy upon which we as citizens can hope to exercise any direct influence, and it is our only channel for affecting international policy. Thirdly, the projects of policy planners are much more likely to prosper if they conform at least occasionally to aspirations which the man on the street fully shares and understands. To him, and to the politician who serves him, the security of the United States is supremely meaningful and important. World security, on the other hand, is an abstraction which gains meaning—at least meaning sufficient to induce him to pay a price for it—only to the extent that he is persuaded that American security is enhanced thereby. The difference may seem superficially a semantic one, but it is more than that. It affects very profoundly the question of the kind and degree of risks one will accept and the character of the price one will pay to achieve security. It certainly affects the basic method by which we proceed to our goal.

Lest we adopt too patronizing an attitude towards the convictions of the layman or the politician, let us consider for a moment the propositions, however dimly he may perceive them, upon which those convictions rest. At least four such propositions may be listed, all of which are basically unaffected by the existence of the atomic bomb.

I. International organization at its existing level of development is obviously inadequate to guarantee either world or American security. This fact explains and partly justifies the preoccupation of most students of international relations with procedures for developing and improving existing bases for international coöperation. But exclusive preoccupation with such ends leaves a large gap which it is inexcusable to ignore, and that for a reason which provides our second proposition.

II. It is clear from any dispassionate and realistic appraisal of the forces at work in international relations today—the kind of appraisal which it is the first responsibility of the specialist in the field to provide—that a highly reliable and effective mechanism for the collective guarantee of security can hardly be deemed to lie within the range of conditions reasonably to be expected within our time. At any rate the degree of probability is not high. The atomic bomb makes that circumstance more tragic, but it does not otherwise alter it. However much the mechanism described deserves working for, it is certainly a matter of ordinary prudence to take heavy insurance against failure or even against too slow a rate of achievement.

III. Whatever our predictions concerning the future of international coöperation, they must take into account the following basic dilemma: The pursuit of security against war—the objective which takes precedence above all others in the modern world—is not inevitably identical with the pursuit of smoother and more intimate international cooperation, the two being especially divergent where the latter holds out little promise of significant success. Where conciliation fails, one must take steps which may make that failure more certain and more complete. Where the opponent refuses to reason, one can only appease or threaten. There are wide variations in the flexibility and subtlety with which the statesman may either appease or threaten, and the degree of skill which he brings to his task is supremely important. However, it is in the main true that appeasement tends to encourage further unreasonable or "impossible" demands; while the threat or warning, however effective at the moment, tends to wound the opponent and to stimulate in him the desire to be less vulnerable to threat in the future. Nevertheless, the statesman may at any time be faced with a choice between these two alternatives and these alone. He will do well to guarantee for himself in advance the maximum of freedom of choice *between* them.

IV. For the purpose of threat or warning, adequate national strength is indispensable. The statesman who possesses it can choose whether to appease or warn; the one who lacks it can only appease. As General Eisenhower so neatly put it, strength is required to coöperate, weakness can only beg.

In a world in which none of the Great Powers felt threatened by one or more of the others, we could expect to see a salutary neglect of security devices resting on the above propositions. But it is clear from the recent behavior of our Government that it feels itself exposed to a threat from the Soviet Union, and it is almost equally clear that the measures which it is pursuing in response to that feeling of exposure enjoy the broadest popular support. Moreover, some of those measures undeniably entail aggravation of the tensions between the Soviet Union and ourselves. Is it possible to look past the difficulties of the moment to see the basic reasons for that concern?

A senior American naval officer told this writer not so long ago that "American strategic calculations concerning the requirements of *great* wars must envisage the Soviet Union as the opponent, if for no other reason than that she is the only foreign Power whose defeat would require great exertions on our part."

That is a good, simple working rule for an admiral. It recalls the old doctrine of the "natural enemy." It reminds us also that there would still be a problem to concern us even if the Soviet Union were something other than what it is; and that the fact that the power system of today is a bipolar one has dominant implications of its own. The main trouble with a bipolar system, as a colleague has so tersely put it, is that the target is all too unambiguous. The admiral's statement reminds us also that concern with security is a concern with possibilities, and not necessarily with high probabilities or certainties.

Nevertheless, if the reason which the admiral gave were the only one which counted, there is no doubt that our attitudes and our efforts concerning security would be profoundly more relaxed than they are. There are special reasons residing in the character of the Soviet state (or, if one insists, in the difference between our two systems) and in the events resulting from that character (or difference in characters) which account for the special dangers and the present acute degree of tension.

There is not space here, or competence on the part of the writer, to permit any analysis of the character of the Soviet state or of Soviet-American relations during the past three years. Nor is such analysis necessary for our purpose. All we need to guide us are a few general observations which will be obvious when pointed out but which may nevertheless strike the reader as having some flavor of novelty.

First of all, one might suggest that students of international relations have perhaps muddied the waters unduly by a somewhat excessive concern with Soviet motives, particularly with the question whether the motives behind Soviet obstreperousness, and worse, are primarily defensive or aggressive. That is not to argue that motives are unimportant. Nor is it to complain that motives are always difficult if not impossible to fathom, which is certainly true. The psychoanalyst is obliged professionally to reach conclusions about motives, and it is noteworthy that his interpretations usually differ from those of the person whose behavior he is examining. What is being suggested here is simply 1, that the act may dwarf in importance, so far as counteraction is concerned, the motive from which it leaps; and 2, that a motive which stems from convictions which we cannot appreciably influence or alter by any reasonable acts on our part ceases thereby to be of much operational significance to us.

The significance of the facts that the Soviet Union is a police state and that its organizing ideology posits among other things the necessity of world revolution has been sufficiently elaborated elsewhere. But a point which is generally overlooked and which is of at least equal significance is the following: the distinctive ideology being all-pervading, it quite naturally includes a special interpretation of previously existing patterns of international relations. That fact means, among other things, that the reassuring analogies which one can draw from western history concerning long periods of amicable relations between states of widely differing ideologies are of much diminished relevance. In almost all those instances we find ministers who otherwise represent the most widely differing persuasions holding a common approach to the conduct of foreign affairs, a common respect for the rules of the game.

Those rules, we are often told, elevated hypocrisy to the status of a first principle. "A diplomat," as the old saw goes, "is an honest man sent abroad to lie for his country." But there is another aphorism to the effect that hypocrisy has at least the merit of giving lip service to virtue. The "hypocrisy" of western statesmen has frequently enough been self-deception. The constant appeal to higher principles in the instruments of diplomacy has almost always been something more than window dressing. The margin of difference between declaration and performance, though wide, nevertheless had limits which the statesman well understood and upon which he could base his expectations. It is a common pattern in all civilizations that behavior falls short of the aspirations reflected in the norms, but the norms are not thereby bereft of importance.

The Communist philosophy explicitly and systematically rejects the previously accepted norms of international conduct. The principle of expediency in the approach to the existing pattern is not simply indulged in, it is avowed and exalted.

The final and conclusive point relevant here is that the Soviet Union is a military state if not a militaristic one. Welfare, in the form of consumers goods and services, is subordinated to military requirements to a degree which also has probably never before been approximated in modern history—certainly not in Nazi Germany, which vaunted "guns before butter." While the milder kinds of Socialists have often been pacifists, no real Communist philosopher from Marx to the present has ever had the slightest use for pacifism. Marx, indeed, and Lenin too, took frequent occasion to bend their matchless scorn upon it.

The points just stated are not matters of opinion. They are the kind of conclusions which any normal intelligence operation provides, except that the factual evidence which supports them is far more abundant and incontrovertible than is usually available to the intelligence officer in his general run of problems. It is the kind of evidence upon which policy, as distinct from hope or yearning, must be based.

These conclusions do not point to the inevitability of war. They do point, however, to a policy the realization of which will at each recurrence of crisis serve to persuade the Soviet leaders that the expedient solution is the peaceful one. Such a policy would no doubt also serve to reduce the frequency of crises. For the saving grace of the Soviet philosophy so far as international relations are concerned is that, unlike the Nazi ideology, it incorporates within itself no time schedule. Hitler had to accomplish his ultimate goals not only within his lifetime but within his years of vigor. The Soviet attitude appears to be much more opportunistic. The Soviets may be unshakably convinced that ultimately there must be war between the Communist world and what they call the "capitalist" one. Since that conviction is a cardinal doctrine of their faith, we can probably do nothing within the present generation to alter it. What we can do, however, is to persuade them each time the question arises that "The time is not yet!"

The problem to which we now return is the problem of how to accomplish this act of persuasion in an atomic age, when the already precious objective of peace is made immeasurably more precious by the immeasurably enhanced horror of the alternative. However, since preoccupation with the horror has brought us nothing positive thus far, and offers exceedingly little promise of doing so in the future, it is time for a shift to a more sober position. There are a large number of questions pressing for an answer, and consideration of many of them requires appraisal of the atomic bomb as an instrument of war—and hence of international politics—rather than as a visitation of a wrathful deity.

No doubt the first question concerns the effect of the atomic bomb upon the basic power relationship between the United States and the Soviet Union. Postponing for a moment such qualifying considerations as stem from our present but admittedly temporary monopoly, we see at once that one of the most fundamental changes created by the atomic bomb is that it makes possible *for the first time* decisive military action between the two great centers of power.

In a brilliant study published during the recent war, Professor William T. R. Fox based much of his analysis of Great Power relationships on the proposition that a war between the Anglo-American bloc on the one side and the Soviet Union on the other would be almost inevitably bound to result in a stalemate, and that common recognition of this fact by both sides would powerfully influence (presumably for the better) relations between them. His explanation follows:

> The pressure which either the Soviet Union or the Western powers can bring to bear upon the other in its main centers of power is surely much less than is implied by the statement that the two are the strongest forces in the world. Not only are the points of direct contact few and inaccessible but the centers are widely separated. The armed power of each can be effectively carried only part of the way to the other. American control over the seaward approaches to the New World will in any foreseeable future render a transoceanic operation by the Soviet Union impossible. The massive superiority of its land army should on the other hand discourage the Western powers from attempting a large-scale amphibious operation against hostile shores controlled by the Red Army.[1]

That proposition was not only true at the time of writing, but it could also be argued that no conceivable evolution of the instruments of war then publicly known could have significantly modified it. To be sure, strategic bombing was gradually developing in effectiveness, and the striking range of bomber aircraft was slowly but steadily increasing. However, with the experience of World War II, none but extremists could argue that strategic bombing was sufficient unto itself for winning a war against a great nation. Moreover, despite the increasing range of bomber aircraft, there were a variety of technical reasons, quite impressive in the aggregate, to support the conclusion that a comprehensive program of strategic bombing over what might be called intercontinental distances would not become practicable "in the foreseeable future." That conclusion assumed,

---

[1] "The Super Powers: The United States, Britain, and The Soviet Union—Their Responsibility for Peace." New York: Harcourt, Brace, 1944, p. 102.

of course, an evolutionary improvement in known types of
bombs and incendiaries, roughly approximating in magnitude the developments of the preceding score of years. At
any rate, it was as nearly certain as any military prediction
can be that a conflict between the two major centers of power
would be a prolonged one—comparable in duration to the
two world wars—and not promising the same finality of
decision achieved in each of those instances.

   The atomic bomb has changed all that. Unless the
number of atomic bombs which it is possible for any nation
to make in, say, 10 years' time is far smaller than the most
restrained estimates would indicate, there can no longer be
any question of the "decisiveness" of a strategic bombing
campaign waged primarily with atomic bombs. Also, for a
variety of reasons which cannot be reviewed here but which
are readily available elsewhere,[2] distance no longer presents
the same kind of barrier to effective strategic bombing with
atomic bombs that it does with chemical bombs. With
atomic bombs, planes already in military service could effectively attack from bases within the continental United States
important targets in the Soviet Union, which the same planes
could not do if they carried only chemical bombs. Thus,
there is no absolute necessity to wage great campaigns merely
to secure advanced bombing bases. Finally, it is difficult to
see how the decisive phases of a war fought with substantial numbers of atomic bombs could be anything but short.

   The corollary of the point made in the previous paragraph is that the atomic bomb has deprived the United States
of what amounted almost to absolute security against attack
upon its continental territories. Its naval supremacy was sufficient to guarantee it both against direct invasion of hostile

   [2] See especially "The Absolute Weapon: Atomic Power and World Order," edited by
Bernard Brodie (New York: Harcourt, Brace, 1946), p. 34–40; also "The Atomic Bomb
and the Armed Services," by Bernard Brodie and Eilene Galloway, Public Affairs Bulletin
No. 55 (Legislative Reference Service, Library of Congress), p. 42–45. The reasons why
the same plane can be effective over much greater distances with atomic bombs than with
chemical bombs concern basically the intricate relationships between such factors as the
amount of bombs which a plane can carry over any given distance, the total military
effort expended in carrying it over that distance, and the tolerable rate of loss of attacking planes. Since the atomic bomb does enormously more damage than an equivalent
load of chemical bombs, the cost per sortie which is acceptable with atomic bombs is
also proportionately greater—great enough, in fact, to include 100 percent loss of planes
on successful attacks. The greater acceptable cost; the fact that the plane itself need not
be retrieved (whatever the arrangements made for the rescue of the crew); and the additional fact that a single atomic bomb, whatever its weight, is always a sufficient payload
for any distance which the plane is capable of carrying it, will have the effect of at least
doubling the maximum effective bombing range of any plane of B-29 size or greater.

land forces and against enemy seizure of bases close to our frontiers for large-scale bombing attack. A potential enemy might count on token raids, but nothing more. America's invulnerability was akin to that which Britain enjoyed through the centuries until the perfecting of the submarine on the eve of World War I. The language which Francis Bacon applied to superior sea power in his own time, that it might take "as much or as little of a war as it liked," still largely held for the United States, alone among nations. But with effective intercontinental bombing available to any enemy who holds in substantial numbers the tools already in our hands, that treasured position is gone. The atomic bomb has in military effect translated the United States into a European Power.

However, though Heaven is lost, not all is lost. There is still the issue of superiority to contend with. Three questions especially concern us. Is clear and conspicuous military superiority possible in an age of atomic bombs? If so, is it possible for the United States to maintain it vis-à-vis its major rival? And what will be the political consequences of an effort to maintain atomic superiority?

It is not possible in a few paragraphs to do more than outline the nature of the problem contained in each of these questions and perhaps to indicate the fallacy of certain prevalent suppositions concerning it. Let us take the third question first.

There has long been a fashion among academic specialists in international relations to deprecate as futile and worse the quest on the part of any nation for military superiority over its rivals. As the argument runs, the attempt is bound to provoke a similar pursuit on the part of the rival, the net result being an armaments race which inevitably results in war. Historical support is of course not lacking, especially if the historical instances be chosen with discrimination. The prevalence of this doctrine has had a great deal to do with our frenetic pursuit of international control of atomic energy at almost any cost, including the cost of neglecting to consider any possible alternatives.

There is of course an important element of truth in the idea. But there is also much taken for granted in it which is not true. It is not true, for example, and has not been true at least since the industrial revolution began, that the so-called Great Powers have been on an approximately equal footing in terms of their ability to compete in the production of those instruments of war that really counted. It could be said, for example, that it was the Washington Naval Treaty of 1922 which made the Pacific phase of World War II possible, for it assured to Japan something much closer to naval parity with the United States than would have been anywhere near her reach in any real building competition ensuing from the absence of such a treaty. The Treaty did avoid for a time a "costly" naval building competition. But was not the war with Japan immeasurably more costly? And would Japan have dared embark upon a war against an America boasting a naval power which was—as it easily could have been, without any untoward strain upon the American economy—two or three times her own?

General propositions should not be pushed too far, including the one just stated, but there is much cant in the field of international studies which needs to be brushed out. Those to whom armaments competition appears disastrous as well as wicked are somewhat inconsistent when they look back nostalgically on the relatively peaceful nineteenth century and on the marvelous role played by Great Britain in helping to preserve that peace. They will speak vaguely of Britain's invulnerability as a contributing factor, as though that invulnerability were something handed down from on high. It was indeed Britain's invulnerability at home which enabled British statesmen to play such an active and on the whole beneficent part in helping preserve the peace of Europe but it was not simply the accident of the Channel which made Britain invulnerable. It was her clear-cut naval superiority over the Channel and adjacent seas, *the impairment of which Britain would not brook*, which gave her that enviable position.

Returning again to the atomic bomb, the issue is not whether our country ought to seek to maintain its present superiority in atomic armaments but whether it has any chance at all of succeeding in such an effort. It has been argued by some (including at one time the present writer) that it was in the very nature of atomic armaments that the kind of clear and decisive military superiority that was feasible in the past—conspicuously in the case of naval armaments—could no longer be realized. The argument was based fundamentally on two considerations: first, that there was "no defense against the atomic bomb," and second, that when a nation had enough bombs to overwhelm its opponent in one surprise attack and was willing to make such attack, it would make little difference whether its opponent had two or three times the number.

There is now reason to believe that the situation is not so simple as all that. A great deal depends on the total number of bombs which it will be possible for the various Great Powers to make in any given period of time. Clearly, a three to one superiority in numbers of bombs would mean one thing if the numbers of bombs on each side were numbered at most in the scores or hundreds, and something quite different (and much less significant) if they were numbered in the thousands. Information which would enable private citizens to make intelligent estimates concerning rate of bomb production has not been made public, but there appear to be hints in various quarters that the maximum feasible rate of bomb production is substantially less than was being generally assumed two years ago. It is also clear that the richer of the known deposits of uranium and thorium are much more accessible to the United States than to the Soviet Union.

One may also assume that the enormous technological lead which the United States has over the Soviet Union— and which shows no conclusive signs of diminishing—is bound to mean a great potential advantage for the United States in the design of the instruments for using the atomic bomb. The bomb by itself has no military utility. It must be delivered to the target in some kind of vehicle which, unless it is a free-flying rocket, is subject to various kinds of attack. Marked superiority in the vehicle or in the means of shooting down the enemy's vehicles may be no less important than superiority in numbers of bombs, especially if those numbers are something less than gigantic. If those several types of superiority are concentrated on the same side, the disparity in atomic fighting power may be sufficient to warrant comparison with outright monopoly.

The Soviet Union has been able, with the assistance of German technicians, to build several types of jet-propelled fighters, and she has also built several large bombers patterned after our B-29, some models of which were impounded by her during the war. But a few German technicians are not going to make the difference between a backward technology and an eagerly progressive one. Our lead in types of aircraft, in the ordnance of combat aviation, and in anti-aircraft materiel should, or rather *could*, be as great during the next 20 years as it was in the recent war. The only question is whether we will make the necessary effort to keep in the lead in our military technology. That the Soviet Union will spare no effort within her capabilities to overtake us goes without saying.

We are often told that our *monopoly* of the atomic bomb is a wasting asset. It is, to be sure, in the sense that some day it is bound to end and we are constantly getting closer to that day. But is our *superiority* similarly a wasting asset? In one respect, at least, we know that it is not, for our fund of bombs is increasing steadily during the period in which the Soviet Union remains without any. On the day that the Soviet Union produces its first bomb, we will have many more than we do at present. What happens thereafter depends on a large number of variables. But looking forward from the present, we may say with a good deal of assurance that our present superiority in atomic armaments will increase considerably before it begins to wane, that it may continue to increase even after the Soviet Union is producing bombs, and that it may be a long time in waning thereafter. At any rate, we know that merely to distinguish— as is usually done—between the monopoly period (in which we are safe) and the post-monopoly period (in which we are lost) is not enough.

One might incidentally point out that it is easy to be over-subtle concerning the political consequences of our present monopoly of the bomb. The duty of the intellectual to get behind the obvious too often betrays him into ignoring the obvious or even denying it. We have heard a good many references to the fact that the atomic bomb, being a weapon of mass destruction, is not really handy for diplomatic maneuvering. We have been told also that since we would never use it against cities inhabited by friendly peoples, it would not help us one whit in stopping Soviet armies from overrunning Western Europe. The latter observation happens not to be strategically correct, since the destruction of *Russian* cities and industries would make a great deal of difference in the ability of the Soviet armies to overrun Western Europe, or to maintain themselves in that area if they got there. But the fact remains that the atomic bomb is today our *only* means for throwing substantial power immediately against the Soviet Union in the event of flagrant Soviet aggression. The Soviets may underestimate the power of the bomb (as may, indeed, our own military leaders), but they cannot be entirely oblivious of that fact. If they choose war now it will be either because they underestimate the bomb even more grossly than they appear to or because they would rather face the hazard now when our bombs are few than later when they are many.

Concerning the effects of the atomic bomb upon our military organization and strategic plans, we must recognize first of all that, to paraphrase Clemenceau, the matter is much too important to be left to the generals—or to the politicians either for that matter. Formulation of security policy demands anticipation of probabilities with due regard to what is politically possible or feasible. But consideration of the latter may too easily degenerate into preoccupation with what is politically safe. Political leaders, moreover, have neither the time nor the inclination to preoccupy themselves with the long-term significance of changes in military technology, and rarely the competence to make anything of it if they do. They must rely upon the advice of their military aides, who belong to a profession long recognized as markedly conservative—though it is easy to exaggerate the degree and character of that conservatism—who have vested service and personal interests which influence them consciously or unconsciously, whose talents are not primarily dialectic, and who are saddled with tremendous responsibility. The responsibility powerfully reinforces the conservative tendencies already present as a result of nurture and training. We are therefore not likely to find military leaders, or the civilian officials whom they advise, accepting readily upon the advent of some revolutionary military device that drastic adjustment which free and objective inquiry may indicate as necessary or at least desirable.

It is a little startling, some three years after Hiroshima, to find the military departments of our government still apparently unprepared to think in terms of what strategic effects are to be expected from the use of any given number of bombs. The national safety will of course demand close secrecy concerning conclusions reached, but in this instance there is reason for believing that "security" is concealing the absence of thinking rather than the import of the ideas derived. For example, in the paper prepared by the War Department in March 1947 on "The Effects of the Atomic Bomb on National Security," there is a reference to something called a "significant" number of bombs. The meaning of "significant" is then explained only as indicating that number of bombs which would "provide an important military capability."[3] The military profession is not the only one which habitually betrays itself with catch phrases, but when we think of the absence of logic usually inherent in such sacrosanct phrases as "balanced fleet" or "balanced force," we cannot be too optimistic about the precision of thought behind the "important military capability."

We know that one bomb will not win a war against a major power, since it took two to produce the surrender of an already defeated Japan. The same may reasonably be held to be true of five or ten. But there appears to be little idea anywhere what number would be "significant" and even less conception of how many it takes to make the weapon "decisive." Much will of course depend on how the bombs are used, but then the significance of the whole issue is that the number available and the estimates concerning the capabilities of that number will in large part govern the way in which they are used.

It is not easy to extrapolate the strategic effectiveness of atomic bombs from the experience with strategic bombing gained in the recent war. There are too many differences, besides that of magnitude of destruction per bomb or per plane, between bombing with chemical bombs and attacking with atomic bombs. It is not even a simple matter to determine the factor of increase in power of the atomic bomb over an equivalent load of chemical bombs. But we do have enough data to provide the basis for some intensive research which might throw some light on the problem. What we need to know is: "How many bombs will do what?" And the "what" must be reckoned in over-all strategic results rather than merely in acres destroyed.

The evidence is presumptive only, but nevertheless impressive, that our military planners are thinking of an atomic bomb which is an "important military capability" but nevertheless only an ancillary rather than a decisive weapon. The chief danger is that the inevitably transitory

---

[3]The War Department Paper was published in the Public Affairs Bulletin No. 55 already cited. The specific reference above is to page 67 of the Bulletin.

nature of the conditions presumed will not be recognized sufficiently or in time. Regardless of what the Soviet Union may accomplish in the field, our own production of atomic bombs is proceeding apace, and the justification for regarding the weapon as an ancillary one is bound to evaporate as our stockpile accumulates.

If we consider national defense policy in its broader aspects, and look beyond the period of American monopoly of atomic weapons, we see that recognition of the loss of American invulnerability to overseas attack and expectation of quick decisions in the event of war will no doubt entail a violent wrench to our defense traditions. Preparedness in the old sense of the term, which meant mainly provision for great expansion of the military services and of military production after the outbreak of hostilities, will appear even less adequate than it has been charged with being in the past. What will that mean for the costs of military preparedness?

Unquestionably the costs will increase, as they have already begun to. But we should not assume that the restraints which have always operated on the growth of military budgets will become inconsequential. There have been no systematic studies of the various factors governing the size of military budgets. It is obvious that periods of international tensions generally stimulate increases in military expenditure, and historians have dwelt on the scale of the armaments races preceding the two world wars. But they have scarcely considered the significance of the fact that in each case the extent of the arming, though large in comparison with more tranquil periods, was relatively small in contrast to the expansion of the war period itself.

We are speaking here partly of ordinary human inertia, even under circumstances where war appears imminent, and in so far as that inertia can be relied upon to be both pronounced and universal it should definitely enter into our calculations. But there is more to the matter than simple inertia. Wartime economies are characteristically fat-consuming. Both the toleration of them by the public and the physical possibility of maintaining their inordinate pace depend on the fact that they are temporary and recognized to be such. If there is to be fat to consume it must first be accumulated. In other words, even from the point of view strictly of defense needs, war economies can be inaugurated too soon as well as too late. And if the relevant comments of General Eisenhower while he was Chief of Staff of the Army can be taken as representative, that fact is recognized by the military themselves.

There is also the problem of avoiding military expenditure which is improvident not only because it is too large but also because it is misdirected. We have heard much, for example, of the business of dispersing our cities as a defense against atomic attack. It is clear that such dispersion would result in a tremendous loss of fixed and sunk capital and, in all probability, in a less efficient spatial arrangement of industries than previously existed. Thus, even if one should make the wholly untenable assumption that wholesale dispersion of our cities and the losses resulting would be tolerated by the public, the project might still appear to be militarily wasteful. A great many combat airplanes could be provided with what it would cost to disperse even a relatively small city. There is no doubt a margin for the dispersion of key industries and services which would not loom large in terms of the economy as a whole but which would nevertheless have important security results. If so, the accomplishment of that objective should remain a maximum as well as a minimum goal.

These observations are of course not very reassuring to those who, like the present writer, deplore the necessity of spending on military protection even so substantial a portion of our national income as we are spending today. The limits referred to are fairly flexible and we are still far from having reached them. And what will occur in this country when the conviction settles upon it that the Soviet Union is producing atomic bombs is the big question of the future. But the error for which we are now paying was after all perpetrated some three centuries ago, when Galileo was permitted to escape burning. Our problem now is to develop the habit of living with the atomic bomb, and the very incomprehensibility of the potential catastrophe inherent in it may well make that task easier.

1954

THE REQUIREMENTS OF DETERRENCE

William W. Kaufmann

William Kaufmann is currently a consultant at the Brookings Institute and a professor at Harvard University. He is a former Professor at MIT, former head of RAND's Social Science Division, and former consultant to RAND, the Central Intelligence Agency, the National Security Council, the Office of Management and Budget and the Office of the Secretary of Defense.

During the past two decades an understanding has developed in the United States not only that an active security policy is essential to the preservation of our society, but also that security wears many faces and can be won in a great variety of ways. Increasingly since the war we have sought to achieve a measure of safety without resorting to violence on a universal scale, and from this effort we have emerged with what is commonly known as a policy of deterrence. Until very recently this policy was concerned with two major contingencies: an attack on Western Europe and a general onslaught against the non-communist world by the Soviet Union. The main instruments of deterrence that we developed for these contingencies were the North Atlantic Treaty Organization and the Strategic Air Command armed with nuclear weapons.

On January 12, 1954, the Secretary of State, Mr. Dulles, delivered an address before the Council on Foreign

Reprinted with permission of Princeton University Press. Copyright © 1956 © 1984 renewed by Princeton University Press.

Relations in which he discussed what has come to be referred to as the doctrine of massive retaliation. Whether correctly or not, this doctrine has been considered a departure from the type of policy of deterrence heretofore followed by the United States, and a prolonged controversy has developed over its meaning, implications, and desirability. In an attempt to clarify his intentions, Mr. Dulles undertook several reformulations and explanations of the doctrine, and various other spokesmen of the administration have offered their interpretations of its significance. But despite these efforts, and perhaps even because of them, a significant residue of confusion and disagreement remains. In the circumstances, there may be some justification for reviewing the meaning and presentation of the doctrine, and for weighing its appropriateness as a policy of deterrence for the United States.

Background of the Doctrine

A brief examination of the background of the doctrine may provide some clues as to its intended meaning. For frequently a policy, which on the face of it seems ambiguous, can be understood in terms of considerations not adverted to in the policy statement itself.

First but not necessarily foremost among these factors was the existence of a new administration in power, pledged not only to perform more efficiently than its predecessor, but also to produce distinctive and economical policies. This situation created within the government an atmosphere favorable to bold and unconventional ideas. By itself, however, it provides little guidance to the meaning of massive retaliation. More important were certain considerations which were bound to impress any Secretary of State, whether Republican or Democratic. There were the areas of the Middle and Far East and Southeast Asia, vitally important to the United States, devoid of powerful local defenses, and subject to heavy pressure from the Soviet Union and Red China. Obviously some measure of protection had to be afforded to these areas. But there was also the recently terminated Korean war, fought to a stalemate at a tremendous sacrifice in American lives and treasure. Its conclusion and its costs strongly suggested that some special means of forestalling another such contingency in these areas had to be found. Otherwise American resources might be dissipated in an endless series of peripheral wars.

There was the defense program which had sprung up in the wake of the Korean conflict: a program which jeopardized the prospects for a balanced budget, required the maintenance of taxes at painfully high levels, and created industrial facilities which under different international conditions might prove redundant and therefore dangerous in terms of economic stability. Its embarrassments and risks certainly invited the institution of a policy that would achieve the same deterrent effects without the accompanying economic and political strains.

Finally, there was the doctrine of containment, which in its original formulation had seemed defective to Mr. Dulles. Containment suggested an essentially defensive posture, a surrender of the initiative to the opponent, almost an invitation to him to do his worst while the United States desperately mended its military and economic fences and tried to meet every form of attack, wherever it might materialize. In the Secretary's view this was an uneconomic and overly demanding policy. Some device had to be found with which to barricade the many avenues of attack open to the Soviet Union and Red China.

Thus, any policy of deterrence formulated by Mr. Dulles was likely to take into account not only the dangerous plight of the Middle East, Southeast Asia, and the Far East, but also the desire to avoid a repetition of the Korean experience, reduce the cost of the military establishment, and replace or at least supplement containment with a more dynamic and efficient approach.

The Content of the Doctrine

In his speech of January 12, the Secretary appeared to have these considerations very much in mind. The time for emergency programs had passed, he said; the problem now was to put American foreign policy on a more effective and less costly basis. The way to do this, he explained, was to place greater reliance on community deterrent power and less reliance upon local defensive power. Local defense, he agreed, would always be important. "But there is no local defense which alone will contain the mighty land power of the Communist world. Local defense must be reinforced by the further deterrent of massive retaliatory power." For if the enemy "could pick his time and his place and his method of warfare—and if our policy was to remain the traditional one of meeting aggression by direct and local opposition—then we had to be ready to fight in the Arctic and in the tropics, in Asia, in the Near East and in Europe; by sea, by land and by air; by old weapons and by new weapons." To avoid this possibility the President and the National Security Council had taken a basic decision, namely, "to depend primarily upon a great capacity to retaliate instantly by means and at places of our own choosing."

As a result of this decision the Department of Defense and the Joint Chiefs of Staff could now shape the military establishment to fit "what is our policy instead of having to try to be ready to meet the enemy's many choices. And that permits of a selection of military means instead of a multiplication of means." Consequently, it would now be possible "to get, and to share, more security at less cost."[1]

Mr. James Reston, reporting from Washington on January 16, took the address to mean that the President and the Secretary of State were telling Moscow and Peiping, "as clearly as Governments ever say these things, that in the event of another proxy or bushfire war in Korea, Indo-China, Iran or anywhere else, the United States might retaliate instantly with atomic weapons against the U.S.S.R. or Red China."[2] Vice-President Nixon put exactly the same interpretation on the doctrine. On March 13, in reply to a speech by Mr. Adlai E. Stevenson, he said:

> Rather than let the Communists nibble us to death all over the world in little wars, we would rely in the future primarily on our massive mobile retaliatory power which we could use in our discretion against the major source of aggression at times and places that we chose.
>
> We adjusted our armed strength to meet the requirements of this new concept and, what was just as important, we let the world and we let the Communists know what we intended to do.[3]

Three days later, at a press conference, and in an article written for the April issue of *Foreign Affairs*, Mr. Dulles

Author's Note: Klaus Knorr of the Center of International Studies contributed greatly to the clarification of my ideas on this subject. However, he is not responsible for the judgments or conclusions that I have reached. For better or for worse, these are my own.

[1] New York Times; January 13, 1954, p. 2.
[2] *Ibid.*, January 17, 1954, Section 4, p. 8.
[3] *Ibid.*, March 14, 1954, p. 44.

provided his own version of what he had intended to say on January 12. In no place, he explained, had he stated that we would retaliate instantly, "although we might indeed retaliate instantly under conditions that call for that. The essential thing is to have the capacity to retaliate instantly." The problem, as he saw it, was to find some way of supplementing local ground defense. And the way to supplement it was "to have a capacity to retaliate at times, places, and with methods of your own choosing." This did not mean that we should eliminate "wholly, by any means, land forces"; it meant rather that "you do not make them your primary reliance because, as against the kind of danger which threatens, it is impossible to match your potential enemy at all points on a basis of man-for-man, gun-for-gun and tank-for-tank. If we try to do that we are going to go bust."[4]

The free world must therefore devise a better strategy for its defense based on its own special assets. These assets include, "especially air and naval power and atomic weapons which are now available in a wide range, suitable not only for strategic bombing but also for extensive tactical use. . . .Properly used, they can produce defensive power able to retaliate at once and effectively against any aggression." The result would be a workable policy of deterrence. For a "would-be aggressor will hesitate to commit aggression if he knows in advance that he thereby not only exposes these particular forces which he chooses to use for his aggression, but also deprives his other assets of 'sanctuary' status. That does not mean turning every local war into a world war. It does not mean that if there is a Communist attack somewhere in Asia, atom or hydrogen bombs will necessarily be dropped on the great industries of China or Russia."[5]

Implications of the Doctrine

What inferences can be drawn from the background of the doctrine and from the various policy statements which now are on the record? Three major assumptions about the communist world stand out quite starkly. The first is that, while communism may take many forms and appear in all sorts of places, its actions are instituted from and controlled by the Soviet Union and Red China. The second

[4] *Ibid.*, March 17, 1954, p. 6.
[5] *Ibid.*, p. 4.

assumption is that, although the leaders of the Soviet Union and Red China may have objectives quite different from our own, their cost-risk calculations must be roughly the same. The third assumption—and it follows from the first two— is that action on the periphery of the communist empire can be forestalled by forecasting to the enemy the costs and risks that he will run—provided always that the costs and risks are of a sufficient magnitude to outweigh the prospective gains.

The main objective of the new policy seems equally clear. It is, quite simply, to prevent any further expansion of the communist empire by giving the Russians and Chinese notice of the losses they may expect to suffer should they attempt to increase their holdings by military means in the Middle East, Southeast Asia, and the Far East. Lesser but by no means negligible objectives are the simplification and clarification of American commitments, and a reduction in the costs of the military establishment.

What are to be the means of massive retaliation does not come out so clearly. But, despite the ambiguity of the Secretary's references to this subject, it seems highly probable that the chief instruments of deterrence will continue to be the Strategic Air Command and its naval counterpart. They are to stand as a constant reminder to Moscow and Peiping that any attack upon what Mr. Finletter calls the gray areas, as well as upon NATO country and the Western hemisphere, will result in nuclear and thermonuclear retribution.

Here, then, is the compass of the doctrine as a policy of deterrence. Relying heavily upon the striking power of SAC, we attempt to seal off the major avenues of attack open to the communists. At the same time, we reduce the burden of our defense by focusing our expenditures on what appears to be the most efficacious arm of the military services, and we release energies and resources for other and more congenial tasks of foreign and domestic policy. The United States gains the opportunity to concentrate its forces and place the communist world on the defensive. Certain risks are taken but the initiative is obtained; we reach a position from which to channel the future course of events in directions of our own choosing.

These, in truth, may be sound strategic principles, but whether they are susceptible to practice depends upon the answers to two questions: first, what requirements must be fulfilled in order for such a policy of deterrence to be effective; secondly, are conditions at the present time such that these requirements can be fulfilled?

The Requirements of Deterrence

In order to evaluate a doctrine like that of massive retaliation it is essential to understand what is involved in a policy of deterrence. Essentially, deterrence means preventing certain types of contingencies from arising. To achieve this objective it becomes necessary to communicate in some way to a prospective antagonist what is likely to happen to him should he create the situation in question. The expectation is that, confronted with this prospect, he will be deterred from taking the action that is regarded as inimical—at least so long as other less intolerable alternatives are open to him.

A deterrence policy thus constitutes a special kind of forecast: a forecast about the costs and risks that will be run under certain conditions, and the advantages that will be gained if those conditions are avoided. The forecast can be made in various ways: by a public statement such as Mr. Dulles delivered; by some pattern of behavior which will lead the antagonist to deduce our intended course of action in various contingencies; or by some combination of diplomatic and other means.

The forecast of intentions can be meant in all seriousness or it can be in the nature of a bluff. Whichever it is should determine to a considerable extent the formulation and communication of the policy. Presumably the precision of the forecast and the manner in which it is communicated will vary with the willingness to live up to the expressed intentions. But whether the forecast is intended or is a bluff, a very real risk and some serious potential costs are attached to a policy of deterrence. The risk is that, despite our best efforts, the antagonist will challenge us to make good on our threat. If we do so, we will have to accept the consequences of executing our threatened action. If we back down and let the challenge go unheeded, we will suffer losses of prestige, we will decrease our capacity for instituting effective deterrence policies in the future, and we will encourage the opponent to take further actions of a detrimental character. This kind of cost can be almost as serious as the cost attached to a fulfillment of the forecast.

In order to minimize this risk, with its attached costs, and at the same time preserve the effectiveness of the policy, it becomes necessary to surround the proposal with an air of credibility. In this connection it must be remembered that a large and varied audience will be observing our behavior and that the reactions of this audience will be crucial to the success or failure of the policy. For the purposes of this discussion, the audience may be broken down very simply into enemy, domestic, and allied categories.

Dealing first with the enemy audience, it is quite obvious that we must know specifically who the opponent is in order to make our policy meaningful to him. If, for example, the Viet Minh had a considerable measure of autonomy from Moscow and Peiping, it might be quite useless to threaten the destruction of those two cities for the purpose of deterring an attack on Laos, Cambodia, or South Vietnam.

But, assuming a knowledge of the antagonist's identity, there are three main areas in which credibility must be established: the areas of capability, cost, and intentions. The enemy must be persuaded that we have the capability to act; that, in acting, we could inflict costs greater than the advantages to be won from attaining the objective; and that we really would act as specified in the stated contingency.

Potential, as against actual capability, cannot be regarded as a convincing instrument of deterrence in the present state of affairs. Nor is it enough simply to have a certain number of planes supplied with fission and fusion bombs. The enemy must be persuaded not only that the instrument exists but also that its power is operational—in the case of SAC, for example, that it can get through to its targets and inflict a most burdensome cost upon him.

Even if capability and cost requirements can be fulfilled, there remains the difficult and delicate problem of making intentions credible. An intelligent opponent—and it would be dangerous indeed to postulate a stupid one in dealing with the communist world—may be expected to use three main sources of information about the intentions of a country such as the United States: its past record of performance in comparable contingencies; the statements and behavior of its government; and the attitudes of public opinion, both domestic and allied. A policy of deterrence consistent with the country's recent behavior in the international arena is likely to seem much more plausible than one which constitutes a sharp break with tradition. Similarly, the credibility of the policy will vary with the degree of consistency in the speech and action of the government and its executive agencies. Nothing can be more crippling to a policy of deterrence than to have the statements of the Secretary of State contradicted or reinterpreted by other officials of national standing. Nor will official statements seem convincing if actions are being taken simultaneously to nullify the statements, or if nothing concrete is being done to support them.

Finally, and perhaps most important in the realm of intentions, a policy of deterrence will seem credible only to the extent that important segments of public opinion in domestic and allied countries support it. In democratic nations, especially, the process of formulating policy is much more than the enunciation of intentions by governmental leaders. Before those intentions can be regarded as policy, there must be genuine evidence of popular support for them from the country at large. This consideration suggests a rather crucial and specific requirement that a policy of deterrence must fulfill. Its potential costs must seem worth incurring. In other words, there must be some relationship between the value of the objective sought and the costs involved in its attainment. A policy of deterrence which does not fulfill this requirement is likely to result only in deterring the deterrer.

Existing Conditions of Deterrence

If these are the requirements that a policy of deterrence must fulfill in order to be credible, and hence effective, it must now be asked whether or not the conditions have existed—or indeed can be created—in which the doctrine of massive retaliation would accomplish the task assigned to it by Mr. Dulles.

In the realm of capabilities it does appear as though we have, in the instrumentalities of SAC, our carrier-based air forces, and our fission and fusion bombs, the means to inflict damage of an incalculable character upon the Soviet Union and of a much lesser extent upon Red China and the satellite countries. However, several factors are now working to limit their utility. SAC's plans and operations still depend to a large extent on the availability of foreign bases.

Consequently, the use of the Sunday punch is subject to some definite constraints. It is quite clear, moreover, that the Soviets are working hard on their active and passive defense measures, and are developing a powerful strategic air force of their own. It may be safe to assume that SAC will get through to its targets now and in the immediate future; but we must also assume that the Soviet strategic air force will be able to retaliate against us with equal devastation. In other words, given these capability conditions, we must face up to the fact that, if we are challenged to fulfill the threat of massive retaliation, we will be likely to suffer costs as great as those we inflict.

An examination of our recent diplomatic record, and indeed of the course of American foreign policy during the past fifteen or twenty years, makes it quite obvious that we do not tend to retaliate massively against anyone except in the face of provocations as extreme as Pearl Harbor. Although World War II garnered a great prestige for the United States, it has been the prestige that invariably accompanies enormous wealth and power rather than the prestige of boldness, sternness, and consistency. And since the war, the record has been a mixed one. Greek-Turkish aid, the Marshall Plan, the Berlin airlift, the North Atlantic Treaty, and intervention in Korea—all have demonstrated a willingness to counter Soviet and Chinese efforts at expansion; but they have also suggested rather strongly that the United States is willing—and, it should be added, able—to meet these moves successfully on the grounds and according to the rules set by the opponent. In fact, Korea and now Indo-China have indicated that we are not prepared in cases of this sort to do more than limit and contain communist thrusts by means of local applications of counterforce. During the Korean war, it is true, we not only tried to prevent the enemy from reaching his objective; we also attempted to punish him for his audacity by removing North Korea from his sphere of influence. Liberation and medium-weight retaliation actually became components of our policy at that point. But when we computed the costs attached to them, and discovered in addition that our antagonist was quite willing to play the game in this more expensive arena, we settled for our original objectives and the stalemate of Panmunjom. In fact, so poignant was the lesson of Korea that in Indo-China we did not intervene directly at all.

This then is the record—the credit, as it were—that we have at our disposal in making credible any policy of deterrence. It is not unimpressive, nor is it conclusive. Governments, attitudes, and behavior can change with extraordinary rapidity, and the past is a most unreliable guide to the future. But this particular record is a condition that exists, and as such it will have much to do with the effectiveness of our program.

Similarly, in the realm of governmental pronouncements and activities, there exist certain conditions which must necessarily affect the credibility of a policy of deterrence. In connection with massive retaliation, Mr. Dulles has not only given varying interpretations of the doctrine; he has seen it alternately upheld and modified by other members of the government. There appears to be some uncertainty within the present administration as to what the future course of American foreign policy should be, and, in these circumstances, both executive and legislature have on occasion spoken with discordant voices. While the Secretary has threatened massive retaliation, the President has spoken of Asians fighting Asians and has placed very definite limits on his power to act in an emergency.

The impression of confusion and cross-purposes given by these and other statements is not by itself too significant, for the exchange value of verbal symbols is no longer as high as it was in the nineteenth century. But in its activities the government has indicated that it holds to other and quite contradictory goals just as firmly as to massive retaliation. The search for a balanced budget, reduced taxes, and a smaller military establishment provides only some of the reasons why the administration finds it difficult to be consistent in its attitudes toward such a policy.

The state of domestic and allied public opinion is somewhat comparable. Revulsion with the Korean war became evident within a year of intervention by the United Nations, and no enthusiasm could be generated either at home or abroad for similar efforts in Indo-China. Fear and hatred of the Soviet Union and Red China may persist, especially in the United States, but these emotions are not so intense that they create a desire for the Western coalition to react to communist expansion massively or otherwise except where vital interests are obviously at stake. And even in the United States, the definition of vital interests remains relatively narrow. The growing desire for peace based on existing arrangements, the belief in the possibility of some kind of *modus vivendi* with the Soviet Union—which has gained strength particularly in Europe—the unwillingness to make sacrifices for countries which show no ability to help themselves, and the increased knowledge of the effects of nuclear weapons—all these attitudes make for reactions of either apathy or outright criticism of the doctrine of massive retaliation.

Appropriateness of Massive Retaliation

If this hasty appraisal of relevant conditions is accurate, we must immediately face the prospect that the leaders of the Soviet Union and Red China will hardly endow the doctrine with much credibility. They will see that we have the capability to implement our threat, but they will also observe that, with their own nuclear capability on the rise, our decision to use the weapons of mass destruction will necessarily come only after an agonizing appraisal of costs and risks, as well as of advantages. Our record of performance after World War II is unlikely to increase their apprehension; Korea and Indo-China are important symbols of our reluctance, not only to intervene in the peripheral areas, but also to expand those conflicts in which we have become engaged. And the behavior of the administration itself, including Mr. Dulles' own reformulations of his policy, will do little to persuade them of the seriousness of American intentions. Finally, the state of domestic and allied opinion will provide them with ample reason to believe that the doctrine is, if not a case of outright bluff, at the very most a proposal that will still have to undergo searching and prolonged debate before becoming accepted policy.

In short the minimum requirements of credibility have not been fulfilled in the case of massive retaliation. What is more, the possibility exists that the Soviet Union and Red China, instead of being deterred, will continue to act as they did in Indo-China and actually push into other peripheral areas not only for gain but also for the purpose of discovering what constitute the limits of our tolerance.

With the doctrine operating under these handicaps, we run, in a particularly aggravated form, all the risks attached to a policy of deterrence. If the communists challenge our sincerity—and they have good reasons for daring to do so—we shall either have to put up or shut up. If we put up, we plunge into all the immeasurable horrors of an atomic war. If we shut up, we suffer a serious loss of prestige and damage our capacity to establish deterrents against further communist expansion. Indeed, given existing conditions, there is no escaping that the doctrine of massive retaliation is likely to confront us continually with having to choose between one or the other of these two most distasteful alternatives.

One way out of this dilemma would be to alter the conditions which make the requirements of credibility so difficult to fulfill. If we could reduce our own vulnerability to atomic attack, increase our offensive capability, either talk less openly and specifically about massive retaliation or act in a manner more consistent with the implications of the doctrine, and at the same time persuade domestic and allied opinion of the desirability of such a Draconian policy—if we could do all this, we might minimize considerably the risk of having our intentions probed. But existing conditions do not appear to be so elastic that we can produce rapid or far-reaching variations in them. What does seem plausible is that the doctrine of massive retaliation as presently formulated is neither feasible nor desirable as a policy of deterrence. Despite the continuing faith of its authors, it cannot be made feasible because of its lack of credibility. And it hardly seems desirable so long as there exist alternative deterrents which are not burdened with comparable risks.

A Role for Massive Retaliation

It should not be inferred from these conclusions that a doctrine such as massive retaliation has no place in a policy of deterrence for the United States. They mean rather that the policy requires rethinking and that massive retaliation should be given a special and concrete assignment within it.

Hardly anyone questions the desirability of having a policy of deterrence; most of us recognize now that it is a mistake to wait passively for the arrival of certain contingencies when the possibility exists of forestalling them. There is an equally general agreement that the immediate costs of a deterrence policy are much smaller than the costs that would result from having to deal with these contingencies. But even with this common ground, there remain several difficult problems to be solved before a satisfactory policy can emerge.

Since there is a large number of contingencies that are likely to affect American interests adversely, and since the United States, however wealthy, cannot effectively prepare for and forestall all of them, it becomes an essential prerequisite of a policy of deterrence to visualize the most significant and probable lines of action open to our opponents. A second requirement is that efficient deterrents be designed for these possibilities. Here two rules of prudence are worth remembering. It is probably hopeless to expect that a single deterrent will cover the entire range of contingencies and still satisfy the criteria of credibility. The attempt to devise such a deterrent is likely to result in either a sparrow hunt with a cannon or an elephant shoot with a popgun. Similarly, it seems futile to expect of a deterrent that it will solve a great many other problems and still prove efficient. To hope, as Mr. Dulles appears to have hoped, that with massive retaliation he could deter the Soviet Union and Red China, and at the same time contribute to the goals of a balanced budget and reduced taxes, is to invite disaster for the deterrent. Effective deterrents have high production costs under existing conditions; they cannot easily be constructed without making sacrifices in other directions.

Is there, in the light of these considerations, a deterrent role for the doctrine of massive retaliation? The answer, surely, is yes, but the role is a limited and specialized one. Although the weapon of strategic air power and nuclear armaments has the capacity to inflict incalculable damage, the threat of its use involves risks of a comparable magnitude. If these risks could be minimized by giving an appearance of credibility to our threat to employ it over a wide range of contingencies, they might be worth taking. But a society equipped with democratic political processes has a limited capacity for bluff, so that massive retaliation cannot be credible and effective as a deterrent unless it is matched against contingencies in which the United States and its allies would actually be prepared to use such a weapon.

Such contingencies are not too difficult to define. They are: an attack on areas which have come to be regarded as of vital interest to us; the use by the communists of nuclear weapons; and that range of actions by the enemy which demonstrates that there is a clear and present danger to our society. The first two are easy to recognize. The third is more elusive and its identification must depend on whether or not there is evidence to suggest that the general situation is deteriorating in such a way that the United States has no real alternatives other than all-out war or ultimate surrender.

The deterrent of massive retaliation directed toward these contingencies has a good prospect of being effective because a majority of people, both here and abroad, are willing to see nuclear weapons used in such cases. And being agreed, they immediately give credibility to the threat. However, it should not be thought that confining massive retaliation to contingencies of the last resort completes the task of setting up this particular deterrent. The more grimly determined we appear to be to meet these contingencies with massive retaliation, the less likely they are to arise. It would seem worthwhile, therefore, to continue and preferably increase our investment in both our offensive striking power and in our active and passive defenses. And, if we are to prevent a rise in the number of allied nationals who deplore the use of SAC under any circumstances, we would do well to increase the stake of our friends in the maintenance and protection of the Western system. Finally, since definitions of vital interests will change through time, we might do worse than to declare a moratorium on public pronouncements dealing with this subject. To the extent that the enemy requires further briefing about our intentions, there are other means and channels of communication which we can employ more effectively—and with less commitment and risk—than the open declaration.

If, as has been suggested here, we confine massive retaliation to contingencies of the last resort, this leaves us with a large gap in our policy of deterrence. The options available to the communists which seem most dangerous to the United States are covered; but it would be to our interest to interdict a number of alternatives that still lie open to them. Among these are conventional warfare against the peripheral areas or segments of the Western bloc, and subversion and civil war instigated in the same areas. Wherever such operations are attempted they hold forth the prospect of a long-term erosion of the American position; at the same time, we suffer serious losses in meeting them and run the risk of creating contingencies of the last resort. Clearly they require that we make a considerable investment of resources in order to prevent their occurrence. Yet massive retaliation is not a weapon that can effectively forestall them. Other types of deterrents have to be devised.

The Availability of Deterrents

In considering the availability of other types of deterrents, we must appreciate that the reservation of massive retaliation for contingencies of the last resort has disadvantages as well as advantages. The communists may be deterred from creating these contingencies, but they may also be encouraged to engage in other operations to the extent that significant costs are not involved. The threat of massive retaliation narrows the scope and character of their actions; it forces them to compete for areas of lesser strategic and economic value. But these limits and constraints do not abolish their freedom of maneuver, as both Korea and Indo-China have demonstrated.

Our problem, therefore, is to construct deterrents that forecast costs sufficient to discourage the enemy, but not great enough to make him turn, whether out of desperation or design, to contingencies of the last resort. We must, in a word, try to fit the punishment to the crime. This is much more difficult in the international arena than in domestic society, where elaborate and reasonably effective systems of legal deterrents have been developed. But it is by no means impossible. Here only a few suggestions can be made about the weapons that we might consider.

It is probably in the military realm that the richest resources of deterrence still lie. If we show a willingness and ability to intervene with great conventional power in the peripheral areas, after the manner of Korea, we will have a reasonable chance of forestalling enemy military action there. Admittedly this suggests offering to compete with the communist world on terms apparently favorable to it. But are the terms as favorable as they seem at first glance? Our effort in Korea was smaller in size and probably less costly in terms of human and material resources than the communist commitment. And it was the communists who first expressed a wish to terminate the conflict. The charade at Kaesong and Panmunjom has made us forget that, in the face of Operation Killer, Mr. Jacob Malik raised the subject of a truce. Even if the debacle of Indo-China has corroded our reputation, the communists cannot have discarded entirely the memory of the Eighth Army under Generals Ridgway and Van Fleet.

In the size and character of German rearmament we also have a weapon of considerable power. The development of the new Wehrmacht will be, in part at least, a function of Soviet behavior, and we might do worse than indicate the correlation. Chiang Kai-shek's troops are a less valuable asset, but they too can play a part in our deterrence policy. Instead of "unleashing" them indiscriminately, we ought to determine the circumstances in which we would be willing to support them, and notify Peiping accordingly. The South Korean army, to the extent that we control it at all, may be drafted to play a similar role. These forces, together with the NATO divisions and our own military power, can provide a very significant deterrent indeed.

In what, for lack of a better term, may be called the social realm, there are several subsidiary deterrents which require consideration. The communist parties in the West, while frequently a nuisance and sometimes a threat, do represent hostages in our hands. The process of destroying their apparatus and dispersing their adherents may be a difficult and costly one. But the threat to do so in prescribed circumstances might well carry weight with the communist leadership. Similarly, the encouragement of defection from, and disaffection within, the satellite countries has excellent deterrent potentialities. The events of June 1953 have already demonstrated that defection and disaffection are possible on a significant scale, and that the Soviets are sensitive to their occurrence. We do not want to be indiscriminate or irresponsible in fostering such activities; but we may wish to advise the enemy as discreetly as possible that there are occasions on which he can expect us to make full use of this subversive potential.

To this arsenal it may be that we can add deterrents of another kind. It was suggested earlier that there are two sides to the coin of deterrence. So far only the threatening face has been considered, but we must examine the side of rewards as well. It is possible, at least in principle, to deter an antagonist from taking inimical action by the offer of a better prospect than the one he presently enjoys. The approach, however, is as familiar to as it is unpopular with Americans. It immediately brings to mind Munich, Yalta, and perhaps even Geneva. The feeling is strong that it is both useless and dangerous to propitiate an opponent such as the communist because in the end he will simply accept our gratuity and proceed to do what he had originally intended. This is an understandable attitude, and it is justified under three conditions: if the antagonist is being driven into his inimical behavior, not by desperate need, but by conscious, grasping ambition; if the reward is not reciprocated by some tangible concession from him; and if the reward is not revocable by the donor. The tragedy of Munich and Yalta is that all of these conditions were fulfilled, so that it is possible to appreciate why there has been such a loss of faith in this approach.

But it does not follow that we have to imitate the past with exact fidelity. We are almost certainly correct in assuming that we cannot shape the communist world to our image by smothering it in a featherbed of concessions. There is no evidence that we are dealing simply with men of good will driven to desperate extremities by exacting social, political, and economic conditions, or that they will surrender their ambitions in the face of changes in those conditions. But we may be quite mistaken if we assume, on the basis of this diagnosis, that concessions are not worth making at all.

Certainly we will decrease the prospects for an effective policy of deterrence if we insist without end that there are no arrangements under which we can live in peace with the communists; for the most dangerous alternatives will begin to look attractive to them in such circumstances. We ought always to keep open the possibility of a genuine *modus vivendi*, and we may actually find it advantageous to take specific steps in that direction. There are, for example, certain revocable rewards at our disposal which, at the present time, will benefit both sides and yet can be withdrawn in the event of hostile action by the communists. The resumption of a carefully screened and regulated trade with Red China might be one such measure. Disarmament is another. Territorial concessions without concrete equivalents are dangerous and undesirable; it is impossible to attach strings to these gifts. But probably there are other realms where we can play the Indian-giver.

In doing so, we may not persuade our antagonist to forego his expansionist goals. But, to the extent that he values our concessions and profits from their availability, we will have created additional means of dissuading him from trying to attain these goals. In conjunction with our other weapons they can give us reasonably powerful means of influencing his calculations of cost and risk without all the hazards inherent in massive retaliation.

Prerequisites of a Policy of Deterrence

Whether or not a program of this general character can be made credible to the communists will depend on our willingness to satisfy the demands that it establishes. In the military realm, if we are to reduce our dangerous dependence on massive retaliation and the instrumentality of SAC, we must strengthen the other arms of the services. The most obvious need is in the ground forces, where we currently lack the necessary divisions for the satisfaction of our overseas commitments and the creation of a powerful and mobile reserve. The tactical air forces probably suffer from undernourishment as well. A general expansion of both organizations seems in order, although their growth should not take place at the expense of SAC. The problem is not to re-slice the present cake; it is to get a larger one with bigger slices available all around.

The question of continental defense in its active and passive aspects has been dealt with elsewhere; it need only be said here that an investment of considerable magnitude in these two activities appears absolutely essential.[6] Similarly, the support of allied forces, military institutions, and economies can hardly be relaxed. Offshore purchases, a continuing supply of military end items, economic assistance to ease the burden of large military establishments, the liberalization of trade if only to prevent the allied nations from becoming attached to the markets of the Soviet bloc— all this and much more will have to be continued. It would seem desirable, too, for American troops to remain in certain areas of the world even if those areas are not ones that we would attempt to hold in the event of a general war. Economies achieved from a concentration of forces in the United States may be more than offset by losses of territory or by the heavy costs involved in trying to prevent their loss at a later date.

In the realm of our policy record there are certain remedial steps that require taking as well. If our career during the past few years has been a chequered one, there is

[6] See Klaus Knorr, "Passive Defense for Atomic War," Memorandum No. 6, Center of International Studies, Princeton University, 1954.

no reason why it should remain so. With a set of deterrence objectives clearly in mind, and with a reasonable amount of self-imposed discipline the government should be able to speak and act in a fairly single-minded fashion. That by itself would be a gain. But we should do more; we should be prepared to seize every favorable opportunity to demonstrate how serious are our deterrent intentions. One of the many tragedies of Indo-China is that we did not seem to weigh seriously enough the implications of non-intervention for a policy of deterrence. In that case it could be argued that the disadvantages of intervention outweighed the advantages; but should contingencies of a similar character arise in the future, despite our best efforts to forestall them, we must remember how much a policy of deterrence depends on the record for its credibility, and evaluate the desirability of intervention from this as well as from other standpoints.

In the realm of governmental attitudes there are obviously several changes that must occur before an effective program of deterrence can be set in motion. First and foremost, we must increase our flexibility and adaptability not only in our estimates of communist behavior and in the ways with which we meet it, but also in our dealings with the wider universe of international relations as it has come to be. An ossification of governmental outlook, a clinging to stereotypes that bear no relation to current realities, a refusal to experiment with new ideas and methods, all preclude the institution of an effective program of deterrence, especially if that program contains not only sanctions but elements of rewards as well. Of equal importance is the development of the will, and the institutions, for regular consultation and planning with the governments of our allies. They have a large stake in the effectiveness of our policy, but they can also affect materially the degree of its credibility. For the communists must know, and regret, that we are very heavily committed to the Western coalition. If they see disagreement within the alliance, as there has been over the doctrine of massive retaliation, they will find it difficult to take our intentions seriously. However delightful it may be to formulate policy in isolation, the luxury is one that we can no longer wholly afford. A willingness to act as the leader of a coalition rather than as the principal of a kindergarten is an essential prerequisite to effective deterrence in the present state of the world.

Advantages and Disadvantages of the Policy

Since a key requirement of an effective policy of deterrence is public support for it both here and abroad, we must deal with the question of whether or not domestic and allied opinion will be prepared to accept the implications of a program much broader than massive retaliation.

There are several reasons why the prospects of public support are good. It seems to be recognized quite generally that there is no easy way of deterring the communists; that if the goal is achieved it will be by complex and expensive means. Some if not all of the components of a wide-ranging program of deterrence have already been accepted. A standing army of considerable size, large air forces and navies, the peacetime draft, alliances, foreign aid, and much of the other paraphernalia of the cold war are now regarded as normal conditions of our existence. But it is useless to pretend that an expansion in the magnitude of these weapons will be greeted with equanimity, unless it can be shown that the advantages of such a step will clearly outweigh its disadvantages.

In the case of an effective deterrence program this is a difficult feat to perform. For its immediate costs would be large and impossible of concealment. The military budget would have to expand; there would almost certainly be an increased appropriation for foreign assistance; and the result would be a further resort to deficit financing and a rise in taxes of all kinds. Hardly anything imaginable could be less popular. Moreover, the risk would remain of the deterrents being ineffective. Guarantees are impossible in this realm; refunds are out of the question if the appliances fail to work. And, if they do work, the returns will be invisible; our gain will be the negative and unexciting one that our position has not deteriorated and the communists have not tried what they might otherwise have been tempted to do.

On the other hand, the demands on our resources and productive facilities are not now so great that an increase in expenditures for defense and economic assistance is beyond our means. Nor will its benefits be any less real because they are intangible. We expand our capacity for deterrence and free ourselves from reliance upon the hazardous policy of massive retaliation. If the contingencies that we wish to deter do after all materialize, our preparations will not have been wasted; and they will probably have cost less than programs hastily instituted to meet a crisis. If the contingencies do not materialize, we will not only have saved ourselves additional and very horrible costs. We will also have increased the chances of constructing a system of international relations more in keeping with our professed desires.

The development of an effective policy of deterrence means discarding ideas of the stretch-out and the long haul, but this should hardly be a source of regret. The first concept assumes that it is possible to assign target dates to aggression; the second presupposes that military preparations should be related simply to fighting a war and not to preventing one as well. A policy of deterrence has contrary assumptions and is incompatible with these approaches. Its immediate costs, therefore, are greater; but the corresponding advantages are so considerable that support for it should not be impossible to mobilize.

The Limits of Deterrence

Whatever the advantages of having a broadly based policy of deterrence, certain factors will limit its utility in the present situation. The Soviet Union and Red China have cut themselves off from the outside world to such an extent that they have become immune to many of the pressures and inducements operative among the non-communist nations. The number of sanctions that we can impose upon them, or the rewards that we can tempt them with, are therefore bound to be limited. It may even be that China, with her great spaces and poverty-stricken economy, will not be sensitive to the final threat of massive retaliation.

Moreover, the means of deterrence that we do have at our disposal are, for the most part, extremely blunt in character. Even if we remit the threat of massive retaliation to contingencies of the last resort, we are left with weapons that we shall be reluctant to use except when confronted with quite critical conditions. Although it will be easier for us to be persuasive in our threat to use them rather than the instruments of massive retaliation, there will always be cases to which they will not plausibly apply. There are, in fact, many avenues of attack open to our antagonist from which it would be wasteful to try to deter him. In the realms of propaganda, infiltration, and the divisive diplomatic maneuver he will have to be granted a pretty free hand. A reduction of his effectiveness along these lines will depend, not on the existence of deterrents, but on our capacity to create conditions in the non-communist world which will make his blandishments and blackmail seem meaningless.

Deterrents are costly to construct and maintain; they are not suitable to the entire range of foreign policy contingencies; frequently, it may be cheaper to devise bulwarks against attack than to attempt to prevent the onslaught. And where the difficulties of the non-communist world result from internal dissatisfactions rather than external pressures, deterrents serve very little purpose at all.

Conclusion

A consideration of these limitations should not be taken to mean that the United States can achieve a reasonable measure of security without an elaborate policy of deterrence. The communist world may actually be changing its stripes, but the evidence of change still is not sufficient to warrant our forgetting the postwar experience. Whatever comfort we may derive from the Geneva Conference, the new orientation of Soviet domestic policy, the soft words from Moscow, and the resumption of disarmament talks, it is outweighed by the menace implicit in the harsh voices of Peiping, the divisive tactics of Mr. Molotov, and, perhaps most important of all, the great change in military technology that is so rapidly overtaking us. The risks inherent in this developing situation are very grave, and we know from the recent past what price must be paid for ignoring them. The outbreak of World War II, Pearl Harbor, the loss of Eastern Europe, and the Korean war itself resulted in part because of a failure by the United States to institute adequate policies of deterrence.

That Mr. Dulles and his predecessors have profited from this experience offers grounds for encouragement. But we must not delude ourselves that deterrents can be constructed on the cheap or that we will be taken at our word when we threaten massive retaliation indiscriminately. The outcry against current doctrine stems from more than fear and partisan politics; it is a reaction against the despair, the futility, and the recklessness that massive retaliation implies. It is, in fact, a demand for reasonable and tolerable substitutes.

We have the resources, the energies, and the skills to create these substitutes; and there are ample reasons for believing that they will perform their appointed tasks. In marshalling our deterrence forces, however, we must remember that they can occupy only a special sector of the foreign policy front. Just as massive retaliation is inadequate as a deterrent, so deterrence is inadequate as a foreign policy. There is a great range of enemy action that we cannot control by threats or rewards. And since we seek far more than security—however vital it may be—there remains a vast field where deterrence has no utility at all. In areas where the communists cannot be efficiently deterred we must create the conditions which will nullify their strategies. In areas where the opportunity exists to enhance the general welfare we must just as surely act. Indeed, here must be the heart of our policy, with deterrence as its discreet, powerful, and versatile guardian.

1961

AFTER DETECTION — WHAT?

Fred Charles Iklé

Fred Iklé is currently the Under Secretary of Defense for Policy. He is a former Director of the U.S. Arms Control and Disarmament Agency, professor of political science at the Massachusetts Institute of Technology and Chairman of Conservation Management Corporation. He serves on the boards of directors of the International Peace Academy, the European-American Institute for Security Research and the Hudson Institute. He is the author of *How Nations Negotiate*.

The current debate on arms control and disarmament puts great stress on the problem of how to detect violations of whatever agreements may be reached. To this end inspection schemes and instruments for detection are developed, their capabilities and limitations discussed, and efforts made to test and improve them. Indeed the technical question of detection dominates not only the domestic debate but also the international disarmament negotiations.

Yet detecting violations is not enough. What counts are the political and military consequences of a violation once it has been detected, since these alone will determine whether or not the violator stands to gain in the end. In entering into an arms-control agreement, we must know not only that we are technically capable of detecting a violation but also that we or the rest of the world will be politically, legally and militarily in a position to react effectively

Reprinted with permission of *Foreign Affairs*. Copyright © 1961 by *Foreign Affairs*.

if a violation is discovered. If we focus all our attention on the technicalities of how to detect a violation, we are in danger of assuming that our reactions and sanctions will be adequate.

A potential violator of an arms-control agreement will not be deterred simply by the risk that his action may be discovered. What will deter him will be the fear that what he gains from the violation will be outweighed by the loss he may suffer from the victim's reaction to it. In other words, even if we can develop an inspection system that makes the probability of detection very high, a nation contemplating a violation will not be deterred if it thinks it can discourage, circumvent or absorb our reaction.

We have learned (almost too late, in the case of the nuclear test ban) that an opponent may thwart our detection techniques by evasive techniques of his own. We should also realize that he may thwart the consequences of detection—which we count on to deter violations—by military or political stratagems. We must study, therefore, not only what our opponent may do to avoid detection, but also what he may do to escape the penalty of being detected.

Let us discuss the question of what may happen when an evasion is detected under four general headings: (1) the reaction of world opinion; (2) the political reaction by the injured country; (3) various military measures that the injured country could undertake in an effort to restore the situation that would have existed without an arms-control agreement; and (4) military and political measures that would go beyond this "restoration."

World opinion, it is sometimes argued, will help to enforce disarmament agreements. World opinion supposedly will turn against the violator, provided he is discovered and "convicted" in an internationally accepted forum. He will lose prestige and influence in the uncommitted countries. In addition, various world-wide political reactions are expected to work to his disadvantage.

"World opinion" is such an amorphous concept that one finds it difficult to determine just how it can injure a violator of arms-control agreements. Speeches or resolutions in the United Nations, or critical editorials in the world press, are not likely to hurt him very much. One reason world opinion is so impotent is that its memory is so short. If the world's reaction cannot be translated immediately into substantive political or military changes damaging to the violator, it will lose all force.

The Soviet suppression of the Hungarian revolution illustrates the point. This gave an exceptionally violent shock to world opinion—in fact, more violent than many possible violations of arms-control agreements are likely to be. This is particularly true since evidence of a violation might often be equivocal and involve technicalities hard for the public to understand. Some of the most cherished beliefs of the West and also of the uncommitted countries were flouted in Hungary: a popular revolt against a dictatorial régime in a small nation was crushed from outside by a large power. Agreements were broken in the most flagrant fashion. One was the promise given by the Soviet-installed Kadar Government to the Jugoslav Government not to take punitive action against Imré Nagy when he left sanctuary in the Jugoslav Embassy. Another was the invitation extended to General Maléter and other delegates of the legal Hungarian Government to negotiate the withdrawal of Soviet forces—a trap to catch and execute them. Yet if one tries to list the penalties that world opinion imposed on the Soviet Union and the Kadar Government for these violations of its most sacred norms and of several important articles of the United Nations Charter, there is very little to record. There was a slight loss in the strength of Communist Parties in Western Europe (confined mostly to intellectuals on the fringe of the Party), but the loss is no longer noticeable. The strain on President Tito's relations with Moscow and the strengthening of NATO ties (particularly with Iceland) were largely ephemeral. Kadar has not been officially recognized as Hungary's legal representative in the United Nations; but he has been sitting in the General Assembly.

Other recent events have aroused world opinion, such as the Peking régime's violent repressions in Tibet and its violations of the Indian border. Yet in February 1960, only a few months after indignation in India had reached its peak, the Communists increased their vote in Kerala from 35 to 43 percent. And many of Communist China's neighbors continued to favor her admission to the United Nations.

Perhaps significantly, when Khrushchev discussed the nuclear test ban before the Supreme Soviet in January 1960, he chose to emphasize the reaction of world opinion as a deterrent to disarmament violations. By arguing that it was a sufficient deterrent, he tried, in effect, to brush aside the problems of inspection and control. But even if one assumed that the reaction of world opinion constituted an adequate sanction—an assumption challenged above—inspection would still be essential. A violator who does not risk being detected obviously does not need to fear world opinion. In any case, the West has paid insufficient attention to the stratagems which a detected violator can pursue to avoid or mitigate whatever action an aroused world opinion might take.

Many devices are available for this purpose. Thus the violator can frustrate the international inspection system and prevent it from reaching an official finding (study of Communist obstruction of inspection in North Korea reveals a large bag of such tricks). Or he can blame the other side for having violated the agreement first, and thus confuse the issue, or even generate an adverse political reaction against the injured party. Or he can accuse the other side of fabricating the evidence as a pretext for breaking the agreement or for covering up some other misdeed. Or he can assert that the agreement is obsolete in view of what he claims are changed political or military conditions and denounce it unilaterally prior to the intended violation (this would be analogous to the Soviet declaration that the Four-Power Agreements on Berlin were no longer valid). Finally, if some unfavorable reaction in world opinion is unavoidable, it may turn out that the violators "will cover themselves with shame"—as Khrushchev argued when he spoke about the nuclear test ban: "If some side violates the assumed commitments, the initiators of this violation will cover themselves with shame, they will be branded by all the peoples of the world." Yet, six weeks before making this assertion that a nuclear test ban would be enforced by world opinion, Khrushchev had this to recommend: "International reactionary circles are still trying to discuss the so-called 'Hungarian question' in the United Nations. Let them keep it as a souvenir if this consoles them"

Not only may the violator be contemptuous of world opinion, but he also may justify his acts on the grounds that they are demanded by the welfare of "the people" or by History—History being his conception of a superior morality that takes precedence over world opinion. "Had we not helped you," Khrushchev told the Hungarian Communists, "we would have been called stupid, and History would not have forgiven us this stupidity."

To be effective, a sanction must be applied as a result of governmental decisions by the injured countries. In democratic countries, government decisions are influenced by active public opinion, or, more precisely, by the conception of public opinion held by the government leaders. In these circumstances, democratic governments might experience serious political difficulties in reacting effectively to a detected evasion:

(1) The injured government must acknowledge the fact that there has been a violation. If the violation is open and well-publicized, no difficulty exists. But if evidence of the violation is equivocal or based on secret intelligence, the government may be reluctant to acknowledge the evasion or feel unsure of its ability to convince public opinion. For example, an admission that the control agreement had failed might be exploited at home by the political opposition, particularly if the agreement had been made originally by the party in power. In such a situation some decision-makers may favor an interpretation which casts doubt on the intelligence data relating to evasion or which belittles the importance of the evasion. Responsible decision-makers seldom distort evidence deliberately.[1] But the interpretation of complicated information is often a matter of judgment and discretion; hence subtle biases may decide the issue. Responsible officials would be particularly disinclined to accept equivocal evidence about an evasion of a disarmament agreement if they had previously been forced to defend the agreement against partisan charges that it might be violated. Yet a democratic government could institute only minor penalties against an evasion without informing legislative bodies and the public about the exact situation and explaining the need for drastic retaliatory or corrective measures.

(2) The injured government must be willing to increase military expenditures and to offend pacifist feelings. Now

---

[1] When Germany violated rearmament restrictions in the 1930s, Winston Churchill suspected that "somewhere between the Intelligence Service and the ministerial chief there has been some watering down or whittling down of the facts." (Speech of May 22, 1935, in "While England Slept," New York: Putman, 1938, p. 190.) Prime Minister Baldwin's later admission suggested that there might have been something deliberate about this "watering down," and perhaps at the highest level.

the reaction to a localized or minor violation need not disturb the defense budget appreciably (the new military equipment needed to counteract the North Korean violations of the rearmament clause was not a heavy burden); but the breaking of a major disarmament agreement will almost certainly require new military measures, perhaps a full-scale program of rearmament. The decision to react firmly and regardless of expense will be a hard one. Public opinion may not approve, especially if the evasion occurred gradually or if it merely consists of a resumption of some activity that had been discontinued—such as testing. If knowledge of the evasion is based exclusively on clandestine intelligence sources that cannot be revealed, the opponent's denial may find receptive ears among domestic opposition groups.

We have already questioned the effectiveness of world opinion as a sanction against arms-control evasions. It is ironic that it may be domestic public opinion—or rather the government's conception of it—that actually prevents effective sanctions being taken. The classic instance of this, and one that may have been a contributing cause of World War II, was England's reluctance to rearm in response to Hitler's violations of the Versailles rearmament restrictions. With what he called "an appalling frankness," Prime Minister Baldwin explained in 1936 why his own government had been unable to react:

You will remember at that time [1932–33] the Disarmament Conference was sitting in Geneva. You will remember at that time there was probably a stronger pacifist feeling running through this country than at any time since the war. You will remember the election at Fulham in the autumn of 1933, when a seat which the National Government held was lost by about 7,000 votes on no issue but the pacifist. . . . I asked myself what chance was there . . . within the next year or two of that feeling being so changed that the country would give a mandate for rearmament? Supposing I had gone to the country and said that Germany was rearming and that we must rearm, does anybody think that this pacific democracy would have rallied to that cry at that moment? I cannot think of anything that would have made the loss of the election from my point of view more certain.[2]

(3) The injured government must accept the new risks created by its reaction to the violation. It may see more than

_____

[2] Baldwin's reply to Churchill as quoted in Churchill, "While England Slept," New York: Putnam, 1938, p. 333.

the domestic difficulties involved. For example, it may have embarked on long-range policies which seem more promising and important than counteracting an accomplished evasion, and it may hesitate to jeopardize them.[3]

It has been argued that all countries will be deterred from violating a major arms-control agreement in present circumstances because to do so would set off an unrestricted arms race that would eventually lead to disaster for the guilty as well as the innocent.[4] But this is an assumption which may not be shared by a country set on violating the agreement. Its leaders may reason that the very prospect of an unrestricted arms race might itself inhibit the injured party from reacting to the violation. And in fact the injured party might feel it safer to write off the violation as a loss rather than risk new dangers by a policy of rearmament— especially if it now finds itself in a weaker military position as a result of having complied with the agreement.

This dilemma is most serious. For example, the nuclear test-ban conference adopted an article on March 19, 1959, upon the insistence of the United States and the United Kingdom, affiming a country's "inherent right" to withdraw from the treaty if its provisions, "including those providing for the timely installation and effective operation of the control system," are not being fulfilled. This article might be of cardinal importance in connection with China's accession to the test-ban treaty, because part of the control system would have to be installed in China. But would it give the Western powers much leverage against Chinese obstructionism? In the absence of a known instance of illegal testing, would the West be willing to withdraw from a test-ban treaty with the Soviet Union, resume testing and risk accelerating the arms race merely because the "timely installation" of the control system was being prevented by China?

(4) The injured government may have to reach agreement with allies before it can react. All disarmament agreements of current interest involve the United States with one

---

[3] Churchill was aware of this when he was pleading for a more effective response to Hitler's treaty violations: 'Then it is said—and I must give this explanation of the extraordinary fact—that 'we were laboring for disarmament,' and it would have spoiled the disarmament hopes if any overt steps to raise our Air Force had been taken." Speech of May 22, 1935, *op. cit.*, p. 190.

[4] For example, the Committee on Science and Technology of the Democratic Advisory Council wrote on March 14, 1960, about the nuclear test ban: "A nation which violates such an a agreement automatically sets into motion an arms race from which there may never be an end."

or more of its allies. It is usually a difficult task to prepare a joint negotiating position vis-à-vis a Communist opponent. Agreeing on a Western response to a violation will raise anew the problem of allied coördination. The stronger and more explicit the reaction proposed, the more difficult it will be to achieve agreement. And all the problems of domestic public opinion and partisan politics discussed above will be evident in the allied nations whose coöperation is required.

The military sanctions against evasion of an arms-control agreement can either be confined to measures that restore the situation that would have existed without the agreement or they can go further. Let us call the former "restorative measures." If the violator resumes testing, the injured country will do likewise; If the violator reoccupies his part of a neutralized zone, the other will move back into his; and if the violator rearms, his opponent will rearm to the same extent.

The problem of deterring violations has often been oversimplified by assuming that a detected evasion would automatically be taken care of by the cancellation of the agreement and the application of such "restorative measures." But three conditions have to be met if "restorative measures" by themselves are to be an adequate deterrent:

(1) The potential violator must fear the risk of being detected.

(2) He must also fear that a detected violation will cause an unwanted response by the injured country.

(3) He must not expect a violation to bring him an irrevocable advantage that would outweigh whatever gain he derives from abiding by the agreement.

The importance of the first condition is fully recognized. The second condition depends on the political factors we have just discussed. Both these conditions are needed for deterring an evasion by any type of sanctions, whether "restorative or "punitive." Here we are interested in the third condition, because if it is not met, "restorative measures" alone are inadequate.

This third condition is not met, for example, if an agreement comprises several arms-control measures in such a way that the separate measures, taken individually, favor either one side or the other. The agreement remains in the interest of both parties only if all measures are observed. Violation of a part of it cannot be deterred by the threat of "restorative measures" confined only to this particular part. Additional sanctions are required. Otherwise the violator can break just those control measures that are not to his advantage. He will stand to gain if his violation remains undiscovered or ignored; and he will also gain if the violated part of the agreement is cancelled, because the residual agreement will then be more to his advantage.

This is precisely what happened with the Korean armistice. The clause prohibiting the introduction of new military equipment was violated by the Communists from the first day, but cancellation of this clause by the United Nations Command did not come until four years later. So the Communists gained on the first count. They also gained on the second count (after the United Nations eventually instituted "restorative measures"), because the residual armistice agreement was more favorable to them than the original agreement. (It was they who had been primarily constrained by the cancelled rearmament clause.)

It might be argued that an arms-control measure can survive only if all its separable components are equally in the interest of both parties. If this argument is true, the future for disarmament agreements is bleak. It is hard enough to arrive at over-all agreements that will not, over time, seem disadvantageous to one side or the other. But individual components of an agreement are inevitably of unequal value to opposing nations. For example, in addition to the Korean armistice, several of the current proposals for disengagement zones are composed of very unequal provisions.

There are other situations where the threat of "restorative measures" would be insufficient to deter an evasion. The violator may gain an irrevocable technological lead or an irreversible strategic advantage. As has often been pointed out, if American and Soviet troops were withdrawn from Western and Eastern Europe, the United States might find it difficult or impossible to return in the event that Soviet troops moved back in. Western alliance arrangements might have lapsed, the American troops might have been demobilized, and in any case they would have to be transported a greater distance—not to mention the Amercan public's unwillingness to send "the boys" back overseas, particularly under a threat of nuclear war.

To sum up, "restorative measures" will not deter a nation contemplating a violation of a disarmament agreement in those situations where our third condition is not met, namely, when the violator expects to gain less from abiding by the agreement than from abandoning it. Indeed, a potential violator might enter into agreements solely in order to seek gains by violating them. He would calculate that there would always be a chance of his escaping detection or that "restorative measures" might be delayed or frustrated for political reasons. And if he lost out on these chances, a mere return to the status quo would leave him no worse off than before he entered into the agreement. The violator, in fact, would be playing a profitable game: "Heads you lose, tails we're even."

Where the threat of "restorative measures" is not enough to deter evasions, additional penalties are required. But to deter a would-be violator effectively they must be credible.

By far the most important and practical penalty would be a general increase in the military effort, going beyond what would be required to restore the pre-agreement situation. (A threat to start a war would not be equally credible and would therefore be less effective.) Suppose the aggrieved nation increases its defense budget by $20 billion. (As a result of the North Korean aggression, the United States increased its national security expenditures from $13 billion to $52 billion.) If the violator does not follow suit, he will become relatively weaker than he was before breaking the disarmament agreement. If he does follow suit, he would, in effect, be "fined" the equivalent of $20 billion, though of course both sides would bear this burden.

The injured country may be able to step up its defense effort in ways that do not require a large increase in the budget and still impose significant penalties on the violator: for example, by changing the deployment and readiness of weapons, or by resuming military activities that were voluntarily limited beforehand. However, in doing this the injured party must be prepared to run the risk that such a "punitive" increase in its defense effort will renew or accelerate the arms race. Actually, the violator may wish to avoid an arms race with so determined an opponent; he may be unwilling or unable to pay his full "fine" and have to accept a loss in relative military strength.

Those who wish to prevent the violation of arms-control agreements must deter potential violators by their evident determination to make a double sacrifice. In the event a violation occurs they must be ready to assume a greater economic burden for defense, and they must risk a step-up in military competition. The willingness to make such sacrifices involves less, however, than would be required to deter limited aggression. To do that successfully a country must be willing not only to accept increased defense costs if deterrence fails, but also to suffer casualties and face the risk that the limited conflict may expand.

Political sanctions are likely to be less effective than an increased defense effort, although they may play an important complementary role. What they might be is difficult to predict in the abstract. If the potential violator is cautious, this uncertainty may help to deter him; if he is adventurous, like Hitler, he will gamble on his ability to meet and overcome the political reaction.

The remaining question is how to make the penalties of evasion seem more inevitable and severe and the gains more dubious. Parliamentary governments are more likely to take strong action against a violation if they are supported by public opinion. The country that is determined to abide by the agreement cannot afford to neglect this research without opening the way for a potential violator to gain and then exploit a technological lead. Unless the public understands this fact, parliamentary governments will be handicapped in maintaining a research effort for weapons whose testing has been prohibited. The same problem would also arise under an agreement which does not prohibit the development of a weapon but does prevent the deployment of it—for example, a ban on placing weapons of mass destruction in orbit.

A program to deter evasion of arms-control agreements, like the one suggested here, does raise some additional problems for which an analogy can be found in the strategy of deterrence against nuclear attack. First, there is the problem of carrying out a threat if deterrence fails, that is, of imposing sanctions in the event of evasion or of retaliating in the event of attack. An advance commitment to carry out the threat is rational and necessary for a policy aimed at deterrence; but carrying out the threat after deterrence has failed may be undesirable or even irrational. Second, a policy of deterrence has to cope with accidental violations of the agreement, just as a policy of deterrence against nuclear attack has to control the risk of accidental war. In the former case, both sides will wish to correct the unintended violation and preserve the agreement; in the latter, both will want to avoid or correct an "accident" before it leads to full exchanges of violence. Third, there is some resemblance between the advantage of a first strike in mutual deterrence against nuclear attack and the advantage of gaining time through an evasion in certain arms-control agreements. None of these analogies is exact, of course. But they do suggest that ideas in the literature on deterrence can be as relevant to the prevention of violations in arms-control agreements as they are to the prevention of war.

1976

FORMULATING STRATEGIC DOCTRINE

Henry S. Rowen

Henry S. Rowen is Professor of Public Management at the Graduate School of Business, Stanford University, and a former President of the RAND Corporation. He is Chairman of the Executive Panel, Office of the Chief of Naval Operations, and a member of the Defense Science Board, Department of Defense, the Council on Foreign Relations, and the International Institute for Strategic Studies.

Should a President in the event of a nuclear attack be left with the single option of ordering the mass destruction of enemy civilians, in the face of the certainty that it would be followed by the mass slaughter of Americans?

U.S. Foreign Policy for the 1970's,
A Report to Congress by Richard M. Nixon,
February 18, 1970.

Obviously a rhetorical question, President Nixon's query in his first foreign policy report posed sharply the

For much of the material on World War II, the author is indebted to Thomas Brown, and for the post-World War II period up to 1963 to William Kaufmann's *The McNamara Strategy* (New York: Harper and Row, 1964). The material on the history of nuclear options in the 1960's owes a great deal to Alain Enthoven, former Assistant Secretary of Defense for Systems Analysis. In addition, much material on this subject has been made public in recent months through Congressional Hearings and Defense Department reports and statements.

The author is also indebted to Graham Allison and Peter Szanton for assistance and comments in the preparation of this paper. Finally, the perspective on nuclear doctrine has been developed in the course of a project on military doctrines and postures that the author has been carrying out with Albert Wohlstetter, who has provided many useful suggestions and comments.

This paper was originally prepared for the President's Commission on the Organization of the Government for the Conduct of Foreign Policy, June 1975.

issue of nuclear options. Evidently no one answered his question because it reappeared in three successive annual foreign policy reports. Not until January of 1974 was it responded to officially. The answer was: No. Secretary of Defense James Schlesinger announced that the U.S. was changing its nuclear plans to provide for a greater range of options, including ones that would be a good deal less "massive" than those that had been available in the past.

Many observers were surprised by the revelation that the U.S. had little flexibility in its nuclear plans. More than a decade had passed since Eisenhower's strategy of "massive retaliation" had been abandoned. In 1961, President Kennedy had adopted a policy of having a wide range of military choices. Through the 1960's Secretary McNamara advocated flexible nuclear plans. One would have thought that President Nixon should have inherited plans for a wide selection of choices from the use of one or a few such weapons on the battlefield, through larger scale use on military targets, to the option of massive attack on Soviet civil society.

Evidently he did not. Though critics were skeptical about the implication of President Nixon's question, the available evidence is clear that the President had not had a wide range of choice for the use of nuclear weapons. Secretary Schlesinger stated this unambiguously:

> In the past we have had massive preplanned nuclear strikes in which one would be dumping literally thousands of weapons on the Soviet Union. Some of these strikes could, to some extent, be withheld from going directly against cities, but that was limited even then.
> With massive strikes of that sort, it would be impossible to ascertain whether the purpose of a strategic strike was limited or not. It was virtually indistinguishable from an attack on cities. One would not have had blast damage in the cities, but one would have considerable fallout and the rest of it.

The advance of pre-planned, non-massive nuclear options does not mean, as the Defense Secretary had pointed out, that they could not be prepared in an emergency. But this is a different matter from thinking through in advance the problems that might arise, working on how they might be dealt with, and training people in possibly needed operations.

This case traces the history of nuclear options over nearly a thirty-year span. The central question is, why is it, in the third decade of the nuclear era, more than a decade after Kennedy's and McNamara's policy of flexible options, four years after President Nixon's query, the Secretary of Defense says that non-massive nuclear options are now in the process of being adopted?

The issue of nuclear options is not only of historical interest; it is a matter of considerable current policy relevance. The role of nuclear weapons in U.S. weapons policy in the years ahead is far from settled. If anything, the future of the subject is likely to be a good deal more complex and difficult than the past has been. Anyone who doubts this should reflect on the problem of the role of nuclear weapons in a world in which many countries, perhaps not all politically stable, possess them.

Section I of this volume is a short primer on the institutional process of nuclear planning. Section II presents an historical overview of this subject. Section III discusses in somewhat greater detail the history of nuclear options in the 1960's under Secretary McNamara. Section IV attempts to draw some lessons from this record on nuclear doctrines.

Nuclear Planning Process

The present process of constructing nuclear plans dates from August, 1960 when Secretary of Defense Gates created the joint Strategic Target Planning Staff (JSTPS) and charged it with producing an integrated plan for the use of nuclear weapons possessed by all of the U.S. military commands and for coordinating this nuclear plan with our allies. The Director of this staff reports to the Joint Chiefs of Staff; from the beginning he has been the Commander of the Strategic Air Command. His Deputy has always been a naval officer. The JSTPS has provided an integrated plan for the forces of the Commander of the Strategic Air Command (CINCSAC), the Commander of U.S. forces in Europe (CINCEUR), the Commander of U.S. naval forces in the Atlantic (CINCLANT) and the Commander of U.S. forces in the Pacific (CINCPAC); he has also coordinated this plan with those of allied forces under the Supreme Allied Commanders in Europe and the Atlantic, SACEUR and SACLANT.

Until recently, the JSTPS operated under a national strategic targeting attack policy that was prepared by higher military and civilian authorities in 1960. This policy set

objectives for the preparation of plans, assigned responsibilities, described the options to be developed, assigned
specific tasks to be performed, and identified the forces
involved. On the basis of this guidance, the Staff maintained
a strategic target list and prepared the Single Integrated
Operational Plan or SIOP, for short. The SIOP specified,
for several options, nuclear weapons to be used, delivery
systems, routes of attack, timing of attack, and the expected
level of target damage to be attained. The options have been
characterized in terms of three classes of targets (nuclear
threat, other military, urban-industrial) and in terms of the
timing of the attack relative to the launch of Soviet forces.
(Timing would affect the size and composition of the U.S.
forces surviving and available for launch.) The policy also
specified the priority to be given to each target class. From
1960 to 1974, the priority in the assignment of weapons was
first, to the urban-industrial targets, and then to nuclear
threat and other military forces.[1] The capability of destroying urban-industrial targets was to be assured even with
inadequate warning of an attack on our strategic forces and
the consequent loss of a sizable portion of them. In short,
highest importance has been consistently given to assuring
a stipulated level of damage to the Soviet civil society and
not to attempting to limit damage to the U.S. or its allies.
However, as noted by Secretary Schlesinger in the quote
above, there has existed the option of withholding strikes
going directly against cities.

The basic planning process, once overall priorities
have been established, is to assign weapons to specific
targets. For example, air defenses might be assigned to early
missile attack because their destruction is important if
bombers are to penetrate reliably. The principle of "cross-
targeting" has been employed in order to have high confidence against possible failure, i.e. the assignment of
weapons to the same target from forces that have very different vulnerabilities on the ground to Soviet attack and different problems of penetration to target. This process
involves multiplying a series of estimated probabilities,
e.g. of survival, reliable launch, penetration to target, and

[1]A high "priority" in this context means "most important." It does not mean first
in time. Presumably the most time urgent targets would be military forces, especially
nuclear threat ones. Highest priority also does not mean that the greatest *weight of effort*
would have to be allocated against urban-industrial targets; rather that the *confidence*
of being able to destroy these targets should be high.

probability of target destruction (given a specific bomb or warhead yield and weapon delivery accuracy). Weapons are then assigned to targets to achieve a given level of expected damage or a given level of damage with a certain level of confidence.[2] The result of this exercise has been the assignment of the weapons in the U.S. nuclear offensive forces (ICBMs, submarine missiles, manned bombers and theater based forces) to the three target classes.

The countries targeted in the SIOP have been the U.S.S.R., the People's Republic of China, and allies of these two powers in Eastern Europe and elsewhere. A good deal of flexibility has been provided for in the separate targeting of countries, (although when the SIOP was first created, plans did not provide for an attack on the U.S.S.R. without also attacking China; this nonseparation reflected widely held American beliefs about the monolithism of the Sino-Soviet bloc).

Over the years the number of weapons in both the U.S. and Soviet forces has increased enormously, as has the number of targets assigned to these weapons, but the number of urban-industrial targets, the most important category as defined by the American political authorities, has increased little. This has made possible the assignment of many more weapons to the lower priority nuclear threat and other military target categories than was possible earlier. So long as our forces survive for launch, the task of producing a high level of urban damage has not been difficult for the U.S. (nor has it, although with a lag, for the Soviet Union). However, the large increase in the number of warheads deliverable against the Soviet Union and increases in the number, hardness, and mobility of Soviet long-range nuclear forces has resulted in a decline in damage expectancies for this class of targets. And a large and growing part of this force, e.g. submarines at sea, cannot be targeted. There has been no comparable decline in the U.S. ability to deliver weapons against Soviet general purpose forces.

Centralizing and integrating nuclear attack planning has meant reconciling the objectives of several U.S. commanders as well as those of other nations, a task of

---

[2] This sequence of probabilities of course assumes a prior one: the political decision to launch an attack had occurred. As later discussion brings out, the probability that a decision to launch a SIOP attack would be made by the political authorities has come increasingly into question.

considerable complexity and delicacy. Each can be expected
to have his own views about what should be done to meet
his responsibilities. Before August, 1960, each theater commander made his own plans for the use of his command's
nuclear weapons. In addition, the commander of SAC had
a separate nuclear plan for employing the major portion of
American nuclear strength. And SACEUR, an allied commander, has long had his own regional plan for the employment of the forces assigned to him, allied as well as U.S.

The new directive on nuclear attack policy announced by Secretary Schlesinger covers all nuclear
weapons, not just those classified as "strategic." It differs from
the earlier directive not only by providing for less than
massive options but, most importantly, by emphasizing the
existence of non-targets, i.e. places that it would be in the
U.S. interest to preserve from destruction. In the past, there
had been constraints, for example, on the amount of fallout
on allied and neutral territory, constraints by SACEUR on
collateral damage in Eastern Europe and constraints on
damage within allied territory; there also was the city
withhold option. However, on the whole, it had been assumed that collateral damage to places of value to an adversary other than designated targets was a "bonus." Now it
is explicitly recognized that it might be very much to the
U.S. advantage to prevent damage to certain places or things
of value in the Soviet Union, e.g. population centers. In
short, collateral damage is now being increasingly seen as
a "minus."

The current policy provides an option for attack on
urban targets, but with emphasis on targeting selected war-
related industrial facilities, not on widespread damage to
populations. This distinction in targeting is becoming
technically feasible because of the increased accuracy of
weapons delivery. High accuracy lowers collateral damage
both directly and indirectly. Directly by preventing bombs
from missing targets and hitting non-targets; indirectly by
making possible the substitution of low yield weapons for
high yield ones and, in some cases, the use of fewer weapons.
In short the linking of "urban" to "industrial" targets in the
hyphenated phrase "urban-industrial" does not follow from
the laws of physics but from a combination of doctrine and
technology specific to a given era. Now both technology and
doctrine are undergoing changes.

The new policy also includes the option of assigning weapons to nuclear threat targets. Most importantly, it includes limited employment options, e.g. those confined to a region or a specific objective.

The World War II Experience

The beginning of understanding of later developments is an appreciation of the significance of the experience of both the British and the Americans in strategic bombing in World War II. Although the RAF did not enter World War II with an area bombing doctrine, it soon adopted one. Britain's employment of bombing against urban areas was, in substantial measure, the unintended product of its poor bombing accuracy. Poor accuracy contributed to civilian casualties in two ways: first, even when strictly military objectives were the targets, a large number of bombs would miss the target and fall almost at random. (In the early part of the War only about one-fifth of the bombs dropped by the RAF fell within five miles of the target.) Second, the known inaccuracy led to the deliberate selection of targets in the middle of builtup areas so that the large numbers of misses would at least do some "good." It was also argued that bombs falling at random on German towns would smash German morale. This made a virtue out of necessity. These indiscriminate raids, carried out in the heat of war, were also a response to the German raids against British cities; they were also the product of British frustration in having no other way to strike directly at Germany until the invasion in 1944. Their continuation was probably dependent on the fact that the Germans could not reply in kind.

The American strategic bombers of the 8th Air Force, using optical means to bomb by day and in good weather, were able to achieve much greater accuracies than the British bombing by night. The Americans attempted to pursue a policy of precision strikes against selected targets, but there was a deterioration in this policy during the course of the war. German air defenses made clear weather attacks costly, intelligence limitations kept some targets from being correctly identified, and a desire to cooperate with the RAF led to strikes on targets which were really surrogates for area attacks on towns (e.g. the marshalling yards in Dresden). In the bombing campaign against Japan, a shift in the tactics of the 20th Air Force occurred when General LeMay replaced General Hansell. U.S. area attacks, for example, the fire raids on Tokyo, then became a matter of policy.

The upshot was that bombing of the war potential of an adversary, i.e. "strategic" bombing, by the end of World War II had come to be associated with large-scale civilian destruction—at least as a byproduct.

Early Nuclear Doctrine: Continuity with World War II

The policy of strategic bombing was disputed during the War on several grounds: on the payoff from allocating resources to long-range bombers versus other military forces; on the efficacy of area attacks versus those against specific war-related factories; on the morality of area attacks. Later analysis intensified doubts about the policy of strategic bombing. Nevertheless, as American concern with the Soviet threat to Western Europe grew in the late 1940's and early 1950's, a capability of strategic bombing emerged as an essential means of coping with that threat. The belief that the Soviet Union had superior conventional strength in Europe and elsewhere around its borders, along with the knowledge that we had clear nuclear superiority, dominated U.S. defense policy for many years. Reliance on the weapon that we had a clear advantage in to counter Soviet strength on the ground seemed obvious. The ability to deliver, say, 100 weapons with yields in the tens of kilotons on Soviet major industrial centers that had the majority of its steel, petroleum refining, aircraft and munitions industries was thought to be an impressive deterrent. If the Soviets were to attack nonetheless, the carrying out of such an attack promised an important advantage—assuming that there was enough strength on the ground to keep the Russians from quickly taking over Western Europe. In short, the nuclear planning task was seen as an extension of strategic bombing in World War II—greatly compressed in time, magnified in effect, and reduced in cost. It was principally the destruction of critical war supporting industries in order to affect Soviet battlefield operations, the longer term ability of its economy to support combat and its will to continue the conflict, The designated ground zeros were almost entirely (1) industrial facilities; (2) "retardation" targets, e.g. transportation links whose destruction was intended to slow the westward movement of Soviet forces; and (3) counterforce targets, the bases of the small and concentrated Soviet long-range air force.

Population damage in this period was viewed largely as a by-product of attacks on industrial and retardation targets.

In the early 1960's the Soviet long-range air force was regarded neither as a major target system nor as a threat to the survival of our own air forces. Here, too, there was an element of continuity with the past; enemy attack on our bases had not been much of a problem throughout most of World War II. However, work done at the Rand Corporation in the early 1950's showed that even a small Soviet long-range air force had the capacity to destroy our strategic bases abroad on which we were then dependent and even threatened our forces in the continental U.S. Although these vulnerabilities were correctable, this work focused attention on what was to be a continuing concern in U.S. defense planning, the possibility of the Soviets developing a capacity to destroy our strategic offensive force by launching a nuclear strike against it. This possibility had implications not only for the survival of our own forces but, more broadly, for the stability of the strategic balance. The existence of vulnerable nuclear forces on both sides would provide an incentive to both to strike first in an ambiguous situation. Concern about our vulnerability led to many actions to reduce the vulnerability of our strategic forces in the 1950's and in the years since then.

A different response to the developing Soviet long-range nuclear threat was a proposal, urged by scientists at M.I.T. and elsewhere, to build a highly effective U.S. continental air defense system. This idea was worked on in the Lincoln Summer Study of 1952 which proposed the construction of a large and costly air defense control system for the U.S. This air defense system was designed primarily to achieve very high effectiveness in defending U.S. cities against nuclear attack by Soviet bombers. Since only a small number of bombs had to get through to these cities in order to do great damage to them, the task faced by this system was formidable. It proved to be infeasible. But as late as the Gaither Committee Report in 1957, even after the development of high-yield fusion weapons and with intercontinental and sea based missiles in the offing, the advocates of defense proposed a very costly program of air defenses, anti-missile defenses and civil defenses to protect U.S. industry and population from attack. (The Report also advocated improved protection for our strategic forces along the lines that had been proposed by Rand.) It is not irrelevant to the current debate about flexible options to observe that many of the enthusiasts for protecting the U.S, population from attack in the 1950's were to shift in the 1960's to the position that populations were the *only* appropriate target for attack in a nuclear war.

The alternative of using nuclear weapons only or mainly on the battlefield did not seem to exist for many years. Individual battlefield targets did not present large concentrations of military value and they were too numerous to warrant expenditure of the small stockpile of nuclear weapons on them. However, the possibility of having weapons for battlefield use, or indeed limiting their use in this way, was of interest to the Army and to some scientists. Project Vista, conducted at the California Institute of Technology in 1951 was an early effort to develop this concept.

In sum, in the period before the H-Bomb was developed in the early 1950's, U.S. doctrine on the bombing of cities was ambiguous. The use of fission weapons delivered by medium and heavy bombers against the Soviet Union was part of the strategy for the defense of Western Europe. Many of the targets were selected with the intention that they have an effect, short or delayed, on the Soviets' ability to carry on a war; they were also to serve as a deterrent to attack. Attack on targets located in population centers would have caused a good deal of population damage. But the numbers of weapons and their yields were still small enough that there was a big difference in the civil damage that would have been produced then and what was to be possible within only a few years.

The possibility of building the H-Bomb produced an intense debate on the uses of nuclear weapons. Many of the opponents saw it as a weapon that could be used only against cities and didn't think it was necessary for that task; fission weapons in larger numbers were good enough for that. Many also opposed attacking cities and favored having more lower-yield fission weapons for use against military targets. The proponents did not argue that they wanted to make it easier to destroy cities; they were mainly interested in a more powerful and efficient technology. Ironically, both sides in the dispute assumed that these weapons would be usable mainly against cities, and big cities at that; both sides missed the main impact that thermonuclear weapons were to have for at least the next quarter century: the development of lightweight, medium and low-yield weapons.

However, the development of thermonuclear weapons by both the U.S. and U.S.S.R. did have consequences for the civil damage that a nuclear war would cause. Between 1954 and 1960, although the number of vehicles in the U.S. strategic force did not change greatly, the total megatonnage in our strategic offensive and defensive forces increased over twentyfold. (The peak in megatonnage—and in "effective megatonnage," another index of damage potential—was in 1960.) With yields in the megatons instead of kilotons, the delivery of only a few hundred weapons could destroy a large part of the industrial capacity and, without large-scale civil defenses, a large part of the populations of even the largest countries.

The discovery that these weapons could not only be made large in yield but light in weight, i.e. that they would have a high yield per pound and could come in small as well as big packages, made long-range ballistic missiles practical, both land and submarine based. It also meant that our strategic bomber force, which was concentrated on a small number of airbases in the U.S., and already vulnerable to a coordinated "sneak" attack by bombers, was highly vulnerable to a coordinated attack with ballistic missiles.

One consequence of the recognition of this new threat was further vulnerability-reducing changes in our strategic nuclear posture throughout the 1950's and 1960's. Another was a reinforcing of the notion that a nuclear strike had to be quick and massive rather than controlled and discriminate because strategic bases and forces could not be expected to survive long in a conflict. Still another was that as the Soviet nuclear force grew it became an important target system. And because the Soviets were slow in reducing the vulnerability of their nuclear forces, it was feasible for us to assign weapons to nuclear threat targets with high damage expectations; this assuming, not unreasonably for some contingencies, given their normal low readiness state, that Soviet forces had not been launched by the time our weapons arrived on target. By the late 1950's, the long-range delivery forces of the U.S. consisted of over 2,000 vehicles, with some vehicles carrying more than one bomb. (About 500 B-52 long-range bombers, 1,485 B-47 and RB-47 medium-range bombers and reconnaissance aircraft, B-58 bombers, and several hundred SNARK, THOR, JUPITER, MACE, MATADOR and REGULUS missiles.) This force could cover many more targets than in the late 1940's and early 1950's when there were few bombs available. Moreover, the large area of destruction produced by megaton yield weapons that became operational in the mid and late 1950's meant that attack on military or industrial targets in or on the edge of cities inevitably produced a great deal of damage to populations. In contrast with the weapons of the late 1940's and early 1950's, now it was virtually impossible to attack specific industrial facilities such as an electric power generating station in a metropolitan area without destroying most of its built-up area and the people in it. Attempts to do precision bombing during World War II had often been frustrated by the need to cope with strong air defenses in daylight bombing and poor accuracy in bombing by night or in bad weather. This had produced widespread civilian damage. With thermonuclear weapons, only a few bombs needed to be delivered to destroy each target, but their effects were much more widespread and destructive.

The idea that cities were the natural targets for thermonuclear weapons was reinforced by the low accuracy expected of ballistic missiles. Mid-1950's U.S. estimates were that these missiles would have average miss distances of three to five miles; but such large inaccuracies could be more than compensated for by the large area of damage produced by high-yield weapons against cities. These weapons would also be effective against "soft" strategic forces such as aircraft on airbases and above ground, fixed missile sites. But missiles could be put under the sea and put underground and hardened, and alert bombers could be gotten off the ground on warning. But cities could not be moved.

The major command responsible for conducting strategic nuclear operations was the Strategic Air Command, the descendant of the 8th and 20th Air Forces that had carried out the U.S. bombing campaigns against Germany and Japan. Its wartime experiences were bound to have an important influence on its doctrine.[3] Shaped by its WW II

---

[3] Characterizing *the* doctrine of a command of service is a tricky business. Within these organizations there are people who have a considerable variety of values, attitudes and expectations—almost as large a variety as is held in American society. Nevertheless,

experience and by the views of its longtime Commander, General LeMay, SAC became committed to a high standard of operational proficiency, a high state of readiness, and the concept of delivering a crushing blow against all sources of the opponent's strength: military, industrial, and governmental controls. The SAC view of strategic bombing was that (1) the Soviets could be deterred from engaging in virtually the entire relevant range of hostile acts, including small non-nuclear attacks, through the threat of large-scale nuclear attack; (2) the side that "prevailed" militarily would dominate in the post-war period; therefore, Soviet military forces were important targets; and (3) urban-industrial facilities and government controls should be hit because their destruction would cripple the Soviet ability to wage war and the ability of its regime to maintain control.

The SAC doctrine was clearly consistent with the overall defensive policy of the Eisenhower Administration. The principal threats to U.S. security were seen as the danger of nuclear war and the danger of excessive military spending forced by competition with the Soviet Union. Having a strong nuclear posture was seen as a way of coping effectively and economically with these dangers. It also was consistent with the "massive retaliation" doctrine enunciated by Secretary of State Dulles (although this doctrine was not regarded by him as an alternative to having more flexible means for dealing with small contingencies). The Eisenhower Administration had adopted a policy of main but not sole reliance on nuclear weapons. Given the available technology and prevailing operational concepts, the existing policy was one, in effect, of planning on inflicting massive civil damage.

The Emergence of Alternative Doctrines in the Late 1950's

Although the belief that thermonuclear weapons meant that nuclear war would involve massive and indiscriminate damage to civil societies was widely shared by the end of the 1950's, cities were proposed as the only nuclear targets by some Naval officers and scientists. Although earlier, in 1948, the Navy had attacked the Air

within a command certain values and operational codes tend to dominate and strongly affect perceptions, attitudes and actions of its members. These are created in a large measure by learned experience and interpretations of experience. Doctrine is, among other things, a codification of learning. However, not everyone in an organization has the same experience or derives the same lessons. Moreover, changes in organizational doctrine have occurred as the result of changes in technology, experience and leadership. The past yields important information about possible future behavior, but it is a far from perfect predictor.

Force's B-56 program in part on the grounds that the B-56 was designed for the mission of delivering nuclear weapons on cities, the invention of the POLARIS submarine missile system produced a shift. Many of the scientists who had opposed the buildup of strategic forces, had fought the development of the H-Bomb, and had favored strong air defense for the U.S., reversed field. The threat to bomb cities shifted from being bad to being good. It was argued that these missiles could be aimed at cities and launched in a deliberate and controlled way. One variant of this general view was that the strategic force need only consist of a small (called a "finite") number of these missiles in contrast to having strategic vehicles for use against Soviet military forces as well as industrial and urban targets. On this view, aiming at long-range air force bases, missile sites, etc. was especially bad because it meant threatening a force vital to the Soviet Union; this would cause it to expand its strategic force; this, in turn, would threaten us and drive up the size and cost of our strategic forces; *ad infinitum.* The result would be an "uncontrollable" arms race as the two sides reacted to each other, all at progressively higher levels of forces and budgets.[4] Moreover, the concealment, mobility, and therefore assumed high degree of protection of the POLARIS meant that it did not present to the Soviets a target which would stimulate them to increase their strategic forces and expenditures.[5] The funds saved by adopting this strategy could then be spent on the traditional forces. i.e. aircraft carriers and other forces which were still needed.

A very different doctrine was developed during the 1950's at Rand and by some Air Force officers. The context of this work was the need for assuring a protected power to retaliate. Within this context, some of the work done emphasized controlled response—but not against cities. It held that a policy of planning for nuclear strikes that had a reflex, "spasm" character, especially against cities, was irrational and unnecessary, indeed suicidal. Instead, attacks on urban targets should be withheld and any such attacks, if carried out at all—which seemed to many analysts highly

---

[4] This theory assumed, unrealistically, that the adversaries did not have available effective means to reduce their force's vulnerability as an alternative to costly multiplication; also that there were no binding constraints on available budgets.

[5] It could, however, result in the Soviets shifting efforts to anti-submarine warfare forces. The net effect of this shift might be no reduction in Soviet military spending or even an increase.

undesirable—should be conducted in a deliberate and controlled way. The importance of the military outcome was stressed both in terms of the ability to erode Soviet military strength and to limit its capacity to do damage to the U.S.

The Army's view of nuclear weapons was ambivalent. It naturally wanted to make use of these modern weapons and, as the weapons stockpile grew and as low-yield, light weapons were developed by the weapons laboratories, a considerable variety of short-range weapons were developed and bought. (And some not of short range; the Army's JUPITER ballistic missile had a nominal range of 1500 miles.) The Army explored many ways in which nuclear weapons might be used on the battlefield, either in conjunction with an all-out nuclear campaign or as an alternative to it. The results were not encouraging. The tactical problems of maneuver, communications and command on the nuclear battlefield appeared formidable—not to mention the difficulties of keeping troops motivated in a nuclear engagement and of limiting collateral damage to civilians in the combat area. Moreover, there had been no assurance that the Soviets would play the preferred game of limiting nuclear weapons to low yields; for example, they might decide to try to blast through the 7th Army in Germany with high-yield weapons. The Army was divided on this matter, but on balance concluded that nonnuclear capabilities should receive most emphasis. Nevertheless, the Army acquired a large number of nuclear weapons; it did so partly because the Eisenhower Administration had adopted a policy of placing primary emphasis on nuclear capabilities and partly as a hedge against the possibility that battlefield use might actually occur.[6]

Despite the emergence of these alternatives, U.S. nuclear strategy by the late 1950's and until 1961 was dominated by the concept of the "Optimum Mix," the planned massive response by SAC to a Soviet attack abroad or against the U.S. by attacking a combination of high priority military, industrial, and government control targets. This strategy was incorporated into NATO's MC 14/2 which

[6] During the course of the 1950's, nuclear weapons were made available for many missions including air defense, anti-submarine warfare, tactical aircraft delivery, carrier based aircraft. Allied forces in NATO had been provided with U.S. nuclear weapons under a "two-key" arrangement which kept them in U.S. custody. By 1961, over 3,000 nuclear weapons had been deployed to Europe for use by U.S. and allied forces. By the late 1960's, the total had risen to 7,000.

called for a nuclear response to any Soviet intrusion, even local, if it persevered.[7] This strategy prevailed to the end of the Eisenhower Administration despite increasing evidence, displayed vividly in Sputnik and ICBM tests, that the Soviets were building a strong capacity to attack the U.S. It persisted despite growing doubts within the Administration about the continued wisdom of the Eisenhower basic national security policy of placing main but not sole reliance on nuclear weapons.[8]

The Expansion of Options in the Early 1960's

The Kennedy Administration made reduced dependence on nuclear threats its major defense policy initiative. This shift was undertaken on two grounds: (1) strengthening deterrence by having more credible means of response to the more probable, i.e. smaller and non-nuclear, kinds of contingencies which are anticipated; (2) having an alternative between suicide and surrender, if deterrence failed. This meant more emphasis on non-nuclear forces. Moreover, deeper investigation into Soviet conventional strength led to a re-evaluation of that strength *vis-à-vis* that of the NATO countries; the result was a considerable deflation of the Soviet side. The task of providing a strong non-nuclear defense of Europe, instead of seeming hopelessly impossible, came to appear to many U.S. planners (but by no means all—and certainly not to all Europeans) to be attainable. There were important NATO weaknesses, such as inadequate stocks of ammunition, which if not remedied could be fatal, but the prospect for an effective non-nuclear defense in many contingencies seemed to be far from hopeless.

[7] In the late 1950's, SACEUR, then General Lauris Norstad, introduced the concept of a "pause" after a Soviet intrusion and before the unleashing of the full power of the West. The concept of the "pause," although never very clearly defined, recognized the possibility that deterrence could fail, that mistakes or accidents could happen and that responsible governments had to have some alternative to rapid commitment to a devastating nuclear war.

[8] This was a doctrine that could be undermined only by growing Soviet ability to inflict damage on the U.S. The major effort made in the 1950's to build a continental air defense system to exact a very high attrition level against long-range Soviet bombers was never very promising. The prospect of doing effective damage limiting through active defense was greatly reduced with the advent of ICBM's because, in the 1950's, effective ABM defense seemed distant at best. The conclusion that damage limiting through active air defense was unpromising led to sharp and continuing cuts in the 1960's and 1970's. These technological developments were much less damaging to more modest possible goals for active defense: the defense of strategic forces or defense against small nuclear powers or accidental or unauthorized small attacks.

Growing Soviet capacity to attack the U.S., of course, undermined even more the doctrine of attacking only Soviet cities.

However, there were still uncertainties and there were some contingencies that almost certainly could not be met at the non-nuclear level. Therefore, deterring non-nuclear attack in some areas and deterring first Soviet use of nuclear weapons in all important areas still required a U.S. nuclear threat.

The upshot was no reduction in nuclear weapons abroad. On the contrary, the number in Europe was increased substantially during the 1960's. This build-up occurred for several reasons: (1) The existing policy was one of adding to theater nuclear stockpiles; a positive effort was needed to reverse it. (2) A policy of defending Europe at the non-nuclear level could not be carried out by the U.S. alone. European cooperation was necessary and the Europeans were suspicious of U.S. motivations in emphasizing non-nuclear forces and, more importantly, they were unwilling to spend money to upgrade their conventional forces. (3) The Administration, faced with European suspicions about its intentions and eager to win support for a buildup of conventional forces, was unwilling to lend support to those on both sides of the Atlantic who charged that this policy was really one of reducing the U.S. commitment to Europe (what later came to be called a "decoupling" of the U.S, from Europe). A change in policy to hold down or to reverse the flow of U.S. nuclear weapons to Europe would have been held by some to signal a dangerous reduction in U.S. commitment to Europe's defense. (4) Although the JCS did not have a sound basis for proposing the continued build-up of nuclear weapons in Europe, Secretary McNamara was not armed with powerful arguments to oppose it.[9] He went along with the increases because he did not think that increasing tactical nuclear weapons made much of a difference one way or another and saw no good grounds for making trouble with the JCS and the Europeans on this issue.

The other key defense initiative taken by the Kennedy Administration was the strengthening of our second strike capacity. Both the POLARIS and MINUTEMAN programs were speeded up and the alertness of the bombers increased. These decisions were motivated by concern for the vulnerability of our strategic force, not by consideration of targeting. They were accompanied by the retirement of the rest of the B-47 force and the phasing out of SNARK,

---

[9] The standard fiscal argument wouldn't work well in this case since most of the cost of these weapons was in the budget of the Atomic Energy Commission.

MACE, MATADOR, THOR, JUPITER, and REGULUS missiles, the stopping of B-52 and B-58 production, and the cancelling of the B-70, SKYBOLT and the nuclear powered airplane. There were also large cuts in air defenses. As a result, the budget for strategic offense and defense forces soon began to shrink both in constant and current dollars during the rest of the 1960's and into the 1970's. However, the programmed force provided a large strategic nuclear force secure for some time into the future against advances in Soviet offensive forces. The combined effect of these changes was to reduce dependence for survival of our strategic forces on warning and quick response. The B-52's still depended on warning and alertness for their survival but the sheltered MINUTEMEN, and especially POLARIS missiles, did not. These changes helped to provide a technological basis for a strategy other than a massive nuclear response.

The importance of having an ability to respond to an attack deliberately and selectively was perceived by Secretary of Defense McNamara. For one thing, there was the possibility of a Soviet nuclear strike limited to our strategic forces; or the possibility of limited nuclear use by the Soviets against U.S. or allied troops in Europe or elsewhere; or the contingency of a large-scale Soviet attack on Europe, a contingency for which we had continually and from the very start said we would use nuclear weapons if non-nuclear means were insufficient; or the possibility of accidental or unauthorized launch of nuclear weapons. On this last possibility, there was no reason to believe that the Russians were casual about control over nuclear forces; on the contrary, they appeared to have tight, centralized control. Nevertheless, circumstances might conceivably arise in which some nuclear weapons might be launched other than through a deliberate Politburo decision. The point was not that contingencies of this sort seemed likely but that if they were to occur and the U.S. had only the choice of a massive nuclear response or doing nothing, the results would be catastrophic.[10]

Consistent with this view, a change in nuclear planning was made in the early 1960's. Basic U.S. options were

[10] By the late 1950's the idea that our strategic forces should be well protected and used in a controlled way had gained wide acceptance. But there were large differences in targeting concepts, described above. Meanwhile, the operators had to work with the equipment on hand which wasn't very compatible with these notions of controlled use. Many of the warheads had multi-megaton yields, missile accuracy was poor, manned bombers and unsheltered missiles, if not launched quickly, risked destruction, and low level penetration of bombers meant ground or near ground bursts which had produced enhanced fallout.

developed that differentiated more clearly between attacks directed against military targets and against cities. Although this meant a shift away from the earlier Optimum Mix, essentially a single option approach as Secretary Schlesinger has pointed out, these were still large options, i.e. they involved thousands of weapons. The principal objective remained deterring Soviet attacks, on allies as well as the U.S., by the threat to carry out large-scale nuclear operations, including attack on urban-industrial targets. A second objective was to attempt to limit damage directly in the event deterrence failed by attacking Soviet nuclear forces, by active defenses and civil defenses (but the last were difficult to sell to Congress). The indirect, and potentially much more powerful way to limit damage was to increase the adversary's incentive to limit damage to us by withholding attack on his cities. This concept was basic to the option of withholding urban attacks.

Despite his continued endorsement of the importance of controlled response as long as he was in office, the emphasis in McNamara's statements on nuclear forces and doctrine shifted after 1963 to that of Assured Destruction. This doctrine held that a nuclear exchange would, with high probability, result in over 100 million fatalities in both the U.S. and the U.S.S.R. and that attempts to limit damage through active and passive defenses could be readily defeated by improvements in offensive forces. The principal test of adequacy of the U.S. strategic force came to be the ability of our programmed force to produce civil damage, even against a greater than expected threat. The damage criterion settled on by McNamara for determining the size of the strategic force was the destruction of 20–25 percent of the Soviet population and 50 percent of its industrial capacity. The programmed forces decided on in the early 1960's readily met this test. So readily that it seemed evident that our forces were more than adequate. The primary purpose of the Assured Destruction capabilities doctrine was to provide a metric for deciding how much force was enough: it provided a basis for denying service and Congressional claims for more money for strategic forces. It also served the purpose of dramatizing for the Congress and the public the awful consequences of large-scale nuclear war and its inappropriateness as an instrument of policy. (However, it was never proposed by McNamara or his staff that nuclear weapons actually be *used* in this way.)

Assured Destruction was symmetrical. It implied that limiting damage to the U.S. population against large direct nuclear attack was infeasible or too costly. Nevertheless, direct damage limiting continued to be asserted as an objective for strategic offensive and defensive forces. However, analyses of the cost of protecting populations versus the costs of destroying them—assuming that the enemy sought to kill people as distinct from regarding population damage as a by-product of attack on military targets—showed the defense to be at a cost disadvantage. It would have to spend a good deal more than the offense, e.g. a factor of three times, at each level of damage. This unfavorable ratio, the high costs of such a defense, perhaps along with the political obstacles to persuading the Congress to support a nationwide fallout shelter program, led McNamara and President Johnson to conclude that damage limiting on a large scale should not be pursued. In a special message on defense to the Congress in February, 1965, Johnson said that we should be alert to the possibility of limiting destruction of ourselves, but that a comprehensive damage limiting program would be costly and uncertain in effectiveness. He also said that defense expenditure would comprise a declining proportion of a growing GNP with the resources freed going to meet other needs.[11]

There were serious problems with the doctrine of Assured Destruction. For one thing, there was a continued affirmation of the U.S. intention to use nuclear weapons for the defense of Europe if needed. But many Europeans—and Americans—continued to believe that Europe, or important parts of it, could not be reliably defended at the nonnuclear level. And it was becoming decreasingly credible that

---

[11] Damage limiting was not abandoned altogether. It might be feasible under favorable circumstances. The most important of these were cases in which mutual interest in survival produced mutual restraint. But for such cases, given the high weapon yields projected in the strategic forces, fallout protection was important. Studies showed such protection to be highly cost-effective, but the combination of low confidence in the prospect of restrained behavior along with the political costs of trying to get fallout shelters, prevented the Johnson Administration from advocating them.

Earlier, a large fallout shelter program had been advocated by the Gaither Committee in 1957 as part of a larger program of strategic offense and defense, and had been rejected by President Eisenhower. In 1961, there had been a brief period of interest in shelters during the period of greatest concern over the escalation of the Berlin crisis.

The principal exception to the movement away from the objective of direct damage limiting during the 1960's was the argument used in 1967 to justify building a "thin" ABM system, justified mainly as an anti-Chinese defense, designed against a small technologically unsophisticated nuclear power but not against deliberate large attack by the Soviet Union. The alternative of a "thick" ABM defense against the Soviet Union was explicitly excluded.

we would commit suicide in the event of an attack on Europe. Would it be deterred if our only nuclear response to an attack abroad were a suicidal one? To be sure, McNamara continued to mention, albeit briefly, the case for flexible nuclear response and of the objective of limiting damage (but we had visibly cut back on active air defenses, civil defenses, and had no plans for anti-missile defense of populations).

Increasingly what was being communicated to the American people, the Europeans, and the Russians, was the prospect of 100 million dead Americans and a similar number of dead Russians (and also of dead Europeans) if a nuclear exchange were to occur. McNamara sought to resolve the conflict between this doctrine and our commitments to allies by persuading our NATO allies to have sufficient non-nuclear strength not to be dependent on the threat of first use of nuclear weapons. Although his arguments were substantively powerful, they were not highly persuasive to the Europeans and, in any case, they left unsolved the problem of what to do if the Soviets used these weapons first. Any nuclear use by the Soviets (or the Chinese for that matter) that left us with a stake in the continuance of our society faced us with the need for having a non-suicidal response capability and policy.

Nuclear Doctrine After 1968

President Nixon's strategic doctrine, labelled Strategic Sufficiency, was put forward in several annual "State of the World" reports. It meant (1) having strategic forces strong enough to inflict enough damage to deter strategic attacks on us and our allies and strong enough to face an aggressor contemplating less than all-out attack with an unacceptable risk of escalation; (2) also having forces strong enough to keep the U.S. allies from being coerced. It contained themes that had been put forward by McNamara earlier: there should be no indiscriminate mass destruction of civilians as the sole response to challenge; the ability to use force in a controlled way helps deterrence; if war comes we need some way of preventing escalation; there should be no policy of launching missiles on warning. But nowhere in his public statements did President Nixon state that actions had been taken consistent with the position he was asserting. He was hardly in a position to do so because the JCS were given no directives to develop flexible options until 1974. Such flexibility as there was, which consisted mostly of some contingency plans outside of the SIOP, had been prepared on the initiative of the JCS and the major commanders.

Strategic Sufficiency as described by Nixon's Secretary of Defense, Melvin Laird, centered on four objectives: (1) having a second-strike capability adequate to deter an all-out surprise attack on our forces; (2) providing no incentive to the Soviet Union to strike first in a crisis; (3) preventing the Soviet Union from having greater ability to do urban-industrial damage to the U.S. than we could do to it; and (4) being able to defend against small attacks or accidental launches. It also included having forces adequate to prevent allies as well as the U.S. from being coerced by having strategic nuclear forces that could enhance theater and allied nuclear forces and also having alternatives to resorting to mass urban and industrial destruction. This version of the doctrine repeated familiar themes: the importance of a second-strike capacity, reducing first-strike incentives, protection against small attacks, the need for flexible options, the contribution of strategic forces to defense of allies. It also echoed the theme of Assured Destruction (while explicitly rejecting it) in stating the objective of the U.S. as being able to do more civil damage to the Soviet Union than *vice versa* (objective 3 above). On balance, while there was a tilt toward a policy of flexibility and discrimination, it was hardly a clear shift in policy.

Secretary Schlesinger's arguments for flexible options are also similar to those used by McNamara; the differences largely reflect changes in the military situation from the 1960's to the 1970's. He has stated two purposes: to help the credibility of deterrence and to help keep conflict at a low level if it were to occur. However, in contrast to the early 1960's, the objectives of limiting damage to the U.S. by having the capacity to deny physically the Soviets the ability to kill U.S. civilians has been rejected. Schlesinger has emphasized that the Soviet force is beyond the U.S. capability to eliminate, not least because it has a large, untargetable submarine component. He also has argued that a policy of flexible options does not require any change in our force structure; i.e. we don't need new forces or new technology in order to be more flexible in employment.[12]

Emphasis on the development of nuclear options would be on contingencies of special concern to our allies, e.g. the deterrence of major attack on Western Europe and an improved ability to respond to such an attack in a non-suicidal way. As in the 1960's, strong non-nuclear capabilities are essential, but smaller nuclear options are also needed for deterrence and for defense. As an example of a class of targets whose destruction might assist the defense of Europe, Schlesinger has mentioned the Soviet oil refining industry, an industry whose output was arguably essential for a successful Soviet attack on Western Europe. Clearly, having the ability to destroy targets such as refineries while preserving non-targets such as people requires precision in attack. In fact, improvements in accuracy have permitted reduction in warhead yields so that such attacks are becoming feasible. (The change from early ballistic missile accuracies is striking.) Another contingency mentioned by Schlesinger is the possibility of a Soviet attack limited to U.S. ICBM's and SAC bomber bases; if the Soviets chose to limit collateral damage, the resulting U.S. fatalities could be held to a small fraction of the fatalities produced from direct attack on U.S. cities. In recent testimony he has compared the population damage from a Soviet SIOP type of attack with American fatalities of around 95–100 million from prompt effects plus fallout with the fatalities from more discriminate attacks. An attack on ICBM silos, SAC bases and ballistic missile submarine bases was estimated as producing 5–6 million

---

[12] Some confusion has been caused by Schlesinger also announcing the development of a new large warhead for the MINUTEMAN, a warhead which has some transient military use in attacking some military targets, such as Soviet hardened missile silos. (Its value is transient because improvement in missile accuracy is increasing missile effectiveness anyway without the need of larger warheads; improvements in accuracy also help make possible large reductions in collateral damage.) He has justified this proposal in terms of perceptions of the U.S.-U.S.S.R. strategic balance; the Soviet missile force has a much larger payload capacity and larger warheads than does the U.S. one. The proposed large warhead should, he has argued, be considered in the context of the Strategic Arms Limitations Talks, a context within which we were trying to get agreement to reduce missile numbers and total payload. We were willing to trade away this addition to our counterforce capibility in SALT, but we needed some currency to trade with. This warhead provided such coin. It had nothing to do with flexible options. Nevertheless, the collocation of these two policy pronouncements caused some confusion in press reporting and hostility among those opposed to nuclear flexibility anyway.

He argued that our strategic force should have some ability to destroy hard targets, even though he prefers to see both sides without major counterforce capabilities. He also favors a program of fallout shelters and population relocation for the contingency of attack limited to military targets.

fatalities; one on ICBM's alone, about 1 million, and on SAC bases alone, about 500,000 fatalities. In short, discriminate attacks are becoming feasible.[13] This does not mean that contingencies such as these are at all likely or that discriminate nuclear capabilities will be used. On the contrary, these are remote possibilities. But these capabilities, it is held, improve deterrence—and could make a large difference in the event of deterrence failing.

Finally, on the subject of obstacles to implementation of a policy of limited options, Schlesinger has mentioned problems of command and control, limitations in existing hardware, and the "mental approach" of the planners. On this last obstacle, it apparently requires significant changes in operational techniques to develop the kinds of options desired; the variety of constraints implied by the new guidance evidently presents difficulties for the planners and operators. Moreover, it is difficult to think through and to anticipate specific contingencies in which small nuclear options might be used. (It is, of course, very much harder to think of realistic contingencies in which massive use of nuclear weapons would take place.) Detailed planning for an actual contingency done in the middle of a crisis isn't likely to be done well. Moreover, much might be done in advance to develop materials and techniques applicable to a wide range of situations. Without this preparation, the alternatives available in the crisis are likely to be a poorly executed attempt to be selective, too massive a use of force, or most likely, governmental paralysis.

A Closer Look at an Earlier Effort to Expand Options

President Kennedy came into office in 1961 committed to the proposition that the U.S. needed a wider range of military capabilities. He and his associates gave highest

---

[13] In order for the Soviets to pursue a selective nuclear policy, they would need (1) to be able to deliver a certain number of nuclear weapons of medium or low yield with precision; and (2) to practice restraint in a conflict, for example, by choosing targets so as to limit collateral damage. On point (1), the Soviets are improving the accuracy of their weapons. The Defense Department has reported that they have achieved or will soon achieve ICBM accuracies of 5000 to 700 meters. As for warhead yields, the constraints imposed by having missiles mobile, e.g. in submarines, and of adopting MIRV's are producing a Soviet trend towards smaller warheads in a significant part of its force. Moreover, the use of air bursts rather than surface bursts would both increase blast effects against military targets and reduce collateral damage from fallout. On point 2, although restraint in a nuclear conflict is by no means assured, it would be powerfully motivated by self interest; there is little in the record of the behavior of Soviet leadership to suggest that it has a taste for suicide.

priority to improving the non-nuclear strength of U.S. forces, an effort which persisted throughout the decade. On nuclear forces, the main effort was on assuring that our strategic forces were well protected against a possible surprise attack. There was no initial commitment by the new Administration to a specific targeting doctrine. There was, however, a disposition to stress control and flexibility in the use of force.

Secretary McNamara's interest in nuclear planning was engaged from the outset. One of the initial ninety-six tasks he set for the Defense Department shortly after taking office was the development of a doctrine for the controlled use of nuclear weapons. In an early briefing on the existing nuclear plans, it was pointed out to him that they didn't offer a choice between attack on urban-industrial targets and attack on military forces. Moreover, they didn't provide for the flexibility to attack some Communist countries without attacking others. As a result, McNamara directed Alain Enthoven, who created and headed the office of Systems Analysis in the office of the Secretary of Defense, to work with the Joint Staff to develop a greater range of options. This was done. McNamara sent the draft guidance to the JCS. It was endorsed by them and was issued.

The new guidance distinguished more clearly among the three tasks described in Section I, attack on (1) nuclear threat targets, (2) other military forces and (3) urban-industrial targets. It also provided options for withholding attack by country and for withholding direct attack on cities. However, the tasks all involved large attacks, and civilian damage, at least from radioactive fallout, would have been very heavy. And there was not a clear distinction between "urban" and "industrial" targets, a distinction that had almost disappeared in the 1950's with the advent of high-yield weapons.

Secretary McNamara also argued the need for nuclear flexibility in a number of major statements. An important occasion was the NATO meeting at Athens in May of 1962. The burden of the Athens message was repeated in a public speech in June in Ann Arbor in which he said:

. . . the mere fact that no nation could rationally take steps leading to nuclear war does not guarantee that a nuclear war cannot take place.

Not only do nations sometimes act in ways that are hard to explain on a rational basis, but even when acting in a "rational" way they sometimes, indeed disturbingly often, act on the basis of misunderstandings of the true facts of the situation . . . The U.S. has come to the conclusion that to the extent feasible basic military strategy in a possible general war should be approached in much the same way that more conventional military operations have been regarded in the past. That is to say, principal military objectives, in the event of a nuclear war stemming from a major attack on the Alliance, should be the destruction of the enemy's military forces, not of his civilian population . . . In other words, we are giving a possible opponent the strongest imaginable incentive to refrain from striking our own cities.

In subsequent annual posture statements he reiterated the need for flexibility:

Furthermore, it is possible that the Soviet's initial strike might be directed solely at our military installations, leaving our cities as hostages for later negotiations. In that event, we might find it to our advantage to direct our immediate retaliatory blow against their military installations, and to withhold our attack on their cities, keeping the forces required to destroy their urban-industrial complex in a protected reserve for some kind of period of time.

Accordingly, we should plan for the 1965–67 time period a force which could: 1. Strike back decisively at the entire Soviet target system simultaneously; or 2. Strike back, first, at the Soviet bomber bases, missiles sites and other military installations associated with their long-range nuclear forces to reduce the power of any follow-up attack—and then, if necessary, strike back at the Soviet urban and industrial complex in a controlled and deliberate way. Such a force would give us the needed flexibility to meet a wide range of possible general war situations.

(FY 1966 Posture Statement)

In talking about global nuclear war, the Soviet leaders always say that they would strike at the entire complex of our military power including government and production centers, meaning our cities. If they were to do so, we would, of course, have no alternative but to retaliate in kind. But we have no way of knowing whether they would actually do so. It would certainly be their interest as well as ours to try to limit the terrible consequences of a nuclear exchange. By building into our forces a flexible capability, we at least eliminate the prospect that we could strike back in only one way, namely, against the entire Soviet target system including their cities. Such a prospect would give the Soviet Union no incentive to withhold attack against our cities in a first strike. We want to give them a better alternative. Whether they would accept it in the crisis of a global nuclear war, no one can say. Considering

what is at stake, we believe it is worth the additional effort on our part
to have this option.

(FY 1964 Posture Statement)

NATO should not only have an improved capability to meet major
non-nuclear assaults with non-nuclear means and forces prepared for
that option, but it should also achieve a true *tactical* nuclear capability
which should include a broad, flexible range of nuclear options, short
of general nuclear war and the means to implement them.

(FY 1966 Posture Statement)

The reaction to this policy initiative was not encouraging. Senators Russell and Margaret Chase Smith
attacked the "no cities" doctrine as a policy of weakness,
a policy which revealed to them a lack of resolve. Senator
Russell, an opponent of flexibility, was no advocate of
Mutual Assured Destruction; he also said that if there were
only two people left in the world both of them should be
Americans. Politicians on the left were no more supportive.
Some of them saw nuclear flexibility as a policy which
legitimized nuclear weapons and made nuclear war more
likely. Many of these were people who, after Sputnik, came
to advocate a policy of planning to bomb populations as
a means of stabilizing deterrence.

Among our allies the reaction was mixed. Some
favored the policy for the reasons McNamara gave. Those
who supported national nuclear forces opposed it because
they depended on the argument of population bombing.
(They also wanted to keep a U.S. nuclear commitment to
Europe, a preference which cut *against* population bombing.) Still others among allies were confused by McNamara's
concepts and suspicious of U.S. motives.

The response of SAC and the JSTPS to this initiative
was mixed. On the one hand, they welcomed the explicit
recognition by the Secretary of Defense of the importance
of the military outcome of a conflict; on the other hand,
there were operational difficulties to be coped with. The constraints on tactics implied by this policy were a problem;
for example, the constraints against ground bursts of nuclear
weapons in order to reduce fallout. Moreover, the SIOP
planning process formally produced a capabilities plan, not
a requirements plan, and in reality it was not unconnected
with the process of generating requirements for delivery
systems. Because McNamara's early formulation didn't

distinguish sharply between capabilities planning and force requirements, one result was varying service responses largely addressed to the subject of requirements. For example, in 1963, General LeMay testified as follows:

> Many people unfortunately measure the effectiveness of a proposed deterrent force by counting the number of enemy citizens to be brought under attack.
> As you know, it doesn't take much of a nuclear force to destroy a large number of enemy cities. But the destruction of cities *per se* does not protect U.S. and allied lives.
> Only the destruction of his military forces can do this. Therefore, an entirely different force capability is required to destroy those weapon systems posing a threat to U.S. and Allied populations.

This looked like a pitch to increase the Air Force strategic budget a lot. But by no means were all of the service reactions similar to LeMay's. The Army favored small strategic offensive forces, large active defenses, and, most importantly, strong general purpose forces. The Navy had earlier argued for small strategic forces but now favored more submarine based missiles (not ICBM's and manned bombers) and more of its type of general purpose forces, e.g. carriers. Those whose primary interest was disarmament favored lowered strategic budgets and this they linked to massive population bombing which they thought could be done cheaply. (Explicitly or implicitly, this meant support for the proliferation of national nuclear forces.) Many analysts at Rand, or who had been at Rand, were against larger strategic budgets and favored better protection and control for the strategic force, and the development of an improved capacity for non-nuclear and limited nuclear responses.

The reaction of the Soviets to the American discussion was first to deny that limitations in war were possible, including the distinction between non-nuclear and nuclear conflict. Later, Soviet commentators shifted to the position that conflicts might be held to the non-nuclear level. But the possibility of a limited nuclear conflict was rejected in the Soviet literature during the 1960's.

On balance, to McNamara it appeared that a policy of nuclear restraint was going to be widely interpreted as implying that we could fight, win and survive a nuclear war and that we should therefore spend much more money on strategic forces, money that would have to come out of conventional force budgets. This forecast, and the general controversy, interfered with a far more important task which was to see to the building up of non-nuclear strength so that nuclear threats would be less necessary. As he saw it, we weren't likely to get both a flexible nuclear policy and stronger conventional forces, and he knew which was the more important. Moreover, the possibility of nuclear war had not seemed completely remote during the crises of 1961 and 1962, and after the Cuban missile crisis of November, 1962 its likelihood seemed to recede. Planning of nuclear options seemed increasingly abstract and remote from the key defense issues. McNamara, therefore, began to stress increasingly the doctrine of having an Assured Destruction capability, the central and overriding importance of having a high confidence capability to inflict great civil damage on the Soviet Union.

McNamara, while increasingly talking about Assured Destruction, apparently remained of the view that any actual U.S. use of nuclear weapons should be controlled and restrained. He apparently also came to believe that the task of preplanning nuclear options was a hopelessly difficult one because the contingencies in which weapons might be used were so unpredictable that nuclear planning could be done only when the contingency arose. The main task for him was trying to assure that major conflicts did not occur, and trying to cope with any that might break out without the use of nuclear weapons. The instruments for this were the general purpose forces. The nuclear forces had little to contribute.

As a result, his interest in improving the flexibility of the SIOP diminished. The planners, who had limited enthusiasm for limited options, read McNamara's Assured Destruction signals as meaning that they did not have to develop a wider range of options. The resulting employment doctrine was not one of flexible options; nor was it really Mutual Assured Destruction either (and still less its mini-variant, Minimum Deterrence). We had a strategic force far too large to be justified by that doctrine and most of our planned targets were military forces. In sum, the nuclear planning process experienced no important change from the early 1960's until 1974. The assignment of weapons to a growing target list went on in accordance with the political direction established in the early 1960's.

Analysis and Conclusions

The record suggests several reasons for the continued existence of plans for the massive use of nuclear weapons only, and for the persistent gaps between these plans and the objectives of policy frequently asserted by senior government officials.

The existence of large gaps between policy and operational behavior is a common phenomenon. High officials place great weight on policy statements. They do so because formulating policy goals and communicating them to the public, to Congress, and not least, members of the bureaucracies, is one of the principal responsibilities. Officials in the Executive Branch are also responsible for the execution of policies. But getting policies executed is usually a more difficult matter than formulating them. The aspect of policy over which Presidents and other high officials have greatest control is making speeches and issuing policy statements. Just about everything else is harder to do.

Moreover, high-level policy statements are usually broad and incorporate multiple and sometime conflicting objectives. They are broad because they are intended to cover a wide range of circumstances, many unforeseeable, at least in detail. They are multiple because the purposes of policy are complex; there are usually trade-offs among different objectives and some may be directly opposed to others. Choices must be made. For example, Secretary McNamara's elaboration of Assured Destruction was designed to educate the Congress and the American people on the catastrophic consequences of nuclear war and to hold down the strategic offense and defense budget; it conflicted directly with his need to assure the Europeans that the U.S. would use nuclear weapons first if needed. Faced with this conflict, he chose to emphasize the first rather than the second strand of policy.

The process of implementation is also affected by the fact that people in operating organizations have perceptions, objectives and constraints which differ from those of higher officials. Moreover, the latter often know little about the operating environment, the perceptions, the goals and problems of the operators. Because policy directives are usually broad, they must be interpreted by middle level officials. Within the limits of general policy, the choices made by subordinates may not correspond at all closely to what was intended by the higher officials. Nor are the choices made in implementation and their consequences always visible at the policy level. Assuring close correspondence between policy and implementation requires an incentive on the part of senior officials to work on the latter, a means of monitoring what is happening, and the will and ability to make adaptations as difficulties with the execution of policy as originally formulated become evident. This sequence can break down at any stage. The implementation of Secretary McNamara's flexible options initiative in the early 1960's was aborted in large measure by the withdrawal of his interest and support. Had his interest been sustained, other obstacles might have emerged.

Moreover, choices among general policies, budget decisions on weapons and forces, and decisions on current plans are different sorts of decisions. Some concern communications to adversaries, allies, the Congress and public; some, capabilities years ahead in the future; and some, actions that might have to be taken in a war that might come at any moment. As a result, the actions taken can appear to flow from inconsistent policies without this really being so. But there can be a spillover from one arena into another. It turned out to be difficult in the early 1960's to operate in the use arena without having an impact on the requirements arena. Perhaps greater awareness of the need to distinguish sharply between these two distinct activities would have helped.

There are other reasons why stated policies might not be implemented. These reasons can be viewed both from the point of view of the *demand* for flexible options and the *costs* of obtaining them.

From the demand side, high officials of the last four Administrations asserted the importance of having more nuclear flexibility. But it is evident that this was not seen as an urgent need. An important operational test was the absence of a Presidential directive to this end before 1974. It was not seen as urgent because of the widely shared belief that major war would not occur. The Soviets would not attack areas vital to our interests and, in particular, they would not use nuclear weapons first. They would not do so despite their great non-nuclear strengh applicable to areas around their borders and despite their rapidly growing nuclear strength. This belief was less firmly held during the crises of the early 1960's and after the Cuban missile crisis in 1962, but most of the time nuclear options were regarded as sound policy, not a compelling matter. Sound policy implied that even a small probability of nuclear war called for choices other than massive nuclear attacks. But other, more immediately pressing matters, e.g. building up non-nuclear forces or coping with Vietnam, usually absorbed the attention and energies of high officials.

On the cost side, the shift in Secretary McNamara's position illustrates one kind of cost, pressures for additional forces and budgets. Another cost is in high-level time and effort to work with operational staffs in order to make the right policy decisions. This is a process which is least costly if proposals "bubble up" from below (as Dean Acheson characterized much of the policy-making in the State Department). But flexible nuclear options was not a policy which the members of the JSTPS or JCS organizations advocated. They had developed some, but by and large small options were not lobbied for by these staffs. They perceived difficult problems in carrying out controlled and discriminate strikes, such strikes placed constraints on them that they wanted to avoid, and the doctrine of the over-whelming massive strike still had a strong hold. Moreover, the operators might have perceived another kind of cost. To them, limited options might have appeared dangerous and unreliable but politicians might not recognize their limitations. Military commanders want to be given well defined tasks to perform, and the authority and resources needed to carry them out. They don't want to be commit-ted to large tasks without adequate authority and means. (One of the lessons many military men and others have derived from Vietnam is that, once the political decision was made to send combat troops, we should have gone in with enough force to settle the conflict quickly instead of getting progressively more involved over time without being able to end the conflict decisively.) From an operator's view-point, a nuclear exchange in which the politicians try to mastermind the conflict while keeping the commanders from carrying out what they regard as necessary military opera-tions could be a frightening prospect. (On the other hand, a massive nuclear war conducted without political guidance and constraints is an even more frightening one.) In short, there were perceived costs on all sides of implementing flex-ible nuclear options.

Other organizational factors probably played a role including the centralizing of nuclear planning in 1960 in Omaha. For one thing, the Strategic Air Command is primarily dedicated to the operation of manned bombers. The problem of reliably delivering a few weapons with a small number of manned bombers against an intact Soviet air-defense system could be formidable. (There might also be certain problems in using missiles instead; for example, in preventing the opponent from believing that a massive attack was being launched against him.) Another possible factor is the difference between the environments in which SAC and the submarine missile force operate and those of the theater commands. The latter are much more involved with and aware of political factors and constraints in their regions than are the former. But actual contingencies arise in particular places, i.e. within theaters and theater commanders might be expected to develop a more discriminate view of the role of military force in dealing with these contingencies and for the role, if any, of nuclear weapons. Long ago it led SACEUR to introduce constraints on the employment of nuclear weapons in Europe. Some theater commanders have come to believe that nuclear weapons have no significant role to play in their area. On the other hand, to have left nuclear planning entirely decentralized would have been inefficient and hazardous, especially in view of the vast increase in Soviet long-range delivery capabilities; also because SAC, and more recently CINCLANT and CINCPAC with their submarine missiles, have controlled most of the nuclear assets. Putting the globally oriented command with the largest forces in charge may have cost something in political sensitivity and tactical nuance, but centralized control made it possible to plan to apply forces in a coordinated manner from a broader perspective. Now the perspectives of the theaters must somehow be given greater weight.

Technological limitations have also been an important obstacle. The operators must work with the equipment made available by those who make the R&D and procurement decisions. Decision-makers in the 1950's made technological choices on warhead yields and delivery systems which severely constrained the operators' choices in the 1960's. This constraint is becoming less binding as R&D and procurement choices in the 1960's provide the operators of the 1970's more choices.

Finally, there has been a conceptual gap. Plausible examples of contingencies in which nuclear weapons might be used by a country with the prospect of a "favorable" outcome have been in short supply. This may be because such contingencies do not exist, or it might reflect a failure of imagination on the part of analysts. But governments often buy military capabilities with only a general idea about their future uses. Weapons often end up having been used for purposes quite different from those intended when bought. One of the things that has inhibited thought is the belief that nuclear war is impossible. Many people have taken comfort in the belief that so long as nuclear war is made as terrible as possible it won't happen. But nuclear contingencies are, one hopes, remote, not impossible. The required intellectual task is one of thinking systematically about nuclear contingencies that might arise, how such contingencies might be prevented from occurring, possible objectives of the adversaries in such contingencies, and how mutually observed constraints might be arrived at and preserved during a conflict. The purpose of such planning is to lower the likelihood of nuclear war while trying to protect various U.S. interests. One of these interests is the survival of American society if nuclear weapons are ever used. It is sometimes argued that thinking about nuclear options makes them more likely. This seems implausible. The purposes here are similar to those in planning nonnuclear options. Officials of several Administrations have attached importance to nonnuclear capabilities and plans not because they wanted to get into a conventional war; they did so because they judged that a non-nuclear response to non-nuclear attack would be much more credible than a nuclear one and that it could be militarily effective in many contingencies. They also have believed that the "firebreak" between non-nuclear and nuclear weapons provides a clear "stopping point" in escalation. This is probably the most important "stopping point," but it is not the only one. There could be limitations in types of targets, in the collateral damage produced, in the geographical area of conflicts, in the use of bases, among others. Limitations apply to nuclear as well as non-nuclear conflict in the sense that there would very likely be strong mutual incentive in finding such limits. The improved capabilities for precision help by making it possible to substitute small warheads for large ones and, as accuracy improves, non-nuclear warheads for nuclear ones. This trend in technology helps to further an important objective of policy, raising the nuclear threshold.

The task of implementing a flexible options policy remains formidable. The sustained attention of senior officials is required and this is a commodity always in short supply. Implementation will require continued monitoring, probably the solving of a number of difficult conceptual and operational problems, and perhaps, some new hardware. It may also require a change in institutional arrangements with the DOD. One possibility is creating a permanently established Nuclear Planning Review Committee charged with oversight responsibilities, a Committee whose members would include both senior military and civilian officials. But, even with some form of added institutionalization, this subject is peculiarly one that requires attention by those at the highest level, the Secretary of Defense and the President.

None of this, of course, assures that, if the U.S. implements a discriminate nuclear and non-nuclear policy, other nuclear powers will build the forces which would be consistent with a policy of discrimination; nor does it assure that the participants in a nuclear engagement would behave with restraint and that civil damage to the participants would be less than catastrophic. But to the extent it is implemented by us, it reduces the likelihood that we would be faced with the choice of holocaust or surrender; to the extent it is not implemented by the Soviet Union or other nations it increases the likelihood that they would be faced with such a choice. Despite the bargaining advantage we might possess in such a situation, we should favor our adversaries as well as ourselves having alternatives to massive destruction.[14]

---

[14] On one issue, controversial a decade ago, there is near consensus now within the U.S. It is that the nuclear forces and deliverable warheads of both the U.S. and the U.S.S.R. are in excess of reasonable levels. Having small, flexible nuclear options today is not nearly as likely to generate strong support for increasing nuclear forces as it was feared a decade ago. The main factor working now for increases in our strategic forces is the increase in Soviet strategic forces. The SALT negotiation process has focused attention on certain indices of strength such as numbers of missiles, numbers of MIRV's, throwweight and the like which only very imperfectly measure the effectiveness of these weapons in realistic contingencies. Ironically, SALT has intensified pressures for us to match the Soviet's higher level in several of these indices.

1975

ASSURING STRATEGIC STABILITY IN AN ERA OF DÉTENTE

Paul H. Nitze

Ambassador-at-Large Paul H. Nitze is currently Special Advisor to The President and The Secretary of State on Arms Control Matters. Ambassador Nitze was a member of the SALT I and SALT II delegations and represented the United States in the Intermediate Range Nuclear Forces talks. He is a former Deputy Secretary of Defense, Secretary of the Navy, and Director of the State Department's Policy Planning Staff.

Even though the translation of the Vladivostok, Accord on strategic arms into a SALT II Treaty has not yet been resolved, I believe it is now timely to take stock of the strategic arms balance toward which the United States and the Soviet Union would be headed under the terms of such a treaty. To that end it is necessary to raise certain basic questions about the maintenance of strategic stability—in terms of minimizing both the possibility of nuclear war and the possibility that nuclear arms may be used by either side as a means of decisive pressure in key areas of the world.

It appears to be the general belief that while such strategic stability may not be assured by the SALT agreements, it is not and will not be substantially endangered— that on the contrary it has been furthered by the SALT negotiations and agreements since 1969—and that in any event the best hope of stability lies in further pursuit

Reprinted with permission of *Foreign Affairs*. Copyright © 1976 by *Foreign Affairs*.

of negotiations with the aim of reducing the level of strategic weapons and delivery systems on both sides.
Unfortunately—and to the profound regret of one who has
participated both in the SALT negotiations and in a series
of earlier U.S. decisions designed to stabilize the nuclear
balance—I believe that each of these conclusions is today
without adequate foundation.

On the contrary, there is every prospect that under
the terms of the SALT agreements the Soviet Union will continue to pursue a nuclear superiority that is not merely quantitative but designed to produce a theoretical war-winning
capability. Further, there is a major risk that if such a condition were achieved, the Soviet Union would adjust its
policies and actions in ways that would undermine the present détente situation, with results that could only resurrect
the danger of nuclear confrontation or, alternatively, increase
the prospect of Soviet expansion through other means of
pressure.

While this highly disturbing prospect does not mean
that strategic arms limitation should for a moment be abandoned as a U.S. (and world) goal, the practical fact we now
face is that a SALT II treaty based on the Vladivostok Accord
would *not* provide a sound foundation for follow-on
negotiations under present trends. If, and only if the United
States now takes action to redress the impending strategic
imbalance, can the Soviet Union be persuaded to abandon
its quest for superiority and to resume the path of meaningful limitations and reductions through negotiation.

Finally, I believe that such corrective action can be
taken: (a) within the framework of the Vladivostok Accord;
(b) with costs that would increase the strategic arms budget
marginally above present levels (themselves less than half
the strategic arms budget we supported from 1956 through
1962, if the dollar values are made comparable); (c) with
results that would encourage the diversion of the Soviet
effort from its present thrust and in directions compatible
with long-range strategic stability. At the close of this article I shall outline the key elements in such a corrective
program.

Let us start with a brief review of the overall state
of Soviet-American relations. The use of the word "détente,"
in its current sense, began in 1971. U.S. efforts to improve

it relations with the Soviet Union go ba
dominated the War and the immediate pos
the early years of the Eisenhower Admir
formed an important strand of U.S. foreign
the Kennedy and Johnson Administratioι
"détente" as currently used implies something
these efforts; it implies that their goal has now l
and that all that remains to be done is to n   ... detente
"irreversible."

The chain of events leading to the present situation
goes back to the Sino-Soviet split and the great buildup of
Soviet forces facing China. There were about 15 Soviet divisions facing China in the mid-1960s; between 1968 and 1972
the number grew to at least 45 divisions. This caused the
Chinese Communists to be deeply concerned about the
danger of an attack by the Soviet Union on China. The
Chinese turned to the one power that could help deter such
an attack; they opened the ping-pong diplomacy that
resulted in the so-called normalization of U.S. relations with
China.

Mr. Nixon was, I think, correct in taking the position that he wished good relations with both China and the
U.S.S.R. and did not want an alliance with either. Moscow,
however, wanted to be sure that the new relationship between China and ourselves did not deepen into something
closer to an alliance and thus impede Soviet policy toward
China. For this and other reasons the Russians began to go
out of their way to be friendly to Mr. Nixon and Mr. Kissinger. They opened up a vista of relaxation of tensions and
of a growing collaboration between the United States and
the Soviet Union. In 1972 not only were the SALT I
agreements—the Anti-Ballistic Missile (ABM) Treaty and
the Interim Agreement—entered into, but also there was
signed at Moscow a document called Basic Principles of Relations Between the United States and the Soviet Union.
Together with a subsequent agreement signed in Washington
in 1973, this laid out what appeared to be a good basis for
continuing relations between the U.S.S.R. and ourselves.
Among other things, these agreements called for collaboration to see to it that crisis situations in other parts of the
world did not build up into confrontation which could
increase the risk of war between the two countries. It was
understood that this collaboration was to have special

eference to Southeast Asia and to the Middle East. These bilateral agreements were accompanied by the Paris Agreements with respect to Vietnam, and the Soviet Union was among those guaranteeing that the Paris Agreements would be implemented and abided by.

These understandings, however, produced no positive Soviet actions. With respect to the final North Vietnamese takeover in Southeast Asia, the Soviets actually took actions to help the North Vietnamese violate the agreements. With respect to the Middle East, it is hard to sustain the argument that is often made that the Soviets exercised restraint in the October 1973 crisis. There appears to have been little that they refrained from doing to encourage and make possible the attack by Egypt and Syria on Israel and the OPEC action on oil prices and the embargo. The Soviets not only trained and equipped the Egyptians and the Syrians for their surprise attack, but also failed to warn us when they knew that an attack was imminent. When the battle turned against the attackers, they threatened to intervene with their forces.

These two experiences in Southeast Asia and in the Middle East are bound to make us skeptical that the Soviet leaders are in fact moving toward any lasting reduction in tensions, or any abandonment of expansionist aims. A further ground for skepticism comes from what Soviet leaders are saying to their own people, and especially what they are saying in authoritative pronouncements aimed at leadership circles. Here readings of the past year are all too clear. To take but one example, there were published in January 1975 companion articles, one by Boris Ponomarev, a deputy member of the Politburo, the other by Aleksandr Sobolev, a leading theoretician, each arguing that the evolution of the correlation of forces—in which they include not only military but economic and social forces—has moved very favorably from the standpoint of the Soviet Union over recent years.[1] Hence, they say, it is now possible to shift the target of communist action from the formerly colonial world to the developed world—particularly Europe. This shift in target is made possible by two things: one of them is

---

[1] B. N. Ponomarev, "The Role of Socialism in Modern World Development," *Problemy Mira i Sotsializma* (Problems of Peace and Socialism), January 1975, pp. 4–13; A. I. Sobolev, "Questions of the Strategy and Tactics of the Class Struggle at the Present Stage of the General Crisis of Capitalism" *Rabochiy Klass in Sovremennyy Mir* (The Working Class and the Contemporary World), January 1975, pp. 3–20.

"détente" and the other is "nuclear parity'" (as they interpret the term, in a way we shall examine shortly).

In the sum total there are strong grounds for concluding that in Soviet eyes "détente" is not that different from
what we used to call the "cold war." When we talked about
the "cold war" we were in part emphasizing the fact that
despite the deep hostility of the U.S.S.R. to the West in
general and to the United States in particular, it would be
a terrible thing if there were to be a "hot war" with the Soviet
Union. When the Soviets use the word "détente" in their
internal writings, they make it clear that they intend "détente"
to mean the same thing as "peaceful coexistence." Peaceful
coexistence they make it clear, implies no change in their
basic objectives, while they expect that current tactics will
weaken the West and strengthen the socialist states.[2]

However one reads these broader signs of present
Soviet behavior, a prime touchstone of the reality of
détente—not only now but for the future—must lie in the
area of strategic arms. If the Soviets are acting (and
negotiating) in a way that gives promise of a stable nuclear
balance (with meaningful reduction in due course), then the
future of détente is clearly much brighter. If they are not,
however, then the disturbing signs must be taken more
seriously, and the long-term dangers are great indeed.

Let us begin by discussing the similarities and contrasts between Soviet and American views on certain
strategic questions.

"Is the avoidance of war—particularly a nuclear
war—between the two countries desirable?" On this question I think both sides are in agreement. However, there is
a certain difference of approach. Clausewitz once said that
the aggressor never wants war; he would prefer to achieve
his objectives without having to fight for them. The Soviets
take seriously their doctrine that the eventual worldwide
triumph of socialism is inevitable; that they are duty bound
to assist this process; and that, as the process progresses,
the potential losers may stand at some point and feel
impelled to fight back. On the U.S. side some say that there
is no alternative to peace and therefore to détente. This

_____

[2] See comments by Aleksey Rumiantsev, at a conference sponsored by *Problemy
Mira i Sotsializma*, Summer 1975.

attitude misses two points. The first is that capitulation is too high a price for free men. The second is that high-quality deterrence, not unilateral restraint to the point of eroding deterrence, is the surest way of avoiding a nuclear war.

This thus leads to a second pair of questions: "Is nuclear war unthinkable? Would it mean the end of civilization as we know it?" We in the United States tend to think that it is, and this view prevailed (except for a small group of believers in preventive war, who never had strong policy influence) even in the periods when the United States enjoyed a nuclear monopoly and, at a later time, a clear theoretical war-winning capability.[3] When the effort was made in the late 1950s and early 1960s to create a significant civil defense capability, public resistance soon aborted the effort, so that today the United States has only the most minute preparations in this area. Rather, Americans have thought throughout the last 30 years in terms of deterring nuclear war, with the debate centering on how much effort is necessary to maintain deterrence, to keep nuclear war unthinkable.

In the Soviet Union, the view has been quite different. Perhaps initially because of the U.S. monopoly, Soviet leaders from the outset discounted the impact of nuclear weapons to their people. But as the Soviet nuclear capability grew, the Soviet leaders still declined to depict nuclear war as unthinkable or the end of civilization. On the contrary, they directed, and still direct, a massive and meticulously planned civil defense effort, with expenditures that run at approximately a billion dollars a year (compared to U.S. civil defense expenditures of approximately $80 million a year).[4] The average Soviet citizen is necessarily drawn into this effort, and the thinking it represents appears to permeate the Soviet leadership. In the Soviet Civil Defense Manual issued in large numbers beginning in 1969 and 1970,

---

[3] To see how top offcials viewed American nuclear power even in the period of American monopoly, one can now consult the recently declassified text of the NSC 68 policy paper dated in the spring of 1950. Even though Soviet nuclear capacity (after the first Soviet test of August 1949) was assessed as small for some years to come, that paper rejected any idea of reliance on American nuclear power for the defense of key areas. To be sure, in the 1950s under John Foster Dulles, the United States had a declaratory policy of "massive retaliation." But in the actual confrontations of that period, this declaratory policy was not in fact followed; instead, conventional force was used, for example in the Lebanon crisis of 1958 and, less directly, in the Offshore Islands crisis of the same year. After 1961 massive retaliation was abandoned.

[4] Eugene Wigner, "The Atom and the Bomb," *Christian Science Monitor*, November 13, 1974, p. 4.

the estimate is made that implementation of the prescribed evacuation and civil defense procedures would limit the civilian casualties to five to eight percent of urban population or three to four percent of the total population—even after a direct U.S. attack on Soviet cities. The Soviets may well overestimate the effectiveness of their civil defense program, but what is plain is that they have made, for 20 years or more, an approach to the problem of nuclear war that does assume, to a degree incomprehensible to Americans (or other Westerners), that nuclear war could happen, and that the Soviet Union could survive.

These differences in approach and attitude appear to be basic and deeply rooted. In essence, Americans think in terms of deterring nuclear war almost exclusively. The Soviet leaders think much more of what might happen in such a war. To the extent that humanitarian and moral objections to the use of nuclear weapons exist in the Soviet Union—as of course they do—such objections are subordinated for practical planning purposes to what Soviet leaders believe to be a realistic view.

It may be argued that these differences are more apparent than real, and that with the passage of time and the emergence of near-equality in the respective nuclear capabilities the differences are today less significant. Unfortunately, as the civil defense picture suggests, the trend in comparative nuclear weapons capabilities has if anything accentuated them.

That this is so can be seen in the more concrete realm of nuclear strategic concepts, and the postures that result from them. Often over-refined or expressed in terms hard for the layman to grasp, the range of strategic nuclear concepts available to any nuclear-weapons nation in fact boils down roughly to five:

1. *Minimum Deterrence.* This means a capacity to destroy a few key cities with little if any counterforce capacity to attack a hostile nation's military forces. In essence, it relies on the threat alone to deter. As between the Soviet Union and the United States, in the event deterrence failed, this level of American capacity would concede to the Soviet Union the potential for a military and political victory. The Soviets would risk U.S. retaliation against a portion of their industry and population, if our action policy in the event deterrence failed turned out to be the same as our declaratory

policy before deterrence failed. To reduce this risk of retaliation, the Soviets could limit their attack to U.S. forces and
continue to hold the U.S. population as hostage. In sum
the effect of this level of deterrence would be to provide
limited deterrence of a full-scale attack on the U.S. population. It would have less strength in deterring a Soviet attack
on U.S. forces or on allies whose security is essential to our
own.

2. *Massive Urban/Industrial Retaliation.* As the
name implies, this posture is designed to destroy many cities,
many millions of people and much productive capacity, and
to do so on an assured second-strike basis. This level of deterrence, sometimes called "Assured Destruction," would concede to the Soviet Union the potential for a military victory
if deterrence failed, but (it would be anticipated) would make
any such victory worthless in political terms. This form of
deterrence differs from minimum deterrence largely in the
degree of damage to Soviet industry and population it would
threaten.

3. *Flexible Response.* In this form of deterrence the
United States would have the capability to react to a Soviet
counterforce attack without going immediately to a countercity attack. It would thus increase the credibility of deterrence. The question of military or political victory if deterrence fails would depend upon the net surviving destructive
capacity of the two sides after the initial counterforce
exchanges. If the net surviving capacity after such a flexible
response were grossly to favor the Soviet Union, or if each
limited exchange placed the United States in a progressively
weaker relative position, we are back to the minimum deterrence or massive urban/industrial retaliation situation,
depending on the amount of surviving effective nuclear
capability on the U.S. side.

4. *Denial of a Nuclear-War-Winning Capability to the
Other Side.* This means a nuclear posture such that, even
if the other side attacked first and sought to destroy one's
own strategic striking power, the result of such a counterforce exchange would be sufficiently even and inconclusive
that the duel would be extremely unattractive to the other
side. This level of deterrence, in addition to deterring an attack
on U.S. population centers, should also deter a Soviet attack
on U.S. forces or those of its allies. In practice, against any
major nuclear nation, the posture would also include a

capacity for effective massive urban/industrial retaliation if such a strategy were called for.

5. *A Nuclear-War-Winning Capability.* This would be a position so superior that, whatever the initial forms of nuclear exchange, one's own surviving capacity would be enough to destroy the war-making ability of the other nation without comparable return damage. Such a U.S. posture would deter any Soviet attack on the United States and could also limit other serious Soviet military initiatives contrary to U.S. and allied interests. However, Soviet weapons technology and program momentum are such that the United States probably could not obtain this capability.

A review of the choices made by the United States and the Soviet Union among these five concepts goes, I believe, further than any other form of analysis in explaining and clarifying the changes in the strategic balance since 1945. Until roughly 1954, the United States retained nuclear superiority without extraordinary effort. By the late 1950s, the vulnerability of American bomber bases (bombers then being the only effective delivery method) emerged as a serious weakness in the American posture.[5] This weakness, and the rapid advances in missile technology of the period, led the United States between 1956 and 1962 to place great emphasis on ensuring the survivability of its nuclear striking power; average strategic obligational authority during these years was about $18 billion a year in 1974 dollars.[6] As a result the feared intercontinental ballistic missile (ICBM) "gap" of the 1960 presidential campaign never in fact became reality, but on the contrary the United States re-established a clearly superior nuclear capability by 1961-62. This was the situation at the time of the only true nuclear confrontation of the postwar period, the Cuban missile crisis of the fall of 1962.

Up to that point something approaching a war-winning capability seemed to most Americans the best possible form of deterrence, and thus desirable. However, as it became clear that the Soviet Union, too, was developing

[5] See Albert Wohlstetter, "The Delicate Balance of Terror." *Foreign Affairs,* January 1959, pp. 211–234.

[6] It should be noted that this figure refers to the amounts obligated annually for equipment, materiel, and personnel that can be directly attributed to the program mission, including all support costs that follow directly from the number of combat units. It does not include allocable costs of such related activities as communications, general support, and intelligence.

massive and survivable missile delivery capabilities, this view changed to the belief that even though a nuclear war might be won in a purely military sense, it could not be won in a political sense. That led to the further view that mutual deterrence through mutually assured destruction was the best feasible objective.

I have explained elsewhere at greater length the decisions of the early 1960s, in which I was one of those who participated with Robert McNamara, then Secretary of Defense.[7] In essence, the United States opted at that point to stress technological improvement rather than expanded force levels. While numerical comparisons were not ignored the basic aim was an underlying condition of what may be called "crisis stability," a situation where neither side could gain from a first strike, and of "mutual assured destruction," where each side would have a fully adequate second-strike capability to deter the other. In such a condition it was believed that neither could realistically threaten the other in the area of strategic weapons, and that the result would be much greater stability and higher chances of the peaceful resolution of crises if they did occur. While nuclear weapons would always be a major deterrent, the conventional arms balance at any point of confrontation would remain important (as it had been in the Berlin crisis of 1958–62 and also in the Cuban missile crisis itself). In short, the aim was to downgrade nuclear weapons as an element in U.S.-Soviet competition and to prepare the way for systematic reductions in nuclear arms. If both sides were to adopt such a concept, it should be possible, over time, to move from what might be called a "high deterrent" posture to a "low deterrent" posture, with the deterrent remaining essentially equivalent on both sides but at successively lower levels.

As the United States thus adjusted its posture, the invitation for the Soviet Union likewise to seek a similar posture—and stop there—was patent both from statements of American policy and from the always-visible American actions. Unfortunately, however the Soviet Union chose to pursue a course that was ambiguous: it could be interpreted as being aimed at overtaking the United States but then stopping at parity; it could, however, be interpreted as being

---

[7] See Paul H. Nitze, "The Vladivostok Accord and SALT II," *The Review of Politics* (University of Notre Dame), April 1975, pp. 147–60, especially pp. 149–50.

aimed at establishing superiority in numbers of launchers and in throw-weight[8] and, perhaps ultimately, a nuclear-war-winning capability on the Soviet side.

It is important to consider the reasons that may have entered into this choice. In part, the Soviet leaders may have been motivated by technological factors—that they had already moved to heavy rockets but were behind in other areas, such as solid propellant technology, accuracy and MIRVing (the development of multiple, independently targetable reentry vehicles). In part, there may have been an element of traditional Soviet emphasis on mass and size. But it is hard to avoid the conclusion that an important factor was the reading the Soviet leaders gave to the Cuban missile crisis and, to a lesser extent, the Berlin crisis. In the latter case, Khrushchev had briefly sought to exploit the first Soviet rocket firings of 1957—by a series of threats to Berlin beginning in late 1958—but then found that the West stood firm and that the United States quickly moved to reestablish its strategic superiority beyond doubt. And in the Cuban missile case, the very introduction of the missiles into Cuba in the fall of 1962 must have reflected a desire to redress the balance by quick and drastic action while the actual outcome of the crisis seemed to the Soviet leaders to spell out that nuclear superiority in a crunch would be an important factor in determining who prevailed.

Harking back to the Soviet penchant for actually visualizing what would happen in the event of nuclear war, it seems highly likely that the Soviet leaders, in those hectic October days of 1962, did something that U.S. leaders, as I know from my participation, did only in more general terms—that is, ask their military just how a nuclear exchange would come out. They must have been told that the United States would be able to achieve what they construed as victory, that the U.S. nuclear posture was such as to be able to destroy a major portion of Soviet striking power and still itself survive in a greatly superior condition for further strikes if needed. And they must have concluded that such a superior capability provided a unique and vital tool for

[8] "Throw-weight" is measure of the weight of effective payload that can be deliverd to an intended distance. In the case of intercontinental ballistic missiles (ICBMs) and submarine-launched ballistic missiles (SLBMs), the throw-weight is a direct measure of such a payload in terms of the potential power of the missiles' boosters. In view of the more variable loads carried by heavy bombers, a formula for equivalence is needed to take account of all factors including explosive power. This point is addressed in footnote 16.

pressure in a confrontation situation. It was a reading markedly different from the American internal one, which laid much less stress on American nuclear superiority and much more on the fact that the United States controlled the sea lanes to Cuba and could also have expected to prevail in any conflict over Cuba waged with conventional arms.[9]

One cannot prove that this was the Soviet reasoning. But the programs they set under way about 1962— above all the new family of weapons systems, embodying not only numbers and size but also greatly advanced technology, the development and deployment of which began to be evident beginning in 1971 but which must have been decided upon some years earlier—seem to reflect a fundamental state of mind on the Soviet side that contains no doubt as to the desirability of a war-winning capability, *if feasible.* Believing that evacuation, civil defense and recuperation measures can minimize the amount of damage sustained in a war, they conclude that they should be prepared if necessary to accept the unavoidable casualties. On the other hand, the loss of a war would be irretrievable. Therefore, the best deterrent is a war-winning capability, if that is attainable.

There have been, and I believe still are, divisions of opinion on the Soviet side as to whether such a capability *is* feasible. There are those who have argued that the United States is a tough opponent with great technical expertise and that the United States can be expected to do whatever is necessary to deny such a war-winning capability to the Soviet side. Others have taken the view that the developing correlation of forces—social, economic and political as well as military and what they call the deepening crisis of capitalism—may prevent the United States and its allies from taking the necessary countermeasures and that the target of a war-winning capability, therefore, is both desirable and feasible. Again, this is not to say that Soviet leaders would desire to initiate a nuclear war even if they had a war-winning capability. They would, however, consider themselves duty bound by Soviet doctrine to exploit fully that strategic advantage through political or limited military means.

---

[9] See Maxwell D. Taylor, "The Legitimate Claims of National Security," *Foreign Affairs,* April 1974, p. 582.

The SALT negotiations got under way in la\
As a participant in those talks from then until mid
I have described elsewhere some of the difficultie\
attended the U.S. side.[10] What was most fundamental
that the U.S. delegation sought at every level and through
every form of contact to bring home to the Soviet delegation, and the leaders behind it, the desirability of limitations which would assure "crisis stability" and "essential
equivalence"—and that the Soviet side stoutly resisted these
efforts.

Indeed, the negotiations very early revealed other
major stumbling blocks. One, in particular, revolved around
the Soviet conception of "strategic parity." In the SALT
negotiations the U.S. delegation consistently argued for the
acceptance by both sides of the concept of "essential
equivalence." By that we meant that both sides did not have
to be exactly equal in each component of their nuclear
capabilities but that overall the nuclear strategic capability
of each side should be essentially equal to that of the other
and at a level, one could hope, lower than that programmed
by the United States. The Soviets have never accepted this
concept, but have argued instead for the concept of "equal
security taking into account geographic and other considerations." In explaining what they meant by "geographic and
other considerations," they said that, "The U.S. is surrounded
by friendly countries. You have friends all around the oceans.
We, the U.S.S.R., are surrounded by enemies. China is an
enemy and Europe is a potential enemy. What we are asking for is that our security be equal to yours taking into
account these considerations." They never went so far as to
say that this really amounts to a requirement for Soviet
superiority in capabilities over the United States, the U.K.,
France and China simultaneously, but watching the way they
added things up and how they justified their position, this
is what it boiled down to.

Yet the two sides were able to reach agreement in May
of 1972 on stringent limitations on the deployment of ABM
interceptor missiles, ABM launchers and ABM radars and
on an Interim Agreement temporarily freezing new offensive missile-launcher starts.

[10] Paul H. Nitze, "The Strategic Balance Between Hope and Skepticism," *Foreign Policy*, Winter 1974–75, pp. 136–56.

After the May 1972 signing of the ABM Treaty and the Interim Agreement, it turned out that the two sides had quite different views as to how the negotiating situation had been left. On the U.S. side, we told the Congress that the Interim Agreement was intended to be merely a short-term freeze on new missile-launcher starts, and that this, together with the ABM Treaty, should create favorable conditions for the prompt negotiation of a more complete and balanced long-term agreement on offensive strategic arms to replace the Interim Agreement and be a complement to the ABM Treaty. Both sides had agreed promptly to negotiate a more complete agreement to replace the Interim Agreement. And the Interim Agreement specifically provided that its provisions were not to prejudice the scope or terms of such a replacement agreement. We thought such a replacement agreement should be based, as was the ABM Treaty, on the principles of equality in capabilities, greater stability in the nuclear relationship between the two sides, and a mutual desire to reduce the resources committed to strategic arms.

However, the Soviet Union had a quite different view. Its negotiators held that in accepting the Interim Agreement we had conceded that the Soviet Union was entitled to an advantage for an indefinite time of some 50 percent in the number of missile launchers and something better than double the average effective size, or throw-weight, of their missiles over ours. In working out a more complete and longer term agreement, in their view, all that was necessary was to add strict and equal limits on bombers and their armaments, provide for the withdrawal of our nuclear forces deployed in support of our allies capable of striking Soviet territory, and halt our B-1 and Trident programs but not the "modernization" of their systems. The difference of position between the two sides was such that it was difficult to see how agreement could be reached.

In the Vladivostok Accord of November 1974 the Soviets did make concessions from their past extremely one-sided negotiating demands. Those concessions were greater than many in the U.S. executive branch expected. However, does the Accord promise to result in achieving the objectives which the United States has for many years thought should be achieved by a long-term agreement on offensive forces? Those objectives were parity, or essential equivalence, between the offensive capabilities on the two sides, the maintenance of high-quality mutual deterrence and a basis for reducing strategic arms expenditures. I believe it does not.

The Vladivostok Accord, in essence, limits the total number of strategic launchers—ICBMs, submarine-launched ballistic missiles (SLBMs) and heavy strategic bombers, to 2,400 on both sides, and the number of MIRVed missile launchers to 1,320 on both sides. It limits the Soviet Union to the number of modern large ballistic launchers (MLBMs) that they now have, while prohibiting the United States from deploying any modern launchers in this category.[11] The Accord calls for air-to-surface missiles with a range greater than 600 kilometers, carried by heavy bombers, to be counted against the 2,400 ceiling. The treaty would allow freedom to mix between the various systems subject to these limitations.

As this article goes to press, there still remain some things to be cleared up: Secretary Kissinger has said that there was a misunderstanding concerning air-to-surface missiles (ASMs), that our understanding was that only *ballistic* air-to-surface missiles of greater than 600-kilometer range are to be included in the 2,400 launcher limit, not *cruise* missiles.[12] That is being argued between the two sides at the present time. There is also a question about mobile missiles, particularly land-mobile missiles: Should they be banned or should they be permitted and counted against the 1,320 and 2,400 ceilings? And there is the open question of what constitutes a "heavy bomber." The Soviets are building a plane called the "Backfire" whose gross take-off weight is three-quarters that of the B-1 and which is two

[11] There has been no agreed definition of a heavy ballistic missile. However, both sides acknowledge that the SS-9 and the SS-18 are MLBMs and that the U.S. Titan missile, while it is considered heavy, does not fall within the definition of "modern." The U.S. has no launchers for MLBMs and is prohibited from converting any of its silos to such launchers. The Soviets are estimated to have had 308 launchers for MLBMs and are permitted to convert the SS-9 launchers into launchers for the even larger and much more capable SS-18s.

[12] There are several relevant points on the 600-km. range and cruise vs. ballistic ASM questions. The inclusion of cruise missiles as well as ballistic missiles in the aggregate would offer a distinct advantage to the U.S.S.R. In the first place, cruise missiles with a range greater than 600 km. would significantly contribute to U.S. bomber penetration in the face of the strong Soviet antiaircraft defenses. Furthermore, the United States needs longer range cruise missiles to reach meaningful targets within the opponents interior than does the Soviet Union. Secondly, the Soviets now have cruise missiles of large size with large conventional warheads having a range close to 600 km. With smaller nuclear warheads their range could be more than doubled. It is not possible to verify the substitution of nuclear warheads for conventional ones, or to tell armed cruise missiles from unarmed ones. In any case, a single cruise missile cannot be equated with a Soviet ICBM carrying 50 times as much warhead weight.

and a half times as big as our FB-111. It is a very competent plane, more competent than some of the planes they now agree should be defined to be heavy bombers. The Soviets say the Backfire should not be included in the category of heavy bombers because "we don't intend to use it in that role." However, it can in fact carry, even without refueling (and it is equipped to be refueled), a significant payload to intercontinental distances if the aircraft is recovered in a third country. The way the Vladivostok Accord reads, air-to-surface missiles in excess of 600 kilometers in range, if not carried on a heavy bomber, are not required to be counted at all. So Backfires and FB-111s with long-range missiles would not count in any way against anything. These problems must be resolved in order to have a meaningful agreement.

Then there are the problems of verification. Messrs. Kissinger and Gromyko have been trying to work out a compromise on the verification issue. I personally take the verification issue less seriously than most because the limits are so high that what could be gained by cheating against them would not appear to be strategically significant.[13] However, we should be careful not to establish a precedent which would cause trouble if more meaningful limitations were agreed upon.

A notable feature of the Vladivostok Accord is that it does not deal with throw-weight. The agreement would not effectively check the deployment of the new Soviet family of large, technically improved and MIRVed offensive missiles. While both sides are permitted equal numbers of MIRVed missiles, the new Soviet SS-19s have three times the

---

[13] The significance of verifiability is a function not only of the confidence one can have in verifying a particular number but of the strategic significance of the number being verified. Fixed ICBM silos are large and the number deployed is therefore readily verifiable; however, the throw-weight of the missiles which can be launched from such silos can vary by a factor of ten.

The provision in the SALT I Interim Agreement that the interior dimensions of silos not be increased by more than 15 percent was an attempt to get at this problem. However, the volume of a missile which can be launched from a silo of given interior dimensions can still vary by a factor of two or three, and the throw-weight of a missile with a given volume can vary by a factor of two. Even if the probable error in directly verifying a throw-weight limitation were 20 percent, such a limitation would be strategically far more significant than any of the preceding limitations.

In addition to throw-weight, there are other significant strategic factors, such as the survivability of the launcher through mobility or hardening, and the accuracy, reliability, and number of RVs (reentry vehicles) carried by a MIRVed missile. None of these other factors is limited under the Vladivostok Accord and, in any case, they are inherently difficult to verify.

throw-weight of the U.S. Minuteman III, and the new SS-18s, seven times. What this comes down to is that under the Accord the Soviets can be expected to have a total of about 15 million pounds of missile throw-weight and bomber throw-weight equivalent. If the Congress goes forward with the B-1 and the Trident system but the United States does not add further strategic programs, the Soviets can be expected to end up with an advantage of at least three-to-one in missile throw-weight and of at least two-to-one in overall throw-weight, including a generous allowance for the throw-weight equivalent of heavy bombers, and two-to-one or three-to-one in MIRVed missile throw-weight. This disparity leaves out of consideration the Backfire, the FB-111, and the highly asymmmetrical advantage in air defenses that the Soviet Union enjoys.[14]

The prospects for SALT III center on reductions in the strategic forces on both sides, an aim of the SALT talks since their inception. My personal view is that meaningful reductions are highly desirable, and that the aim of reductions should be to increase strategic stability. But this aim is not served by reducing numbers of launchers, unless throw-weight is also reduced and made more equal.[15]

The agreed reduction of the throw-weight of large, land-based MIRVed missiles, however, would increase stability. I see no reason why the Soviet Union needs to replace its SS-9s with SS-18s, nor why it needs to replace a large number of its SS-11s with SS-19s. Although it is perfectly feasible and permissible under the Vladivostok Accord for us to develop missiles of equally large or even greater throw-weight than the SS-19s and fit them in Minuteman III silos, would it not be far better for both sides if there were sub-limits of, say, 50 on the number of SS-18s the Soviets were permitted to deploy and 500 or less on the number of SS-19 and SS-17 class ICBMs that either side was permitted to deploy? Even in a context of no other changes

[14] In mid-1973 the United States had 602 fighter interceptors and 481 surface-to-air missiles, compared to the Soviet Union's 3,000 fighter interceptors and 10,000 surface-to-air missiles. Edward Luttwak, *The U.S.-U.S.S.R. Nuclear Weapons Balance,* The Washington Papers, Beverly Hills: Sage Publications, 1974.

[15] Indeed, if total throw-weight is not reduced while the number of launchers is, the fewer launchers become more vulnerable and critical to each side and crisis stability is actually lessened. See Lt. Gen. (then Col.) Glenn A. Kent, "On the Interaction of Opposing Forces under Possible Arms Agreements," Occasional Papers in International Affairs, No. 5, Center for International Affairs, Harvard University, March 1963.

in the postures of the two countries, the reduction in missiles to these numbers would change the missile throw-weight asymmetry to one-and-a-half to one.

It might then be more feasible to work out subsequent reductions in numbers of vehicles which would include the Soviet older un-MIRVed missiles, such as the SS-9, along with our Minuteman II and Titan. But in the absence of throw-weight limitations of some sort, reduction per se will not improve stability.

However, the Russians are opposed to considering throw-weight limitations and have also taken the position that a future negotiation for reductions has to take into account all forward-based systems—all the systems we have in Europe and in East Asia, and on aircraft carriers. Thus, it is hard to see how we can have high hopes of getting anything in SALT III that will provide relief for the anticipated strain on the U.S. strategic posture as the Soviet deployments proceed and as their accuracy improves.

The country as a whole has looked at strategic nuclear problems during the last six years in the context of SALT, hoping to make the maintenance of our national security easier through negotiations. It now appears, however, for the reasons outlined above, that we are not likely to get relief from our nuclear strategic problems through this route. Therefore, we have to look at our strategic nuclear posture in much the way we used to look at it before the SALT negotiations began and determine what is needed in the way of a nuclear strategy for the United States and what kind of posture is needed to support it. A fundamental aim of nuclear strategy and the military posture to back it up must be deterrence: the failure to deter would be of enormous cost to the United States and to the world.

Once again, two important distinctions should be borne in mind: the distinction between the concept of "deterrence" and the concept of "military strategy," and the accompanying distinction between "declaratory policy" and "action policy." Deterrence is a political concept; it deals with attempts by indications of capability and will to dissuade the potential enemy from taking certain actions. Military strategy deals with the military actions one would, in fact, take if deterrence fails. A responsible objective of military strategy in this event would be to bring the war to an end in circumstances least damaging to the future of our society.

From the U.S. standpoint, just to level a number of Soviet cities with the anticipation that most of our cities would then be destroyed would not necessarily be the implementation of a rational military strategy. Deterrence through the threat of such destruction thus rests on the belief that in that kind of crisis the United States would act irrationally and in revenge. Yet serious dangers can arise if there is such a disparity between declaratory deterrence policy and the actual military strategy a nation's leaders would adopt if deterrence fails—*or* if there is a belief by the other side that such a disparity would be likely. I think former Secretary James Schlesinger's flexible response program was, in effect, an attempt to get our declaratory policy closer to a credible action policy and thus improve deterrence.

Ultimately, the quality of that deterrence depends importantly on the character and strength of the U.S. nuclear posture versus that of the Soviet Union. In assessing its adequacy, one may start by considering our ability to hold Soviet population and industry as hostages, in the face of Soviet measures to deter or hedge against U.S. retaliation directed at such targets.

In 1970 and 1971—when the focus was almost exclusively on "mutual assured destruction"—the congressional debates on whether or not to deploy a U.S. anti-ballistic missile system recognized clearly the importance to deterrence of hostage populations. Critics of the ABM argued—and with decisive impact on the outcome of the debate—that an effective ABM defense of urban/industrial centers could be destabilizing to the nuclear balance: if side *A* (whether the United States or the U.S.S.R.) deployed an ABM defense of its cities; side *B* could no longer hold side *A*'s population as a hostage to deter an attack by *A* on *B*. And in 1972 the same argument carried weight in the negotiation and ratification of the ABM limits in the SALT I agreements.

Yet today the Soviet Union has adopted programs that have much the same effect on the situation as an ABM program would have. And as the Soviet civil defense program becomes more effective it tends to destabilize the deterrent relationship for the same reason: the United States can then no longer hold as significant a proportion of the Soviet

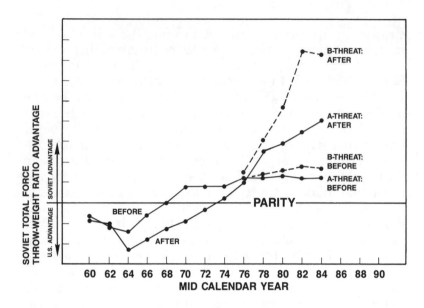

TABLE I
SOVIET — U.S. Throw-Weight Ratios

population as a hostage to deter a Soviet attack. Concurrently, Soviet industrial vulnerability has been reduced by deliberate policies, apparently adopted largely for military reasons, of locating three-quarters of new Soviet industry in small and medium-sized towns. The civil defense program also provides for evacuation of some industry and materials in time of crisis.

In sum, the ability of U.S. nuclear power to destroy without question the bulk of Soviet industry and a large proportion of the Soviet population is by no means as clear as it once was, even if one assumes most of U.S. striking power to be available and directed to this end.

A more crucial test, however, is to consider the possible results of a large-scale nuclear exchange in which one side sought to destroy as much of the other side's striking power as possible, in order to leave itself in the strongest possible position after the exchange. As already noted, such a counterforce strategy appears to fit with Soviet ways of thinking and planning; it is a strategy we must take into account.

Tables I and II, on these two pages, apply this test over a period of years running from 1960 to (as it happens)

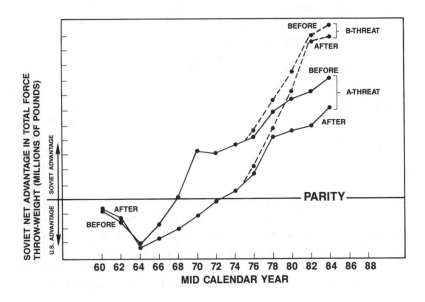

TABLE II
SOVIET — U.S. Throw-Weight Differentials

1984. For past periods, fairly assured estimates are available for both sides. For future years, a median estimate of U.S. programs, based on published data, has been used, while on the Soviet side there are two alternative projections— an "A-threat" based on a representative estimate of Soviet force deployments and accuracy capabilities, and a "B-threat" reflecting the possibility of increased Soviet emphasis on accuracy and other strategic force factors. Both forces are assessed in terms of total available throw-weight, measuring this directly for assumed missile inventories and making full allowance for the bomber equivalent of missile throw-weight for both sides.[16]

[16] A B-52 has been assigned an equivalent throw-weight of 10,000 lbs. and a B-1 about 19,000 lbs. The SRAM air-to-surface missile has a yield about equal to that of a Minuteman III warhead; hence, for every three SRAMs carried by a bomber, that bomber is given a throw-weight equivalent equal to the throw-weight of one Minuteman III. Laydown bombs are assumed to have roughly the yield of Minuteman II; hence, for each laydown bomb carried by a bomber it is given a throw-weight equivalent equal to the throw-weight of a Minuteman II. The alert bomber force is assumed to be 40 percent of the B-52 inventory and 60 percent of the B-1 inventory, degraded to incorporate penetration factors.

The Tables assume an exchange in which the Soviet Union has attacked U.S. forces, and the United States has retaliated by trying to reduce Soviet strategic throw-weight to the greatest extent possible. To assess the opposing forces *before* attack in terms of their relative throw-weight is of course only a partial measure of their comparative original capability. In working out what would actually happen in the assumed exchange, full account has been taken of all relevant factors—in particular the number, yield, accuracy and reliability of the reentry vehicles associated with that throw-weight, and the hardness of the targets against which they are assumed to have been targeted.

It is the situation *after* attack, of course, that is most important. And, here, since the targets remaining after the exchange would almost all be soft ones, missile accuracy and other refinements in the original postures no longer have the same significance. Surviving throw-weight thus becomes an appropriate *total* measure of the residual capability on both sides.

As worked out by Mr. T. K. Jones, who served as my senior technical advisor when I was a member of the U.S. SALT delegation, the results of such an assessment are shown in Table I, expressed in terms of the ratios, and Table II, expressed in terms of the absolute units of weight—by which one side exceeds the other before and after attack in the various periods and alternative cases examined.[17]

Based on this method of assessment, the United States in 1960 held a slight but increasing advantage over the Soviet Union, and this advantage became greatest in about mid-1964. Thereafter, however, Soviet programs—greatly accelerated, as earlier noted, after the Cuban missile crisis—started to reverse the trend, so that by mid-1968 the total deployed throw-weights on both sides, before a hypothetical nuclear exchange, were roughly equal. However, as the "after" curve shows, the U.S. operational military advantage persisted for some time thereafter, offsetting the Soviet

---

[17] I regret that, even if space permitted, the full assumptions used in Mr. Jones' study cannot be spelled out here. Security considerations necessarily enter in for some of the underlying data. I have myself gone over Mr. Jones' data and assumptions with care and believe that they represent a careful and objective analysis of the relevant factors. Above all, since his methods are self-consistent from one period to the next, they show a valid trend-line and pace of change—which I believe the more expert readers of this article will find conform to their more general judgments.

superiority in deployed throw-weight. For example, if in 1970 the Soviets had attacked U.S. forces, their entire prewar advantage would have been eliminated, leaving the United States with substantial superiority at the end of the exchange. However, this situation began to be reversed in 1973, with the Soviets gaining the military capability to end an exchange with an advantage in their favor. Moreover, in 1976 the "before" and "after" curves of Table I cross, signifying that the Soviets could, by initiating such an exchange, increase the ratio of advantage they held at the start of the exchange. By 1977, after a Soviet-initiated counterforce strike against the United States to which the United States responded with a counterforce strike, the Soviet Union would have remaining forces sufficient to destroy Chinese and European NATO nuclear capability, attack U.S. population and conventional military targets, and still have a remaning force throw-weight in excess of that of the United States. And after 1977 the Soviet advantage after the assumed attack mounts rapidly.

In addition to the ratios and absolute differences that apply to the remaining throw-weights of the two sides, there is a third factor which should be borne in mind. That factor is the absolute level of the forces remaining to the weaker side. If that absolute level is high, continues under effective command and control, and is comprised of a number of reentry vehicles (RVs) adequate to threaten a major portion of the other side's military and urban/industrial targets, this will be conducive to continued effective deterrence even if the ratios are unfavorable. These considerations reinforce the desirability of survivable systems and methods of deployment.

In sum, the trends in relative military strength are such that, unless we move promptly to reverse them, the United States is moving toward a posture of minimum deterrence in which we would be conceding to the Soviet Union the potential for a military and political victory if deterrence failed. While it is probably not possible and may not be politically desirable for the United States to strive for a nuclear-war-winning capability, there are courses of action available to the United States whereby we could deny to the Soviets such a capability and remove the one-sided instability caused by their throw-weight advantage and by their civil defense program.

To restore stability and the effectiveness of the U.S. deterrent: (1) the survivability and capability of the U.S. strategic forces must be such that the Soviet Union could not foresee a military advantage in attacking our forces, and (2) we must eliminate or compensate for the one-sided instability caused by the Soviet civil defense program. Specifically, we must remove the possibility that the Soviet Union could profitably attack U.S. forces with a fraction of their forces and still maintain reserves adequate for other contingencies.

As to the civil-defense aspect, the absence of a U.S. capability to protect its own population gives the Soviet Union an asymmetrical possibility of holding the U.S. population as a hostage to deter retaliation following a Soviet attack on U.S. forces. Although the most ecnomical and rapidly implementable approach to removing this one-sided instability would be for the United States to pursue a more active civil defense program of its own, such a program does not appear to be politically possible at this time. Its future political acceptability will be a function of the emerging threat and its appreciation by U.S. leadership and by the public.

Two more practicable avenues of action suggest themselves. First, all of the options which would be effective in diminishing the one-sided Soviet advantage involve some improvement in the *accuracy* of U.S. missiles. Differential accuracy improvements can, at least temporarily, compensate for throw-weight inequality.

This is a controversial issue which has been studied extensively. The results of one such study by a member of Congress are shown in the *Congressional Record* of May 20, 1975. According to that study the United States presently holds a 4:1 superiority in the hard-target kill capability of missile forces. The Congressman notes in his opposition to a U.S. high-accuracy maneuvering reentry vehicle (MaRV) program that MaRV would by the late 1980s improve U.S. accuracy to 0.2 n.m. (120 feet), incorrectly estimating that this would increase the U.S. advantage to 7:1 over the U.S.S.R.—assuming the latter was unable to develop MaRV by that time. However, the Congressman's data also predict that the hard-target kill capability of the Soviet missile force will by the 1980s have increased 100-fold, so that if the United States took no action to improve the accuracy of its missiles, the Soviet Union would have an advantage of 25:1. While it is unnecessary to equip more than a portion of U.S. missiles with high accuracy RVs, it is clear that substantial accuracy improvements are essential to avoid major Soviet superiority in a critical respect.

Others argue that improvements in U.S. missile accuracy would be "destabilizing." More specifically, such programs "could spur Soviet countermeasures such as new programs to increase their second-strike capabilities by going to (1) more sea-launched strategic missiles, (2) air- and sea-launched cruise missiles, (3) expanded strategic bomber forces, and (4) mobile ICBMs."[18] These arguments ignore the central fact that deterrence is already being seriously undermined by unilateral actions of the Soviet Union. Hence, further self-restraint by the United States cannot but worsen this condition.

Moreover, the Soviet programs cited as consequences of U.S. accuracy improvement are in fact stabilizing rather than destabilizing. Under the SALT agreements on force ceilings, such reactions would compel offsetting reductions in the Soviet silo-based ICBM force, thereby reducing their total force throw-weight. Moreover, the replacement ICBM systems are not likely to achieve accuracy equal to that of the silo-based ICBMs, while throw-weight moved to bombers and cruise missiles, because of the long flight time to targets, cannot be effectively used in a first-strike counterforce role.

In sum, even on the information furnished by those generally opposing improved accuracy of U.S. missiles, improvement *is* necessary to avoid a major Soviet advantage, and the logical Soviet counter to such improvements would move the Soviets in a direction which would stabilize the strategic relationship and reduce the Soviet throw-weight advantage.

Second, the prospective Soviet advantage would be offset by measures to decrease the *vulnerability* of U.S. strategic nuclear forces. Here there are several ongoing programs already under way, notably the development of the Trident submarine and the B-1 bomber; both these delivery systems will be inherently less vulnerable to a counterforce attack than fixed ICBM installations, the submarine by

---

[18] Additional views of Representative Schroeder, "Alternative Defense Posture Statement," Report 94–199 of House Armed Services Committee, May 10, 1975, p. 130.

reason of its mobility at sea and the B-1 by virtue of its mobility and escape speed as well as the potential capacity to maintain a portion of the B-1 force airborne in time of crisis. In addition, programs to increase the pre-launch survivability of U.S. bomber forces generally, as well as programs to increase air defense capability through the so-called AWACS system, operate to reduce vulnerability of the total U.S. force. To a considerable extent, however, these programs are already taken into account in the calculations shown on Tables I and II—if they were to be delayed, the effect would be negative, and the contrary if they were to be stepped up and accelerated.

I believe, however, that these measures do not go far enough. The most vulnerable U.S. delivery system today is that of our fixed and hardened ICBM installations, including Minuteman silos. Under present trends, it is only a question of time until a combination of the large throw-weight available to the Soviets and improved accuracy will threaten the destruction of a high percentage of these installations—so that today there is considerable talk in some quarters of actually phasing out U.S. ICBM installations.

I believe such action would be unwise, and that it is entirely feasible, at not excessive cost, to adopt a new system of deployment that would not only permit the retention of our ICBMs—which contribute heavily to the total U.S. throw-weight—but would actually make these a more critical and effective component of the U.S. striking force. The system that would accomplish these ends would be a proliferation of low-cost shelters for what is called a multiple launch-point system. The essence of such a system would be to construct a large number of shelter installations, so that the smaller number of actual missile launchers could be readily moved and deployed among these installations on a random pattern deliberately varied at adequate intervals of time.

The ingredients for such a system are, I believe, already in existence, notably through the availability of sufficiently large areas of western desert land now owned by the Department of Defense. On this land there could be created a large number of hardened shelters, or alternatively the missiles themselves could be encased in hardened capsules redeployable among a large number of "soft" shelters. Preliminary study indicates that the research, development and procurement costs of a system along these would average approximately $1.5 billion a year in 1975 dollars over the next eight to ten years. Inasmuch as the current level of obligational authority for strategic weapons systems is on the order of $7 billion per year—much less, as already noted, than the comparable amounts obligated annually in 1956–62—I believe this is a cost we should be prepared to accept.

The objective of creating such a new system of deployment would be to greatly increase the throw-weight costs to the Soviets of destroying a sustantial portion of our deterrent forces. This is achieved with a multiple launch-point system, since in order to destroy the system virtually all of the relevant shelter installations would need to be destroyed. There would be many more hardened shelters or encapsulated missiles than the present number of fixed installations, so that the Soviets would be required to commit a larger portion of their throw-weight to this task than they would to the task of attacking fixed installations—the trade-off of U.S. throw-weight destroyed to Soviet throw-weight used would greatly favor the United States. Thus the Soviet advantage in a counterforce exchange would be drastically reduced or eliminated.

Furthermore, I believe that such a U.S. move would be likely to lead to Soviet countermoves that would have a constructive impact on the overall balance. The logical answer to such a U.S. move would be for the Soviet side to substitute either multiple launch-point missiles or SLBMs for a portion of their large fixed ICBMs. They would thereby increase the survivability of their systems, but at the cost of substantially reducing their throw-weight advantage. Such moves by both sides would greatly improve crisis stability and thus significantly reduce the risk of a nuclear war.

In essence, the multiple launch-point idea is a method of preserving and increasing the effectiveness of land-based systems by making them partially mobile. It is, however, necessary to take account of the usual argument advanced for banning land-based mobile missile systems. This argument is that it is more difficult to verify with confidence the number of mobile and thus deployable launchers deployed by either side than it is to verify the number of fixed silos. The merit of this argument fades in a situation where up to 10 or 12 million pounds of MIRVed throw-weight can be expected to be available to the Soviet side under the limits contemplated by the Vladivostok Accord. With improved accuracy, less than four million pounds of MIRVed throw-weight could threaten the destruction of a high percentage of the fixed silos on the U.S. side. No practicable addition through unverified mobile launchers to the 10 to 12 million pounds of throw-weight permitted the Soviet side would compensate strategically for the additional throw-weight requirement that a U.S. multiple launch-point system would impose. A significant portion of a U.S. multiple launch-point system should survive even if the Soviet Union were to devote to the task of attacking it double the four million pounds of MIRVed throw-weight it would have to allocate to the destruction of our Minuteman silos.[19]

Undoubtedly, there are other programs which would also be necessary. In particular, it would seem to be essential, if the Soviet Union is to be permitted an unlimited

---

[19] Under the Vladivostok Accord, both sides are permitted 1,320 MIRVed missile launchers. The maximum MIRVed throw-weight the Soviets could obtain within this limit with the missiles they are currently testing and beginning to deploy is:

  4,500,000 pounds on 308 SS-18s (about 15,000 pounds each)
  7,100,000 pounds on 1,012 SS-19s (about 7,000 pounds each)

for a total MIRVed throw-weight of 11.6 million pounds. However, it is unlikely that the Soviets will reach this maximum, as they are currently deploying some SS-17s, which will have a throw-weight of about 5,000 pounds, and they may choose not to MIRV all of their SS-18s. A more likely figure is less than ten million pounds of MIRVed throw-weight.

A reliable megaton-range RV with a CEP (circular error probable, a measure of accuracy) of 0.125 nautical miles has a probability of damage of 85 percent against a silo of 1,500 psi (pounds per square inch) hardness. The targeting of two such RVs on the silo would give a probability of damage of about 92 percent taking into account both reliability and accuracy. An SS-18 missile may have up to eight megaton-range RVs (International Institute for Strategic Studies, *The Military Balance, 1974–75*); thus a megaton-range RV may require around 2,000 pounds of throw-weight. The net throw-weight required, then, to threaten 92 percent destruction of 1,000 hard silos would be approximately four million pounds, assuming the Soviets achieve CEPs averaging an eighth of a mile.

A multiple launch-point ICBM system with 600-psi hard shelters or encapsulated missiles in soft shelters would require considerably more throw-weight for its destruction. To barrage attack such a mobile system deployed on 6,000 square nautical miles of land as an area target would require about 19,000 megaton-range RVs to achieve a 92 percent damage level. The throw-weight required for this force would be considerably above the Soviet available force. Even as low a damage level as 20 percent would require almost 4,000 megaton-range RVs, a throw-weight of at least eight million pounds.

Assuming the same factors for accuracy and reliability as used above in calculating the potential results of an attack on silo-based ICBMs, an equal probability of damage (85 percent for a single reliable RV) can be achieved against a 600-psi shelter with a 290-kiloton weapon. Since a Minuteman III, with a total of three RVs of less than 200-kt yield, has a throw-weight of about 2,000 pounds, an RV of 290-kt yield might require about 800 pounds of throw-weight. Thus a U.S. deployment of some 10,000 shelters would require eight million pounds of Soviet MIRVed throw-weight to threaten destruction of 72 percent of the multiple launch-point system. The entire ten million pound force would raise the level of destruction to only 77 percent. The cost of adding RVs to the Soviet attack force should be substantially greater than the cost to the United States of adding shelters. In any case, it would appear technologically infeasible to reduce the throw-weight required per RV to less than 300 pounds, even if accuracies were eventually to approach zero CEP.

number of Backfires, that we not grant them a free ride for their bomber forces. This would require a reversal of congressional action limiting support for the AWACS program. But taking everything into consideration, the magnitude of the U.S. effort required would be far less than that which we undertook in the 1957–1962 period in response to Sputnik and the then-threatened vulnerability of our bomber force.

Some of my friends argue that those knowledgeable about such matters should bear in mind the horrors of a nuclear war, and should call for U.S. restraint in the hope the U.S.S.R. will follow our lead. Having been in charge of the U.S. Strategic Bombing Survey team of 500 physicists and engineers who measured the detailed effects of the two nuclear weapons used at Nagasaki and Hiroshima, the only two such weapons ever used in anger, and having been associated with many of the subsequent studies of the probable effects of the more modern weapons, I am fully sensitive to the first point. But to minimize the risks of nuclear war, it would seem to me wise to assure that no enemy could believe he could profit from such a war.

As to the second point, Helmut Sonnenfeldt, Counselor for the State Department, recently described the preconditions for the U.S. détente policy in the following terms:

The course on which we embarked requires toughness of mind and steadfastness of purpose. It demands a sober view not only of Soviet strengths but of our own. It is an attempt to evolve a balance of incentives for positive behavior and penalties for belligerence; the objective being to instill in the minds of our potential adversaries an appreciation of the benefits of cooperation rather than conflict and thus lessen the threat of war . . . . Interests will be respected only if it is clear that they can be defended. Restraint will prevail only if its absence is known to carry heavy risks.[20]

Unfortunately, I believe the record shows that neither negotiations nor unilateral restraint have operated to dissuade Soviet leaders from seeking a nuclear-war-winning capability—or from the view that with such a capability they could effectively use pressure tactics to get their way in crisis situations.

[20] Helmut Sonnenfeldt, "The Meaning of Détente," *Naval War College Review*, July–August 1975, pp. 3–8.

Hence it is urgent that the United States take positive steps to maintain strategic stability and high-quality deterrence. If the trends in Soviet thinking continue to evolve in the manner indicated by the internal statements of Soviet leaders, and if the trends in relative military capability continue to evolve in the fashion suggested by the prior analysis, the foundations for hope in the evolution of a true relaxation of tensions between the U.S.S.R. and much of the rest of the world will be seriously in doubt.

1978

WHAT SALT CAN
(AND CANNOT) DO

Aaron L. Friedberg

Aaron L. Friedberg, is currently a MacArthur Fellow at the Center
for International Affairs, Harvard University. He has served as a consultant to the National Security Council and the Department of Defense.

Arms control is in trouble. In 1972 both the interim
SALT I agreement and the treaty limiting antiballistic missile
systems (ABMs) passed the Senate by a margin of 88 to 2.
But the current strategic arms limitation treaty now lumber-
ing its way toward Capitol Hill faces stiff opposition. The
very idea of negotiating serious arms control agreements
with the Russians, once unquestioned, now seems dubious
or, at best, passé.

One reason for this unfortunate and possibly dangerous state of affairs is that arms control advocates have failed
to adapt to changing times. They have clung firmly and often
rather smugly to technically elegant but politically naive proposals for coping with the problems that nuclear weapons
pose. Unlike their critics, who begin with a set of explicit
assumptions about Soviet intentions, the arms controllers
(many of whom are former scientists and technical specialists) have focused almost exclusively on Soviet capabilities,
on the performance of individual weapons, and on the

Reprinted with permission from *Foreign Policy* 33 (Winter 1978–79).
Copyright © 1978 by the Carnegie Endowment for International Peace.

interactions between opposing weapons systems. Their interest in what the Russians hope to achieve through a military build-up is purely secondary. Because they pay little attention to the political dimension of the military balance, many traditional arms control advocates continue to view the undiminished Soviet appetite for the instruments of military power as a temporary aberration that will disappear if it is only ignored.

Today, faced with harsh and telling criticism from opponents of the entire SALT process, many arms controllers merely recite tired and unconvincing arguments in favor of further agreements or fall into a numbed silence. This need not be the case. Despite the attacks of the critics and the silence of the proponents, there is still a great deal to be said in favor of strategic arms control.

In the past, arms control in general and SALT in particular have been dramatically oversold. No matter what the present negotiations produce, the superpower competition for global political influence will continue, as will the competition for more narrow military advantages. SALT cannot, as some enthusiasts once claimed, cement an amicable political relationship between the United States and the Soviet Union. Nor can it, as Richard Burt has pointed out, ensure the absolute "technical stability" of the strategic balance.[1]

What the SALT process can do is to help the competing superpowers mark some channels of cooperation in what must for the foreseeable future remain a sea of conflict. These channel markers can serve to restrain the flow of the strategic arms competition, deflecting its path periodically and warning the participants away from especially hazardous waters. Eventually, arms control agreements may help to transform the turbulent international environment. But for now it is in the narrow but important realm of improving the stability of the strategic balance that SALT must play its role.

To understand the present debate over SALT, it is important first to examine the two basic arguments being made against the strategic arms control process. Critics claim that SALT has failed to suppress technical developments that

---

[1] Richard Burt, "Asking SALT to do too Much," *Washington Review of Strategic and International Studies*, January 1978, p. 30.

now pose a serious threat to U.S. security. They contend that negotiated agreements cannot prevent dangerous qualitative improvements in Soviet strategic forces. Moreover, say the critics, the steps the United States must take to offset those improvements will make future treaties virtually impossible to verify and thus to negotiate. For these reasons, it is argued, the United States should abandon the SALT process.

At a more general level, critics assert that SALT has always presumed a basic U.S.-Soviet agreement on fundamental strategic issues. That presumption, say the critics, has been decisively disproved by the events of the past six years. The Soviets have not been content with strategic parity or stable deterrence, and they continue to take steps that threaten the balance of power, both in their deployment of intercontinental strike forces and in their military activities in Europe and the Third World. The opponents of arms control argue that further American participation in SALT would be pointless at best: The two sides have nothing to talk about. At worst, they warn, the Russians may use arms control negotiations to deceive and manipulate their more gullible and optimistic partner.

High Hopes and Overblown Rhetoric

Both these arguments are given strength by a series of ongoing technical military developments that have come increasingly into view since the first SALT agreements were signed. Specifically, SALT has stopped neither the United States nor the Soviet Union from developing and deploying large numbers of highly accurate multiple independently targetable reentry vehicles (MIRVs). The first SALT accord also failed to prevent the Russians from deploying a new generation of MIRVed heavy missiles. The negotiations have thus failed to prevent the emergence of a thoretical Soviet first-strike threat against the American land-based missile force.

Arms control negotiations have also produced no visible change in the USSR's strategic doctrine or in the overall Soviet political-military worldview. Some Russian military affairs experts continue to stress the importance of being able to fight and win a nuclear war with the West. These commentators deny that a strategic balance based on the mutual vulnerability of the American and Soviet civilian populations is either militarily stable or politically desirable.

And they continue to emphasize the importance of military power in affecting the so-called "correlation of forces"— globally and in local situations.

Such statements are more than idle talk. They are reflected in Soviet defense programs and in specific foreign policy decisions. Thus, the Soviets have pushed ahead with the acquisition of counterforce weapons and have moved to improve their chances of winning a nuclear conflict by building up a significant civil defense capability and experimenting with antisatellite warfare techniques. Meanwhile, Soviet conventional and medium-range missile forces in Europe have been expanded. Finally, the Russians have shown an increasing willingness and ability to use military power to influence events in the Third World.

Clearly, the critics of arms control are right on a number of important issues. SALT has not stabilized the strategic balance, ended the continuing Soviet military build-up, or converted the Russians into international good citizens.

The lofty expectations engendered by the 1972 SALT agreements have not been fulfilled, nor are they likely to be in the near future. But it is those expectations rather than the arms control process itself that deserve to be most harshly criticized. The high hopes and overblown rhetoric of the early 1970s are today commonly acknowledged to have been unrealistic. The problems of controlling technical progress are now more fully understood, and the traditional conservative nature of Soviet thinking on questions of strategy and stability is more widely recognized.

Given what has been learned in the past six years, what can the United States reasonably expect to obtain from arms control negotiations with the Russians?

It is important to state quite clearly what SALT is not and cannot be:

• Arms control is neither a carrot to tempt the Soviets into good behavior nor a stick to beat them into line. Unless the United States obtains a significant strategic advantage over the Russians (or vice versa), the overall negotiating situation will remain more or less symmetrical. Both sides may need and want a SALT agreement, but neither will have sufficient leverage to extract unilateral concessions from the other—on military issues or on larger political questions. Put another way, SALT cannot be effectively linked to other, nonstrategic problems as long as the capabilities of the two participants remain roughly equal.

• SALT is not a barometer or a polygraph, nor is an arms control agreement a compact between trusting friends. A willingness to participate in serious negotiations should not be taken as an indication that the Russians have reformed, that they accept the global status quo, or even that they are content with the present state of the strategic balance. Soviet attempts to stretch the limits of any SALT agreement and perhaps even to get away with some subtle violations of the rules should be met firmly but calmly. It should come as no surprise to discover that the Soviets are clever, alert, and opportunistic. That is why the United States insists on independently verifiable agreements. Conversely, aggressive and deceitful Soviet behavior in other arenas does not mean that further arms control agreements are impossible. SALT is only one part of a complex and fragmented picture, not a universal glue with which some larger U.S.-Soviet rapprochement can be held together.

• The strategic arms limitation talks are not a school. Soviet ideas about the utility of military force, the nature of war, and the advantages of offense over defense and defense over deterrence all spring from long traditions and from a unique set of political and geographic circumstances. Except on some peripheral issues, and even then in a very indirect way, the United States is not going to educate the Soviet Union.

• SALT is not the cool, technical, rational bargaining forum in which the details of a permanent stable military balance can be drawn up. The hope of the classical arms control theorists, that self-interest would draw the two superpowers toward steps that would ultimately stabilize the entire strategic balance, cannot be fulfilled. This is true for two reasons. As the critics point out, the Soviets do not yet accept the virtues of strategic stability as it has come to be defined by Western theorists. They can therefore be expected to continue in their efforts to protect Soviet society from the effects of a nuclear war and in their attempts to acquire offensive forces capable of suppressing an American attack.

Moreover, the dynamic of technological progress and the difficulty of restraining it make a final, stable balance all but impossible to achieve. SALT can help to control the effects of technical advance, but it cannot legislate an end to change.

Centerpiece, Not Cornerstone
Three conclusions flow from these observations. First, SALT cannot end the arms race, and—second—it is unlikely to bring significant reductions in spending on strategic weapons. Because political and technical factors make absolute stability impossible, the strategic arms competition will continue, and it will continue to be expensive. Negotiated agreements can help prevent an unrestrained explosion in spending (a world without SALT would undoubtedly be more costly for both sides), but even maintaining and upgrading existing forces will remain an expensive proposition. Finally, SALT cannot serve any grand political function. Arms control negotiations may well be the centerpiece of the superpower relationship, but they cannot be the cornerstone on which a larger edifice is built.

What can the SALT process do? Essentially, what it has been doing all along—playing a limited but important role in improving strategic stability and thereby reducing the chances of nuclear war.

SALT has helped to stabilize the overall size of strategic forces, albeit at a high level. Actually, the current round of negotiations seems certain to lower ceilings on the number of delivery vehicles that each side may deploy by about 10 per cent.

Arms control negotiations have in the past constrained some costly and potentially dangerous technological developments. Bernard Brodie said of the 1972 treaty limiting the deployment of ballistic missile defenses: "The ABM appears to have been a target of opportunity, torpedoed at just the right time and by the right means. It should be the prime function of an intelligently directed arms control program to be looking out for such targets."[2]

Future targets of opportunity for the strategic arms control process may include antisatellite (ASAT) warfare techniques (although these are being handled in a forum outside SALT) and further improvements in warhead accuracy.

As was the case with the ABM, the Soviets have taken an early lead in testing ASAT technology and moving toward the deployment of operational antisatellite weapons. In theory an effective ASAT capability would fit neatly into a pre-emptive, war-fighting strategy just as a working ABM

[2] Bernard Brodie, "The Objectives of Arms Control," *International Security*, Summer 1976, p. 36.

system would have been in keeping with Soviet ideas on the value of active defense. In practice, the fear of being outpaced by the mobilized American research and development establishment may dampen Soviet enthusiasm for further ASAT experiments. The Russians may be willing, as they were on the ABM, to agree to a treaty limiting weapons to which they have no theoretical objections and which, under more favorable circumstances, they might very much like to have. Whatever the motivations of the two sides, an agreement to ban antisatellite weapons would prevent the emergence of a new threat to stability.

Through bilateral discussions it may also be possible to negotiate outright prohibitions on various types of weapons that neither side wants but both, in the absence of firm limitations, might feel compelled to deploy. Orbiting nuclear weapons have been outlawed in the past. Depressed trajectory submarine-launched ballistic missiles and intercontinental rockets designed for use on surface ships and airplanes may soon be eliminated.

By limiting numbers, restraining some destabilizing technological developments and eliminating certain types of weapons, the SALT process can help to reduce mutual uncertainties. The character and direction of the arms competition can be controlled, at least in part. While each country will have to accept limitations on its own freedom of action, both will have a better idea of the threats they will have to face in the future.

SALT can also help establish restraints on certain kinds of potentially provocative behavior—restraints that, while by no means absolute and foolproof, are nonetheless real. Through the Standing Consultative Commission (SCC), created as part of the 1972 ABM treaty, each superpower can question the other's compliance with the provisions of their mutual agreements. Attempts at missile silo concealment, ABM radar experiments, and efforts to interfere with surveillance satellites can currently be discussed. Other forms of dangerous activity, such as simultaneous missile tests that could be mistaken for the first salvo of a surprise attack, will soon be added to this list.

Without negotiated agreements detailing which activities are proscribed, there would be no real grounds for protesting against offensive Soviet behavior. And without the SCC or something like it, the United States would have no forum where it can forcefully voice its objections to Russian violations. The Soviets can be expected to probe around the edges of any arms control treaty they sign. But the record shows that when they can be carefully watched and, if necessary, called to account, they will live up to the letter of a SALT agreement.

A Difficult Business

The fact that there is a process by which the two superpowers define illegitimate behavior is at least as important as the agreements that emerge from it. When the United States and the Soviet Union agree simultaneously to forgo certain options, they tacitly acknowledge that they share some overlapping, if not identical, interests. By encouraging the recognition of coincident interests, by reminding the superpowers that their fates are inextricably linked, SALT exerts a modest but undeniable stabilizing influence.

This recitation of the virtues of arms control should not be taken as an attempt to refute all the charges of the critics. It is true that the United States may sometimes have to take unilateral actions (such as deploying some form of mobile missile) to offset the destabilizing influence of technological progress. And it is also true that the Soviet Union has a much different and, from the American point of view, more dangerous approach to the strategic arms competition than does the United States. But this does not mean that worthwhile arms control treaties are impossible. As long as the two sides have interests that overlap for whatever reason, there will be a possibility for significant, stabilizing agreements.

Americans should not deceive themselves about what negotiations can achieve. But neither should they shy away from the difficult business of controlling nuclear arms simply because they have given up hope or because they are afraid of being tricked. Above all, the United States should not rule out the possibility of more profound accommodations as the Soviets realize that they cannot gain real strategic advantage over the West.

The SALT treaty currently being discussed can help to improve the stability of the strategic balance. A move to scuttle SALT II and, in effect, to abandon arms control, would be an example of all those things critics of the negotiating process fear and warn against. It would be a failure of will, a failure of nerve, and, most important, a failure of imagination that the United States can ill afford.

1981

A MODEST PROPOSAL

George F. Kennan

George Kennan is Emeritus Professor at the Institute for Advanced Study, Princeton, and co-chairman of the American Committee on East-West Accord. He has served as the U.S. Ambassador to Yugoslavia and the Union of Soviet Socialist Republics. Professor Kennan is a past President of the American Academy of Arts and Letters. He has written extensively. For this essay Professor Kennan was awarded the Albert Einstein Peace Prize in 1981.

Adequate words are lacking to express the full seriousness of our present situation. It is not just that our government and the Soviet government are for the moment on a collision course politically; it is not just that the process of direct communication between them seems to have broken down entirely; it is not just that complications in other parts of the world could easily throw them into insoluble conflicts at any moment; it is also—and even more importantly—the fact that the ultimate sanction behind the policies of both these governments is a type and volume of weaponry that could not possibly be used without utter disaster for everyone concerned.

For over thirty years wise and farseeing people have been warning us about the futility of any war fought with these weapons and about the dangers involved in their very cultivation. Some of the first of these voices were those of

Reprinted by permission of George F. Kennan. Copyright © 1981 by George F. Kennan.

great scientists, including outstandingly Albert Einstein himself. But there has been no lack of others. Every president of this country, from Dwight Eisenhower to Jimmy Carter, has tried to remind us that there could be no such thing as victory in a war fought with such weapons. So have a great many other eminent persons.

When one looks back today over the history of these warnings, one has the impression that something has now been lost of the sense of urgency, the hopes and the excitement that initially inspired them. One senses, even on the part of those who today most acutely perceive the problem and are inwardly most exercised about it, a certain discouragement, resignation, perhaps even despair, when it comes to the question of raising the subject publicly again. What's to be gained by it? people ask. The danger is obvious. So much has already been said. What does it do to continue to beat this drum? Look, after all, at the record. Over all these years the competition in the development of nuclear weaponry has proceeded steadily, relentlessly, without the faintest regard for all these warning voices. We have gone on piling weapon upon weapon, missile upon missile, new levels of destructiveness upon old ones. We have done this helplessly, almost involuntarily: like the victims of some sort of hypnotism, like men in a dream, like lemmings heading for the sea, like the children of Hamelin marching blindly behind their Pied Piper. And the result is that today we have achieved, we and the Russians together, in the numbers of these devices, in their means of delivery, and above all in their destructiveness, levels of redundancy of such grotesque dimensions as to defy rational understanding.

I say redundancy. I know of no better way to describe it. But actually the word is too mild. It implies that there could be levels of these weapons that would not be redundant. Personally, I doubt that there could. I question whether these devices are really weapons at all. A true weapon is at best something with which you endeavor to affect the behavior of another society by influencing usefully the minds, the calculations, the intentions, of the men who control it; it is not something with which you destroy indiscriminately the lives, the substance, the culture, the civilization, the hopes of entire peoples. What a confession of intellectual poverty it would be—what a bankruptcy of intelligent statesmanship—if we had to admit that such blind, senseless, and irreparable destruction was the best use we could make of what we have come to view as the leading element of our military strength! To my mind, the nuclear bomb is the most useless weapon ever invented. It can be employed to no constructive purpose. It is not even an effective defense against itself. It is only something with which, in a moment of petulance or panic, you perpetrate upon the helpless people of another country such fearful acts of destruction as no sane person would ever wish to have upon his conscience.

There are those who will agree, with a sigh, to much of what I have just said, but will point to the need for something called deterrence. Deterrence is, of course, a concept which by implication attributes to others—to others who, like ourselves, were born of women, walk on two legs, and love their children, to human beings, in short—the most fiendish and inhuman of tendencies. But all right: accepting for the sake of argument the incredible iniquity of these adversaries, no one could deny, I think that the present Soviet and American arsenals, presenting over a million times the destructive power of the Hiroshima bomb, are simply fantastically redundant to the purpose in question. If the same relative proportions were to be preserved, something well less than 20 percent of these stocks would surely suffice for the most sanguine concepts of deterrence, whether as between the two nuclear superpowers or with relation to any of those other governments that have been so ill-advised as to enter upon the nuclear path. Whatever their suspicions of each other, there can be no excuse on the part of these two governments for holding, poised against each other and poised in a sense against the whole Northern Hemisphere, quantities of these weapons so vastly in excess of any demonstrable requirements.

How have we got ourselves into this dangerous mess?

Let us not confuse the question by blaming it all on our Soviet adversaries. They have, of course, their share of the blame, and not least in their cavalier dismissal of the Baruch Plan so many years ago. They too have make their mistakes; and I should be the last to deny it. But we must remember that it has been we Americans who, at almost every step of the road, have taken the lead in the development of this sort of weaponry. It was we who first produced and tested such a device; we who were the first to raise its destructiveness to a new level with the hydrogen bomb; we who have declined every proposal for the renunciation of the principle of "first use"; and we alone, so help us God, who have used the weapon in anger against others, and against tens of thousands of helpless noncombatants at that.

I know that reasons were offered for some of these things. I know that others might have taken this sort of lead had we not done so. But let us not, in the face of this record, so lose ourselves in self-righteousness and hypocrisy as to forget the measure of our own complicity in creating the situation we face today.

What is it, then, if not our own will, and not the supposed wickedness of our opponents, that has brought us to this pass?

The answer, I think, is clear. It is primarily the inner momentum, the independent momentum, of the weapons race itself—the compulsions that arise and take charge of great powers when they enter upon a competition with each other in the building up of major armaments of any sort.

This is nothing new. I am a diplomatic historian. I see this same phenomenon playing its fateful part in the relations among the great European powers as much as a century ago. I see this competitive build-up of armaments conceived initially as a means to an end, soon becoming the end in itself. I see it taking possession of men's imagination and behavior, becoming a force in its own right, detaching itself from the political differences that initially inspired it, and then leading both parties, invariably and inexorably, to the war they no longer know how to avoid.

This compulsion is a species of fixation, brewed out of many components. There are fears, resentments, national pride, personal pride. There are misreadings of the adversary's intentions—sometimes even the refusal to consider them at all. There is the tendency of national communities to idealize themselves and to dehumanize the opponent. There is the blinkered, narrow vision of the professional military planner, and his tendency to make war inevitable by assuming its inevitability. Tossed together, these components form a powerful brew. They guide the fears and the ambitions of men. They seize the policies of governments and whip them around like trees before the tempest.

Is it possible to break out of this charmed and vicious circle? It is sobering to recognize that no country, at least to my knowledge, has yet done so. But no country, for that matter, has ever been faced with such great catastrophe, such plain and inalterable catastrophe, at the end of the line. Others, in earlier decades, could befuddle themselves with dreams of something called "victory." We, perhaps fortunately, are denied this seductive prospect. We have to break out of the circle. We have no other choice.

How are we to do it?

I must confess that I see no possibility of doing this by means of discussions along the lines of the negotiations that have been in progress, off and on, over this past decade, under the acronym of SALT. I regret, to be sure, that the most recent SALT agreement has not been ratified. I regret it, because if the benefits to be expected from it were slight, the disadvantages were even slighter; and it had a symbolic value which should not have been so lightly sacrificed. But I have, I repeat, no illusions that negotiations on the SALT pattern—negotiations, that is, in which each side is obsessed with the chimera of relative advantage and strives only to retain a maximum of the weaponry for itself while putting its opponent to the maximum disadvantage—I have no illusion that such negotiations could ever be adequate to get us out of this hole. They are not a way of escape from the weapons race; they are an integral part of it. The weapon of mass destruction is not just a weapon like other weapons; there is a point where difference of degree becomes difference of essence.

Whoever does not understand that when it comes to nuclear weapons the whole concept of relative advantage is illusory—whoever does not understand that when you are talking about preposterous quantities of overkill the relative sizes of arsenals have no serious meaning—whoever does not understand that the danger lies not in the possibility that someone else might have more missiles and warheads then you do, but in the very existence of these unconscionable quantities of highly poisonous explosives, and their existence, above all, in hands as weak and shaky and undependable as those of ourselves or our adversaries or any other mere human beings: whoever does not understand these things is never going to guide us out of this increasingly dark and menacing forest of bewilderment into which we have all wandered.

I can see no way out of this dilemma other than by a bold and sweeping departure—a departure that would cut surgically through all the exaggerated anxieties, the self-engendered anxieties, the self-engendered nightmares, and the sophisticated mathematics of destruction in which we have all been entangled over these recent years, and would permit us to move smartly, with courage and decision, to the heart of the problem.

President Reagan recently said, and I think very wisely, that he would "negotiate as long as necessary to reduce the numbers of nuclear weapons to a point where neither side threatens the survival of the other." Now that is, of course, precisely the thought to which these present observations of mine are addressed. And I wonder whether the negotiations would really have to be at such great length. What I would like to see the President do, after proper consultation with the Congress, would be to propose to the Soviet government an immediate across-the-boards reduction by 50 percent of the nuclear arsenals now being maintained by the two superpowers—a reduction affecting in equal measure all forms of their delivery—all this to be implemented at once and without further wrangling among the experts, and to be subject to such national means of verification as now lie at the disposal of the two powers.

Whether the balance of reduction would be precisely even—whether it could be construed to favor statistically one side or the other—would not be the question. Once we start thinking that way, we would be back on the same old fateful track that has brought us where we are today. Whatever the precise result of such a reduction, there would still be plenty of overkill left so much so that if this first operation were successful, I would then like to see a second one put in hand to rid us of at least two thirds of what would be left.

Now, I have, of course, no idea of the scientific aspects of such an operation; but I can imagine that serious problems might be presented by the task of removing, and disposing safely of the radioactive contents of the many thousands of warheads that would have to be dismantled. Should this be the case, I would like to see the president couple his appeal for a 50 percent reduction with the proposal that there be established a joint Soviet-American scientific committee, under the chairmanship of a distinguished neutral figure to study jointly and in all humility the problem not only of the safe disposal of these wastes, but also the question of how they could utilized in such a way as to make a positive contribution to human life, either in the two countries themselves or—perhaps preferably—elsewhere. In such a joint scientific venture we might both atone for some of our past follies and lay the foundation for a more constructive future relationship.

It will be said; this proposal, whatever its merits, deals with only a part of the problem. This is perfectly true. Behind it, even if it were to be implemented, there would still lurk the serious political differences that now divide us from the Soviet government. Behind it would still lie the problems recently treated, and still to be treated, in the SALT forum. Behind it would still lie the great question of the acceptability of war itself, any war, even a conventional one, as a means of solving problems among great industrial powers in this age of high technology. What has been suggested here would not prejudice the continued treatment of these questions just as they might be treated today, in whatever forums and under whatever safeguards the two powers find necessary. The conflicts and arguments over these questions could all still proceed to the heart's content of all those who view them with such passionate commitment. The stakes would simply be smaller; and that would be a great relief to all of us.

What I have suggested is, of course, only a beginning. But a beginning has to be made somewhere, and if it has to be made, is it not best that it should be made where the dangers are the greatest, and their necessity the least? If a step of this nature would be successfully taken, people might find heart to tackle with greater confidence and determination the many problems that would still remain.

It will also be argued that there would be risks involved. Possibly so, I do not see them. I do not deny the possibility. But if there are, so what? Is it possible to conceive of any dangers greater than those that lie at the end of the collision course on which we are now embarked? And if not, why choose the greater—why choose, in fact, the greatest—of all risks, in the hopes of avoiding the lesser ones?

We are confronted here with two courses. At the end of the one lies hope—faint hope, if you will—uncertain hope, hope surrounded with dangers, if you insist—but hope, nevertheless. At the end of the other lies, so far as I am able to see, no hope at all. Can there be—in the light of our duty not just to ourselves (for we are all going to die sooner or later) but of our duty to our own kind, our duty to the continuity of the generations, our duty to the great experiment of civilized life on this planet—can there be, in the light of these claims on our loyalty, any question as to which course we should adopt?

In the final week of his life, Albert Einstein signed the last of the collective appeals against the development of nuclear weapons that he was ever to sign. He was dead before it could see publication. It was an appeal drafted, I gather, by Bertrand Russell. I had my differences with Russell at the time, as I do now in retrospect. But I would like to quote one sentence from the final paragraph of that statement, not just because it was the last Einstein ever signed, but because it sums up, I think, all that I have been trying to say on the subject. It reads as follows:

We appeal, as human beings to human beings: Remember your humanity and forget the rest.

1981

MUTUAL DETERRENCE AND STRATEGIC ARMS LIMITATION IN SOVIET POLICY

Raymond L. Garthoff

Raymond L. Garthoff is a Senior Fellow at the Brookings Institution. He is a retired Foreign Service officer, former Deputy Director of the Bureau of Politico-Military Affairs in the State Department, a member of the SALT I Delegation and U.S. Ambassador to Bulgaria. He is author of *Soviet Military Policy*, *Soviet Strategy in the Nuclear Age*, *Soviet Military Doctrine* and other works.

One of the most controversial—and important—questions underlying debate on Soviet intentions, American relations with the Soviet Union, and arms control and strategic arms limitations in particular, has concerned the Soviet views on mutual deterrence and parity. Do the political and military leaders in Moscow accept mutual deterrence? Do they see it as a basis on which to negotiate strategic arms limitation and reduction (in SALT and the successor negotiations)? Or do they hold a fundamentally different view of the strategic relationship between the two superpowers, and did they "take us for a ride" in SALT? Are they prepared to accept parity or will they strive for military superiority? Continuing Soviet military programs, and published Soviet writings on military doctrine for waging

Reprinted with permission of Allen and Unwin. Copyright © 1981 by Allen and Unwin. This essay originally appeared in *Soviet Military Thinking* edited by Derek Laebaert.

war, have convinced some—and troubled others—as to
Soviet aims.

The present essay seeks to illuminate Soviet thinking
on the subject, with consideration of the interrelationship of
Soviet ideological beliefs, political imperatives and calculation, military views and doctrine, and their intersection and
reconciliation in Soviet policy. For reasons that should become
clear in the discussion, it is important to examine the subject as it has evolved over the last two decades, in order better to inform our understanding of the present and ability
to estimate future prospects.

The central conclusion of this analysis is that since
the late 1960s, when SALT was launched, the Soviet political
and military leadership has recognized that in the contemporary world: (1) a nuclear war would be catastrophic, with
no real victor, and must not occur; (2) there is parity in a
strategic "balance" between the two superpowers and, as a
result, mutual deterrence; (3) the nuclear strategic balance
is not transitory, but also not automatically enduring, and
continuing military efforts are required to assure its stability; and (4) agreed strategic arms limitations can make a contribution, possibly a significant one, to reducing these otherwise necessary reciprocal military efforts. This view is even
more solidly held in the 1980s. Increasingly in the late 1970s,
and especially in the 1980s, however, the Soviets believe that
the leaders of the United States are no longer prepared to
accept parity and strategic arms limitations reflecting and
perpetuating a balance, but instead seek to regain military
superiority.

The Soviet leaders believe that peaceful coexistence—
with continued political and ideological competition—is the
preferable alternative to an unrestrained arms race and to
recurring high-risk political-military confrontation, and that
detente and a relaxation of tensions is in the interests of the
USSR. This does not mean that Soviet foreign policy is
passive or rests on satisfaction with the *status quo*. But Soviet
leaders believe that the need to avoid a nuclear war can best
be served by prudent actions within a framework of mutual
strategic deterrence between the Soviet Union and the United
States, preferably reinforced by nuclear arms reductions and
optimally by an elimination of nuclear weapons.

Detente seemed well established by the Brezhnev-
Nixon summits of 1972 and 1973, and SALT I was seen by

both sides as a major achievement of the new relationship between the two powers. It was not long, however, before this relationship began to be subject to growing strains. A decline in relations was arrested but briefly in mid-1979 by the Brezhnev-Carter summit and the signing of the SALT II treaty. By the beginning of 1980 the Soviet invasion of Afghanistan had provoked a sharp American reaction and retaliation across the range of political, economic and cultural relations, including shelving in the Senate the already beleaguered SALT II treaty without its ratification.

Under the Reagan Administration, the SALT II treaty was rejected, although the modest constraints on offensive arms introduced by SALT I and II were maintained precariously by tacit observance. The process of negotiated strategic arms limitation was resumed in START (Strategic Arms Reduction Talks) from mid-1982 to the end of 1983, and again in the NST (Nuclear and Space Arms Talks) since 1985. But prospects for a new agreement in the 1980s remain bleak. Indeed, it is uncertain whether the remnants of strategic arms control built in the 1970s, including the one really significant agreement, the ABM Treaty, will survive until a more propitious time to build on them. Under these circumstances both the United States and the Soviet Union have come to place even greater reliance on unilateral military programs— always the fundamental underpinning of mutual deterrence.

Questions of War and Peace in Soviet Ideology and Policy

Marxism-Leninism is based on historical determinism, a belief that socio-economic forces, through a struggle of classes, are the driving force of history. With the advent of the Soviet Union as a socialist state, the question of war between states as a possible form of class struggle arose— indeed, it was the central fact of life to the Bolshevik leaders. Successive Soviet leaders have seen the greatest danger to the socialist cause (identified with the Soviet Union) as coming from the capitalist military threat—and the one mortal danger faced during the first half-century of Soviet rule after the victorious conclusion of the Russian Civil War was the attack by Germany in World War II. Since World War II, the greatest threat in Soviet eyes has been the unparalleled destructive power of the American nuclear arsenal. Marxist-Leninist ideology sanctions the use of military power (and any other means) available to the socialist (Soviet) leaders whenever, *but only if*, expedient in advancing the socialist cause and not jeopardizing the security of achievements already gained, above all the security of the Soviet Union. Military power is considered necessary to *deter* possible attack and to *defend* the socialist cause, and its use is sanctioned if that is deemed expedient to *advance* that cause. Military power is *not*, however, seen as the decisive element in advancing the historical process, which it is believed will progress when conditions are ripe through indigenous progressive revolutionary action.

With the failure of "world revolution" after the successful conclusion of the Russian Civil War, the new Soviet state turned to recovery and then to achievement of "socialism in one country." Priority was given to economic development and to assurance of political control. The key role of military power on behalf of world socialism was seen as guaranteeing the survival of the first socialist state. Although the term was not then in vogue, *deterrence* of renewed military intervention by the capitalist powers was the underlying strategic conception. Later, when attacked, the role of the armed forces was of course defense and defeat of the attacker. The same deterrent conception has governed the period since World War II, except that there now exists a socialist camp or commonwealth, and of course it is recognized that military power in the nuclear age is enormously more dangerous and important. The principal role of Soviet military power has consistently been to dissuade imperialist powers from resort to *their* military power against the Soviet Union (and, later, also against the other countries of the socialist camp) in an effort to thwart the progressive course of history driven by social-economic revolutionary dynamics—not by military conquest.

The Soviets also see other important ideologically sanctioned uses of military force, but the basic Marxist-Leninist ideological framework predicates a fundamentally deterrent role for Soviet military power.[1]

The Soviets have, nonetheless, faced a doctrinal dilemma. While jettisoning Stalinist views on the inevitability of war and the necessary or desirable role of war as a

---

[1] In addition to the very summary discussion in these paragraphs, see Raymond L. Garthoff, *Soviet Military Policy: A Historical Analysis* (New York: Praeger, 1966), chapters 1, 4, 10 and 12.

catalyst of socialist advance in the world, as Communists they must assume that socialism is destined to survive and to triumph, even if a world nuclear catastrophe occurs. If they openly discarded that view, it could place in question not only their whole world-view but also their basis for legitimacy. Hence there are occasional reaffirmations of confidence in the ultimate triumph of socialism even if a world nuclear war should, despite Soviet efforts to prevent it, occur. The Soviet leaders have, nonetheless, increasingly acknowledged that general nuclear war would threaten the whole existence and future of world civilization and mankind, and begun to draw further conclusions from that fact deepening Soviet interest in strategic arms limitations and reductions and leading to a new conception of requirements for security.

Military Views

Lenin embraced the observation of Clausewitz that "war is a continuation of policy by other means," and this indeed represents a natural Marxist-Leninist conception.[2] Remarkably, some Soviet writers (mainly but not exclusively civilians) over two decades ago were so impressed by the inexpediency and enormous dangers of any nuclear world war (or indeed any war which could escalate into such a war) that they seemed to challenge this view. They, in turn, were sometimes criticized and refuted by other spokesmen, mainly military. Yet the question kept arising. Why? Mainly because the two sides were not engaged in a theoretical disputation, but in a political argument with considerable potential importance for military programs and policy. In fact, both sides accepted the basic premise that war is a matter of policy or political motivation; both sides also have accepted the fact that resort to nuclear war would not be expedient as a matter of policy. The real underlying debate has been over whether war is recognized as so unpromising and dangerous that it can never occur. Such a question has profound implications for military requirements. Is a force dedicated to deterrence enough? And if war were to occur, is a war-waging capability needed to seek a Pyrrhic "victory?"

In the early and mid-1960s, after general acceptance of the theses on the noninevitability, nonnecessity and non-

---

[2] See Raymond L. Garthoff, *Soviet Military Doctrine* (Glencoe, Il.: Free Press, 1953), pp. 9-19, 51-57.

expediency of nuclear war, Khrushchev and others began to argue further that nuclear war would spell the end of world civilization, and was therefore not only unacceptable but unthinkable.[3] One civilian commentator on political-military subjects in 1963 carried this argument to the point of paraphrasing Clausewitz (and Lenin) to say "War can only be the continuation of madness."[4] This statement, along with a number of others, was made in the context of ideological-political Soviet polemics with the Chinese communists. The more orthodox Soviet military line was, while agreeing that nuclear war precisely as a continuation of politics made no sense *as a policy option for the USSR*, to insist that such a war could occur and on the need for powerful Soviet military forces to deter such a war, or if deterrence failed to defeat an attacker.[5] Thus, military spokesmen distinguished between war as a continuation of policy, which was reaffirmed, and war as a useful instrument of policy, which it was agreed not to be;[6] but stressed the need to deter, and to be able to wage and seek to win a war if it could not be averted.

In 1965, the late Major General Nikolai Talensky, former editor of the military theoretical journal *Military Thought* (at the time of military doctrinal rejuvenation after Stalin's death in the mid-1950s) and an outspoken "revisionist," argued: "In our days there is no more dangerous illusion than the idea that thermonuclear war can still serve as an instrument of politics, that it is possible to achieve political aims by using nuclear weapons and still survive."[7] Several Soviet military writers subsequently attacked General Talensky's position (and criticized him by name), arguing not that his position was theoretically wrong, but

---

[3] In fact, this view began to be developed by some Soviet leaders even before Stalin's death, and was prematurely (in political terms) stated by Malenkov in 1954. See Raymond L. Garthoff, "The Death of Stalin and the Birth of Mutual Deterrence," *Survey*, no. 111, Spring 1980, pp. 10–16.

[4] Boris Dmitriyev, "Brass Hats: Peking and Clausewitz," *Izvestiya (News)*, September 25, 1963. ("Boris Dmitriyev" is the pen-name of a Soviet diplomat and scholar specializing in American political-military affairs).

[5] For example, Marshal Sergei S. Biryuzov (then Chief of the General Staff), "Politics and Nuclear Weapons," *Izvestiya*, December 11, 1963.

[6] For example, Major General N. Sushko and Major T. Kondratkov, "War and Politics in the 'Nuclear Age,'" *Kommunist vooruzhennykh sil (Communist of the Armed Forces)*, no. 2, January 1964, pp. 14–23.

[7] Major General N. A. Talensky, "The Late War: Some Reflections," *Mezhdunarodnaya zhizn' (International Affairs)*, no. 5, May 1965, p. 23.

that it was practically dangerous because it undercut the rationale for maintaining necessary large military forces.[8]

Some of the discussions in the 1960s, especially non-public military writings, made clear that the military were taking issue not with the assessment of the catastrophic consequences of a nuclear war, nor with the need to avoid such a war, but with discussions which made war "unthinkable" and therefore cast doubt on the need for Soviet military programs and requirements; war was seen as deterred (by Soviet military strength) and therefore unlikely, but not inconceivable, and hence requiring Soviet strategic planning, weapons development, maintaining and improving forces, and morale-sustaining statements of confidence in victory if war should come.[9]

The debate was renewed in the early and mid-1970s—during and after SALT I and the rise of detente (especially in 1973-74 after the Prevention of Nuclear War agreement). A number of prominent commentators, mainly civilian, some with positions close to political leaders, again stressed the cataclysmic nature of a nuclear world war, and clearly indicated there would be no meaningful "victor" in such a war.[10] And again there were a number of counterarguments, usually by writers on military theory, mainly challenging implications of these discussions for Soviet military strength as a deterrent, but also as a war—waging and war-winning force if a world nuclear war

---

[8] Lt. Colonel Ye. I. Rybkin, "On the Nature of Nuclear Missile War," *Kommunist vooruzhennykh sil*, no. 17, September 1965; Colonel I. Sidel'nikov, "V. I. Lenin on the Class Approach in Determining the Nature of Wars," *Krasnaya zvezda (Red Star)*, September 22, 1965; Colonel I. Grudinin, "On the Question of the Essence of War," *Krasnaya zvezda*, July 12, 1966; and Editorial, "Theory, Politics, and Ideology: On the Essence of War," *Krasnaya zvezda*, January 24, 1967.

[9] See the discussion in Raymond L. Garthoff, "Mutual Deterrence and Strategic Arms Limitation in Soviet Policy," *International Security*, vol. 3, no. 1, Summer 1978, pp. 117–21. This article was an early version of the present paper, and dealt more fully with the formative debates in the 1960s.

[10] In particular, Aleksandr Bovin, Georgy Arbatov and Veniamin Dolgin; see A. I. Krylov, "October and the Strategy of Peace," *Voprosy filosof ii (Problems of Philosophy)*, no. 3, March 1968; G. A. Arbatov, "The Stalemate of the Policy of Force," *Problemy mira i sotsializma (Problems of Peace and Socialism)*, no. 2, February 1975 and "Soviet—American Relations in a New Stage," *Pravda*, July 22, 1973; A. Bovin, "Internationalism and Coexistence," *Novoye vremya (New Times)*, no. 30, July 1973, and "Peace and Social Progress," *Izvestiya*, July 11, 1973 (only in the first edition, substituting a *different* article, also by Bovin, in later editions!), and "Socialist, Class Politics," *Molodoi kommunist (The Young Communist)*, no. 4, April 1974; and V. G. Dolgin, "Peaceful Coexistence and the Factors Contributing to its Deepening and Development," *Voprosy filosof ii*, no. 1, January 1974. There have been many others, usually with the discussion not developed so fully as in these articles.

should ever occur.[11] By 1976, however, the direct challenges were stilled. Indeed, later (as we shall see) some of these same military writers made a rather sharp turn accepting views which they had previously criticized.

Subsequent theoretical discussions reconciled the earlier opposing views and clarified the issue. Dr. Trofimeriko, for example, cited "the Leninist thesis on the fact that war is a continuation of policy . . . by forcible means," but went on to note that it is no longer "in practice a usable instrument of policy when an aggressor in the course of struggle for 'victory' can himself be annihilated." He identified the chief reason for the abandonment of war as an expedient, usable instrument not in the destructive nature of the weapons themselves, arguing that "imperialism would not hesitate to resort to any weapon to realize its designs"; but rather in the fact that "the other side," the Soviet Union, "has analogous means at its disposal in a potential conflict,"[12] thus justifying the need to maintain a strong (and perhaps even war-waging) military force as a deterrent in order to buttress mutual deterrence.[13]

Soviet military doctrine has continued to be predicated on the assumption that if a general nuclear war should occur, all elements of the armed forces would contribute to waging a decisive struggle aimed at defeating world imperialism. Soviet military power, and the constant enhancement of its capability and readiness, is thus justified primarily for deterrence, as well as to wage a war if one should come despite Soviet efforts to prevent it. This view has been consistently held by the Soviet military and political leaders. It is not accurate, as some Western commentators

[11] For example, see Major General K. Bochkarev, "The Question of the Sociological Aspect of the Struggle against the Forces of Aggression and War," *Voyennaya mysl'* (*Military Thought*), no. 9, September 1968, pp. 3–16; Bochkarev, "Nuclear Arms and the Fate of Social Progress," *Sovetskaya Kirgiziya* (*Soviet Kirgizia*), August 25, 1970; Major General A. Milovidov, "A Philosophical Analysis of Military Thought," *Krasnaya Zvezda*, May 17, 1973; Colonel I. Sidel'nikov, "Peaceful Coexistence and the People's Security," *Krasnaya zvez da*, August 14, 1973; Colonel Ye. Rybkin, "The Leninist Conception of Nuclear War and the Present Day," *Kommunist vooruzhennykh sil*, no. 20, October 1973; Rear Admiral V. Shelyag, "Two World Outlooks—Two Views on War," *Krasnaya zvezda*, February 7, 1974; and Colonel T. Kondratkov, "War as a Continuation of Policy," *Soviet Military Review*, no. 2, February 1974.

[12] G. A. Trofimenko, *SShA: Politika, voina, ideologiya* (*The USA: Politics, War and Ideology*) (Moscow: Mysl', 1976), pp. 292–93.

[13] See also [Colonel] T. R. Kondratkov, "Social-Philosophical Aspects of Problems of War and Peace," *Voprosy filosofii*, no: 4, April 1975, and [Major General] A. S. Milovidov and Ye. A. Zhdanov, "Social-Philosophical Problems of War and Peace," *Voprosy filosofii*, no. 10, October 1980, esp. pp. 36–37.

have done, to counterpose Soviet military interest in a "war-fighting" (and hopefully "war-winning") posture to a "deterrent" one. At least until very recently, the Soviets have seen the former capability as providing the most credible deterrent, as well as serving as a contingent resort in the event of war. The emphasis has, however, steadily shifted from the mid-1970s to the mid-1980s toward the absolute need to prevent nuclear war, even to the extent of repeated authoritative statements by successive Soviet leaders, and military chiefs, on the unwinnability of nuclear war. We shall return to this later.

The three editions of the basic Soviet work on military doctrine in the 1960s, *Military Strategy*, edited by a commission headed by the late Marshal Sokolovsky, show Soviet military recognition of the emergence of mutual deterrence (as well as an equivocal and changing view on its public embrace). In the first edition, in 1962, a passage appeared which not only attributed the concept to Western strategists and leaders, but also endorsed it.[14] In a section on "Contemporary Means of Armed Combat and Their Effect on the Nature of War," all three editions stressed the colossal and unacceptable consequences of a world nuclear war. In addition to citing U.S. and other sources on tens of millions of casualties, the second edition added a quotation from Khrushchev (made in the interval after publication of the first edition), stating that at the beginning of 1963 the United States had more than 40,000 nuclear weapons, and "the USSR also has more than enough of these means," so that "scientists have calculated that 700–800 million people would die as a result of the initial strikes alone, and all the large cities of many countries."[15] In the third edition, while this (as well as all references to or statements by Khrushchev) was deleted, a new passage was added which, if less graphic, was even more explicit on "the *unacceptability* of a world nuclear war" to the USSR, and "the *necessity* for its prevention."[16] Thus, the most authoritative Soviet open military publication of the 1960s, with changing shadings, was quite forthright in recognizing the fact of mutual deterrence, despite some reticence to endorse the concept as formulated

[14] Marshal V. D. Sokolovsky (ed.), *Voyennaya strategiya (Military Strategy)* (Moscow: Voenizdat, 1962), pp. 74–75.
[15] Ibid., 2d edition, 1963, pp. 244.
[16] Ibid., 3d edition, 1968, p. 239; emphases added.

in the West and continuing attention to doctrine on waging war if it should occur.

One of the discussants in the "debate" of the mid-1970s over the proper interpretation of the application of Clausewitz's thesis returned to this point in 1979, adumbrating the formula by which that debate had ended. Aleksandr Bovin, political observer for *Izvestiya*, noted that the dictum "War is a continuation of policy by other means, by means of force" has two meanings. One meaning, which is unaffected by such things as changes in military technology, is that every war is a continuation of the policy of the state that pursues it. The other meaning is that war represents a choice of conducting a policy by one or another means, including the possible choice of use of military force. As to this latter sense, Bovin states that while such a choice sometimes made sense in Clausewitz's day, it no longer does:

Now take the present situation: Can one consider a general nuclear-missile war as a normal, sensible means of pursuing some particular political aim? Obviously one cannot do this because the consequences of such a war would be a catastrophe for mankind, and in the current situation the one to risk making a first nuclear strike would inevitably be doomed to destruction by the forces available for a retaliatory strike. This is in fact what is called the balance of terror, and although this position is far from ideal . . . it does nonetheless exist.[17]

There is still a new more nuanced "debate" on the theme of Clausewitz's dictum, as seen in the following rather different (although not contradictory) way of saying essentially the same thing: Possibly related to the above statement by Bovin in late 1979, General Sidel'nikov (who as a colonel had taken issue with Bovin by name on the same issue in 1973!) wrote in *Red Star* in early 1980 a rebuttal to the "Western" notion that "the thesis on war as the continuation of policy by means of force has allegedly outlived its usefulness." His argument is that "a new world war can and must be prevented and that it must not—precisely, must not—arise as a continuation of policy, must not be chosen as a means of achieving political aims." He was clear, in agreement with Bovin, that war is no longer a rational

---

[17] Aleksandr Bovin, "Détente: Results of the 1970s," *Radio Moscow*, Domestic Service, December 25, 1979; and see Bovin, "The SALT II Treaty," *Radio Moscow*, June 19, 1979, and Bovin, "The Permanent Significance of Lenin's Ideas," *Kommunist* no. 10, July 1980, pp. 77–78.

choice. But what if the *other* side initiates war? Indeed, Sidel'nikov stated his concern that the United States might unleash such a war in pursuit of an anti-Soviet policy. "And if imperialist aggressive forces again [he had cited Hitler's attack] try to test our strength and foist a war on us, on the part of the Soviet Union that war would be a continuation of the policy the sole aim of which is to defend the socialist Fatherland and the achievements of socialism."[18]

In an interesting analysis published in 1980, General Milovidov and an associate argued that Clausewitz' formulation on war as a continuation of policy is now obsolete, but *Lenin's* formulation on war as a continuation of policy is not. While this distinction may seem tendentious, the authors indicate that what they meant is that while war can never lose its political relationship, war has now lost its utility as a political instrument to serve the aims of imperialism. They do not mean that war remains a feasible instrument for socialism; on the contrary, they stress that the question of the consequences of a nuclear war would be disastrous. Indeed, they conclude that nuclear missile weapons have led to a change in the relationship between the aims of war and the means of warfare: "For the first time, a situation was created when the means of waging war outgrew the aims of war," making a choice of resort to war inadmissible.[19]

By 1986, Bovin again cited Clausewitz's axiom, and conceded it was "as axiomatic as ever;" nonetheless, precisely because Clausewitz relates war to policy aims, he argued that even posing the question of choice of nuclear war has now become "obsolete." "There is not, nor can there be, *any* political end for whose sake the future of mankind may be risked. A nuclear missile war cannot be perceived as a viable choice or a rational means for the continuation of policy." Indeed, he even states 'Nor is there *anything* more important than peace if the alternative to peace is a nuclear missile war.[20]

---

[18] Major General I. Sidel'nikov, "Who Needs Military Superiority and Why," *Krasnaya zvezda*, January 15, 1980. General Sidel'nikov was at the time chief of the Propaganda Department of the Main Political Administration of the armed forces. The chief role of that department is internal indoctrination and morale-building in the Soviet armed forces.

[19] Milovidov and Zhdanov, *Voprosy filosofii*, no. 10, 1980, pp. 39–40.

[20] A. Bovin, "Imperative of the Nuclear Age," *Izvestiya*, April 23, 1986; emphasis added.

It is thus quite clear from Soviet military and political discussions that acceptance of the Clausewitzian (and Leninist) conceptions of the nature and role of war is not only compatible with mutual deterrence, but reinforces its paramount feature: recognition of the necessity of avoiding and preventing general nuclear war. The most important aspect of this particular question is the unfounded contention of some prominent Western commentators, such as Professor Richard Pipes, widely cited, that "as long as the Russians persist in adhering to the Clausewitzian maxim on the function of war, mutual deterrence does not really exist."[21] On the contrary, the Soviet literature clearly shows that there is no contradiction between being "Clausewitzian" and recognizing the validity of mutual deterrence.

Mutual deterrence in Soviet writings is usually expressed in terms of assured retaliatory capability which would devastate the aggressor, because this formulation (rather than "mutual assured destruction" capability) is more responsive to ideological sensitivity over the idea that the USSR could be considered a potential aggressor and thus needs to be deterred. (Only adversaries—the United States, more broadly the imperialists, and for a time also the Chinese communists—are described as potential aggressors.) In addition, this formulation avoids identification with the specific content of the American concept of "mutual assured destruction," often expressed in terms of a countervalue capability for destroying a specified percentage of the opponent's industry and population. This U.S. interpretation is more limited than the Soviet recognition of mutual deterrence, which rests simply on mutual capability for devastating retaliation unacceptable to a rational potential initiator for war, without calculations of arbitrary industrial and population losses that theoretically would be acceptable costs.[22]

[21] Richard Pipes, "Why the Soviet Union Thinks It Could Fight and Win a Nuclear War," *Commentary*, vol. 72, no. 7, July 1977, p. 34.

[22] This distinction of the U.S. and Soviet formulations of mutual deterrence was expressed in this way in my original article (*International Security*, vol. 3, no. 1, Summer 1978, p. 124), with no specific Soviet source references. Five years later, a Soviet analyst used almost exactly the same terms to describe the U.S. and Soviet conceptions: "Then, as now, both sides in the nuclear confrontation possessed an assumed capability to inflict an annihilating retaliatory strike on an aggressor (the Soviet formulation), or to inflict 'unacceptable damage' on the attacker as long as the situation of 'mutual assured destruction' exists (the American formulation)." See G. Gerasimov, "Current Problems of World Politics," *Mirovaya ekonomika i mezhdunarodnyye otnosheniya (The World Economy and International Relations)*, no. 7, July 1983, p. 99.

Some observers have posited a possible Soviet conception of "deterrence by denial," as contrasted with the American conception of "deterrence by punishment." (Neither of course is a Soviet, nor for that matter an official American, expression.) "Deterrence by denial" is conceived as seeking to deter by maintaining a capability for thwarting and defeating a potential attack; "deterrence by punishment" seeks to deter by relying instead on a capability for devastating punitive retaliation. Soviet force posture and "war-waging" military doctrine does suggest the possible applicability of this idea, but Soviet statements on deterrence are usually couched in terms of retaliatory punishment, and it is not clear that such a distinction reflects a Soviet way of thinking.

The political leaders in their programmatic statements endorse the idea that deterrence requires strong and ready combat capability, but do not go on to discuss meeting requirements for waging and winning a war. Brezhnev, for example, stated simply: "Any potential aggressor is well aware that any attempt to launch a nuclear missile attack on our country would be met by devastating retaliation."[23]

Mutual Deterrence and the Initial Soviet SALT Decision

There is reason to believe that the United States' proposals in 1967–68 to hold bilateral strategic arms limitations talks (SALT), and in particular the emphasis on avoiding an arms race in ABM systems, coincided with internal Soviet consideration of the implications for their own security, and for their future military programs, of the emerging attainment of mutual deterrence. While the transition to *mutual* deterrence had been long anticipated in the United States, it nevertheless meant adjustment from previous U.S. superiority and an unmatched American assured retaliatory capability. For the Soviets, however, it meant the achievement for the first time of a real second-strike capability, and in their view greatly enhanced security not only against a possible American first strike, but also against diplomatic-military pressures supported by the superior U.S. "position of strength" based on its monopoly of a secure second-strike capacity.

[23] L. I. Brezhnev, in *Materialy XXIV s'yezda KPSS (Materials of the Twenty-Fourth Congress of the CPSU)* (Moscow: Politizdat, 1971), p. 81, and see A. N. Kosygin, ibid., p. 186.

In the exchanges in 1967–69 leading up to the SALT talks and in their critical opening phase, the Soviet leadership showed an increasingly clear acceptance of, and commitment to, mutual deterrence, and an awareness of the role strategic arms limitations could play in reinforcing mutual deterrence.

In the first Soviet response to the U.S. SALT proposal, in early 1967, the discourse was primarily in traditional disarmament terms. By the time the Soviets were prepared to meet, in 1968, both sides had expressed interest in a wider dialogue on the strategic relationship, and in confidential exchanges had agreed that a main objective of the strategic arms talks would be to achieve and maintain stable strategic deterrence between the United States and USSR through agreed limitations on the deployment of strategic offensive and defensive arms, balanced so that neither side could obtain any military advantage and so that equal security should be assured for both sides.[24]

In the very first business meeting of the two SALT delegations in Helsinki (on November 18, 1969), both sides—and not by prearrangement—stated that mutual deterrence was the underpinning of strategic arms limitation. The Soviet delegation, in a prepared statement cleared by the highest political and military leaders in Moscow, expressed the Soviet view that:

Even in the event that one of the sides were the first to be subjected to attack, it would undoubtedly retain the ability to inflict a retaliatory strike of annihilating power. Thus, evidently, we all agree that war between our two countries would be disastrous for both sides. And it would be tantamount to suicide for the one who decided to start such a war.[25]

The Soviets prior to SALT had often described their own posture as one of deterrence, and had in their open military publications described deterrence, avoidance of war and readiness to rebuff any aggressor as the main objectives of their defense policy and posture.[26] But the above-cited

---

[24] See Raymond L. Garthoff, "SALT I: An Evaluation," *World Politics*, vol. 31, no. 1, October 1978, esp. pp. 1–5.

[25] By happenstance, the initial Soviet statement can be cited, as it was the only one not stamped "Sekretno"; from that time on, copies of formal statements exchanged between the delegations were marked "Secret" ("Sekretno").

[26] For an example that coincided closely with the first Soviet response to the U.S. proposal for SALT, see "Theory, Politics, and Ideology: On the Essence of War," *Krasnaya zvezda*, January 24, 1967.

explicit formulation of mutual deterrence had never before been so clearly expressed by authoritative Soviet spokesmen. The public military press, in particular, avoided positive references to *mutual* deterrence and *mutual* assured destruction, for reasons discussed earlier.

It is, therefore, of considerable interest and significance that during the key formative period of Soviet policy toward negotiations on strategic arms limitation there were very clear and explicit endorsements by influential Soviet *military* leaders of mutual assured retaliation and mutual deterrence in *Military Thought*, the important confidential Soviet General Staff journal.

At the very time the decision on whether to enter SALT talks was still being debated and decided in Moscow, although without reference to that fact, Marshal Nikolai I. Krylov, Commander in Chief of the Strategic Missile Forces, wrote in *Military Thought* in November 1967:

Under contemporary circumstances, with the existence of a system for detecting missile launches, an attempt by an aggressor to inflict a surprise preemptive strike cannot give him a decisive advantage for the achievement of victory in war, and moreover will not save him from great destruction and human losses.[27]

Later, in mid-1968, General Vasendin and Colonel Kuznetsov similarly stated: "Everyone knows that in contemporary conditions in an armed conflict of adversaries comparatively equal in power (in number and especially in quality of weapons) an immediate retaliatory strike of enormous destructive power is inevitable."[28]

These professional discussions, soberly stated in terms clearly applying to *both* sides, are quite different from the tone of articles in the public military press with their political purposes and stress on deterring the *other* side. Similarly, in May 1969, General of the Army Semyon P. Ivanov, commandant of the prestigious Military Academy of the General Staff, and previously deputy chief of the General Staff and chief of its Operations Division, wrote: "With the existing level of development of nuclear missile weapons and their reliable cover below ground and under

[27] Marshal N. I. Krylov, "The Nuclear Missile Shield of the Soviet State," *Voyennaya mysl'*, no. 11, November 1967, p. 20.
[28] Major General N. Vasendin and Colonel N. Kuznetsov, "Contemporary War and Surprise," *Voyennaya mysl'*, no. 6, June 1968, p. 42.

water it is impossible in practice to destroy them completely, and consequently it is also impossible to prevent an annihilating retaliatory strike."[29] In the same issue of _Military Thought_, its chief editor, then Major General V. I. Zemskov, after citing the build-up of U.S. and Soviet strategic forces in the 1960s, declared:

This growth in nuclear potential, in the estimate of foreign specialists, led to a situation in which a kind of "nuclear balance" was created between the major nuclear powers. In military-political circles of the United States, there has long been a lack of confidence in the supremacy of their nuclear-missile capabilities. Precisely for this reason they talk about a nuclear balance, the essence of which consists in the following: the capabilities for mutual destruction in a limited time by nuclear strikes on the main vitally important regions of the countries and the main groupings of armed forces are relatively equal. The presence of stockpiles of nuclear weapons and means of their delivery are such that their complete use theoretically makes it possible to destroy every living thing on our planet.

A nuclear war, states the Declaration of the Conference of Representatives of Communists and Workers Parties of 1960, "can inflict unprecedented destruction on entire countries and turn the largest centers of world production and world culture into ruins. Such a war would result in the death and suffering of hundreds of millions of people, including those in countries not participating in the war." A nuclear war, as in general any war, cannot and must not serve as a method of resolving international disputes.

Realistically considering this, the Communist Party of the Soviet Union and the Soviet Government are pursuing a consistent line toward preventing a world war, including a nuclear war, and toward excluding it from the life of society.[30]

This passage makes an interesting transition from attribution of concepts of a "nuclear balance," parity, and mutual deterrence to Western sources, to the Soviet and other communist parties' declaration of the devastation that would be caused by a world nuclear war, and from that to the Soviet policy aim of prevention of a world nuclear war. Later in the article, in discussing Soviet military policy, he stated:

The degree of probability of a particular type of war does not, of course, remain the same for each historical period, and changes under the influence of a number of political and military-technical factors. Of special importance in this connection can be the disruption of the

[29] General of the Army S. P. Ivanov, "Soviet Military Doctrine and Strategy," _Voyennaya mysl'_, no. 5, May 1969, p. 47.

[30] Major General V. I. Zemskov, "Wars of the Contemporary Era," _Voyennaya mysl'_, no. 5, May 1969, p. 57.

"nuclear balance." It is possible, for example, in case of further sharp increase of nuclear potential or *the creation by one of the sides of highly effective means of anti-ballistic missile defense while the other side lags considerably in solution of these tasks. A change of the "nuclear balance" in favor of the countries of imperialism would increase greatly the danger of a nuclear war.*[31]

It is clear from these passages that General Zemskov believed in 1969 that there was a "nuclear balance" providing mutual potential destruction and therefore mutual deterrence, but that it was at least at that time a somewhat precarious balance from the *Soviet* standpoint, and particularly if the United States, which was well ahead of the USSR in developing antiballistic missile technology, should deploy an effective ABM defense. There is a clear relationship between this discussion and the Soviet decision, taken by that time and soon to become evident in SALT, that ballistic missile defenses of the two sides should if possible be sharply limited through a strategic arms limitation agreement so as not to risk restoring the United States to a position of superiority that could imperil the still reversible state of mutual assured retaliation and mutual deterrence.

A related point of considerable interest was made explicit in these same confidential discussions in *Military Thought*. The reader may have noted the reference by Marshal Krylov to "the existence of a system for detecting missile launches" as one element in his conclusion on mutual deterrence. In his discussion, he explained further that he has in mind, and that the USSR had, under at least some unspecified contingency guidance, a policy of "launch on warning" or "launch under attack" (though he does not use either Western expression):

It must be stressed that under present conditions, when the Soviet Armed Forces are in constant combat readiness, any aggressor who initiates a nuclear war will not remain unpunished, a severe and inevitable retribution awaits him. With the presence in the armament of the troops of launchers and missiles completely ready for operation, as well as of systems for detecting enemy missile launches and other types of reconnaissance, *an aggressor is no longer able suddenly to destroy the missiles before their launch on the territory of the country against which the aggression is committed. They will have time during the flight of the missiles of the aggressor to leave their launchers and inflict a retaliatory strike against the enemy.*[32]

---

[31] Ibid., p. 59; emphasis added.

[32] Krylov, *Voyennaya mysl',* no. 11, 1967, p. 20; emphasis added. Krylov also indicated a "fallback" reliance on hardening of missile launchers, "even in the most unfavorable circumstances, if a portion of missiles is unable to be launched before the strike by the missiles of the aggressor."

Again, the previously cited 1968 article by General Vasendin and Colonel Kuznetsov also was explicit on the importance (and existence) of contemporary means of reconnaissance, detection, warning, and control of one's own forces in assuring retaliation (in a passage immediately preceding the one earlier quoted):

With contemporary means of reconnaissance, early detection, warning, and control should an aggressor succeed in placing into action the chief means of destruction (mass missile launches, takeoffs of aircraft, launch of space vehicles, etc.), this does not mean that he will not receive deserved retribution.[33]

General of the Army Ivanov also stated: "Contemporary means of *early detection*, moreover, make it possible to discover the *initiation* of an enemy nuclear attack and to take necessary retaliatory measures in a timely manner."[34] Although less explicit, a "launch under attack" concept is implied in these passages as well.

During the SALT I negotiations, in 1970, the Soviet delegation referred in passing to the existence and continuous improvement of early-warning systems, owing to which ICBM silos might be empty by the time they were hit by an attacker's strike, the ICBMs having been launched by that time. The U.S. delegation commented on this statement and expressed the hope that no government would launch its ICBM force solely on the possibly fallible reading of signals from its early-warning systems. It expressed the view that such a strategic doctrine seemed inconsistent with a proper concern for the problems of accidental or unauthorized launches or provocative third-party attack, which both delegations had been discussing. The Soviet delegation clearly was not authorized to enter a discussion of this subject, and had not intended in its initial statement to do so. Accordingly, it replied with an attempt to disassociate the question from accidental, unauthorized or provocative attacks, and referred awkwardly to unofficial *American* statements (not made in SALT) about possible launch on warning. The U.S. delegation then provided an official disavowal of the concept by Secretary of Defense Laird, with further criticism of the idea as potentially dangerous for

---

[33] Vasendin and Kuznetsov, *Voyennaya mysl'*, no. 6, 1968, p. 42.
[34] Ivanov, *Voyennaya mysl'*, no. 5, 1969, p. 47; emphasis added.

automatic escalation or for starting a war by accident.[35] But efforts to elicit a statement on Soviet policy with respect to the concept met with silence, and in an unofficial comment General (now Marshal) Ogarkov, the senior Soviet military representative, remarked to his American counterpart that such operational matters went beyond the proper purview of SALT, and that as military men they both surely understood the matter.[36]

These indications in *Military Thought* and in the exchanges in SALT that the Soviet authorities consider seriously a launch on warning concept helps to explain their relatively less excited concern over ICBM silo vulnerability. It raises the further question whether a concept which evidently arose at a time of relative Soviet inferiority may have continued since as a justification for keeping such a large ensiloed ICBM force (still today constituting 75 percent of Soviet strategic force capability) after the United States has deployed considerable counterforce capacity and is further developing and planning to deploy highly effective counterforce capabilities which could threaten the entire Soviet ICBM force—*if* it remained in its silos and tried to "ride out" a U.S. attack. The U.S. pursuit of such a capability with the MK-12A warhead for Minuteman III, the MX missile, and Trident II thus may serve to increase Soviet reliance on a launch under attack concept.

It should be noted that the Soviet military had first developed a concept of preemptive action in response to an imminent and irrevocable enemy decision to attack in the mid-1950s.[37] It was explicitly not a euphemism for a surprise first strike, but represented a last-minute seizure of the

---

[35] Secretary of Defense Harold Brown a decade later was much more ambiguous in congressional testimony as to conditions under which the United States might or might not launch its ICBMs before Soviet missiles struck ICBM silos in the U.S. See George C. Wilson, "Brown Cautious on Response to Attack," *Washington Post*, October 24, 1977. In a speech on June 23, 1978, Brown also stated: "The Soviets would have to consider the possibility that our Minuteman missiles would no longer be in their silos when their ICBMs arrived. We have not adopted a doctrine of launch under attack but they surely would have to take such a possibility into consideration." See also *Report of the Secretary of Defense Harold Brown to the Congress on the FY 1980 Budget*, January 25, 1979, p. 15; and *Report of the Secretary of Defense Harold Brown to the Congress on the FY 1981 Budget*, January 29, 1980, p. 86.

[36] This comment is the one referred to somewhat inaccurately by John Newhouse, in *Cold Dawn: The Story of SALT* (New York: Holt, Rinehart & Winston, 1973), p. 192, and often cited. It did not refer to "military hardware," but to military operational concepts, specifically, to launch on warning. Also, Ogarkov did not refer to excluding *his own* (or any) civilian colleagues, as the Newhouse account suggests.

[37] See Raymond L. Garthoff, *Soviet Strategy in the Nuclear Age* (New York: Praeger, 1958), pp. 84–87.

initiative to forestall an enemy attack. This concept, developed in the premissile age, and explicitly discussed only in
Military Thought in the 1950s, was evidently modified, if
not entirely superseded, in the 1960s by the concept of launch
on warning or under attack. From this standpoint, launch
under attack may be a step toward stability from preemption, but it remains a potentially destabilizing and dangerous
possibility and the United States should seek ways to discourage the Soviets from any degree of reliance on it.
Inherently, the *possibility* of launch on warning (or launch
on first impact, or on multiple impacts, etc.) *does* contribute
to the uncertainties any potential attacker must consider and
that is good, but it would be dangerous if in fact resorted
to in defense against anything except a proven assault.

The Soviet concept of launch on warning (or under
attack) has never meant a commitment to launch without
deliberate decision, but represented a contingent response
if a major enemy attack were detected. In addition to the
means of detection, reconnaissance, and control highlighted
in the statements cited, it also was necessary to have, and
by the early 1970s the Soviets were acquiring, rapid response
missile systems unlike the slow reaction liquid-fuelled Soviet
missiles of the early and mid-1960s.

By the late 1970s and early 1980s, political figures
were also occasionally referring in public statements to
retaliatory launch under attack, as a presumptive consideration for any would-be attacker. For example, an official of
the Central Committee staff, in arguing against the idea of
limited nuclear attack options, stated that scenarios for
limited strategic counterforce strikes are totally unrealistic
"deceptions," since "in reality nothing could hold back war
if it began in some such 'limited' framework. Only maniacs
ready to sacrifice hundreds of millions of lives, if indeed
not all mankind, could think in such terms. No one should
forget that an aggressor's missiles could not reach their
targets before an all-destructive retaliatory salvo would
follow."[38]

Soviet military theorists and leaders, including those
we have cited above, continue to discuss ways and means
of waging and seeking to win a general nuclear war should

[38] V. Kortunov, "Disastrous Relapses Into a Policy of Strength," *Kommunist*, no.
10, July 1980, pp. 103–04.

one occur. For reasons discussed earlier, they see no inconsistency in recognizing that such war would be an unprecedented disaster endangering all mankind, and therefore in supporting mutual deterrence based on mutual retaliatory capability, while also preparing to attempt to cope with the eventuality of war if deterrence should fail and war should come, and to seek to emerge from any war "victorious," that is, less totally destroyed than the United States.

In April 1969, an article by Anatoly A. Gromyko (son of the Foreign Minister, then at the Academy of Sciences Institute of USA Studies), appeared in *Military Thought*. Articles in this journal by nonmilitary contributors are uncommon; clearly the purpose of Gromyko's contribution was to present a rationale for SALT in terms appealing to its select military readership. The thrust of his argument was that U.S. reaction to the build-up in Soviet strategic power (ICBMs were specifically noted) had led not only to the need for the United States to shift from "massive retaliation" to "flexible response" concepts and to accepting "mutual assured destruction," but also had compelled the United States to seek strategic arms limitations and to curb the strategic arms race. (Incidentally, he suggested that Secretary McNamara had been forced out of his position as secretary of defense because of hard-line opposition by "the military-industrial complex" and others to his "realism" in recognizing the emergence of mutual deterrence.) More broadly, he argued in terms of differentiation among various elements of the U.S. policymaking and policy-influencing elite which—by implication—should be recognized by the military readers, rather than assuming that all were single-mindedly hostile to arms limitations and to any improvement of relations with the USSR.[39]

The Soviet military have had an active interest and role in SALT.[40] The strong endorsement of mutual deterrence made by the Soviet side from the very outset of the SALT talks, including by senior Soviet military representatives at SALT, has been noted. This was backed up by further concrete signals, including above all the Soviet indications

---

[39] Anatoly A. Gromyko, "American Theoreticians between 'Total War' and Peace," *Voyennaya mysl'*, no. 4, April 1969, pp. 86–92.
[40] See Raymond L. Garthoff, "The Soviet Military and SALT," in Jiri Valenta and William Potter, eds., *Soviet Decisionmaking for National Security* (Boston, Mass.: Allen and Unwin, 1984), pp. 136–61.

(also from the very outset of SALT in late 1969) that they were opposed to a nationwide ABM deployment which not only could fuel the competition in strategic offensive arms, but also could upset mutual assured retaliation. The explicit prohibition on such nationwide ABM deployments contained in Article I of the ABM treaty was, in fact, included on Soviet initiative.[41]

The Soviet decision in SALT to seek, and then to commit themselves by treaty of indefinite duration, to limit ABM deployment to a minimal defense of the national capital, was based on a far-reaching change in Soviet military doctrine in the late 1960s.[42] In essence, the Soviets saw parity, mutual deterrence, and Western recognition of their significance in its turn to a strategy of flexible response and conventional war options, as meaning that both sides would see their interests best served by avoiding a general nuclear war even if hostilities occurred. While of course there could be no guarantee that nuclear war would not eventuate, military planning should at least base its preferred strategies on its avoidance. Conventional capabilities assumed renewed importance. And, most significant of all, in order to buttress mutual deterrence of nuclear war it was more important to assure strategic retaliatory capability than to try to limit damage. An absence, or minimization, of reciprocal strategic antiballistic missile defenses would assure retaliation; deployment of such strategic defenses could make such retaliation less sure. In this key respect assuring deterrence thus became more important in the eyes of the Soviet political and military leaders than pursuing requirements for waging a nuclear war.

This change in position also affected the choice between preemption and launch under attack. When all-out nuclear war was assumed to be the only or even the most likely form of war, as it had been in the early 1960s, preempting at a time when the enemy was about to launch an attack made sense: going first in the last resort. But if general nuclear war could be averted, and preferably would be, it became more prudent to rely on launch under attack.

[41] See Raymond L. Garthoff, "Negotiating with the Russians: Some Lessons from SALT," *International Security*, vol. 1, no. 4, Spring 1977, p. 17.
[42] On the evolution of Soviet thinking on ABM, and the critical change in the late 1960s, see Raymond L. Garthoff, "BMD and East-West Relations," in Ashton B. Carter and David N. Schwartz, editors, *Ballistic Missile Defense* (Washington, D. C.: Brookings Institution, 1984), pp. 286–314.

Technically this was also becoming more feasible. Launch under attack of course also covered the contingency of not learning about an imminent enemy surprise strike in time to be able to preempt.

Launch under attack also had a more specific implication for the Soviet position on sharply constraining ABM defenses. In particular, as noted earlier, it helps to explain the lack of Soviet interest in ABM defenses for ICBMs in silos. The Soviet solution was not to plan to defend all those silos, but to fire the missiles from them before they could be destroyed by attacking missiles. In the longer run, mobile missile systems could provide even more leeway.

We do not have to *infer* from such things as the Soviet acceptance of the ABM treaty that there is a Soviet interest in mutual deterrence based on assured mutual retaliatory capability; there is a clear case for it in changes in Soviet military doctrine reflected in confidential Soviet military discussions preceding (and, as we shall see, following) SALT I, and from the SALT negotiating history as well.

Parity and the Renunciation of Superiority

In the Soviet view—shared by military and civilian leaders—just as in the mainstream of thinking in the United States in the 1970s, overall "parity" has existed since the early 1970s. There are those—again, both in Moscow and in Washington—who are apprehensive as to whether this parity will be upset by some successful effort of the other side. But successive U.S. secretaries of defense and chairmen of the Joint Chiefs of Staff have agreed, even when sounding such an alarm for the future (fortunately, one that seems each few years to recede to a few years hence), that "at present" there is an overall strategic parity—that while each side has certain areas of superiority they balance out to yield parity overall.

Parity was, of course, for the Soviet side a significant advance over the previous U.S. unilateral superiority. Soviet political leaders from the ebullient Khrushchev of the late 1950s on had been claiming various partial superiorities, and overall parity. But only in the early to mid-1970s did the Soviet military leaders admit that an assured retaliatory capability for the USSR had not come about until "the 1960s," or the late 1960s. By the late 1970s and early 1980s commentators began to acknowledge that it was only in the early

1970s that "the USSR achieved nuclear missile parity with the United States."[43] And the Soviet military have acknowledged throughout the 1970s that while each side has certain areas of superiority, these balance out to yield an overall parity. Nevertheless, uncertainties remain as to the future.

In an interesting article on "Military Strategy and Military Technology" in *Military Thought* in April 1973, Major General Mikhail I. Cherednichenko, a well-known Soviet military theoretician, described the evolution of mutual deterrence as a product of the 1960s—implicitly admitting that previously only the United States had had an assured retaliatory capability. In his words:

The Sixties were characterized by the further development of weapons and military hardware. . . . Possessing powerful strategic nuclear weapons which were kept at a high state of combat readiness, the Soviet Armed Forces acquired the capability of delivering a devastating nuclear response to an aggressor under any and all circumstances, even under conditions of a surprise nuclear attack, and of inflicting on the aggressor a critical level of damage. An unusual situation developed: *an aggressor who would initiate a nuclear war would irrevocably be subjected to a devastating retaliatory nuclear strike by the other side. It would prove unrealistic for an aggressor to count on victory in such a war*, in view of the enormous risk for the aggressor's own continued existence.[44]

General Cherednichenko saw mutual deterrence mainly as a product of advances in military technology permitting the USSR to match the long-standing U.S. retaliatory capability. With reference to SALT I, signed a year earlier, he specifically comments that "Definite successes have been achieved in strategic arms limitation negotiations." But in seeking "to prevent military superiority by aggressive [Western] forces," he also argues implicitly for the need to maintain Soviet military efforts to that end. SALT I was seen not as central, but as contributing to mutual deterrence by reducing the uncertainties generated by unlimited strategic technological competition—a contribution to preventing "the possibility of unexpected major technological achievements" by the United States which could give it military superiority.[45]

---

[43] See Kortunov, *Kommunist*, no. 10, 1980, p. 99.
[44] Major General M. I. Cherednichenko, "Military Strategy and Military Technology," *Voyennaya mysl'*, no. 4, April 1973, p. 42; emphasis added.
[45] Ibid.

The 1970s and 1980s have seen hopeful further developments in Soviet acceptance of the implications of mutual deterrence for strategic and political objectives. This may in time facilitate strategic arms limitation and reductions, or at least mute and stabilize the competition.

Soviet military and political leaders ceased to call for strategic superiority as an objective after the 24th Party Congress in April 1971 (which also marked a turning point in SALT). Instead, mutual deterrence, a balance, parity and equal security are advocated. To be sure, this is often expressed in terms of implying that it is only the West which has aggressive aims which are restrained by mutual deterrence. But it is none the less an important advance. Brezhnev stated the general Soviet political view in 1975 in these words:

International détente has become possible because a new relation of forces has been established in the world arena. Now the leaders of the bourgeois world can no longer entertain serious intentions of resolving the historic dispute between capitalism and socialism by force of arms. The senselessness and extreme danger of further tension are becoming increasingly obvious under conditions where both sides possess weapons of colossal destructive power.[46]

This view has been reiterated by all Soviet leaders in the years since then. Notwithstanding the fact that each side sees only a need to deter the other, both recognize the fact of mutual strategic "sufficiency" and assured retaliatory capability and the resulting mutual deterrence.

On the eve of the Carter administration, in a major policy address at Tula, Brezhnev authoritatively disavowed the aim of military superiority aimed at a first strike, reaffirming the aim of deterrence:

Of course, Comrades, we are improving our defenses. It cannot be otherwise. We have never neglected and will never neglect the security of our country and the security of our allies. But the allegations that the Soviet Union is going beyond what is sufficient for defense, that it is striving for superiority in arms, with the aim of delivering a "first strike," are absurd and utterly unfounded. . . . Our efforts are aimed at preventing both first and second strikes and at preventing nuclear war altogether. . . . The Soviet Union's defense potential must be sufficient to deter anyone from disturbing our peaceful life. Not a course aimed

[46] L. I. Brezhnev, "In the Name of Peace and Happiness for Soviet People," *Pravda*, June 14, 1975. See also Brezhnev, *Pravda*, July 22, 1974, and *Pravda*, November 25, 1976.

at superiority in arms, but a course aimed at their reduction, at lessening military confrontation—that is our policy.[47]

The Soviet position was spelled out more fully in *Pravda*
shortly after the Tula speech by the American affairs expert,
Academician Georgy Arbatov. He vigorously refuted arguments that the USSR was seeking superiority, and accurately
described in some detail areas of the strategic balance in
which the USSR leads (the overall number of ICBM and
SLBM missile launchers; strategic missile "throw-weight")
and in which the United States leads (numbers of strategic
bombers and bomber "throw-weight"; numbers of missile
warheads; forward submarine bases; "and much else"). Thus,
he noted, that "while enjoying an approximate equality
(parity) in general, the two countries have within this parity considerable differences (asymmetries) in various components of their armed forces, connected with differences
in geographic situations, the nature of possible threats to
their security, technical characteristics of individual weapons
systems, and even in traditions of military organization."
The main thing, though, is "the existence of an approximate
balance, that is, a parity in the relation of forces about which
the USSR and the United States came to agreement with the
signing of the principle of equal rights to security."[48] Again
on the occasion of the sixtieth anniversary of the Bolshevik
Revolution, Brezhnev returned to this theme, stating:

> The Soviet Union is effectively looking after its own defense, but it does
> not and will not seek military superiority over the other side. We do
> not want to upset the approximate balance of military strength existing
> at present . . . between the USSR and the United States. But in return
> we insist that no one else should seek to upset it in his favor.[49]

This was a more far-reaching statement than his earlier one
at Tula, denying an aim of superiority "with the aim of a
first strike": it denies superiority as a current or future aim
for *any* purpose, as have many subsequent authoritative
Soviet statements. Soviet renunciation of an aim of military
superiority is frequently coupled with assurance that the
Soviet Union will not, of course, permit the United States

---

[47] L. I. Brezhnev, "Outstanding Exploit of the Defenders of Tula," *Pravda*, January
19, 1977.

[48] G. A. Arbatov, "The Great Lie of the Opponents of Détente," *Pravda*, February
5, 1977.

[49] L. I. Brezhnev, "The Great October Revolution and the Progress of Mankind,"
Pravda, November 3, 1977.

to acquire superiority. As Marshal Kulikov wrote in 1978: "The Soviet state, effectively looking after its defense, is not seeking to achieve military superiority over the other side, but at the same time, it cannot permit the approximate balance which has taken shape . . . between the USSR and the United States to be upset to the disadvantage of our security."[50]

Soviet assertions that their strategic aims and programs are in pursuit of parity and not superiority must of course be judged on the merits of an objective evaluation of actual developments, rather than being accepted on faith. But such assertions are not without significance. Numerous authoritative commentators since 1977 have echoed these themes of Soviet acceptance of parity, equal security and the nonpursuit of superiority.

Especially interesting have been discussions in the military press. Even before Brezhnev's Tula speech, in early 1977, *Red Star* carried two commentaries observing that "parity" was a reality and had been the basis for U.S.-Soviet relations "in recent years," and that the military power of the United States and the USSR was regarded by "unbiased experts" as "about equal."[51]

Appearing about the same time as the Tula speech, although signed to press a month earlier, was an interesting article in the *Military-Historical Journal* by Colonel Yevgeny Rybkin, long regarded in the West as a "Red Hawk." Colonel Rybkin, a professor on the Lenin Military-Political Academy staff, and later at the Institute of Military History, citing Lenin that "war is a continuation of policy," but in apparent modification of some of Rybkin's own earlier expressed views, noted the essential need for the possibility of peaceful coexistence and the prevention of war.[52] The point of particular interest to the present discussion is not only Rybkin's conclusion that "Rejection of a nuclear war . . . is dictated by the new realities of the era," but that " 'nuclear parity,' " as it is called, has been established between the USSR and the United States, that is, a certain balance of power, which

[50] Marshal Viktor G. Kulikov, "Sixty Years on Guard over the Achievements of the October Revolution," *Partiinaya zhizn' (Party Life)*, no. 3, February 1978, p. 28.

[51] TASS, "Who Sets the Tone?" *Krasnaya zvezda*, January 12, 1977, and Yury Kornilov, "Myths and Facts," *Krasnaya zvezda*, January 14, 1977.

[52] Colonel Ye. Rybkin, "The 25th Congress of the CPSU and the Problem of Peaceful Coexistence between Socialism and Capitalism," *Voyenno-istoricheskii zhurnal (The Military-Historical Journal)*, no. 1, January 1977, pp. 5 ff. This issue went to press on December 17, 1976.

was officially recognized at the Soviet-American [Summit] talks in 1972–74, with a mutual agreement not to disrupt this balance." Moreover, in arguing that there is "an objective need to end the arms race," Rybkin stated that "the quantity of nuclear weapons has reached such a level that a further increase would in practice make no change," and he cited Brezhnev's statement of July 1974 that "a sufficient quantity of arms has been amassed to destroy everything alive on earth several times over."[53] (Brezhnev, incidentally, had echoed his own 1974 remarks a few weeks earlier in a speech in Bucharest.)[54]

An important official of the Central Committee staff in 1980 stated in *Kommunist*, the chief theoretical journal of the Communist Party, that it had become an "historical phenomenon" that in our time, regardless of how intense the arms race became, "*whoever* attempted to achieve military superiority could not attain it. The capability of the putative adversaries for mutual annihilation makes this objective obviously inadmissible."[55] This formulation made crystal clear that the unattainability of superiority applies to *both* sides, and that a state of mutual deterrence is seen to prevail.

Marshal Ogarkov, then Chief of the General Staff and First Deputy Minister of Defense, in the authoritative Defense Ministry *Soviet Military Encyclopedia* article on "Military Strategy," expressed determination not to permit "the probable enemy" to gain military-technical superiority, but "Soviet military strategy . . . does *not* have as its own objective the attainment of military-technical superiority over other countries."[56] Since 1977, this has been standard Soviet military doctrine.

In addition to numerous authoritative Soviet political and military renunciations of the objective of military superiority, and reaffirmation of the existence of parity and of the aim of preserving that parity,[57] the official US-USSR communique issued in Vienna on June 18, 1979, at the

[53] Ibid., p. 8 (the original Brezhnev statement is in *Pravda*, July 22, 1974).
[54] L. I. Brezhnev, *Radio Moscow* (TASS), November 24, 1976.
[55] Kortunov, *Kommunist*, no. 10, 1980, p. 99.
[56] Marshal N. V. Ogarkov, "Military Strategy," *Sovetskaya voyennaya entsiklopediya (The Soviet Military Encyclopedia)* (Moscow: Voyenizdat, 1979), vol. 7, p. 564; emphasis added.
[57] To cite but a few in the late 1970s: Marshal N. Ogarkov, *Pravda*, August 2, 1979; Marshal D. Ustinov, *Pravda*, October 25, 1979; Ogarkov, *Partiinaya zhizn'*, no. 2, February 1979, p. 27; and Lt. General (ret.) M. Mil'shtein, *SShA*, no. 10, October 1978, p. 10.

conclusion of the summit at which the SALT II treaty was signed, included a commitment by both sides that each "is not striving and will not strive for military superiority, since that can only result in dangerous instability, generating higher levels of armaments with no benefit to the security of either side."[58] This statement has often since been cited by Soviet writers. For example, General Sidel'nikov cited it approvingly in his article earlier quoted for his defense of Clausewitz's maxim. He strongly endorsed maintaining the existing "approximate balance" and "parity" in military forces between the United States and the USSR. In addition to restating the now familiar position that "the Soviet Union has not set itself the task of achieving military superiority," he questioned the very meaningfulness of the concept: "One would think that any realistically minded person would realize that under contemporary conditions the course toward military superiority is an entirely senseless course . . . when one considers that arsenals of weapons of mass destruction of truly monstrous and devastating destructive power have already been created in the world then the very concept of 'military superiority' should be erased from the military lexicon."[59]

Another prominent Soviet military writer, Major General Rair Simonyan, a professor at the Frunze Academy, also argued: "Given parity of strategic forces, when both sides possess weapons capable of destroying many times over all life on earth, neither the addition of new armaments nor an increase in their destructive power can bring any substantial military—and still less political—advantage."[60] He also cited and explicitly agreed with a U.S. statement that: "In the contemporary world it is impossible to insure security by means of an arms buildup."[61] An editorial in *Red Star* in 1977, in arguing the need not to be complacent in the quest for peace, commented: "After all, it is a case of the fate of world civilization and the future of all mankind."[62] Thus by the late 1970s we see a new readiness by military as well

---

[58] *Vienna Summit, June 15–18, 1979* (Washington, D. C.: U.S. Department of State, Selected Documents No. 13, 1979), p. 7.

[59] Sidel'nikov, *Krasnaya zvezda*, January 15, 1980. See also V. Kuznetsov, *Novoye vremya*, no. 37, September 7, 1979, p. 31 for a similar statement.

[60] Major General R. Simonyan, "Disarmament—Demand of the Times: Concerning the Risk of Confrontation," *Pravda*, June 14, 1977.

[61] Ibid.

[62] Editorial, "Vigilance Must Be Raised Higher!" *Krasnaya zvezda*, June 22, 1977.

as civilian commentators to accept strategic parity, mutual deterrence and the inadmissibility of nuclear war. And an article in the Soviet armed forces journal in 1981 specifically endorsed *"strategic parity* as a factor of *mutual deterrence"* which, it stated, "makes possible the process of *strategic arms limitation."*[63]

It is of some interest and significance that over the past decade there has developed a new stress on the need to go *beyond* codification of a nuclear balance on the basis of parity at the very high levels currently existing. A writer in *Pravda* in 1976 argued: "Trying to justify the arms race, certain political circles in Western countries propagandize some sort of balance of terror which is supposedly necessary to maintain peace and to insure the security of peoples. But such a balance is an unreliable foundation for security. The real way to achieve security is to observe the principle of the non-use of force."[64] This argument does not *oppose* a nuclear balance based on parity from the standpoint of seeking superiority, but on the contrary argues for a need to go beyond it to disarmament:

The accumulated means of mass destruction are such that an exchange of nuclear strikes contradicts even the most narrowly construed national security interests and seriously threatens the lives of peoples. . . .

The "balance of terror" cannot guarantee security. . . . There is a danger of their [the accumulated weapons] accidental or unsanctioned use. The numbers of these weapons are constantly growing. . . .

In other words, if one wants to live in security, struggle to resolve the problems of disarmament.[65]

Soviet objections to the "balance of terror" and indefinite reliance on mutual deterrence extend beyond concerns and continuing risks of possible resort to nuclear warfare or accidental occurrence precipitating nuclear war. "The conception of preserving peace on the basis of an 'equilibrium of fear' or 'balance of terror' occupies an important

---

[63] S. Tarov, "Constructive Initiatives," *Krasnaya zvezda*, February 13, 1981; emphasis added.

[64] V. Larin, "A Topical Proposal," *Pravda*, October 27, 1976; see also A. Bovin, *Radio Moscow*, June 19, 1979; B. Andrianov and V. Nekrasov, *Radio Moscow*, June 18, 1979; G. Shakhnazarov, "The Arms Race Is a Danger to the Peoples," *Krasnaya zvezda*, June 14, 1979; and Dr. [Colonel] V. Kulish, "A Balance of Trust and not a Balance of Terror," *Novoye vremya*, no. 22, May 1979, pp. 4–6.

[65] Yu. Nilov, "The Time Has Come to Call a Halt", *Novoye vremya*, no. 23, June 1977, p. 6.

place in the arsenal of the enemies of disarmament."[66] The concept of the "balance of terror" and mutual deterrence is, it is argued, used by Western opponents of detente and disarmament to legitimize the arms race.[67] Nevertheless, Soviet critics usually note, that while the "balance of terror" is an uneasy peace owing to the tension engendered by being under a nuclear sword of Damocles, and much less satisfactory than one marked by trust and disarmament, still "such a balance is peace."[68] Thus, the Soviet position is to accept that "nuclear missile parity is a condition contributing to the success of a policy of peace," and that détente reflects the strategic nuclear balance of parity, while advocating steps beyond that situation toward greater cooperation and disarmament.[69] Brezhnev, in his speech on the sixtieth anniversary of the Bolshevik Revolution, after renouncing an aim of superiority and stating that the Soviets "did not want to upset the approximate balance of military strength that now exists," went on to state: "Needless to say, maintaining the existing balance is not an end in itself. We are in favor of starting a downward turn in the curve of the arms race and of gradually reducing the level of the military confrontation. We want to reduce substantially, and then to eliminate, the threat of nuclear war—the most formidable danger for mankind."[70] To the Twenty-Sixth Congress of the Communist Party in February 1981, while calling for further steps in arms limitation, Brezhnev declared that "The military and strategic equilibrium prevailing between the Soviet Union and the United States ... objectively serves to safeguard world peace."[71] This has remained the Soviet position in the 1980s.

An early sophisticated argument along this line was made in the mid-1970s by two retired military men now with the Institute of the USA and Canada, General Mil'shtein and Colonel Semeyko. They stressed the importance of the Soviet-American agreements of 1972 and the Prevention of Nuclear War Agreement of 1973, which they said were made

---

[66] N. I. Lebedev and S. V. Kortunov, "The Problem of Disarmament and the Ideological Struggle—A Critique of the Apologists for the Arms Race," *Novaya i noveishaya istoriya (Modern and Contemporary History)*, no. 4, July–August 1980, pp. 8–9.
[67] Ibid.; and see Milovidov and Zhadanov, *Voprosy filosofii*, no. 10, 1980, p. 49.
[68] Bovin, *Kommunist*, no. 10, 1980, p. 78.
[69] Ibid.; and see the Resolution of the Central Committee of the CPSU, June 23, 1980, text in *Kommunist*, no. 10, July 1980, pp. 8–10.
[70] Brezhnev, *Pravda*, November 3, 1977.
[71] Brezhnev, *Pravda*, February 24, 1981.

possible only by "proceeding from their mutual recognition of the fact that nuclear war would have devastating consequences for mankind and from the need to reduce and in the final analysis to eliminate the danger of nuclear war."[72] Mil'shtein and Semeyko were realistic in their criticism of nuclear deterrence as not being an "ideal solution." "Of course, the concept of 'nuclear deterrence,' which presupposes the existence of enormous nuclear forces capable of 'assured destruction' is not an ideal solution to the problem of peace and the prevention of nuclear conflict."[73] They, and many other Soviet commentators in the 1970s, argued that influential elements in the United States have tried to escape mutual deterrence by pursuing limited nuclear options, "selective targeting" concepts and the like.

Soviet commentaries in 1980–81 also criticized the American Presidential Directive PD-59 from this standpoint, arguing that its underlying purpose has been to cultivate acceptability for the idea of selective limited use of nuclear weapons, under the umbrella of the "balance of terror" which could still deter resort to all-out use of nuclear weapons.[74] Soviet political and military leaders, indeed, have showed great concern over what Brezhnev called "military doctrines dangerous to the cause of peace" (in referring to President Carter's Directive PD-59); as then Defense Minister Marshal Ustinov stressed: "a so-called local nuclear conflict would always be fraught with the threat of escalation into a world nuclear war."[75] The Soviets reject any concept accepting use of nuclear weapons, endorsing a need to move from mutual deterrence on the path of detente, arms limitation, disarmament and peaceful coexistence. "Preventing nuclear war in any of its forms, large or small, and the limitation of the arms race, are the central problems of Soviet-American relations."[76]

---

[72] [Lt. General] M. A. Mil'shtein and (Colonelj L. S. Semeyko, "The Problem of the Inadmissibility of a Nuclear Conflict (On New Approaches in the United States)," *SShA (USA)*, no. 11, November 1974, p. 4.

[73] Ibid., p. 9; see also [Colonel] D. Proektor, "Two Approaches to Military Policy," *Novoye vremya*, no. 48, November 1978.

[74] For example, see Col. Lev Semeyko, "The International Situation—Questions and Answers," *Radio Moscow*, September 5, 1980. For a prescient anticipation of PD-59, see [Lt. Gen.] M. A. Mil'shtein," Some characteristics of Contemporary US Military Doctrine," *SShA*, no. 5, May 1980, pp. 12–15.

[75] Brezhnev, *Pravda*, February 24, 1981; and Ustinov, *Pravda*, February 21, 1981.

[76] Mil'shtein and Semeyko, *SShA*, no. 11, 1984, pp. 10–12.

At the Vienna Summit meeting of President Carter and President Brezhnev in 1979 the Soviet side was not yet ready to agree to inclusion in a formal joint statement with the United States of a statement that there could be no victor in a nuclear war, although they did include a statement that "both sides recognized that nuclear war would be a disaster for all mankind," as well as a commitment by both sides not to seek military superiority.[77]

By the time of the 26th Party Congress in 1981, Brezhnev declared that "to count on victory in a nuclear war is dangerous madness."[78] A few months later he repeated that statement, and added that "only he who has decided to commit suicide can start a nuclear war in the hope of emerging a victor. No matter what strength an attacker possesses, no matter what method of unleashing war he chooses, he will not attain his aims. Retribution will inevitably ensue."[79] Party leaders Andropov and Chernenko made similar statements in major party pronouncements on Lenin's anniversary.[80]

At the Summit meeting of President Reagan and General Secretary Mikhail Gorbachev in 1985, it was reportedly Gorbachev who took the initiative in proposing inclusion in the joint statement that the two sides "agreed that a nuclear war cannot be won and must never be fought," as well as reaffirming that they would "not seek to achieve military superiority."[81]

By the mid-1980s even Soviet military spokesmen were saying that today "what is at issue is no longer victory or defeat, but annihilation or existence." Lieutenant General Dmitri Volkogonov, deputy chief of the Main Political Administration and a well-known military theorist, made that statement in 1985 in a major article on "War and Peace in the 'Nuclear Age'" on the seventieth anniversary of Lenin's principal military writing, "Socialism and War."[82] He reaffirmed as valid today Lenin's Clausewitzian definition of war

---

[77] See Raymond L. Garthoff, *Detente and Confrontation*, p. 738.

[78] L. Brezhnev, *Pravda*, February 24, 1981.

[79] L. Brezhnev, *Pravda*, October 21, 1981.

[80] K. U. Chernenko, *Pravda*, April 23, 1981; and Yu. V. Andropov, *Pravda*, April 23, 1982.

[81] "Joint Statement, Nov. 21, 1985," *Department of State Bulletin*, vol. 86, no. 2106, January 1986, p. 8. Gorbachev's initiative in seeking inclusion of these statements was disclosed by a Soviet participant in the delegation.

[82] Lt. Gen. D. Volkogonov, "War and Peace in the 'Nuclear Age,'" *Krasnaya zvezda*, August 30, 1985. All subsequent quotations in this and the succeeding paragraph are from this article.

as the continuation of policy by violent means, but went on to stress that "it is becoming increasingly obvious that a nuclear war can no longer be used by an aggressor as a means for resolving political tasks." He cited Brezhnev's 26th Congress statement that "counting on victory in a nuclear war is dangerous madness," and as noted above went beyond to question even the concept of "victory" for anyone. He also repeated the judgment that "The arms buildup above a certain level ceases to play a decisive military role." As he put it, "Indeed, life on earth can be annihilated only once, not twice or three times over." And he cited a statement attributed to Lenin that the militarization of science and technology can undermine "the very conditions of the existence of human society," which he depicted as displaying striking sagacity. No matter how one interprets this or other statements by Lenin, what is significant is the ideological basis being provided to support the current Soviet view and to discourage any challenges to it.

Deterrence is the underlying military policy, and "the only objective material basis for deterrence of war today is the capability of socialism to maintain strategic parity in nuclear means." General Volkogonov emphasized, as do all Soviet writers, the existence of a "prevailing approximate parity in strategic nuclear forces" as depriving the imperialists of any realistic hope for achieving victory and thus deterring war and preserving the peace. Far from seeing this as a transient development, he drew from it a far-reaching theoretical proposition: "Essentially, this dialectical interconnection between a balance of strategic forces and attainment of international security emerges as one of the laws governing the preservation of peace in the world." But while deterrence is seen as the necessary bedrock, Volkogonov also stressed that "the dominating imperative of 'the nuclear age' is that real security lies not in the search for ways to achieve victory in war, but in the ability to prevent a nuclear cataclysm."

This discussion is indicative of the trend in Soviet military and political thinking in the mid-1980s. This approach has received authoritative advocacy from successive Soviet political leaders, including General Secretary Mikhail Gorbachev.

By the time of the 27th Party Congress in 1986, Gorbachev not only spoke of "the complete *unacceptability* of nuclear war," but also of the insufficiency for security of defense or deterrence in the nuclear age. "The character of contemporary weapons," he said, "does not permit *any* state hope of defending itself by military-technical means alone, even by creating the most powerful defense."[83] While accepting the reality of mutual deterrence "when the whole world has become a nuclear hostage," he argued that "security cannot indefinitely be built on fear of retaliation, that is on doctrine of 'deterrence' or "intimidation.'" Moreover, "these doctrines [deterrence] encourage the arms race, which sooner or later can get out of control." Rather, "Ensuring security more and more becomes a political task and can only be solved by political means. Above all, the will is needed to take the path of disarmament."[84] And "it is more than time to begin a practical withdrawal from balancing on the brink of war, from a balance of terror, to normal civilized forms of mutual relations between states of the two systems."[85]

By this time the Soviet leadership had established the maintenance of strategic parity with the United States as a foundation for stability, deterrence, arms control, and security, and endorsed all these aims. An article in May 1986 in the authoritative journal *Kommunist* is worth citing at some length:

Life has so developed that both of our countries must proceed from the fact that strategic parity is a natural condition. Without a military-strategic balance the maintenance of international stability is unthinkable. Without it it would hardly have been possible to conclude a number of treaties and agreements on the limitation of the arms race. An approximate equivalence of forces must be accepted as a foundation for international security, as a self-evident imperative.

But for this new thinking, it is necessary to understand that for reliable defense today a considerably reduced number of arms is sufficient. Indeed, and this is obvious to everyone, the present level of the balance of nuclear potentials of the two sides is much too high. For the present this ensures both sides with equal danger. But only for the time being. A continuation of the arms race will inevitably increase this equal danger and it could lead to such extremes that even parity would cease to be a military-political deterrent.[86]

---

[83] M. S. Gorbachev, *Politicheskii doklad tsental'nogo komiteta KPSS XXVII s'yezdu kommunisticheskoi partii Sovetskogo Soyuza (Political Report of the Central Committee of the CPSU to the 27th Congress of the Communist Party of the Soviet Union)* (Moscow: Politizdat, 1986), pp. 15 and 81.

[84] Ibid., pp. 81–82.

[85] Ibid., p. 15.

[86] L. Tolkunov, "The Dilemma of the Age," *Kommunist* no. 7, May 1986, pp. 85–86. Lev Tolkunov is chairman of one of the houses of the Supreme Soviet, and an influential member of the Party Central Committee.

Similarly, the new Party Program adopted at the 27th Party Congress in 1986 described "The establishment of military-strategic parity between the USSR and the United States and the Warsaw Pact and NATO" not only as "a historic achievement of socialism," but also argued that the preservation of parity is "an important factor for safeguarding peace and international security."[87]

Maintaining Mutual Deterrence

The Soviet leadership, like its U.S. counterpart, continues to look in the first instance and in the final account to its own unilateral military strength as the guarantor of deterrence of the other side and, hence, of mutual deterrence. Soviet generals have often cited a statement made by General Secretary Brezhnev in 1970: "We have created strategic forces which constitute a reliable means of deterring any aggressor. We shall respond to any and all attempts from any quarter to obtain military superiority over the USSR with a suitable increase in military strength to guarantee our defense. We cannot do otherwise." This, of course, remains a postulate of Soviet policy—as, indeed, of parallel U.S. policy.

In both the Soviet Union and the United States, elements of the professional military leadership, especially at the outset, were somewhat skeptical of the role that arms control—especially bilateral (or multilateral) negotiated commitments to strategic arms limitations—can play in securing such deterrence. At the same time, there is good evidence that national leaderships, including senior professional military men, came increasingly in the 1970s to accept negotiated strategic arms limitations as a contributing element in providing more stable and less costly deterrent military forces. As one of the leading Soviet civilian commentators on strategic matters put it (in 1976): "Under contemporary circumstances a real possibility to find a common interest with a potential adversary is to be found in the area of . . . the stabilization of the military balance by means of limiting the arms race."[89]

---

[87] "Program of the CPSU, New Edition, Adopted by the 27th Congress of the CPSU," *Pravda*, March 7, 1986.

[88] L. l. Brezhnev, *Leninskim kursom (A Leninist Course)*, vol. 3 (Moscow: Politizdat, 1970), p. 541.

[89] G. A. Trofimenko, *SShA: Politika, voina, ideologiya*, p. 324.

Let us recall the important discussion by General Zemskov in *Military Thought,* in 1969. He spoke of the particular importance of the possible "disruption" of the nuclear balance in case of "the creation by one of the sides of highly effective means of anti-ballistic missile defense while the other side lags considerably in solution of these tasks" and that it would "increase greatly the danger of a nuclear war" if the West achieved such an advantage.[90] It is clear that this reflected a view held at the highest political and military levels, and the congruence of Soviet and American views and objectives led to the ABM Treaty signed in May 1972.

Many Soviet writers have noted the effect of SALT in reflecting and supporting parity and the nuclear balance. Trofimenko expressed with particular precision the effect of the ABM Treaty on mutual deterrence, as seen by the Soviets. He described "a situation of equality of strategic capabilities of the USSR and the United States stemming from the essential equality in the balance of strategic arms (in particular, since each of the sides under any circumstances retains the capability for a retaliatory strike on the vital centers of the other)." While this situation had developed by the late 1960s, and was only implicitly codified in the SALT I agreements in late 1972, Trofimenko spoke of "the equalizing of capabilities of the USSR and the U.S. for a retaliatory strike (in particular as a result of the prohibition on the creation of nation-wide ABM systems through the 1972 Treaty),"[91] and further:

The conclusion of the ABM Treaty and its subsequent Protocol [reducing the number of permitted ABM defense areas from two to one for each side] for all practical purposes cast off the key link of "offense—defense" in the field of strategic systems. By relinquishing deployment of nation-wide ABM systems, the two sides eliminated one of the main motivating stimuli to the further build-up of efforts in the field of offensive systems.[92]

This recognition of the key significance of the ABM Treaty in "preventing the emergence of a chain reaction of competition between offensive and defensive arms" was specifically cited by Marshal Grechko, then Minister of Defense, and General of the Army (now Marshal) Kulikov,

[90] Zemskov, *Voyennaya mysl',* no. 5, 1969, p. 59.
[91] Trofimenko, *SShA: Politika, voina, ideologiya,* pp. 317, 318.
[92] Ibid., pp. 324–25.

then Chief of the General Staff, in endorsing the treaty when it was formally considered by the Supreme Soviet in the ratification process.[93] Aleksandr Bovin, following the signing of the SALT II treaty in 1979, similarly commented on the contribution of the SALT I ABM treaty:

This Agreement introduced into the nuclear arms race for the first time some elements, albeit modest, of restraint, certainty, and predictability. . . . Let us suppose that a potential enemy—for us this is the United States, and for the Americans it is the Soviet Union—were to deploy an antimissile defense system which protects the country's basic vital centers, including the areas where ICBMs are deployed. . . . The other of course would not be reconciled to lagging behind strategically. As a result, instead of stability there would be a forced arms race, both in defensive and offensive arms. Since the destabilizing significance of antimissile defense systems was understood, both the Soviet Union and the United States virtually gave up deploying them, or to be precise each side has the right to deploy only one such complex.

Thus since 1972 the strategic situation has become more simple: Each side must reckon with the fact that the one who decided on a first strike would have a counterstrike delivered against him which would be unacceptable in its consequences. In other words, it is precisely the preservation of a retaliatory strike potential which is seen as the best guarantee of security. This is that very balance of terror about which we have all read and heard, and under conditions of which we live.[94]

We should recall the second element in General Zemskov's analysis in 1969. In addition to noting the possibility of the disruption of the nuclear balance if one side obtained an effective ABM capability and the other did not, he also had noted such a danger "in case of a further sharp increase of nuclear [strike] potential" by one side.[95] And this is the risk Soviet military planners have seen in the qualitative and quantitative superiority of the United States in MIRVed systems throughout the 1970s, and in other new offensive systems in the 1980s.

There are many indications of this concern in Soviet discussions. One worth citing is the statement by the now retired former General Staff Colonel Vasily M. Kulish, writing soon after the SALT I agreements had been reached:

[93] The quotation is from General of the Army Viktor G. Kulikov, cited in *Izvestiya*, August 24, 1972; a similar statement by Marshal Andrei A. Grechko appears in *Pravda*, September 30, 1972.
[94] Bovin, *Radio Moscow*, June 19, 1979.
[95] Zemskov, *Voyennaya mysl'*, no. 5, 1969, p. 59.

The appearance of new types of weapons could seriously affect the relation of military forces between the two world systems. . . . Far-
reaching international consequences could arise in the event that one
side possessed qualitatively new strategic weapons which could serve
to neutralize the ability of the opposing side to carry out effective
retaliatory operations . . . even a relatively small and brief superiority by the United States over the Soviet Union in the development of
certain "old" or "new" types and systems of weapons that significantly
increase the strategic effectiveness of American military power could
exert a destabilizing influence on the international political situation
throughout the entire world and present extremely unfavorable consequences for the cause of peace and socialism.[96]

The main concern of the Soviet leadership is U.S.
political-military strategic *intentions*. They are also concerned over growing U.S. counterforce *capabilities* and
parallel U.S. advocacy of counterforce *concepts*, both because
of threatened destabilization of the existing balance and
because of what they suspect as to the underlying U.S. intentions. Dr. Trofimenko, for example, concludes that the
"genuine parity" reflected and bolstered by the SALT ABM
treaty "does not suit American theoreticians." He has argued
that:

the true nature of American strategic missile targeting is a most important state secret, and the American command can target its missiles in
any way it wishes without speaking out publicly about it. Hence the
public campaign of the Pentagon connected with the advertised "retarget-
ing" [of the Schlesinger Doctrine] is . . . a conscious effort to put
psychological pressure on the other side.[97]

The reversal of U.S. stated policy on the destabilizing nature of counterforce capabilities and the open pursuit
of such capabilities after 1974 considerably raised Soviet
suspicions, especially because it initially accompanied the
failure in the latter half of the 1970s to reach a SALT agreement based on the Vladivostok accords.

The change of U.S. policy on counterforce also
illustrates a hazard of "the SALT dialogue." In the course
of the SALT I discussions, the Soviet delegation evinced concern over apparent U.S. programs for improving the accuracy
of missiles to the extent of giving them counterforce
capabilities. In accordance with authoritatively stated United

---

[96] Colonel V. M. Kulish, in *Voyennaya sila i mezhdunarodnye otnosheniya (Military
Force and International Relations)* (Moscow: IMO, 1972), p. 59.
[97] Trofimenko, *SShA: Politika, voina, ideologiya*, p. 319.

States policy at that time, the U.S. delegation vigorously argued that it was *not* U.S. policy to seek such accuracies, which would be destabilizing, and cited a publicly released letter from President Nixon to Senator Brooke which stated that the United States would *not* develop such capabilities. Yet less than three years later, in 1974, President Nixon reversed this policy, and programs were announced and pursued to attain the very capabilities previously denounced as destabilizing by the same administration.

In the Soviet perception, the United States continued, notwithstanding SALT and detente, to seek military superiority even in the 1970s, and more openly in the post-détente 1980s. Although some highly placed U.S. leaders and others are considered to have "soberly" evaluated the strategic situation and given up pursuit of supremacy in the 1970s, powerful forces are believed to have continued to seek advantage and superiority in order to compel Soviet acquiescence in U.S. policy preferences. Moreover, actual American military policy and programs are seen as seeking to upset or to circumvent the nuclear mutual deterrence balance.

A series of developments after the SALT I agreements were signed in 1972 are seen in this light, above all the open pursuit of counterforce capabilities through increasingly accurate and numerous MIRV systems. At the outset of SALT II in late 1972, the Soviet side did probe for reciprocal restraints on MIRV (and MARV) as well as more generally on new strategic programs of both sides. These efforts were swamped by the tough overall initial Soviet position in SALT II, the lack of synchronization of MIRV technology, with the United States unwilling to restrain its advantages for early deployment, and the priority given in the negotiations by the United States to attempts to move toward equalization of missile throw-weight.[98]

American counterforce capabilities developed and deployed since the mid-1970s constitute a powerful threat to the overall Soviet ICBM force, bomber force and submarine force (particularly since the latter two are not kept on the same degree of airfield alert or deployment at sea as are their U.S. counterparts). While Americans focus on growing Minuteman vulnerability, the Soviets recognize that

---

[98] Based on the author's participation in the first phase of the SALT II negotiations.

ICBMs are less than one fourth of the U.S. strategic force, and it is far more ominous for the Soviet side that its ICBM force will soon be vulnerable, because far more Soviet strategic eggs are in the fixed land-based ICBM force basket—about 75 percent of their total strategic force. Also, as noted above, other Soviet intercontinental forces are less numerous, less capable and more vulnerable. Given the concerns in the United States over the Soviet threat to U.S. ICBMs, it is no wonder that conservative Soviet military planners and responsive political leaders would be concerned over existing and growing U.S. capabilities. From the vantage-point of Moscow, while a general nuclear balance had come into being by the late 1960s, and parity was recognized in the SALT accords and consolidated by Soviet military modernization programs of the 1970s, major continuing Soviet efforts were needed to keep up the balance.

Numerous Soviet commentaries have noted the Mark 12A warhead for Minuteman III, the MX, the Trident I and II, Pershing II, and the cruise missiles as indications that the United States is seeking to upset parity and reacquire military superiority. Some of these protestations may be inflated for propaganda effect, but it is highly likely that even before the collapse of the SALT II treaty, and even taking account of their own military programs set in train in the late 1970s, Soviet military men have been concerned over whether the United States could gain an advantage.

We in the United States are accustomed to regarding the later 1970s as a time of a "relentless Soviet military buildup," and of American relaxation in military programs—in the eyes of the Reagan Administration a decade of neglect and passivity. Yet, in fact, the United States added *more* strategic warheads to its force during the decade of the 1970s, the decade of detente and SALT, than did the Soviet Union. Moreover, we now know that the Soviet Union was cutting *back* in the pace of its military buildup during the second half of the decade.

In 1975, the Soviet leadership made a decision of considerable importance: to reduce military spending from an annual rate of increase of four to five percent to about two percent, and to level off the procurement of military weapons and equipment. Paradoxically, just as this policy began to be implemented in 1976–77 the United States began to publicize a campaign decrying a spending gap, and depicting an allegedly undiminished Soviet rate of military spending as evidence of a relentless Soviet military buildup despite detente and SALT.[99] Regrettably, United States intelligence estimators did not detect and establish this Soviet cutback until 1982–83—but to the Soviets it appeared that the United States was using a false charge of a growing Soviet military buildup as a screen and support for the American and NATO military buildup that began in the late 1970s and burgeoned in the 1980s.[100] The Soviet perspective, while no doubt biased, is more readily understood against this background.

It should be emphasized that measuring a military balance and parity is a far more subjective matter than most people realize. Moreover, adversaries are bound not only to see the balance differently, but to resolve uncertainties in favor of the other side in the interests of prudence—and then, often, to use such "worst case" estimates not only for hedging in setting their own military requirements, but also to infer the adversaries intentions as well as capabilities from such weighted estimates.[101] And Soviet and American military and political leaders have seen the military balance very differently—each side tends to look at the balance as if through the two ends of a telescope, at the adversary's capabilities through a magnifying lens and then at one's own forces through the minifying reverse lens. Moreover, different historical, cultural-ideological, geopolitical and other filters importantly affect judgments. This occurred on both sides in the last half of the 1970s with respect to buildup and capabilities, and in the first half of the 1980s with respect to intentions.[102]

The process of "hedging" on parity by seeking a margin of insurance is occasionally recognized by Soviet commentators, but without much sympathy and without admitting that it affects their own defense programming.

---

[99] See Raymond L. Garthoff, *Detente and Confrontation*, pp. 794–96.
[100] Ibid., pp. 795 and 800.
[101] See Raymond L. Garthoff, "Worst-Case Assumptions: Uses, Abuses and Consequences" in Gwyn Prins, *The Nuclear Crisis Reader* (New York, N. Y.: Vintage/Random House, 1984), pp. 98–108.
[102] For a more comprehensive discussion of the problem of determining a military strategic balance, and of conflicting Soviet and American viewpoints, see Raymond L. Garthoff, *Perspectives on the Strategic Balance* (Washington, D. C.: Brookings Institution, 1983), and for further discussion of diverging American and Soviet military thinking and views of the strategic balance, see Garthoff, *Détente and Confrontation*, pp. 768–800.

Indeed, it is usually dismissed as a U.S. pretext for seeking superiority.[103] But it does tend to influence military force planning in both countries.

There is, in addition, a strong temptation more or less consciously to manipulate "the threat" by the other side to justify one's own military programs. This also has been only too evident on both sides in this period, especially in the 1980s.

Thus, from their perspective Soviet leaders and military and political commentators since the late 1970s have perceived the leaders of the United States to be following a "course directed at overthrowing the existing approximate balance of forces between the USSR and the United States and at achieving American military superiority."[104] The Central Committee in June 1980 charged that the United States was seeking to upset "the existing strategic balance in the world," and reaffirmed the need for strengthened Soviet defense capability "to defeat imperialist plans to attain military superiority."[105] Many Soviet commentators have since 1980 referred to the alleged U.S. attempt "to destabilize global strategic parity in its own favor," and failure to recognize that "security in the age of nuclear parity is based on stability, and stability is based on the mutual acknowledgement of equality and on abandoning the aspiration for superiority."[106] Beginning in 1980–81, Soviet military men began to become increasingly concerned as the United States buildup became large and sustained. Yet successive Soviet leaderships under Brezhnev, Andropov, Chernenko and Gorbachev, while rhetorically vowing to maintain parity, did not accept plans for a comparable Soviet buildup.

Military leaders, and other Soviet leaders and commentators, display considerable suspicion of U.S. intentions, and concern not only over growing U.S. capabilities, but also as to *why* this continued increase in capabilities is sought. To be sure, some of these expressions of concern doubtless

---

[103] V. Nekrasov, "An Absurd but Dangerous Myth," *Kommunist*, no. 12, August 1979, p. 98.

[104] Editorial, "On the US President's State of the Union Message," *Pravda*, January 29, 1980. In this connection it cited the president's statement that the United States should be prepared to pay any price that may be required to remain "the strongest country in the world."

[105] *Kommunist*, no. 10, July 1980, pp. 8 and 10.

[106] Vladimir B. Lomeyko, "International Observers Roundtable," *Radio Moscow*, Domestic Service, February 10, 1980.

serve other purposes, such as argument to support requested Soviet military programs. But many have the ring of sincerity about them and many cite incontrovertible evidence to support their arguments on capabilities, as well as "evidence" which to the Soviets seem to be convincing signs of nefarious U.S. objectives and intentions.[107]

During the Reagan Administration the sustained American military buildup has stilled any doubts in Moscow that there is a major United States effort to regain strategic superiority. While seeing the Reagan Administration's military program as essentially continuing and building on those of its predecessor, Soviet observers see radical change in two other respects, changes that imparted a still more ominous cast to the whole direction of U.S. military strategy.

The first significant new departure was the attitude toward strategic arms limitation. While the SALT negotiations and agreements of the 1970s had not effectively curbed a continuing competition in offensive arms, they had at least delimited and moderated that competition. At least equally important, the Soviet leaders saw the American interest and efforts in SALT through four administrations from the late 1960s to the end of the 1970s as an indication that the leaders of the United States saw a role for negotiated mutual strategic arms limitation, and accepted the underlying premises of cooperation in pursuing common interests in reducing risks of war. The Reagan Administration from the outset vied in showing a range of attitudes from lack of interest to downright hostility, not only toward the "fatally flawed" SALT II treaty, but toward the entire process of collaborative arms control. When it did enter the Intermediate-Range Nuclear Forces (INF) talks in November 1981 it was patently in order to sustain sufficient European political support to proceed with INF deployments, not to reach agreement on limitations. And when strategic arms talks (rechristened Strategic Arms Reductions Talks, START, by the Americans) were resumed in June 1982, the terms proposed did not lead the Soviet leaders to see a serious American interest in agreement. Both negotiations were broken off by the Soviets at the end of 1983.

---

[107] For a comprehensive analysis of Soviet perceptions of American military policy and doctrine, see Raymond L. Garthoff, "Soviet Perceptions of Western Strategic Thought and Doctrine," in *Soviet Military Doctrine and Western Security Policy* (Paris: Atlantic Institute for International Affairs, forthcoming). The paragraphs following draw upon that analysis.

The combined Nuclear and Space Arms Talks (NST) that began in March 1985 also did not lead anywhere—in part owing to the other new development.

The second significant new departure of the Reagan Administration was the president's flamboyant advocacy of a strategic defense initiative (SDI), as it came to be called officially, better known (and termed in most Soviet commentary) as "Star Wars." The Star Wars initiative directly challenged the whole rationale of the ABM Treaty banning a ballistic missile defense of the territories of the two countries. It marked not only an intention to override the restraints of that treaty of indefinite duration, but also directly challenged the idea of mutual vulnerability and mutual deterrence that underlay it. Above all it was seen in Moscow as embodying an American desire, and intention if possible, to regain the option of a counterforce first strike by threatening to foil a surviving Soviet retaliatory strike by means of ballistic missile defenses. Soviet scientific studies, as most independent American studies, concluded that attainment of a really effective defense against an enemy first strike—as President Reagan described his aim—was not a promising prospect. But an intensive major effort probably would be able to produce a workable defense of some degree of effectiveness, one that might be considered adequate for damage limitation against a degraded second, retaliatory strike. Thus the real American objective was perceived as a defensive shield to augment a strengthened sword and permit use politically, or even militarily, of a coercive first strike capability.[108] This aim seemed strengthened in later months and years as U.S. spokesmen increasingly shied away from the idea that the SDI could *replace* a nuclear offensive deterrent, as Reagan had suggested, and claimed instead it would *supplement* offensive forces and strengthen deterrence (interpreted by the Soviets to mean coercion).

[108] The most authoritative and complete Soviet analysis has been a report prepared by a distinguished group of Soviet scientists led by R. A. Sagdeyev, Director of the Institute of Space Research, and A. A. Kokoshin, a deputy director of the Institute of USA and Canada, under the auspices of the Committee of Soviet Scientists for Defense of Peace and Against Nuclear War. The report is titled: *Strategicheskiye i mezhdunarodno-politicheskiye posledstviya sozdaniya kosmicheskoi protivoraketnoi sistemy s ispol'sovaniyam oruzhiya napravlennoi peredachi energii (Strategic and International-Political Consequences of the Creation of a Space-based Antiballistic Missile System Using Directed Energy Weapons)*. Moscow: Institute kosmicheskikh issledovanii Akademiya Nauk, 1984, 42 pp. This interpretation had been given authoritatively by General Secretary Yury Andropov only a few days after the Star Wars speech; see "Replies of Yu. V. Andropov to Questions from a Correspondent of Pravda," *Pravda*, March 27, 1983.

Space weapons, seen as a principal element in the SDI, have come to be suspected of development also as offensive arms, "space strike weapons." Thus, for example, Marshal Akhromeyev, first deputy Minister of Defense and Chief of the General Staff, has written that: "Reagan's so-called 'Strategic Defense Initiative,' which envisages the creation of a large-scale ABM defense system and, most important, the deployment of strike weapons in space, also pursues aggressive aims. The main purpose of this program is perfectly clear: to make possible a sudden nuclear attack on the Soviet Union with minimal risk to the United States."[109] Defense Minister Marshal Sergei Sokolov declared that "From the military view-point, the American "Star Wars' plan is an integral part of U.S. nuclear strategy, a first-strike strategy."[110]

The Soviet military, as well as political, leaders see the Star Wars program as a U.S. attempt to capitalize on technological superiorities in seeking a military superiority in order to gain political dominance. Even if doomed to failure (and the Soviets may not be quite so certain of this outcome as they say), it would at least disrupt the offensive-defensive connection stabilized by the ABM Treaty. Again to cite the defense minister, Marshal Sokolov has stressed that "the creation by one of the sides of a large-scale ABM system will break this interconnection ['that objectively exists between offensive and defensive arms'], will destabilize the strategic situation, and will require the other side to reestablish the situation either by building up its strategic offensive arms, or supplementing them with antiballistic missile systems, or most likely both."[111]

The SDI is also seen as both undermining the existing ABM Treaty, and precluding further steps in strategic offensive arms limitations. As Gorbachev put it: "The creation of space weapons can have only one result: the arms race will become even more intensive and will embrace new spheres."[112] Indeed, Soviet commentators not only see an intensification of the arms race as the inescapable result of the SDI, but also as part of its purpose: "The real purpose

---

[109] Marshal S. Akhromeyev, "A Great Victory and Its Lessons," *Izvestiya*, May 7, 1985.
[110] "Replies of Marshal of the Soviet Union S. L. Sokolov, Minister of Defense of the USSR to Questions of a TASS Correspondent," *Krasnaya zvezda*, May 5, 1985.
[111] Ibid.
[112] "Interview of M. S. Gorbachev with the Editor of Pravda," *Pravda*, April 8, 1985.

behind Reagan's space fantasies is to pave the way for renouncing existing accords and whipping up the arms race in all kinds of strategic weapons, offensive and defensive."[113]

Finally, complementing and supporting both the American abandonment of serious arms control, and the intention to escape the constraints of the ABM Treaty, was an escalation of charges of Soviet noncompliance with the ABM Treaty, SALT II, and other arms control agreements. The first official U.S. charge of Soviet violations of arms control agreements came in January 1974, just as the SDI program was first presented to Congress. The Soviets have depicted, and probably perceived, these charges to be leveled primarily for political reasons, to contribute to the confrontational atmosphere needed to sustain the major U.S. military buildup and to foist the blame on the Soviet Union for the erosion and eventual collapse of arms control, including the ABM Treaty.

The Soviet leaders explicitly tie these military developments to the aims of the Reagan Administration to mount a "crusade" against Soviet socialism, and "to destroy socialism as a social-political system."[114] Thus in addition to intensifying military competition, and making arms control impossible, the U.S. Star Wars program is seen as reflecting and intensifying political confrontation.

In the mid-1980s, in Moscow, the question is no longer, as it was fifteen years earlier, whether strategic arms limitation is a potentially useful instrument to serve mutual deterrence and mutual security. Now the question is not whether negotiated mutual arms control can be useful, but whether it is attainable, given what they see to be a higher American preference for pushing a technological arms race and seeking unilateral security.

---

[113] A. Bovin, "Fantasies and Reality," *Izvestiya*, April 21, 1985.

[114] See Marshal S. L. Sokolov, "Great Victory: Conclusions and Lessons," *Kommunist*, no. 6, April 1985, pp. 64–65; and Marshal S. Akhromeyev, *Izvestiya*, May 7, 1985.

The Star Wars speech of March 1983 had followed closely after the most direct political challenge by Reagan to the legitimacy of Soviet rule, a speech in which he declared the Soviet leaders to be "the focus of evil in the world," and the Soviet Union "an evil empire." And in a third speech a week later, nominally addressed to arms control, the president attacked what he called a "relentless military buildup" by the Soviet Union, and called for "peace through [American military] strength," rather than arms control. See President Reagan, "National Security, Address to the Nation," March 23, 1983, *Weekly Compilation of Presidential Documents*, no. 19, March 28, 1983, pp. 442–48; "Remarks at the Annual Convention [of the National Association of Evangelicals] in Orlando, Fla., March 8, 1983," ibid., vol. 19, March 14, 1983, p. 369, and "Remarks to the Los Angeles World Affairs Council," March 31, 1983, ibid., vol. 19, April 4, 1983, p. 484.

We do not need to accept at face value Soviet protestation of innocence on their own part for their share of
responsibility for the arms race and deterioration of relations, nor their accusations of U.S. culpability, in order to
recognize that the Soviet *perception* of developments
undoubtedly differs significantly from our own. There are
now strong pressures to ensure, by unilateral Soviet military
programs if necessary, that the United States does not upset
parity and achieve military superiority. Nonetheless, Soviet
declared acceptance of parity and mutual deterrence, renunciation of the goal of superiority, and professed support of
negotiated strategic arms limitation are now clearer than they
were when SALT began. Moreover, recognition by the Gorbachev regime of the economic problems of the country add
powerfully to other incentives to reach agreed arms limitations and reductions. The intensified efforts of both sides
in the 1980s to rely more upon unilateral military programs
than on negotiated constraints to secure deterrence com-
pounds the difficulty of resuming a serious negotiation of
strategic arms limitations and reductions. So does the inex-
orable march of military technology. Maintaining parity and
mutual deterrence is not easy, even if mutual deterrence is
recognized as preferable to the attainable alternatives; and
negotiating agreed restraints is, while the best way to support it, also the most difficult.

Conclusion

A number of American commentators have argued
that the Soviets, and in particular the Soviet military, reject
mutual deterrence, and some have therefore questioned the
basis for possible agreed strategic arms limitation. These
writers were not sufficiently aware of the record. It has
sometimes been alleged that Soviet statements on such propositions as mutual deterrence and the unacceptability of
general nuclear war are "for export," and they are contrasted
with selected open Soviet military discussions. Authoritative
statements of successive Soviet political leaders on such occasions as Party Congresses, and by Soviet military leaders,
and finally the evidence from such sources as the confidential USSR Ministry of Defense organ *Military Thought*,
dispel such erroneous assumptions.

The record indicates that the Soviet political and
military leadership accepts a strategic nuclear balance and

parity between the USSR and the United States not only as a fact, but as the probable and desirable prospect for the foreseeable future. They are pursuing extensive military programs to ensure that they do not fail to maintain their side of the balance, which they see as in some jeopardy given U.S. programs. They state that they seek to stabilize and to maintain parity and mutual deterrence, and that they do not seek superiority. They also support strategic arms limitations and reductions. There may be differing judgments on whether those statements should be taken at full value. Moreover, rhetorical acceptance and avowal of parity and mutual deterrence, and profession of support for strategic arms limitation, *even if genuine* and even if voiced by both sides, does not assure that agreements on curbing the arms competition or reducing tensions can be negotiated. Each side also sees the military balance, and the forces required for parity, differently. Still, there is at least a potential basis to direct argument to the requirements for parity, stability and security, rather than to assume that there is no basis for dialogue and negotiation. Finally, it is simply not the case that such avowed Soviet objectives are inconsistent with Soviet military doctrine or with communist ideology.

In Marxist-Leninist eyes, military power is not and should not be the driving element in world politics. With "imperialist" military power held in check, the decisive social-economic forces of history would determine the future of the world. Nuclear war is the one threat to *any* ideological goal. In the Soviet view, the United States came to accept mutual deterrence, and some strategic arms limitations, not because it is our preference, but because we had no alternative given the general world "correlation of forces," and Soviet strategic nuclear power in particular. Now they fear that the United States thinks that it can regain superiority and that it is unprepared to accept parity. Pursuit of such superiority requires countermeasures and the arms race is intensified. This is economically, politically and potentially militarily destabilizing, and not in the real security interest of anyone.

Much of what has been said in the preceding paragraphs could easily be turned around to describe U.S. views of the situation. This is not owing to any careless resort to a "mirror image." There are, in fact, a number of parallel perceptions—and misperceptions—held by both sides.

Despite greatly differing ultimate national goals, some of the principal problems in strategic arms control are due not to differing operative aims of the two sides, but to differing perceptions, to mutual suspicions, and to the difficulties of gearing very different military forces and programs into balanced and mutually acceptable strategic arms limitations and reductions.

To illuminate Soviet thinking on this matter is one step to understanding the problem and to finding its solution, and it has been the purpose of this essay to contribute to that understanding.

1982

DEFENSE POLICY AND ARMS CONTROL: DEFINING THE PROBLEM

Richard Burt

Richard Burt is the United States Ambassador to the Federal Republic of Germany. He is the former Assistant Secretary of State for European and Canadian Affairs, Director of the Bureau of Political Military Affairs, Assistant Director of the International Institute for Strategic Studies and National Security Affairs correspondent for *The New York Times*.

Few concepts have gained greater allegiance from political elites around the world in the last two decades than arms control, or more specifically, formal diplomatic negotiations aimed at limiting military forces. It is curious, then, that after the two superpowers succeeded in achieving a second strategic arms limitation accord (SALT II), arms control seems to have fallen into disrepute. In national politics, negotiations and their outcomes have become the subject of intense controversy. In the analytical community, meanwhile, thinking about arms control suffers from an unmistakable malaise.

However, it is not really so difficult to explain this state of affairs. During the last decade, we learned that negotiating for East-West arms control can be an exhausting and time-consuming process. Following the conclusion of the first SALT accords in 1972, it was widely assumed that

Reprinted with permission of Richard Burt. Originally published in *Arms Control and Defense Postures in the 1980's*. Copyright © 1982 by Westview Press.

a follow-on agreement would be obtained in a few years at most. Yet SALT II took nearly twice as long to negotiate as its predecessor. The Vienna force-reduction talks, the negotiations on a comprehensive test ban (CTB), and recent U.S.-Soviet attempts to regulate naval forces in the Indian Ocean and to control conventional arms transfers have made little or no progress.

But while some observers may be disappointed with the pace of arms control, others are distressed with its lack of impact on overall East-West relations. Ten years ago, SALT and other negotiating processes were viewed not only as instruments for controling military forces, but also as foundation blocks for building a "structure of peace" among the superpowers and their allies. Accordingly, SALT I was described as part of a wider process of U.S.-Soviet détente that promised to reduce competition in a number of arenas, including regional conflicts in the Third World. Soviet actions during the 1973 war in the Middle East, Moscow's intervention in conflicts in Angola and the Horn of Africa, and, most recently, its invasion of Afghanistan have all but demolished the notion that arms control and détente are synonymous. Instead, the contentious idea that arms control is more necessary in times of superpower stress has risen to take its place.

U.S.-Soviet tensions clearly are responsible, in part, for the controversy that surrounds arms control. But thoughtful and substantive criticism is now being directed toward arms control itself. One reason that arms control is in crisis is that, as Raymond Aron has pointed out, SALT and other negotiating enterprises have "accompanied and concealed" a tremendous expansion of Soviet military power during the last decade. For example, whatever SALT has achieved, it has not succeeded in stopping the Soviet Union in the last decade from deploying some 1,000 new land- and sea-based missile launchers or from increasing its number of deliverable warheads threefold. More important, there is now a consensus that regardless of SALT II, the Soviet Union has been able to acquire a sufficient number of accurate, high-yield warheads to threaten the bulk of U.S. land-based missiles. What this means for strategic stability, Moscow's risk-taking propensities, and U.S. political resolve is a matter of debate, but there can be little doubt that the creeping vulnerability of the *Minuteman* force will raise perplexing problems for defense planners during the next decade.

The growth of Soviet capabilities elsewhere will create other challenges for U. S. defense policy. In Europe, the continuing modernization of Warsaw pact ground and air forces threatens to neutralize any gains in Western capabilities that may arise out of NATO's (the North Atlantic Treaty Organization's) long-term defense improvement program. A much more troubling development, however, is the growth—in size and quality—of the Soviet long- and short-range theater nuclear arsenal. Militarily, missile systems like the SS-20 and SS-21, and the Su-19 aircraft not only represent a substantial improvement in existing Soviet capabilities, but could also provide the Soviet Union, for the first time, with a credible capability to suppress the Alliance's in-theater escalation potential. The political implications of this development for the Alliance thus go beyond a simple concern about an "imbalance" in one category of forces and raise questions about the continued credibility of the U.S. "extended" deterrent.

The growth of Soviet naval and projection capabilities is a third area of concern. Although less impressive than Soviet advances in strategic and theater nuclear capabilities, Soviet advances in the ability to project power into distant areas may constitute the most troublesome military challenge during the next decade. Continuing conflict in the Middle East and Persian Gulf, Southern Africa, and Southeast Asia is likely and future Russian planners may find that Soviet gains in strategic and theater nuclear capabilities provide an "umbrella" from under which to conduct regional operations. New airlift and sealift capabilities, meanwhile, will provide the Soviet Union with the means to carry out these operations.

What is so striking is that existing arms control processes seem almost, irrelevant to these emerging problems. It is even more disturbing, however, that arms control not only seems insensitive to a new class of military concerns, but may also reduce the ability of the United States and its allies to respond to these problems through unilateral military initiatives. For example, the 1972 SALT interim agreement on offensive missiles did little, if anything, to slow the Soviet Union down in attaining a capacity to threaten the *Minuteman* force through the deployment of the SS-18 and SS-19 intercontinental ballistic missile systems (ICBMs). Yet, for better or worse, the companion ABM (anti-ballistic missile) Treaty did foreclose a promising option for solving this problem: the deployment of hard-site ballistic missile defenses. Although both the Ford and the Carter administrations sought to curb the growth of Soviet ICBM capabilities in follow-on negotiations, the SALT II Treaty again fails to protect the *Minuteman* force from becoming vulnerable to preemptive attack.

As with the ABM Treaty, the SALT II accord seems to have already complicated unilateral U.S. efforts to come to grips with the problem by imposing constraints on the deployment of a mobile ICBM force. For a start, the Protocol attached to the treaty prohibits the deployment of mobile land-based launchers and air-to-surface ballistic missiles through 1981—a wholly theoretical constraint. A more practical constraint is the incompatibility of various mobile-missile basing modes with the verification requirements of the new treaty. The Carter administration ruled out the most secure (and least expensive) land-based mode—the multiple protective shelter or "shell game" system—on the ground that it would pose severe monitoring difficulties for future arms control regimes. Regardless of whether this assessment is correct, the administration initiated another approach to basing the new MX—the so-called "race track," a horizontal shelter system—that will be more costly, require more land, and is likely to arouse greater local opposition. All of these considerations could delay deployment of a survivable land-based missile or, possibly, cancel the systems altogether.

SALT's almost pernicious impact on *Minuteman* vulnerability is mirrored, in some respects, by its consequences for the changing nuclear balance in the European theater. As in the case of central strategic forces, the new treaty does little to arrest the growth of Soviet medium-range capabilities directed against Western Europe. In some ways, the accord actually seems to exacerbate the increasing problems confronting the Alliance in responding to the SS-20, the *Backfire* bomber, and other systems. Although the Carter administration insisted that the inclusion of sea- and ground-launched cruise missiles limitations in SALT II would not prejudice the ability of the United States to exploit such systems in theater nuclear roles after 1981, the political costs of protecting those systems from further limitation in any SALT III negotiation are likely to be high.

The mutual and balanced force reduction (MBFR) exercise in Vienna, meanwhile, is not only failing to help solve nuclear problems in Central Europe, but a negotiating outcome there could also conflict with Alliance efforts to stabilize the conventional balance in the region. The outcome that the West hopes to achieve in the negotiations—"parity" in manpower levels—seems increasingly irrelevant to the challenge of defending Central Europe from the type of "Blitzkrieg" that NATO confronts. Moreover, it is also possible that an MBFR agreement could hinder current efforts to improve NATO readiness and staying power, such as building up European reserves and augmenting U.S. reinforcements.

The negotiations on limiting Soviet and U.S. naval forces in the Indian Ocean and regional arms transfers were only underway for a short period of time before they were shelved by the Carter administration. Nevertheless, some of the same problems that beset SALT and MBFR talks surfaced again in these two negotiating enterprises. In areas around the Indian Ocean, greater regional conflict, together with the growing dependence of the West on oil from the Persian Gulf, have forged a strong argument for augmenting U.S. naval and air presence there. Yet an Indian Ocean accord that "stabilized" the presence of superpower navies in the region (and also neglected to control forces around the Indian Ocean littoral) would clearly hamper any serious U.S. effort to plan and prepare for contingencies in the region. The same is probably true of any accord controlling arms transfers. The fall of the Shah of Iran demonstrated the limits to which U.S. arms sales can be used as a surrogate for American military power, but in an era when direct military intervention remains an unpopular option for projecting force, arms sales—as the Egyptian-Israeli peace process underscores—continue to be an especially important military and diplomatic instrument. When the United States lacks the interest and the ability to use surrogates in regional conflicts, agreements that limit U.S. access to local allies are likely to have particularly adverse consequences.

In sum, the problem with existing arms control exercises is not that they are merely failing to respond to the challenges to U.S. security that are likely to be dominating security planning in the 1980s. As we shall see below, it has been a mistake to believe that negotiations by themselves can cope with these problems. The bigger problem is that, in many instances, arms control seems increasingly to impede efforts to cope with these challenges through other means.

What Arms Control Can Do

It has now become commonplace for analysts and government officials to argue, as did Leslie H. Gelb, former director of the Bureau of Politico-Military Affairs, that "as a result of a specialization of a narrow mandate, people all too often focus exclusively either on military programs or on arms control while losing sight of the other. Yet neither new forces nor arms control agreements are an end in itself. They are only means to an end, which is to ensure national security." But recognizing that a sort of analytical and bureaucratic "decoupling" between arms control and defense planning has occurred is only the first step toward finding a solution to the problem Gelb described. The second, more difficult step is to recognize that the conflicts and inconsistencies that plague arms control and defense planning flow, in the main, from misconceptions about what negotiations can accomplish. Thus, while it is now an article of faith that arms control cannot serve as a substitute for an adequate defense posture, U.S. negotiating strategy and conduct in many areas has assumed that this *is* the case. Indeed, some of the basic beliefs that underpin U.S. thinking about arms control seem to rule out the possibility of achieving greater compatibility between negotiating policy and military strategy.

A central fallacy of the existing approach to arms control is the belief that the primary function of negotiations is to alleviate sources of military instability. Probably the most conspicuous aspect of the SALT enterprise is the absence of any shared consensus between the two sides over the role and utility of long-range nuclear weapons—in particular, the meaning of "strategic stability." And without such a consensus, negotiators have failed to work out solutions to such problems as ICBM vulnerability. In March 1977, for example, the Carter administration tabled a proposal that, from the U.S. perspective, would have restructured both sides' arsenals along more stable lines: the most threatening (and vulnerable) component of both sides' forces—land-based ICBMs—would have been de-emphasized while each would have been free to build up its more secure sea-based and bomber forces.

Although some U.S. officials argued that Moscow's rejection of the socalled "comprehensive proposal" simply reflected a lack of imagination, there were sound strategic reasons for turning the American action down. For a start, given technological and geographical reasons, the idea of placing greater reliance on sea-launched ballistic missiles (SLBMs) and bombers undoubtedly appeared unattractive to Soviet planners. More important, from a doctrinal perspective, the Soviets probably viewed the growing vulnerability of U.S. ICBMs as a stabilizing rather than a dangerous development. What the March 1977 episode, along with the experience at MBFR, reveals is that lacking a consensus among negotiators over what "stability" constitutes, the most likely outcomes of arms control are agreements like the SALT II Treaty—accords that ratify rather than restructure prevailing trends in the military balance. This is surely why the Vienna talks have so far failed to produce an accord; while there are good reasons for the West to insist on manpower parity in the center region, the Soviet Union possesses equally strong incentives for maintaining its existing position of superiority.

The foregoing should not be interpreted to suggest that arms control outcomes do not have a military impact. Agreements, such as the 1972 ABM Treaty, can of course have a major impact on the plans of both sides. But, as in the case of the ABM Treaty, it is probably a mistake to view new agreements as part of a process of doctrinal convergence. The hypothesis that Moscow, by accepting severe restrictions on ABM deployment, agreed, in effect, to a system of "nuclear mutual vulnerability" must be judged against its continuing efforts in the area of air defenses, civil defense, antisubmarine warfare, and antisatellite systems. A much more plausible explanation for Moscow's decision to enter into the treaty is that with the U.S. *Safeguard* system ready to undergo deployment, the Soviet Union made a hard-headed decision to close off competition in ABMs. Again, the lesson is not that arms control outcomes reflect a narrowing of strategic beliefs, but that nations can sometimes reach agreement for very different reasons.

A second fallacy that proceeds from the notion of arms control as a solution to defense problems is the idea that military programs that threaten existing negotiations somehow endanger deterrence. As suggested above, the most common result of arms control is not enhanced stability but the registration of reality; agreements are often controversial because, more than anything else, they spotlight military deficiencies. But when looking at the impact of military programs on arms control negotiations, there is a common tendency to confuse means and ends. Weapons that for one reason or another pose threats to existing negotiations are viewed as threatening stability when, in fact, the impact of their deployment might be just the opposite. An example is the U.S. cruise missile program. It is easy to understand why the cruise missile complicated efforts to complete the SALT II Treaty. The relatively small size of the missile posed challenges to verification, and its utility in both strategic and theater roles (armed with nuclear and conventional warheads) created daunting problems of categorization. The irony, of course, is that although cruise missiles posed a threat to SALT, their deployment in large numbers would be more likely to strengthen than to weaken deterrence. While cruise missiles are clearly second-strike strategic weapons, their ability to offer more durable basing modes at land and sea and their possible marriage to a new family of conventional munitions would certainly be desirable in theater roles. They might even raise the nuclear "threshold."

There can be little doubt that what some people refer to as the "qualitative arms race" can, at times, create military problems. New weapons technologies can increase first-strike incentives and produce such unwanted side effects as collateral damage. In the longer term, they can also force wrenching changes in prevailing patterns of military thought, as laser and charged-particle defensive systems might necessitate within a decade or more from now. At the same time, technological superiority continues to be an official goal of U.S. defense policy. Had the SALT process been underway in the early 1960s, the Soviet Union, together with many arms control proponents in the United States, would have probably maintained that the deployment of *Polaris* nuclear powered ballistic missile submarines (SSBNs) created verification difficulties and also represented another destabilizing round of the "qualitative arms race." SLBMs did represent a a new departure in military technology, but in an era of growing ICBM vulnerability, their deployment can hardly be viewed as anything but a beneficial development. If arms control is not a substitute for unilateral defense initiatives, then the political price of negotiating the fielding of new systems must be measured against the security benefits that will be gained from their deployment.

The cruise missile case is also useful in highlighting the tendency of negotiations to distort, simplify, and most important, compartmentalize military reality. As the acronym implies, the SALT process uses as its central organizing principle the idea that there is a distinct class of U.S. and Soviet forces known as "strategic weapons." Although that description of the state of technology was generally accurate during the 1960s, a new class of more accurate and flexible systems, such as the cruise missile, is making the time-honored distinction between "strategic" and "general purpose" forces obsolete. Moreover, new munitions, such as fuel-air explosives and enhanced radiation weapons, are blurring distinctions between nuclear and conventional weapons.

As a result, the preoccupation of the SALT process with the "homeland-to-homeland" nuclear balance between the two superpowers has made it increasingly difficult to cope with weapons technologies that are relevant in both "central strategic" and regional military contingencies. SALT outcomes that limit these systems are unattractive because they foreclose options for upgrading theater defenses. At the same time, agreements that exclude these systems are equally unattractive, because, as the controversy over the *Backfire* at SALT II illustrated, neither side likes the idea of allowing the other to increase its intercontinental-range arsenal under the guise of expanding its theater forces. Because the United States has nuclear commitments to the defense of Western Europe, the notion of a "homeland-to-homeland" balance fostered by SALT has never been terribly attractive. During a period in which the systems limited by the process were not directly relevant to the defense of the theater, bilateral agreements were bearable. But in a period when it no longer is possible to compartmentalize the U.S.-Soviet strategic balance, new SALT agreements seem certain to challenge the military and political cohesion of the Western alliance.

If SALT points out the problems of trying to limit a functional category of arms, such as strategic weapons, the MBFR exercise underlines the dangers of geographical compartmentalization. Since the talks got underway in 1973, analysts have complained about the geographical asymmetries inherent in efforts to limit forces in an artificially bounded chunk of Central Europe. Some critics have worried, for example, that if any agreement covering U.S. and Soviet forces were reached, the United States would be forced to withdraw forces beyond the Atlantic while the Soviet Union would only have to move its forces back into the Western Military District. Most Western governments, however, have viewed this as an acceptable price to pay in order to achieve some semblance of manpower parity in the center region.

In a similar way, military reality was also distorted by the artificial geographical boundaries of the short-lived Indian Ocean negotiations. Discussing naval forces at sea without reference to shifting capabilities on land can probably only work against the West. For the foreseeable future, carrier-based aircraft will probably provide the only immediate air power that the United States will be able to bring to bear within the region. In the most critical areas on the Indian Ocean littoral and the Persian Gulf, Soviet land-based air could be decisive.

A more basic question is whether the attempt to freeze the existing naval balance at some rough level of "parity" is even a desirable goal in applying arms control to the Indian Ocean. In both SALT and MBFR, parity can be justified as a negotiating outcome, because both the United States and the Soviet Union possess roughly similar interests in guaranteeing their own security and that of their respective allies in Europe. However, the stakes for the two sides in the Indian Ocean, and more particularly the Persian Gulf and the Middle East, seem quite disparate. Although closer to the Soviet Union, the Gulf is far more important to the West. Arguably, then, the United States might need to maintain superior forces in the region.

It is also questionable whether equality is a desirable goal in approaching any negotiations on conventional arms transfers. As both political and military instruments, arms transfers confer influence in peacetime and, on occasion, leverage in time of conflict. Although the United States and the Soviet Union are commonly lumped together as the "two superpowers," they obviously differ in their ability to use military supply relationships to their own advantage. In such regions as Latin America, where the United States has long enjoyed greater access, the proposal for putting the superpowers on equal footing as regards arms sales seems to make particularly little sense.

The Bureaucratic Factor

Although the fallacies outlined above primarily stem from a conceptual tendency to make arms control an end in itself, they have been strongly reinforced by bureaucratic behavior. For example, while few analysts believe that the U.S.-Soviet balance in central strategic forces should be viewed in isolation from other aspects of the East-West military balance, it is almost inevitable that officials deeply immersed in the day-to-day complexities of SALT have paid little attention to the wider implications of negotiating outcomes. Thus, until European governments began to anxiously question the implications for Alliance security of cruise missile constraints at SALT, the Carter administration had not seriously considered how the negotiating process had begun to "spill over" into the realm of theater nuclear forces. Similarly, the administration was also late in recognizing the psychological and military problems posed for Europe by the SS-20—probably because the weapon had not emerged as a factor in either SALT or MBFR.

The tendency to seek parity in negotiations, even when parity might be an inappropriate goal, can also be explained in bureaucratic terms because diplomats are naturally attracted to proposals that appear equitable; that is, proposals that have a chance of being accepted. Finally, it is also understandable that officials responsible for arms control have a natural aversion to new weapons technologies—particularly to systems that appear to threaten central organizing concepts, such as the cruise missile at SALT, or pose verification problems, like the MX. Whatever case can be made for such weapons on strategic grounds, they make negotiations more difficult and, in the minds of negotiators, this is a much weightier consideration.

These factors help explain why, in a bureaucratic sense, the establishment of an arms control process is in some ways more important than whether the process produces an agreement. To begin with, the creation of an arms control process allows new participants to shape policy in the area under discussion. In the absence of arms control, decisions over military posture and weapons development and deployment are dominated by the Defense Department, with the armed services possessing a large voice in most matters. But once a "defense problem" is transformed into an "arms control issue," questions like the future of U.S. naval forces in the Indian Ocean also become the concern of the State Department and the ACDA. Indeed, both the State Department and ACDA have a vested interest in proliferating arms control negotiations, if only to maximize their impact on defense policy.

Just as there are strong bureaucratic incentives to begin negotiations, there are also payoffs to be gained from continuing them. Some years back, political scientists noted that in major weapons system procurement programs, military organizations often lost sight of the original military rationale for new systems and that "getting the job done" became the measure of bureaucratic success. Thus, even though the supersonic B-70 bomber was obsolete compared to Soviet high-altitude surface-to-air missiles (SAMSs) by the time it was ready for deployment, the organizational and personal stakes involved in the B-70 program made it almost impossible to turn the program off. In such a way, it was argued, developing inertia to weapons procurement was difficult to resist. By the same token, there has also been a bureaucratic inertia with regard to arms control when the goal of achieving agreement has supplanted an earlier strategic objective. A basic rationale for plunging into the MBFR exercise in the early 1970s, for example, was to dampen enthusiasm in the Senate for unilateral withdrawal of U.S. troops from Europe. That rationale has ceased to exist, but the MBFR dynamic continues.

These factors are useful in explaining why arms control can sometimes become a bureaucratic end in itself, but they do not shed much light on how negotiations become decoupled from defense planning in the first place. At the heart of the matter are deep-seated differences of view over such basic questions as the utility of military force, the severity of the Soviet military threat, and the nature of U.S.-Soviet arms competition. On one end of the spectrum, there are those who argue that military force is of declining relevance in the post-Cold War era, that the Soviet Union is beset with all sorts of domestic problems and new foreign threats, such as China, and that the arms race is essentially a mechanistic game of "monkey-see, monkey-do." On the other end of the spectrum, observers argue that the utility of force has not declined, but the willingness of the United States to use force has been diminished. The Soviet Union is depicted as a stronger, increasingly more assertive power and the arms race is said, in fact, not to be a race at all, but a much more complex phenomenon in which both sides are running at different speeds and for different reasons. There is no way that government can resolve these differences, but what is surprising is how the structure of the national security establishment seems to widen them. Not only are arms control and defense planning functions currently fragmented throughout the government, but the nature of the interagency process seems more designed to create differences than to reach consensus.

In part, the existence of the ACDA is responsible for this state of affairs. Having no responsibility for either threat assessment or force planning, but possessing strong vested interests in negotiations, ACDA has little reason to get involved in the difficult trade-offs between arms control and unilateral military flexibility. This was not always the case. When it was created in 1961, the agency was seen as an instrument for bringing arms control issues to the attention of the national security establishment. But ACDA may have become a victim of its own success, or more precisely, the success of arms control. As arms control has moved from being a diplomatic experiment to a central fixture of U.S. foreign policy, ACDA's role has been displaced by arms control units within the Pentagon, the State Department, and the National Security Council. In order to justify its existence, therefore, the agency has had to become ever more doctrinaire in its adherence to the primacy of arms control. This not only has created unnecessary bureaucratic frictions, but has also, in many cases, curiously reduced the influence of the agency. The innovation of arms control impact statements has further accelerated the agency's estrangement from the defense planning community, because the process actually encourages the agency to adopt a different perspective on weapons issues than the Defense Department. The fact that ACDA and the Defense Department report to different committees on Capitol Hill and possess different congressional constituencies only serves to deepen this split.

In the Pentagon itself, other divisions are at work. It is no coincidence (as the Soviets are fond of saying) that the rise of arms control as a central policy objective accompanied the expansion of civilian control in the Pentagon. The so-called "McNamara Revolution" of the 1960s not only brought managerial reforms to defense management, but also a new sympathy for negotiated military restraint. Understandably, the military services viewed arms control as part of a larger threat to their traditional prerogatives. And they were correct in doing so. By framing military issues as arms control problems, civilian-dominated organizations, such as the Office of International Security Affairs, were able to gain considerable influence at the expense of the joint Chiefs of Staff. Thus, like ACDA in the wider interagency process, the armed services, along with the joint Chiefs, were gradually pushed to adopt extreme positions on arms control. As in the budgetary process, their views gradually lost credibility and they came to be seen as obstacles to agreement. In the process, the professional military has inevitably come to view arms control as a threat rather than an opportunity.

Finding a New Balance

The central argument of this essay has been that arms control and defense planning are out of kilter largely because misunderstandings about what can be achieved in negotiations have been reinforced by bureaucratic behavior. There are some ways that these problems might be solved.

The central reality of arms control is that only rarely do negotiated outcomes address pressing military concerns. To reiterate, arms control is primarily useful for registering and codifying an existing balance of forces. This can be a useful outcome. At SALT, the belief that U.S. and Soviet strategic forces are roughly equivalent (at least in size) is probably critical to the maintenance of détente, however tenuous. In the same way, an MBFR agreement that provided for equal manpower ceilings (assuming the use of a mutually acceptable data base) would also create a condition of "optical parity" that would surely enhance political confidence in both Eastern and Western Europe. Moreover, arms control agreements can create a degree of predictability that is useful both politically and militarily. In criticizing arms control, it is easy to lose sight of the uncertainty that plagued political leaders and military planners during the first half of the 1960s. In the early part of the decade the tendency to exaggerate Soviet strategic programs led the United States to rush ahead with programs that by 1965 seemed unnecessary. However, American overreaction in the early 1960s probably fostered a tendency in the latter half of the decade to underestimate Soviet strategic ambitions, an even more dangerous development. Whatever else SALT II does, it will enable political and military authorities to agree on the character of the strategic environment in the mid-1980s.

But "optical parity" and predictability are not the same things as the maintenance of deterrence. In strategic forces, the maintenance of credible deterrence requires the deployment of U.S. land-based systems in a more survivable basing mode and, more controversial, an enhanced ability to threaten hard targets in the Soviet Union. In the European theater, deterrence also requires more survivable nuclear forces. It is possible that many options for bolstering deterrence in these areas could complicate future arms control efforts. There is no obvious solution to this dilemma. Some observers, despite the lessons of SALT II, seem interested in shaping a new set of grandiose goals for a new round of negotiations. In the view of this writer, that would be a major mistake. Asking too much from SALT III not only runs the risk of raising expectations that will surely be disappointed, but also places a national security burden on SALT that it cannot bear.

If there is a solution, it probably lies in asking arms control to do less instead of more. Thus, at SALT III, the United States should not seek severe quantitative reductions or tighter qualitative constraints. An accord that would provide both sides with some flexibility for dealing unilaterally with their separately perceived military problems might not only be more negotiable but also, probably, more conducive to overall stability. Scaling down ambitions for arms control will not totally eliminate the very real tensions between efforts to achieve "optical parity" at SALT and unilateral efforts to strengthen deterrence. But the first step toward wisdom in this area is to recognize that such tensions exist.

Using Arms Control to Bolster Deterrence

While negotiations alone are unlikely to produce solutions to military problems, arms control, in conjunction with U.S. defense initiatives, can offer some promising approaches to coping with new Soviet challenges. Probably the strongest military argument that can be made for SALT II is that by putting a ceiling on Soviet missile warheads, the agreement could potentially enhance the survivability of the MX (if the ceiling were extended beyond 1985). Without a limit on warhead fractionation, the argument goes, the Soviet Union could counter any deceptive basing system for a mobile missile by massively expanding its warhead inventory. There may be other ways that arms control outcomes could work synergistically with unilateral defense decisions. For example, a SALT III limitation on Soviet air defenses, particularly around hard targets, would ensure the continuing effectiveness of cruise missiles. At the same time, it would probably be a mistake to allow U.S. forces to become overly dependent on arms control constraints accepted by the Soviet Union. Although Moscow has agreed to warhead fractionation limits at SALT, the MX will not undergo deployment until after the treaty is due to run out. Thus, as SALT negotiations continue, the Soviets could either refuse to agree to further limits on fractionation or, more likely, exact a steep price in concessions elsewhere and demand major concessions in other areas as a price for enabling the United States to proceed with the MX.

The main way in which defense programs and arms control can interact positively is by enhancing U.S. negotiating leverage. As the ABM case suggests, weapons programs can provide incentives for the Soviet Union to consider negotiating outcomes that do more than simply ratify prevailing strategic trends. It has been suggested, for example, that Carter's MX decision could force the Soviet Union, for the first time, to think seriously about the merit of severe constraints on MIRVed (multiple independently targetable reentry vehicles) ICBMs. Yet, "bargaining chip" negotiating strategies must be approached with caution. In the ABM case, the United States possessed a system that was technologically vastly superior to what Moscow had and, equally important, its deployment lay right around the corner. These conditions are absent in the MX case. First, with the MX only now undergoing full-scale development, it is unrealistic to expect the system to provide the U.S. side with much negotiating leverage in the immediate future. Second, the system's hardtarget capability will not be qualitatively different than Soviet systems undergoing deployment at the same time. Thus, it is probably unrealistic to expect that the Soviet Union would react to the threat of MX deployment by agreeing to a scheme for de-emphasizing land-based ICBMs. It would be a much more painful response to the MX if the Soviet Union were to find a more survivable basing mode for its own ICBMs.

Political problems also can arise from the inappropriate use of "bargaining chips." This is perhaps most clearly illustrated in the current effort by NATO to agree on a plan for modernizing long-range theater nuclear forces. Because of the sensitivity of nuclear deployment issues in various European states, governments are attracted to the idea of coupling an Alliance decision to proceed with the deployment of a new, long-range system with an arms control offer to the East. While this strategy might allow the Alliance to overcome domestic opposition in West Germany and Holland to modernizing U.S. nuclear forces in Central Europe, in the longer run, it could backfire. The problem is that it is hard to see why, at this stage, Moscow would be interested in any arms control proposal aimed at limiting long-range theater forces. Just as the MX, with an initial operating capability (IOC) of 1986, is unlikely to arrest Moscow's current deployment of the SS-18, an extended-range *Pershing*, with an IOC in the early 1980s, is unlikely to coerce Moscow into dismantling its existing SS-20s. At most, if the Alliance proceeds with the deployment of several hundred medium-range systems during the next few years, it is conceivable that Moscow would accept some upper limits on the size of its long-range theater forces. But even this outcome may not be possible. By hoping (and in some cases, pretending) that there is a negotiating solution to the SS-20 problem, when in all reality there is not, the Alliance runs the risk of being criticized for using arms control as a "fig leaf" to justify new military programs.

Refocusing, Restructuring, and Stopping Arms Control

While it has become conventional wisdom that arms control considerations should be taken into account in shaping defense policy and programs, it is interesting that so little thought is given to how existing negotiations should be adapted to changing the military realities. Although a second SALT treaty has been completed, the principal problems that dragged out the talks, such as verification, Soviet ICBM preponderance, and the "gray area" weapons, loom as even bigger obstacles in SALT III. Thus, even if the United States entered the negotiations with fairly modest goals, SALT III could quickly become bogged down. In such circumstances, it would seem worth exploring whether a more piecemeal approach to SALT III—one that attempts to address one issue at a time—makes more sense than seeking a more "comprehensive" arrangement that tries to deal with several issues simultaneously. In a more sequential approach to SALT III, negotiators might first grapple with theater nuclear concerns, such as the status of cruise missiles, in the Protocol, while deferring discussion on "deep cuts" in central forces to a later phase of the talks.

It might also be profitable to change existing approaches at MBFR. Given the character of the Warsaw Pact threat, arms control outcomes that constrain the use, rather than the size, of military forces in Central Europe would be very useful. This, of course, is the essential function of "confidence building measures" ("associated measures" in MBFR parlance). Negotiated limits on force deployment and maneuver have only recently come under serious study, but if associated measures do offer a real possibility of complicating Soviet surprise attack options while enhancing tactical warning, then this is an avenue worth pursuing in Vienna.

In the future, MBFR may not be the best place to negotiate arms control in Europe. The French proposal for an arms control forum reaching "from the Atlantic to the Urals" makes far more strategic sense than continuing to do business in Vienna, especially if equipment limits, instead of manpower or confidence-building measures, are going to be the focus for negotiations.

The possibility of revising existing arms control arrangements to bring them more into line with emerging military realities should not be overlooked. Revision of the

ABM Treaty to facilitate the deployment of hard-site missile defenses is an especially interesting option. So far, it has received little serious consideration out of a fear that tampering with the 1972 treaty could lead to an unraveling of the entire agreement. But the deployment of hard-site defenses might not only enhance the survivability of multiple-launch point ICBM basing systems; it also might even rule out the need for deceptive basing modes altogether by giving fixed silos a new lease on life.

Finally, while some negotiations might be usefully rechanneled and replaced, others should probably be abandoned for good. Controling American and Soviet naval deployments in the Indian Ocean, for example, is an effete idea. Not only is the concept of a "naval balance" in the region analytically unsound, but the goal of the negotiations—to freeze U.S. and Soviet naval forces at their existing levels—is most likely incompatible with growing U.S. security concerns in the region. At the very time that the region is taking on greater importance to the West, the Iranian revolution, radical currents in Arab politics, and local suspicions have made naval forces probably the only reliable way for the United States to project power into the area. When the United States has finally sorted out what it needs to be able to do in the region and has implemented these steps, then it might be useful to take another look at arms control.

From the standpoint of organization structure and process, the goal of harnessing arms control to defense planning is hindered in two ways. First, parochialism in negotiating perspectives makes it almost impossible to come up with any comprehensive strategy for arms control. Second, bureaucratic frictions and disconnections often make it difficult to mesh negotiating objectives with defense planning goals. In other words, means need to be found for increasing communication among arms controllers and between arms controllers and defense planners.

To begin with, ways must be found to minimize the bureaucratic polarization between arms controllers and defense planners. In retrospect, the creation of the ACDA may have been a mistake. By its very existence and role in the interagency process, the agency reinforces the idea that negotiations offer an alternative path to international security. Although it would be counter productive at this point to attempt to disband the agency or to incorporate it into the State Department, some marginal changes could bring the agency back into the mainstream of the policy process. For symbolic reasons, it is probably wise to insist that directors of the agency be civilians, but perhaps ACDA's charter could be amended to require that the deputy director be a serving military officer. Such a change might work two ways: it would bring an operational military perspective to senior levels of the agency and it would also give military officers a deeper insight into arms control.

Indeed, one of the most conspicuous failures of the present system is its failure to elicit and profit from high-level military participation. In striking contrast to the Soviet pattern, U.S. arms control has become a mostly civilian enterprise, viewed with suspicion and sometimes open hostility by the military services. This is the fault of both uniformed officers and their civilian counterparts. Rather than concerning itself with the broad policy implications of negotiations, the military establishment is overly preoccupied with how arms control will affect specific hardware programs. Yet, the parochial concerns of the military are often justified by the way arms controllers use negotiations to gain leverage over military force planning and weapons decisions. There is no easy solution to this problem, but it is clear that the joint Chiefs of Staff and senior elements of the armed services must be given a larger role in arms control planning and the negotiations themselves. This not only means giving the armed services a larger advisory capacity, but greater responsibility in the actual conduct of negotiations as well. Greater military responsibility for arms control would foster greater harmony between defense and arms control objectives and negotiating outcomes that might win greater support within the military establishment.

The role of the State Department also needs to be examined. Even more than ACDA, the proliferating number of new negotiations has worked to enhance the influence of the State Department on defense questions. This has led to a significant expansion in the number of State Department officials focusing on military problems, particularly in the Bureau of Politico-Military Affairs. There has always been a notorious shortage of skilled defense professionals within the foreign service, so an increased competence within the State Department in this area is a healthy development.

But the role of the department and, in particular, the Bureau of Politico-Military Affairs, should be kept in perspective. In the 1960s, there was legitimate concern that the Pentagon's Office of International Security Affairs was becoming a "little State Department." Now the State Department's Bureau of Politico-Military Affairs seems to be evolving into a "little Defense Department." The bureau does have an important role to play in assessing the political implications of proposed defense policies and programs. But it risks compromising this function by becoming a competitive center for defense analysis.

While some of these steps might help to break down a few of the barriers that have grown up within the bureaucracy, the tendency to compartmentalize different aspects of the arms control process will remain a serious problem. Conceptually, it is appealing to think about formulating a comprehensive arms control strategy that will be aimed at ensuring that negotiating goals in different settings remain coherent and compatible. But even if it were possible to formulate such a strategy, it would probably be too vague to be of much use. Instead of a "grand design" for arms control, it would be much more useful to institute a continuous system of monitoring existing negotiating processes. The system would examine a number of important questions: the relevance of existing U.S. arms control goals to changing military circumstances; the effect of various negotiating outcomes on planned and future American forces; the implications of negotiating outcomes for other arms control efforts; and finally, apparent changes in Soviet arms control policy. Of course, all of these questions are randomly examined in different parts of the government. But a high-level security planning office, perhaps situated in the National Security Council, that could centralize and coordinate the monitoring process might be able to produce new and far more useful variants of the Arms Control Impact Statement: not analyses of the narrow impact of new weapons on negotiations, but studies of the impact of arms control on American security.

Rediscovering Defense Policy

It is too easy to blame the defense policy dilemmas now confronting the United States on an unblinking enthusiasm for arms control alone. In fact, one reason that arms control has become such a dominant factor in national security planning is that in many areas, negotiations have proceeded in a defense policy vacuum. Arms control, in other words, has often become a surrogate to thinking about defense problems. It is easy to see why this has happened. Unlike before, today there is no general doctrine, such as "containment," around which to organize defense policy. Nor do military planners have the luxury of strategic superiority with which to avoid difficult choices. Instead, in an era of unprecedented Soviet military growth, the United States, still recovering from the shock of Vietnam, is profoundly uncertain over the meaning of the Soviet buildup and how to respond to it. Arms control, by promising to cope with the Soviet challenge while also restraining the United States from making an unnecessary military response, has seemed to offer an opportunity to escape from a divisive and enervating debate over defense policy.

But if the thesis of this essay is correct—that arms control, in the final analysis, is mostly useful in only defining military problems—then negotiations cannot be used as a crutch. For arms control to play a useful role, U.S. goals in such areas as strategic doctrine, theater nuclear and conventional forces, as well as maritime and projection capabilities, must be outlined with far greater precision than they have been before.

One of the most difficult issues that must be addressed is the impact of growing Soviet strategic counterforce capabilities on the credibility of deterrence in the 1980s. While the so-called "Schlesinger Doctrine" of flexible strategic options aroused intense controversy a few years ago, today it is an accepted part of U.S. nuclear strategy. But beyond this, it has become difficult to discuss, in concrete terms, what the prevailing U.S. strategy for nuclear targeting is. For example, how far down the road will the Carter administration's concept of a "countervailing strategy" take the United States in matching the Soviet Union's war-fighting approach to strategic deployment and employment? In the MX decision and other actions, such as recognizing the contribution that civil defense can make to strategic stability, the Carter administration seemed to toy with what could become a radical shift in deterrence strategy. But so far, the far-reaching implications of any such a shift have escaped real debate.

The relationship between strategic balance and U.S. deterrence doctrine for European security is another area which has escaped close scrutiny in recent years. What special demands does the requirement of "extended" deterrence place on strategic force design? The answer to this question may be important to the future of theater forces. In an era of strategic parity, it is questionable whether theater forces can any longer be considered as escalatory instruments. Escalation control and battle management obviously become more attractive, and these goals should thus be weighed heavily in decisions on the sizing and design of theater forces. At present, the NATO Alliance is still caught up in difficult and complex consultations over the deployment of a few hundred long-range systems that would be able to reach the Soviet homeland. While immensely important, the long-range tactical nuclear forces (TNF) issue should not be allowed to obscure the fact that the Alliance confronts a Soviet program for modernizing theater nuclear forces across the board. Again, lacking any overall consensus on the role of theater nuclear forces, if an effort is made to take a comprehensive look at the adequacy of NATO's existing posture—examining such controversial issues as whether "combined" nuclear and conventional options are now necessary to maintain deterrence—the most important implications of the Soviet actions are likely to be missed.

Basic issues could also be ignored in the area of conventional forces. The Alliance is engaged on a long-term defense improvement program, but that effort is proceeding with minimum discussion over NATO strategy. Although suggestions for radically transforming the Alliance along the lines suggested by Steven Canby and other critics are in many cases politically unfeasible, it is clear that NATO's existing adherence to linear and firepower-dominated concepts of defense need to be reexamined.

Finally, despite years of analysis, the great debate over whether sea control or projection should take precedence in naval force design is still unresolved. Although the growth of Soviet maritime power has made the sea control mission seem a more pressing requirement than ever before, resource constraints, the concurrent growth in Soviet projection capabilities, and political instability in the Southern Hemisphere have also made "strategic access" an equally important concern. The problem of course, is that even if these doctrinal issues are resolved, some basic force structure questions will have to be addressed, such as the familiar question of whether large-ship, small-fleet navies are more desirable than small-ship, large-fleet ones. In the area of projection, meanwhile, other problems need to be addressed, particularly whether the most important contingencies in the Persian Gulf and elsewhere are likely to be ones in which small, rapidly deployed forces will be decisive or whether larger, more slowly available forces with greater staying power will be crucial.

At present, these questions are being resolved on an expedient, piecemeal basis. Unless more coherent, long-term plans linking military purposes and force structure and sizing are adopted, arms control inevitably will be forced to take on a burden it is unsuited to bear. In the end, national security, along with arms control, will suffer.

1983

THE DANGER OF THERMONUCLEAR WAR: AN OPEN LETTER TO DR. SIDNEY DRELL

Andrei Sakharov

Andrei Sakharov distinguished Soviet physicist and winner of the 1975 Nobel Peace Prize, is currently in internal exile in Gorki. Among his works available in English are *Alarm and Hope* and *Collected Scientific Works*. This essay was written for publication in response to the materials noted below which Professor Drell of Stanford had sent to him. The translation from the Russian was done by Richard Lourie and Efrem Yankelevich.

Dr. Drell's speech at Grace Cathedral is unpublished but available from him on request. His opening statement before the Subcommittee on Investigations and Oversight of the House Committee on Science and Technology is contained in the Committee's record of those hearings, *The Consequences of Nuclear War on the Global Environment*, September 15, 1982. A more comprehensive statement of Dr. Drell's views will be found in his Danz Lectures, published by the University of Washington Press in June 1983 under the title *Facing the Treat of Nuclear Weapons*.

The Editor is grateful to Professor Drell and to Strobe Talbott for their help in refining the translation of technical terms, and in preparing the explanatory Editor's Notes, for which of course the Editor takes responsibility.

Dear Friend:

I have read your two splendid lectures—the speech on nuclear weapons at Grace Cathedral, October 23, 1982,

Reprinted with permission of *Foreign Affairs*. Copyright © 1983 by Andrei Sakharov.

and the opening statement to Hearings on the Consequences of Nuclear War before the Subcommittee on Investigations and Oversight. What you say and write about the appalling dangers of nuclear war is very close to my heart and has disturbed me profoundly for many years now. I decided to address an open letter to you, feeling it necessary to take part in the discussion of this problem, one of the most important facing mankind.

In full agreement with your general theses, I will express certain considerations of a more specific nature which, I think, need to be taken into account when making decisions. These considerations in part contradict some of your statements and in part supplement and, possibly, amplify them. It seems to me that my opinion communicated here in open discussion can prove of interest in view of my scientific, technological, and psychological experience, acquired in the period when I took part in work on thermonuclear weapons, and also because I am one of the few independent participants in this discussion in the U.S.S.R.

I fully agree with your assessment of the danger of nuclear war. In view of the critical importance of this thesis, I will dwell on it in some detail, perhaps repeating what is already well known.

Here, and later on, I use the terms "nuclear war" and "thermonuclear war" nearly interchangeably. Nuclear weapons mean atomic and thermonuclear weapons; conventional weapons mean any weapons with the exception of three types with the capability of mass destruction—nuclear, chemical, and bacteriological weapons.

A large nuclear war would be a calamity of indescribable proportions and absolutely unpredictable consequences, with the uncertainties tending toward the worse.

According to data from United Nations experts, by the end of 1980 the world's overall supply of nuclear weapons consisted of 50,000 nuclear charges.[1] The total power of these charges (most of which are in the 0.04- to 20-megaton range) amounts to 13,000 megatons according to the experts' estimates. The figures you have presented are

[1] *Editor's Note.* "Charge" is a standard Soviet term—used frequently in arms control negotiations—embracing warheads on ballistic missiles and also armaments aboard bombers, which may be in bomb or missile form. There is a separate Russian word for warheads.

not in conflict with those estimates. In this regard you mention that the total power of all the explosives used in the Second World War did not exceed six megatons (three megatons, according to the experts estimates with which I am familiar). However, when making this comparison one must take into account the greater relative efficacy of smaller charges with the same total power, but that does not alter the qualitative conclusions about the colossal destructive power of the nuclear weapons that have been amassed.

You also cite data according to which the U.S.S.R. at the present time (1982) has 8,000 thermonuclear charges deployed and the United States 9,000.[2] Many of these charges are warheads on ballistic missiles, and many of these are multiple independently-targetable reentry vehicles (MIRVs). It should be noted that the basis of the U.S.S.R.'s arsenal (70 percent, according to statements by TASS) consists of gigantic land-based missiles (in silos) and somewhat smaller intermediate-range missiles, on mobile launchers. Eighty Percent of the U.S. arsenal consists of submarine-based nuclear missiles, much smaller but less vulnerable than silo-based missiles, and also of strategic bombers carrying nuclear bombs, some of which are apparently very powerful. It is doubtful whether masses of aircraft could penetrate Soviet territory deeply—but a more precise assessment of their capabilities must take the possibilities of cruise missiles into account; these would probably be able to penetrate the enemy's air defense systems.

Currently, the most powerful American ICBMs (I am not speaking of the planned MX) possess several times less throw-weight than the principal land-based Soviet missiles.[3] The American ones carry fewer MIRVs, and the yield of their warheads is less. (It is assumed that when dividing the throw-weight of a missile among several warheads—let's say ten—the aggregate yield of the multlple warheads is less than the yield of a large single warhead on the same missile. But

---

[2] *Editor's Note.* These totals refer to the number of charges deployed on intercontinental ballistic missiles, submarine-launched ballistic missiles, and intercontinental-range bombers.

[3] *Editor's Note.* The term "throw-weight" is normally defined as the weight of effective payload that can be delivered to an intended distance; effective payload may include penetration aids and navigational equipment as well as the nuclear charge itself. The term "yield" refers to destructive power and the term "compact targets" as used in this paragraph, clearly refers to military targets in general and to specially hardened ICBM sites in particular.

MIRVs greatly increase the ability of one side to attack compact targets on the other. MIRVs are also highly destructive against targets spread out over a wide area such as large cities. The aggregate yield may be less than that of a large single warhead, but the destructiveness will remain high because of the multiple blasts spread out over the area. I have dwelt on these details since they may prove of substance in further discussion.)

You cite the estimates of the international journal of the Royal Swedish Academy, according to which an attack on the principal cities of the Northern Hemisphere by 5,000 warheads with a total power of 2,000 megatons will kill 750 million people as a result of the shock wave alone.[4]

I would like to add the following to that estimate:

1. The overall number of long-range nuclear weapons possessed by the five nuclear powers is three or four times greater than the figure used in the Swedish estimate and their overall power is six to seven times greater. The accepted average number of casualties per missile—250,000 people—cannot be considered an overestimate if one compares the accepted average power of a thermonuclear charge of 400 kilotons with the power of the 17-kiloton explosion at Hiroshima and the number of victims from its shock waves, no fewer than 40,000.

2. An extremely important factor in the destructive capability of nuclear weapons is thermal radiation. The fires at Hiroshima were the cause of a signficant portion (up to 50 percent) of the fatalities. With the increase of the charges' power, the relative role of thermal radiation increases. Therefore, this factor significantly increases the number of direct casualties.

3. During an attack on especially dense, compact enemy targets (like silo-based missile launchers, command points, communication centers, government institutions, shelters, and other of the more important targets) it must be assumed that a significant portion of the explosions will be ground-level or low. In such cases there inevitably will be "traces," bands of dust fallout raised by the explosion from the surface and "impregnated" by the products of uranium fission. Therefore, although the direct radioactive effect of

---

[4] *Editor's Note.* This estimate is contained in the publication of the Royal Swedish Academy, *Ambio*, Vol. XI. Nos. 2–3, 1982.

a nuclear charge takes place in a zone where everything alive is, in any case, annihilated by the shock wave and by fire, its indirect effect—through fallout—proves very substantial. The area contaminated by fallout so that the total dose of radiation exceeds the safety limit of 300 roentgens is, for a typical one-megaton nuclear charge, thousands of square kilometers!

During the ground-level test of the Soviet thermonuclear charge in August 1953, tens of thousands of people were evacuated beforehand from the zone where fallout was possible. People were only able to return to the settlement of Kara-aul in the spring of 1954! In war conditions an orderly evacuation is impossible. Hundreds of millions will flee in panic, often from one contaminated zone into another. Hundreds of millions of people will inevitably become the victims of radioactive irradiation, the mass migrations of people will make the chaos, the deterioration of sanitary conditions and the hunger all the greater. The genetic consequencess of irradiation will threaten man as a biological species and all animal and plant life on the Earth.

I entirely agree with your basic idea that mankind has *never* encountered anything even remotely resembling a large nuclear war in scale and horror.

No matter how appalling the direct consequencess of nuclear explosions, we cannot exclude that the indirect effects will be even more substantial. The indirect effects could be fatal for modern society, which is extraordinarily complex and thus highly vulnerable.

The general ecological consequences are just as dangerous, although by virtue of the complex nature of ecological interdependencies, forecasts and estimates are extremely difficult here. I will mention some of the problems discussed in the literature (in your talks, in particular) without assessing their seriousness, although I am certain that many of the dangers indicated are entirely real:

1. Continuous forest fires could destroy the greater part of the planet's forests. The smoke involved would destroy the transparency of the atmosphere. A night lasting many weeks would ensue on Earth followed by a lack of oxygen in the atmosphere. As a result, this factor alone, if real, could destroy life on the planet. In less pronounced form, this factor could have important ecological, economic, and psychological consequences.

2. High-altitude wartime nuclear explosions in space (particularly the thermonuclear explosion of ABM missiles and the explosion of attacking missiles whose purpose is to disrupt enemy radar) could possibly destroy or seriously damage the ozone layer protecting Earth from the sun's ultraviolet radiation. Estimates of this danger are very imprecise—if the maximal estimates are true then this factor is sufficient to destroy life.

3. Disruption of transportation and communication could prove critical in the complex modern world.

4. No doubt there will be a (complete or partial) disruption in the production and distribution of food, in water supply and sewage, in fuel and electric service, and in medicine and clothing—all on a continent-wide scale. The public health-care system will be disrupted, sanitary conditions will revert to a medieval level and may become even worse than that. It will be impossible in practice to provide medical assistance to the hundreds of millions who have been wounded, burned, or exposed to radiation.

5. Hunger and epidemics in a context of chaos and devastation could take more lives than the nuclear explosions would take directly. It is also not out of the question that, along with the "ordinary" diseases which will inevitably spread far and wide—influenza, cholera, dysentery, typhus, anthrax, plague, and others—entirely new diseases could arise as the result of the radiation-caused mutation of viruses as well as especially dangerous forms of the old diseases against which people and animals would have no immunity.

6. It is especially difficult to foresee mankind's maintaining any social stability in conditions of universal chaos. Great gangs will kill and terrorize people and struggle among themselves in keeping with the laws of the criminal world: "You die today, I'll die tomorrow."

Of course, our experience of social upheaval and war demonstrates that mankind possesses unexpected reserves; people's vitality in extreme situations surpasses what could have been imagined a priori. But even if mankind were able to preserve itself as a social body, which seems highly unlikely, the most important social institutions—the foundation of civilization—would be destroyed.

In sum, it should be said that all-out nuclear war would mean the destruction of contemporary civilization, hurl man back centuries, cause the deaths of hundreds of millions or billions of people, and, with a certain degree of probability, would cause man to be destroyed as a biological species and could even cause the annihilation of life on earth.

Clearly it is meaningless to speak of victory in a large nuclear war which is collective suicide.

I think that basically my point of view coincides with yours as well as with the opinion of a great many people on earth.

I am also in complete agreement with your other conclusions. I agree that if the "nuclear threshold" is crossed, i.e., if any country uses a nuclear weapon even on a limited scale, the further course of events would be difficult to control and the most probable result would be swift escalation leading from a nuclear war initially limited in scale or by region to an all-out nuclear war, i.e., to general suicide.

It is relatively unimportant how the "nuclear threshold" is crossed—as a result of a preventive nuclear strike or in the course of a war fought with conventional weapons, when a country is threatened with defeat, or simply as a result of an accident (technical or organizational).

In view of the above, I am convinced that the following basic tenet of yours is true: *Nuclear weapons only make sense as a means of deterring nuclear aggression by a potential enemy*, i.e., a nuclear war cannot be planned with the aim of winning it. Nuclear weapons cannot be viewed as a means of restraining aggression carried out by means of conventional weapons.

Of course you realize that this last statement is in contradiction to the West's actual strategy in the last few decades. For a long time, beginning as far back as the end of the 1940s, the West has not been relying on its "conventional" armed forces as a means sufficient for repelling a potential aggressor and for restraining expansion. There are many reasons for this—the West's lack of political, military, and economic unity; the striving to avoid a peacetime militarization of the economy, society, technology, and science; the low numerical levels of the Western nations' armies. All that at a time when the U.S.S.R. and the other countries of the socialist camp have armies with great numerical strength and are rearming them intensively, sparing no resources. It is possible that for a limited period of time the mutual nuclear terror had a certain restraining effect on the course of world events. But, at the present time, the balance of nuclear terror is a dangerous remnant of the past! In order to avoid aggression with conventional weapons one cannot threaten to use nuclear weapons if their use is inadmissible. One of the conclusions that follows here—and a conclusion you draw—is that it is necessary to restore strategic parity in the field of conventional weapons. This you expressed somewhat differently, and without stressing the point.

Meanwhile this is a very important and non-trivial statement which must be dwelt on in some detail.

The restoration of strategic parity is only possible by investing large resources and by an essential change in the psychological atmosphere in the West. There must be a readiness to make certain limited economic sacrifices and, most important, an understanding of the seriousness of the situation and of the necessity for some restructuring. In the final analysis, this is necessary to prevent nuclear war, and war in general. Will the West's politicians be able to carry out such a restructuring? Will the press, the public, and our fellow scientists help them (and not hinder them as is frequently now the case)? Can they succeed in convincing those who doubt the necessity of such restructuring? A great deal depends on it—the opportunity for the West to conduct a nuclear arms policy that will be conclusive to the lessening of the danger of nuclear disaster.

In any case, I am very glad that you (and earlier, in another context, Professor Panofsky) have spoken out in favor of strategic parity in the area of conventional weapons.[5] In conclusion, I should stress especially that a restructuring of strategy could of course only be carried out gradually and very carefully in order to prevent a loss of parity in some of the intermediate phases.

As I have understood them, your further thoughts on nuclear weapons *per se* amount to the following:

It is necessary to conduct a balanced reduction of the nuclear arsenal, and a first stage in this process of nuclear disarmament might be a mutual freeze on the currently existing nuclear arsenals. I will quote you: "Decisions in the

---

[5] *Editor's Note.* The reference here is to Wolfgang K. H. Panofsky, Professor of Physics at Stanford and Director of the Stanford Linear Accelerator Center. Professor Panofsky notes that the statement accurately reflects his views.

area of nuclear weapons should be based simply on the criterion of achieving a reliable deterrent and not on other additional demands relating to nuclear war since, generally speaking, such demands are not limited by anything and are not realistic." This is one of your central theses.

For talks on nuclear disarmament you propose that one quite simple—and, within the limits of the possible, fair—criterion for assessing nuclear strength be worked out. As that criterion you propose taking the sum total of the number of delivery vehicles and the total number of nuclear charges which can be delivered (probably one should assume the maximal number of certain standard or conventional charges which can be delivered by a given type of missile with a corresponding division of the usable weight).

I will begin by discussing that latter proposal of yours (made jointly with your student, Kent Wisner).[6] This proposal seems practical to me. Your criterion takes into account delivery vehicles of various throw-weights by assigning them various weight factors. This is very important—the assigning of an equal weight factor to both the small American missiles and the large Soviet missiles was one of the points for which I, at one time, criticized the SALT I Treaty (while in general viewing the very fact of the talks and the concluding of the Treaty in a positive light). Here, in distinction to criteria using the power of the charge, as a rule not published officially, the number of deliverable charges is easy to determine. Your criterion also takes into account the fact that, for example, five missiles each carrying one warhead have a significant tactical advantage over one large missile carrying five warheads. Of course, the criterion you propose does not encompass all the parameters like distance, accuracy, or degree of vulnerability—they will have to be allowed for supplementarily or, in some cases, not taken into account so as to facilitate agreements.

I hope that your (or some analogous) criterion will be accepted as the basis for negotiations both on intercontinental missiles and (independently) on medium-range missiles. In both cases it will be much more difficult than it now is to insist on unfair conditions in the agreements

---

[6] *Editor's Note.* The proposal was originally set forth in Sidney D. Drell and Kent F. Wisner, "A New Formula for Nuclear Arms Control," *International Security,* Winter 1980/81, pp. 186–194, and is refined in Dr. Drell's "L+ RV: A Formula for Arms Control," *The Bulletin of Atomic Scientists,* April 1982, pp. 28–34.

and possible to move from word to deed more swiftly. Most likely, the very acceptance of your (or an analogous) criterion will require a diplomatic and propaganda struggle—but it's worth it.

From this relatively specific question I will move to one more general, more complex and controversial. Is it actually possible when making decisions in the area of nuclear weapons to ignore all the considerations and requirements relevant to the possible scenarios for a nuclear war and simply limit oneself to the criterion of achieving a reliable deterrent—when that criterion is understood to mean an arsenal sufficient to deal a devastating blow in response? Your answer to this question—while perhaps formulating it somewhat differently—is positive and you draw far-reaching conclusions.

There is no doubt that at present the United States already posseses a large number of submarine-based missiles and charges carried by strategic bombers which are not vulnerable to the U.S.S.R. and, in addition, has silo-based missiles though they are smaller than the U.S.S.R.'s—all these in such amounts that, were those charges used against the U.S.S.R., nothing, roughly speaking, would be left of it. You maintain that this has *already* created a reliable deterrent—independently of what the U.S.S.R. and the United States have and what they lack! Therefore, you specifically consider the building of the MX missile unnecessary and similarly consider irrelevant the arguments which are advanced in support of developing it—the U.S.S.R.'s substantial arsenal of intercontinental missiles with large throw-weight which the United States does not have; and the fact that Soviet missiles and MX missiles have multiple warheads so that one missile can destroy several enemy silos during a missile duel. Therefore you consider it acceptable (with certain reservations) for the United States to freeze the nuclear arsenals of the United States and the U.S.S.R. at their current numerical levels.[7]

---

[7] *Editor's Note.* Professor Drell notes that maintaining the U.S. and Soviet nuclear arsenals at their present numerical levels is not the same as the kind of "freeze" usually discussed today—in that it would not preclude changes in the types of weapons within the numerical level. As to a strict "freeze" as usually discussed, Professor Drell's position, stated in his Grace Cathedral speech, is that "the freeze movement has been very helpful in creating . . . a constituency for arms control. Though I recognize some deficiencies of the freeze as literal policy, I support it and will vote for it as a mandate for arms control . . . ."

Your line of reasoning seems to me very strong and convincing. But I think that the concept presented fails to take into account all the complex realities of the opposition that involves two world systems and that there is the necessity (despite your stance) for a more specific and comprehensive unbiased consideration than a simple orientation toward a "reliable deterrent" (in the meaning of the word as formulated above, i.e., the possibility of dealing a devastating retaliatory strike). I will endeavor to explain this statement.

Precisely because an all-out nuclear war means collective suicide, we can imagine that a potential aggressor might count on a lack of resolve on the part of the country under attack to take the step leading to that suicide, i.e., it could count on its victim capitulating for the sake of saving what could be saved. Given that, if the aggressor has a military advantage in some of the variants of conventional warfare or—which is also possible *in principle*—in some of the variants of partial (limited) nuclear war, he would attempt to use the fear of further escalation to force the enemy to fight the war on his (the aggressor's) own terms. There would be little cause for joy if, ultimately, the aggressor's hopes proved false and the aggressor country perished along with the rest of mankind.

You consider it necessary to achieve a restoration of strategic parity in the field of conventional arms. Now take the next logical step—while nuclear weapons exist it is also necessary to have strategic parity in relation to those variants of limited or regional nuclear warfare which a potential enemy could impose, i.e., it is really *necessary* to examine in detail the various scenarios for both conventional and nuclear war and to analyze the various contingencies. It is of course not possible to analyze fully all these possibilities or to ensure security entirely. But I am attempting to warn of the opposite extreme—"Closing one's eyes" and relying on one's potential enemy to be perfectly sensible. As always in life's complex problems, some sort of compromise is needed.

Of course I realize that in attempting not to lag behind a potential enemy in any way, we condemn ourselves to an arms race that is tragic in a world with so many critical problems admitting of no delay. But the main danger is slipping into an all-out nuclear war. *If* the probability of such an outcome could be reduced at the cost of another ten or fifteen years of the arms race, then perhaps that price must be paid while, at the same time, diplomatic, economic, ideological, political, cultural, and social efforts are made to prevent a war.

Of course it would be wiser to agree now to reduce nuclear and conventional weapons and to eliminate nuclear weapons entirely. But is that now possible in a world poisoned with fear and mistrust, a world where the West fears aggression from the U.S.S.R., the U.S.S.R. fears aggression from the West and from China, and where China fears it from the U.S.S.R., and no verbal assurances and treaties can eliminate those dangers entirely?

I know that pacifist sentiments are very strong in the West. I deeply sympathize with people's yearning for peace, for a solution to world problems by peaceful means; I share those aspirations fully. But, at the same time, I am certain that it is absolutely necessary to be mindful of the specific political, military, and strategic realities of the present day and to do so objectively without making any sort of allowances for either side; this also means that one should not proceed from an a prior assumption of any special peace-loving nature in the socialist countries due to their supposed progressiveness or the horrors and losses they have experienced in war. Objective reality is much more complicated and far from anything so simple. People both in the socialist and the Western countries have a passionate inward aspiration for peace. This is an extremely important factor, but, I repeat, itself alone does not exclude the possibility of a tragic outcome.

What is necessary now, I believe, is the enormous practical task of education so that specific, exact, and historically and politically meaningful objective information can be made available to all people, information that will enjoy their trust and not be veiled with dogma and propaganda. Here one must take into account that, in the countries of the West, pro-Soviet propaganda has been conducted for quite a long time and is very goal-oriented and clever, and that pro-Soviet elements have penetrated many key positions, particularly in the mass media.

The history of the pacifist campaigns against the deployment of missiles in Europe is telling in many respects.

After all, many of those participating in those campaigns entirely ignore the initial cause of NATO's "dual decision"— the change in strategic parity in the 1970s in favor of the U.S.S.R.—and, when protesting NATO's plans, they have not advanced any demands on the U.S.S.R. Another example: President Carter's attempt to take a minimal step toward achieving balance in the area of conventional arms, i.e., to introduce draft registration, met with stiff resistance. Meanwhile, balance in the area of conventional arms is a necessary prerequisite for reducing nuclear arsenals. For public opinion in the West to assess global problems correctly, in particular the problems of strategic parity both in conventional and in nuclear weapons, a more objective approach, one which takes the real world strategic situation into account, is vitally needed.

A second group of problems in the field of nuclear weapons about which I should make a few supplementary remarks here concerns the talks on nuclear disarmament. For these talks to be successful the West should have something that it can give up! The case of the "Euromissiles" once again demonstrates how difficult it is to negotiate from a position of weakness. Only very recently has the U.S.S.R. apparently ceased to insist on its unsubstantiated thesis that a rough nuclear parity now exists and therefore everything should be left as it is.

Now, the next welcome step should be the reduction of the number of missiles—which must include a fair assessment of the *quality* of missiles and other means of delivery (i.e., the number of charges deliverable by each carrier, its range and accuracy, and its degree of vulnerability—the last being greater for aircraft and less for missiles;[8] most likely, it would be expedient to use your criterion, or analogous ones). And what is absolutely at issue here is not moving the missiles beyond the Urals but *destroying* them. After all, rebasing is too "reversible." Of course, one also must not consider powerful Soviet missiles, with mobile launchers and several warheads, as being equal to the now-existing Pershing I, the British and French missiles, or the bombs on short-

---

[8] *Editor's Note:* The reference to greater relative vulnerability of aircraft vis-à-vis missiles apparently refers to vulnerability to defensive measures in the execution of a mission.

range bombers—as the Soviet side sometimes attempts to do for purposes of propaganda.

No less important a problem is that of the powerful silo-based missiles. At present the U.S.S.R. has a great advantage in this area. Perhaps talks about the limitation and reduction of these most destructive missiles could become easier if the United States were to have MX missiles, albeit only potentially (indeed, that would be best of all).

A few words about the military capabilities of powerful missiles: they can be used to deliver the largest thermonuclear charges for destroying cities and other major enemy targets—while for exhausting the enemy's ABM systems there will most likely be a simultaneous use of a "rain" of smaller missiles, false targets and so on. (Much is written about the possibility of developing ABM systems using super-powerful lasers, accelerated particle beams, and so forth. But the creation of an effective defense against missiles along these lines seems highly doubtful to me.) We present the following estimates to give an idea of what a powerful missile attack on a city would be like. Assuming that the maximal power of an individual charge carried by a large rocket would be of a magnitude of 15–25 megatons, we find that the area of complete destruction of dwellings would be 250–400 square kilometers, the area affected by thermal radiation would be 300–500 square kilometers, the zone of radioactive traces (in case of a ground-level explosion) would be 500–1000 kilometers long and 50–100 kilometers wide!

Of equal importance is the fact that powerful MIRVed missiles could be used to destroy compact enemy targets, in particular, similar silo-based enemy missiles. Here is a rough estimate of an attack of that type on launch sites. One hundred MX missiles (the number proposed by the Reagan Administration for the first round of deployment) could carry one thousand 600-kiloton warheads.

Considering the ellipse of concentration[9] and the hardness assumed for the Soviet launch sites, each of the warheads has, according to the data published in the

---

[9] *Editor's Note.* This phrase is a literal translation from the Russian. It apparently refers to the shape and size of the area in which a given missile is likely to land in accordance with its accuracy characteristics. The comparable American term is "circular error probable," or "CEP," defined as the area within which a given missile has a 50-percent chance of landing. Such an area is in fact usually elliptical in shape rather than circular.

American press, a 60-percent probability of destroying one launch site. During an attack on 500 Soviet launch sites, with two warheads targeted for each site, 16 percent will remain undamaged, i.e., "only" 80 missiles.

A specific danger associated with silo-based missiles is that they can be destroyed relatively easily as a result of enemy attack, as I have just demonstrated. At the same time, they can be used to destroy enemy launch sites in an amount four to five times larger than the number of missiles used for the attack. A country with large numbers of silo-based missiles (at the present time this is primarily the U.S.S.R., but if the United States carries out a major MX program, then it too) could be "tempted" to use such missiles first before the enemy destroys them. In such circumstances the presence of silo-based missiles constitutes a destabilizing factor.

In view of the above, it seems very important to me to strive for the abolition of powerful silo-based missiles at the talks on nuclear disarmament. While the U.S.S.R. is the leader in this field there is very little chance of its easily relinquishing that lead. If it is necessary to spend a few billion dollars on MX missiles to alter this situation, then perhaps this is what the West must do. But, at the same time, if the Soviets, in deed and not just in word, take significant verifiable measures for reducing the number of land-based missiles (more precisely, for destroying them), then the West should not only abolish MX missiles (or not build them!) but carry out other significant disarmament programs as well.

On the whole I am convinced that nuclear disarmament talks are of enormous importance and of the highest priority. They must be conducted continuously—in the brighter periods of international relations but also in the periods when relations are strained—and conducted with persistence, foresight, firmness and, at the same time, with flexibility and initiative. In so doing, political figures should not think of exploiting those talks, and the nuclear problem in general, for their own immediate political gains but only for the long-term interests of their country and the world. And the planning of the talks should be included in one's general nuclear strategy as its most important part—on this point as well I am in agreement with you!

The third group of problems which should be discussed here is political and social in nature. A nuclear war could result from a conventional war, while a conventional war is, as is well known, a result of politics. We all know that the world is not at peace. There are a variety of reasons for this—national, economic, and social reasons, as well as the tyranny of dictators.

Many of the tragic events now occurring have their roots in the distant past. It would absolutely be wrong to see only Moscow's hand everywhere. Still, when examining the general trend of events since 1945 there has been a relentless expansion of the Soviet sphere of influence—objectively, this is nothing but Soviet expansion on a world scale. This process has spread as the U.S.S.R. has grown stronger economically (though that strength is one-sided), and in scientific, technological and military terms, and has today assumed proportions dangerously harmful to international equilibrium. The West has grounds to worry that the world's sea routes, Arab oils and the uranium, diamonds, and other resources of South Africa are now threatened.

One of the basic problems of this age is the fate of the developing countries, the greater part of mankind. But, in fact, for the U.S.S.R., and to some degree for the West as well, this problem has become exploitable and expendable in the struggle for dominance and strategic interests. Millions of people are dying of hunger every year, hundreds of millions suffer from malnutrition and hopeless poverty. The West provides the developing countries with economic and technological aid, but this remains entirely insufficient due largely to the rising price of crude oil. Aid from the U.S.S.R. and the socialist countries is smaller in scale and, to a greater degree than the West's aid, military in nature and bloc-oriented. And, very importantly, that aid is in no way coordinated with world efforts.

The hot spots of local conflicts are not dying but are rather threatening to grow into global wars. All this is greatly alarming.

The most acutely negative manifestation of Soviet policies was the invasion of Afghanistan which began in December 1970 with the murder of the head of state. Three years of appallingly cruel anti-guerrilla war have brought incalculable suffering to the Afghan people, as attested by the more than four million refugees in Pakistan and Iran.

It was precisely the general upsetting of world equilibrium caused by the invasion of Afghanistan and by other concurrent events which was the fundamental reason that the SALT II agreement was not ratified. I am with you in regretting this but I cannot disregard the reasons I have just described.

Yet another subject closely connected to the problem of peace is the openness of society and human rights. I use the term the "openness of society" to mean precisely what the great Niels Bohr meant by it when introducing it more than 30 years ago.

In 1948, the U.N.'s member states adopted the Universal Declaration of Human Rights and stressed its significance for maintaining peace. In 1975, the relationship of human rights and international security was proclaimed by the Helsinki Final Act, which was signed by 35 countries including the U.S.S.R. and the United States. Among those rights are: the right to freedom of conscience; the right to receive and impart information within a country and across frontiers; the right to a free choice of one's country of residence and domicile within a country; freedom of religion; and freedom from psychiatric persecution.

Finally, citizens have the right to control their national leaders' decision-making in matters on which the fate of the world depends. But we don't even know how, or by whom, the decision to invade Afghanistan was made! People in our country do not have even a fraction of the information about events in the world and in their own country which the citizens of the West have at their disposal. The opportunity to criticize the policy of one's national leaders in matters of war and peace as you do freely is, in our country, entirely absent. Not only critical statements but those merely factual in nature, made on even much less important questions, often entail arrest and a long sentence of confinement or psychiatric prison.

In keeping with the general nature of this letter, I refrain here from citing many specific examples, but must mention the fate of Anatoly Shcharansky, who is wasting away in Chistopol Prison for the right to be visited by his mother and to write to her, and Yuri Orlov[10] who, now for a third time, has been put for six months in the punishment

---

[10] *Editor's Note.* At the time this open letter was written, Shcharansky was on a hunger strike because he was denied all contact with his family. Shcharansky now lives in Israel and Orlov in the United States. Both men were freed in exchange for Soviet spies.

block of a Perm labor camp, after having been beaten unmercifully in the presence of a warden.

In December 1982 there was an amnesty to honor the U.S.S.R.'s sixtieth anniversary but, just as in 1977 and in the preceding amnesties, there was a point made of excluding prisoners of conscience. So distant is the U.S.S.R. from the principles it proclaims, a country which bears such great responsibility for the fate of the world!

In conclusion I again stress how important it is that the world realize the absolute inadmissibility of nuclear war, the collective suicide of mankind. It is impossible to win a nuclear war. What is necessary is to strive, systematically though carefully, for complete nuclear disarmament based on strategic parity in conventional weapons. As long as there are nuclear weapons in the world, there must be a strategic parity of nuclear forces so that neither side will venture to embark on a limited or regional nuclear war. Genuine security is possible only when based on a stabilization of international relations, a repudiation of expansionist policies, the strengthening of international trust, openness and pluralization in the socialist societies, the observance of human rights throughout the world, the rapprochement—convergence—of the scocialist and capitalist systems, and worldwide coordinated efforts to solve global problems.

February 2, 1983   *Andrei Sakharov*

1983

THE MILITARY ROLE OF NUCLEAR WEAPONS: PERCEPTIONS AND MISPERCEPTIONS

Robert S. McNamara

Robert S. McNamara was Secretary of Defense from 1961 to 1968 and President of the World Bank from 1968 to mid-1981.

The public, on both sides of the Atlantic, is engaged in debate on controversial questions relating to nuclear weapons: the desirability of a nuclear freeze; the deployment of Pershing II and cruise missiles to Western Europe; the production of the MX missile and the B-1 bomber; the development of the neutron bomb; and proposals to reduce the risk of nuclear war by such measures as the withdrawal of tactical nuclear weapons from forward areas and the declaration of a strategy of "no launch on warning."

These questions, however, cannot be thoughtfully discussed, and certainly not adequately answered, until there has been general agreement on the military role of nuclear weapons. If there is confusion in the public mind on this matter, it only mirrors the disagreement among those most familiar with such weapons and their implications.

I would ask the reader momentarily to guess whether the following three statements come from leaders in peace movements:

Reprinted with permission of Mr. McNamara. Copyright © 1983 by Robert S. McNamara.

At the theatre or tactical level any nuclear exchange, however limited it might be, is bound to leave NATO worse off in comparison to the Warsaw Pact, in terms both of military and civilian casualties and destruction . . . To initiate use of nuclear weapons . . . seems to me to be criminally irresponsible.

I am in favor of retaining nuclear weapons as potential tools, but not permitting them to become battlefield weapons. I am not opposed to the strategic employment of these weapons; however, I am firmly opposed to their tactical use on our soil.

The European allies should not keep asking us to multiply strategic assurances that we cannot possibly mean, or if we do mean, we should not want to execute because if we execute, we risk the destruction of civilization.

The answer is that none do. The first is by Field Marshall Lord Carver Chief of the British Defence Staff from 1973 to 1976; the second by General Johannes Steinhoff, former Chief of Staff of the Federal German Air Force; and the third by former Secretary of State Henry A. Kissinger.[1]

And, if one were to accept all three propositions, there follows logically the statement of Admiral Noel A. Gayler, former Commander in Chief of U.S. forces in the Pacific: "There is no sensible military use of any of our nuclear forces. Their only reasonable use is to deter our opponent from using his nuclear forces."[2]

On the other hand, a number of statements by senior officials in the Reagan Administration have suggested that a nuclear war could be limited, Secretary of Defense Caspar Weinberger contends that: "The nuclear option [i.e., early first use of nuclear weapons] remains an important element in deterring Soviet [conventional] attack."[3] And in the same vein, former Secretary of State Alexander Haig, also a former NATO Supreme Commander, concedes that it is unlikely nuclear war could be limited, but argues that "adoption of a policy of no first use would remove a threat which

---

[1] Lord Carver's statement is in *The Sunday Times* (London), February 21, 1982; General Steinhoff's is quoted in Hans Gunther Brauch, "The Enhanced Radiation Warhead: A West German Perspective," *Arms Control Today*, June 1978, p.3; and Mr. Kissinger's in Henry A. Kissinger, "NATO Defense and the Soviet Threat," *Survival*, Nov./Dec. 1979, p. 266 (address in Brussels).

[2] *Congressional Record*, 97th Cong., 1st sess., July 17, 1981, Washington; GPO, 1981, p. S 7835.

[3] Secretary of Defense, *Annual Report to the Congress, FY 1984*, U.S. Department of Defense, February 1, 1983, Washington: GPO, 1983.

deters Soviet aggression and, therefore, would increase the danger of war."[4]

More broadly, President Reagan—in proposing a program to develop an anti-ballistic missile defense in March 1983—said that "our objective should be to move to an impenetrable defense against Soviet nuclear strikes, thereby totally neutralizing their offensive nuclear forces." He added that it would be in our interest for the Soviets to possess a similar defense, thus stating in effect that the Soviet Union and the United States would both be better off if nuclear weapons were totally eliminated. (Under such circumstances, NATO would depend, of course, solely on conventional forces for deterrence of Soviet aggression.) And on June 16, 1983, the President made an even more categorical statement in favor of a non-nuclear world: "I pray for the day when nuclear weapons will no longer exist anywhere on earth."[5]

A similar thought has been expressed by Melvin Laird, Secretary of Defense in the Nixon Administration: "A worldwide zero nuclear option with adequate verification should now be our goal. . . . These weapons . . . are useless for military purposes."[6]

These quotations from European and American political and military leaders show the depth of doubt and division that exists today. It is clear that there are three quite contradictory and mutually exclusive views of the military role of nuclear weapons:

> • Such weapons can be used in a controlled or selective way, i.e., they have a war-fighting role in defense of the NATO nations, Therefore, a strategy of "flexible response," which has been the foundation of NATO's war plans since 1967, including possible "early first use of nuclear weapons," should be continued. Underlying this policy is the belief that NATO can achieve "escalation dominance"—i.e., NATO can prevent the Warsaw Pact from extending the use of nuclear weapons beyond the level NATO chooses, with the implication that a nuclear war once started can remain limited.

[4] Speech in Washington, April 6, 1982.
[5] *The New York Times*, June 17, 1983.
[6] *The Washington Post*, April 12, 1982.

• Any use of nuclear weapons by the United States or the Soviet Union is likely to lead to uncontrolled escalation with unacceptable damage to both sides. Therefore, nuclear weapons have no military use other than to deter first use of such weapons by one's adversary.

• Although initiating the use of nuclear weapons is likely to lead to uncontrolled escalation, with devastation of both societies, the threat of such use by NATO acts as a deterrent to both Soviet conventional and nuclear aggression. It is not practical to build up an equivalent deterrent in the form of conventional forces; therefore the threat of early use of nuclear weapons should never be withdrawn.

I propose to examine these views by exploring four questions:

• What is NATO's present nuclear strategy and how did it evolve?

• Can NATO initiate the use of nuclear weapons, in response to a Soviet attack, with benefit to the Alliance?

• Even if the "first use" of nuclear weapons is not to NATO's advantage, does not the threat of such use add to the deterrent and would not the removal of the threat increase the risk of war?

• If it is not to NATO's advantage to respond to a Soviet conventional attack by the use of nuclear weapons, can NATO's conventional forces, within realistic political and financial constraints, be strengthened sufficiently to substitute for the nuclear threat as a deterrent to Soviet aggression?

Questions of the military utility of nuclear weapons are addressed most realistically in the context of the possibility of warfare in Europe. Throughout the postwar period the security of Europe has been the centerpiece of U.S. foreign policy; it is likely to remain so indefinitely. In no other region have the two great powers deployed so many nuclear weapons. In no other part of the world are military doctrines which specify the use of nuclear weapons granted such wide-ranging credibility.

The use of nuclear weapons has been an integral part of NATO's military strategy since virtually the inception of the alliance.[7]

Shortly after the North Atlantic Treaty was ratified in 1949, estimates were made of the size of the Soviet military threat as a basis for developing NATO's military strategy and force structure. Believing that the U.S.S.R. could muster as many as 175 divisions against Western Europe, NATO military planners concluded that the Alliance would require 96 of its own divisions—which were larger than those of the Soviet Union—in order to mount an adequate defense. This estimate was accepted by the NATO ministers in February 1952 at their annual meeting in Lisbon.

It soon became clear, however, that the member nations were not willing to meet these so-called Lisbon force goals. Instead, the Alliance turned consciously to nuclear weapons as a substitute for the financial and manpower sacrifices which would have been necessary to mount an adequate conventional defense.

That budgetary considerations were a key factor in NATO's decision to rely on nuclear weapons is evident from the following statement by then Secretary of State John Foster Dulles:

The total cost of our security efforts (and those of our Allies) . . . could not be continued long without grave budgetary, economic, and social consequences. But before military planning could be changed the President and his advisers . . . had to make some basic policy decisions. This has been done. The basic decision was to depend primarily upon a greater (nuclear) capacity to retaliate instantly by means and at places of our own choosing. As a result it is now possible to get and to share more basic security at less cost.[8]

Nor was this new emphasis only rhetorical. A Presidential Directive (NSC-162/2) ordered the Joint Chiefs of Staff to plan on using nuclear armaments whenever it would be to the U.S. advantage to do so. Changes were made in the organization and plans of the U.S. Army so that it would

---

[7] An excellent brief history of NATO's conception of the role of nuclear wapons is presented in J. Michael Legge, "Theater Nuclear Weapons and the NATO Strategy of Flexible Response," Santa Monica (Calif.): RAND Corporation, R-2964-FF, April 1983. For this section I have also drawn on unpublished writings of David A. Rosenenberg and David Schwartz.

[8] John Foster Dulles, "The Evolution of Foreign Policy," Department of State Bulletin 36, No. 761, January 25, 1954. p. 108.

be better able to fight on nuclear battlefields. By late 1953, substantial numbers of tactical nuclear weapons—artillery shells, bombs, short-range missiles, nuclear mines, and others—were beginning to be deployed in Europe. The buildup of NATO tactical nuclear weapons continued steadily, peaking in the mid-1960s at around 7,000. Although large numbers of conventional forces were retained on the continent, until the early 1960s their only purpose was seen to be to contain an attack long enough for nuclear strikes to defeat the aggressor.

If there were any doubts about the seriousness of NATO's nuclear threats in the 1950s, they should have been dispelled by the following statement by General Bernard Montgomery, the Deputy Supreme Allied Commander in Europe, who said in late 1954:

I want to make it absolutely clear that we at SHAPE are basing all our operational planning on using atomic and thermonuclear weapons in our own defense. With us it is no longer: "They may possibly be used," It is very definitely: "They will be used, if we are atacked."[9]

By December 1954, the NATO ministers felt comfortable enough with the nuclear strategy to reduce the force level objective from 96 to 30 active divisions. Two years later, the Alliance formally adopted the policy of "massive retaliation" in a document known as MC 14/2.

Whether the balance of nuclear forces between the Warsaw Pact and NATO, as it was developing during the mid-1950s, justified adoption of NATO's nuclear strategy is arguable. But its merit had become questionable to many by the early 1960s. Soon after taking office in January 1961, the Kennedy Administration began a detailed analysis of the policy's strengths and weaknesses.

These studies revealed two major deficiencies in the reasoning that had led to the adoption of MC 14/2: first, the relative balance of NATO and Warsaw Pact conventional forces was far less unfavorable from a Western perspective than had been assumed (the power of Soviet forces had been overestimated and that of NATO forces underestimated); and second, there was great uncertainty as to whether and, if so, how nuclear weapons could be used to NATO's advantage.

---

[9] Address to the Royal United Services Institute, London: cited in Robert E. Osgood, *NATO: The Entangling Alliance*, Chicago: University of Chicago Press, 1962, p. 110.

President Kennedy, therefore, authorized me as Secretary of Defense to propose, at a meeting of the NATO ministers in Athens in May 1962, to substitute a strategy of "flexible response" for the existing doctrine of "massive retaliation."

The new strategy required a buildup of NATO's conventional forces, but on a scale that we believed to be practical on both financial and political grounds. Instead of the early massive use of nuclear weapons, it permitted a substantial raising of the nuclear threshold by planning for the critical initial responses to Soviet aggression to be made by conventional forces alone. The strategy was based on the expectation that NATO's conventional capabilities could be improved sufficiently so that the use of nuclear weapons would be unnecessary. But, under the new doctrine, even if this expectation turned out to be false, any use of nuclear weapons would be "late and limited."

Our proposal of the new strategy was the result of the recognition by U.S. civilian and military officials that NATO's vastly superior nuclear capabilities, measured in terms of numbers of weapons, did not translate into usable military power. Moreover, we understood that the initial use of even a small number of strategic or tactical nuclear weapons implied risks which could threaten the very survival of the nation. Consequently, we, in effect, proposed confining nuclear weapons to only two roles in the NATO context:

• deterring the Soviets' initiation of nuclear war;

• as a weapon of last resort, if conventional defense failed, to persuade the aggressor to terminate the conflict on acceptable terms.

The proposed change in NATO's strategy met with strong opposition.

Some opponents argued that the United States was seeking to "decouple" itself from the defense of Europe. These critics shared our view that a "tactical" nuclear war in Europe would quickly escalate to a strategic exchange involving the U.S. and Soviet homelands, but they saw this danger as the primary factor which deterred Soviet aggression. Any reduction in this prospect, they argued, might cause the Soviets to believe that hostilities could be confined to Central Europe, and thus tempt them into adventures.

Other critics maintained that the proposed buildup of NATO's conventional forces was totally beyond what the Alliance would be willing to support. Still others argued that we had greatly exaggerated the dangers of limited uses of nuclear weapons.

The argument raged for five years. It was not until 1967 that NATO adopted the strategy of "flexible response," inscribing it in a document known as MC 14/3.

The revised strategy proposed to deter aggression by maintaining forces adequate to counter an attack at whatever level the aggressor chose to fight. Should such a direct confrontation not prove successful, the strategy proposed to escalate as necessary, including the initial use of nuclear weapons, forcing the aggressor to confront costs and risks disproportionate to his initial objectives. At all times, however, the flexible response strategy specified that efforts should be made to control the scope and intensity of combat. Thus, for example, initial nuclear attacks presumably would be made by short-range tactical systems in an attempt to confine the effects of nuclear warfare to the battlefield. Even so, the strategy retained the ultimate escalatory threat of a strategic exchange between U.S. and Soviet homelands to make clear the final magnitude of the dangers being contemplated.

"Flexible response" has remained NATO's official doctrine for more than 15 years. Its essential element, however— building sufficient conventional capabilities to offset those of the Warsaw Pact—has never been achieved. Indeed, during the late 1960s and early 1970s, the Alliance may have fallen farther behind its opponent. Although NATO has made considerable strides in improving its conventional posture in more recent years, most military experts believe that the conventional balance continues to favor the Warsaw Pact; they thus conclude that an attack by Soviet conventional forces would require the use of nuclear weapons, most likely within a matter of hours. NATO's operational war plans reflect this belief. The substantial raising of the "nuclear threshold," as was envisioned when "flexible response" was first conceived, has not become a reality.

Before turning to the question whether NATO can initiate the use of nuclear weapons—in response to a Soviet attack—with benefit to the Alliance, I should perhaps comment on the evolution of Soviet nuclear strategy over the past three decades.[10]

For much of the postwar period, Soviet military doctrine appears to have assumed that war between the great powers would include the use of nuclear weapons. Soviet publications stressed the use of both long- and intermediate-range nuclear weapons in the initial hours of a conflict, to destroy concentrations of enemy forces and the ports, airfields, and other facilities necessary to support military operations. And these publications emphasized as well the use of tactical nuclear weapons on the battlefield.

The way that Soviet soldiers trained, the protective clothing and decontamination equipment with which they were equipped, and the nature of their military exercises—which for years always included a nuclear phase—suggested that the written expressions of Soviet military doctrine constituted deadly serious descriptions of the way the U.S.S.R. planned to fight the next war.

In fact, until the mid-1960s, writings of Soviet military officials consistently maintained that the only conflict possible between the great powers was an all-out nuclear war. They asserted, moreover, that it was possible to prevail in such a conflict, and they urged the military and social preparations necessary to ensure that the U.S.S.R. emerged triumphant from any nuclear conflict. It was these writings which, in the late 1970s, were used so devastatingly by opponents of nuclear arms control in the debate on the SALT II Treaty.[11]

By that time, however, this portrayal of Soviet military doctrine was becoming badly out of date.

Official Soviet doctrine changed slightly in the mid-1960s as Soviet writers began to admit the possibility of a "war by stages" in Europe, in which the first phase would be a conventional one. Although they asserted that this initial stage would be very short, and further noted that the conflict "inevitably" would escalate to all-out nuclear war, the previous doctrinal rigidity had been broken.

Soviet experts and military officials debated the inevitability of nuclear escalation throughout the 1960s and

[10] Much of the following discussion is based on James M. McConnell, "The shift in Soviet Military Development from Nuclear to Conventional," manuscript to be published in *International Security.*

[11] See, for example, Richard H. Pipes, "Why the Soviet Union Thinks It Could Fight and Win a Nuclear War," *Commentary,* July 1977, p. 21.

much of the 1970s. By the time of a famous speech of Leonid Brezhnev at Tula in 1977, the question seems to have been settled: Soviet theorists then admitted the possibility of a major protracted war between East and West in which nuclear weapons would not be used.

Indeed, the Soviets now officially maintain that they would not be the first to make use of nuclear weapons. As stated by Defense Minister Ustinov in 1982: "Only extraordinary circumstances—a direct nuclear aggression against the Soviet state or its allies—can compel us to resort to a retaliatory nuclear strike as a last means of self-defense."[12]

This is a new position for the U.S.S.R. It was first articulated by Brezhnev at the U.N. Special Session on Disarmament in June 1982. Previously, Soviet spokesmen had only been willing to say that they would not use nuclear weapons against non-nuclear powers.

Along with this shift has come the explicit and repeated renunciation of what Soviet spokesmen had declared for more than two decades: that it was possible to fight and win a nuclear war. All Soviet writers and political leaders addressing this question now solemnly declare that "there will be no victors in a nuclear war."

Does this doctrinal shift suggest that the U.S.S.R. is no longer prepared for nuclear war in Europe? Certainly not. In addition to the deployment of intermediate-range SS-20 missiles, the Soviets are busily modernizing their shorter-range nuclear-armed missiles in Europe (SS-21s, SS-22s and SS-23s). Two types of artillery tubes capable of firing nuclear charges have been seen with Soviet units in Eastern Europe in larger numbers in recent years. And there are now many more aircraft capable of delivering nuclear bombs deployed with Soviet forces in Europe than was the case not many years ago.

The U.S.S.R. is obviously prepared to respond if NATO chooses to initiate nuclear war. I turn, then, to the question of whether NATO can initiate the use of nuclear weapons, in response to a Soviet conventional attack, with benefit to the Alliance.

Doubts about the wisdom of NATO's strategy of flexible response, never far from the surface, emerged as a major

[12] D. F. Ustinov, "We Serve the Homeland and the Cause of Communism," *Ivestia* May 27, 1982.

issue in the late 1970s; debate has intensified in the ensuing years. The debate hinges on assessments of the military value of nuclear weapons.[13]

The nuclear balance has changed substantially since the Kennedy Administration first proposed a strategy of flexible response. Both sides have virtually completely refurbished their inventories, increasing the number of weapons of all three different types—battlefield, intermediate-range and strategic—and vastly improving the performance characteristics of both the weapons themselves and their delivery systems. Because the Soviet Union was so far behind the United States in the early 1960s, the quantitative changes, at least, appear to have been more favorable for the U.S.S.R. The ratio of warheads on strategic and intermediate-range launchers, for example, has shifted from a very great U.S. advantage in 1962 to a far more modest advantage at present.

As the Soviet Union moved toward and then achieved rough parity in strategic and intermediate-range forces, a crucial element of the flexible response strategy became less and less credible.

It will be recalled that the strategy calls for the Alliance to initiate nuclear war with battlefield weapons if conventional defenses fail, and to escalate the type of nuclear weapons used (and therefore the targets of those weapons), as necessary, up to and including the use of strategic forces against targets in the U.S.S.R. itself. Given the tremendous devastation which those Soviet strategic forces that survived a U.S. first strike would now be able to inflict on this country, it is difficult to imagine any U.S. President, under any circumstances, initiating a strategic strike except in retaliation against a Soviet nuclear strike. It is this reasoning which led to the much criticized statement by Henry Kissinger in Brussels in 1979, quoted earlier. Kissinger's speech was criticized not for its logic however, only for frankness.

In short, a key element of the flexible response strategy has been overtaken by a change in the physical realities of the nuclear balance. With huge survivable arsenals on both sides, strategic nuclear weapons have lost whatever military utility may once have been attributed to

[13] For this section, I have drawn on *Arms Control and National Security*, Washington: Arms Control Association, 1983; the unpublished writings of William W. Kaufmann and Leon V. Segal; and recent discussions with military and civilian experts, not all of whom agree with one another.

them. Their sole purpose, at present, is to deter the other side's first use of its strategic forces.

Thus, given that NATO would not be the first to use strategic nuclear weapons, is it conceivable that the first use of tactical weapons would be to its military advantage?

The roughly 6,000 NATO nuclear weapons now deployed in Europe consist of warheads for air-defense missiles, nuclear mines (known as atomic demolition munitions), warheads for shorter range missiles, nuclear bombs, and nuclear-armed artillery shells. The North Atlantic Assembly recently published a rough estimate of the distribution of these weapons.[14] It is shown in the table below.

U.S. NUCLEAR WARHEADS LOCATED IN EUROPE IN 1981

Bombs to be delivered by aircraft	1069
Artillery Shells (203mm and 155mm)	2000
Missiles: Pershing IA	270
Lance and Honest John	910
Air Defense and Atomic Demolition Charges	1750
Total	5999

According to these figures, nuclear artillery shells comprise the largest portion of the stockpile, about one-third of the total. They are also the weapons which cause the greatest worry.

There are two types of nuclear artillery shells in the NATO inventory: those for 155mm howitzers and those for 203mm cannons. Both the howitzers and cannons are dual-capable: they can be used to fire shells containing conventional explosives as well as nuclear weapons. The precise ranges of these systems are classified, but most accounts put them at around ten miles. Because of the short range of nuclear artillery, the guns and their nuclear shells tend to be deployed close to the potential front lines of any conflict in Europe—there are, in effect, approximately 2,000 short-range nuclear warheads concentrated at a few sites close to the German border.

[14] North Atlantic Assembly's Special Committee on Nuclear Weapons in Europe, *Second Interim Report on Nuclear Weapons in Europe*, Report to the Committee on Foreign Relations, U.S. Senate, 98th Cong., 1st sess, Washington: GPO, 1983, p. 59.

Atomic demolition munitions (ADMs) also raise particular concerns. These weapons are about 25 years old and probably no longer reliable. Intended to block mountain passes and other "choke points" on potential Soviet invasion routes, their effects would be felt on NATO territory. Moreover, to be effective they would have to be emplaced before a war actually began. Such an action could aggravate a crisis and would probably contribute to the likelihood of the war starting. At the same time, because ADMs would have to be used at the very onset of the conflict, their use would mean that NATO had not tested the ability of its conventional forces to contain a Warsaw Pact invasion.

Similar problems beset nuclear-armed air defense systems. They are old and probably unreliable. And they are intended for use at the onset of a conflict—to disrupt the large-scale air attacks that would accompany a Warsaw Pact invasion—thus negating the strategy of "flexible response."

In an acute crisis in which the risk of war seemed to be rising, these characteristics of nuclear artillery, mines, and air defense systems would be likely to lead to pressures on NATO's political leaders, particularly the U.S. President, to delegate the authority to release these weapons to the military commanders on the scene. Whether such authority were delegated or not, it is these characteristics—most importantly the vulnerability of NATO's nuclear artillery—which lead many observers to predict that the Alliance would use tactical nuclear weapons within hours of the start of a war in Europe. In effect, whether its military or civilian leaders retained decision authority, NATO would be likely to face the choice of either using its battlefield nuclear weapons or seeing them overrun or destroyed by the enemy.

In terms of their military utility, NATO has not found it possible to develop plans for the use of nuclear artillery which would both assure a clear advantage to the Alliance and at the same time avoid the very high risk of escalating to all-out nuclear war.

Current guidelines on the initial use of nuclear weapons date from the early 1970s.[15] A former member of the High Level Group, a special official committee established

---

[15] *NATO Facts and Figures.* 10th edition, Brussels: NATO Information Service, 1981, pp. 152–54.

by NATO in 1978 to examine the Alliance's nuclear posture, stated recently that despite discussions lasting for years, "NATO has not yet managed to agree on guidelines for the follow-on use of nuclear weapons if a first attempt to communicate NATO's intentions through a controlled demonstrative use did not succeed in persuading the adversary to halt hostilities."[16]

Two problems stand in the way.

First, since the assumption is made that NATO will be responding to a Warsaw Pact invasion of Western Europe, and since the artillery has short range, the nuclear explosions would occur on NATO's own territory. If a substantial portion of the 2,000 nuclear artillery shells were fired, not only would the Warsaw Pact likely suffer heavy casualties among its military personnel, but large numbers of NATO's civilian and military personnel also would likely be killed and injured. There also would be considerable damage to property, farmland and urbanized areas.[17]

Moreover, there is no reason to believe that the Warsaw Pact, now possessing tactical and intermediate-range nuclear forces at least comparable to those of NATO, would not respond to NATO's initiation of nuclear war with major nuclear attacks of its own. These attacks would probably seek most importantly to reduce NATO's ability to fight a nuclear war by destroying command and control facilities, nuclear weapon storage sites, and the aircraft, missiles, and artillery which would deliver NATO's nuclear weapons. Direct support facilities like ports and airfields would likely also be attacked in the initial Warsaw Pact nuclear offensive. Thus the war would escalate from the battlefield to the rest of Western Europe (and probably to Eastern Europe as well, as NATO retaliated).

What would be the consequences of such a conflict? In 1955 an exercise called "Carte Blanche" simulated the use

---

[16] *Second Interim Report on Nuclear Weapons in Europe, op. cit.*, p. 7.

[17] A 100-kiloton tactical nuclear weapon would be needed to destroy approximately 50 to 100 armored fighting vehicles (e.g., tanks) in dispersed formation, the equivalent of a regiment. Such a weapon would create general destruction (of structures and people) in a circle with a diameter of 4.5 miles (an area of 15 square miles). A blast circle of this size, in typical Western European countries, would be likely to include two or three villages or towns of several thousand persons. In addition, depending on the nature of the weapon and height of burst, a much larger area could be affected by fallout. Several hundred of such tactical nuclear weapons would be required to counter an armored development in Europe. See Seymour J. Deitchman, *New Technology and Military Power*, Boulder (Colo.): Westview Press 1979, p. 12.

of 335 nuclear weapons, 80 percent of which were assumed to detonate on German territory. In terms of immediate casualties (ignoring the victims of radiation, disease, and so forth), it was estimated that between 1.5 and 1.7 million people would die and another 3.5 million would be wounded—more than five times the German civilian casualties in World War II—in the first two days. This exercise prompted Helmut Schmidt to remark that the use of tactical nuclear weapons "will not defend Europe but destroy it."[18]

Additional studies throughout the 1960s confirmed these results. They prompted two of my former aides in the Pentagon to write in 1971:

Even under the most favorable asumptions, it appeared that between 2 and 20 million Europeans would be killed, with widespread damage to the economy of the affected area and a high risk of 100 million dead if the war escalated to attacks on cities.[19]

Have the more modern weapons deployed on both sides in the 1970s changed the likely results of nuclear war in Europe? Not at all! A group of experts was assembled recently by the U.N. Secretary General to study nuclear war. They simulated a conflict in which 1,500 nuclear artillery shells and 200 nuclear bombs were used by the two sides against each other's military targets. The experts concluded that as a result of such a conflict there would be a minimum of five to six million immediate civilian casualties and 400,000 military casualties, and that at least an additional 1.1 million civilians would suffer from radiation disease.[20]

It should be remembered that all these scenarios, as horrible as they would be, involve the use of only a small portion of the tactical nuclear weapons deployed in Europe, and assume further that none of the roughly 20,000 nuclear warheads in the U.S. and U.S.S.R.'s central strategic arsenals would be used. Yet portions of those central forces are intended for European contingencies: the United States has allocated 400 of its submarine-based Poseidon warheads for

---

[18] Helmut Schmidt, *Defense or Retaliation?* New York: Praeger, 1962, p. 101: Schmidt's comment and the exercise result are cited in Jeffrey Record, *U.S. Nuclear Weapons in Europe*, Washington: Brookings, 1974.
[19] Alain C. Enthoven and K. Wayne Smith, *How Much is Enough?* New York: Harper & Row, 1971, p. 128.
[20] *General and Complete Disamament: A Comprehensive Study on Nuclear Weapons: Report of the Secretary General, Fall 1980*, New York: United Nations, 1981.

use by NATO; the Soviet Union, it is believed, envisions as many as several hundred of its ICBMs being used against targets in Europe.

Is it realistic to expect that a nuclear war could be limited to the detonation of tens or even hundreds of nuclear weapons, even though each side would have tens of thousands of weapons remaining available for use?

The answer is clearly no. Such an expectation requires the assumption that even though the initial strikes would have inflicted large-scale casualties and damage to both sides, one or the other—feeling disadvantaged—would give in. But under such circumstances, leaders on both sides would be under unimaginable pressure to avenge their losses and secure the interests being challenged, and each would fear that the opponent might launch a larger attack at any moment. Moreover, they would both be operating with only partial information because of the disruption to communications caused by the chaos on the battlefield (to say nothing of possible strikes against communications facilities). Under such conditions, it is highly likely that rather than surrender, each side would launch a larger attack, hoping that this step would bring the action to a halt by causing the opponent to capitulate.[21]

It was assessments like these which led not only Field Marshall Lord Carver, but Lord Louis Mountbatten and several other of the eight retired Chiefs of the British Defence Staff as well, to indicate that under no circumstances would they have recommended that NATO initiate the use of nuclear weapons.

And it was similar considerations which led me to the same conclusions in 1961 and 1962.

It is inconceivable to me, as it has been to others who have studied the matter, that "limited" nuclear wars would remain limited—any decision to use nuclear weapons would imply a high probability of the same cataclysmic consequences as a total nuclear exchange. In sum, I know of no plan which gives reasonable assurance that nuclear weapons can be used beneficially in NATO's defense.

I do not believe the Soviet Union wishes war with the West. And certainly the West will not attack the U.S.S.R,

---

[21] This discussion is based on a presentation by Vice Admiral John M. Lee (Ret.) in St. Petersburg, Florida, December 17, 1981.

or its allies. But dangerous frictions between the Warsaw Pact and NATO have developed in the past and are likely to do so in the future. If deterrence fails and conflict develops, the present NATO strategy carries with it a high risk that Western civilization, as we know it, will be destroyed.

If there is a case for NATO retaining its present strategy, that case must rest on the strategy's contribution to the deterrence of Soviet aggression being worth the risk of nuclear war in the event deterrence fails.

The question of what deters Soviet aggression is an extremely difficult one. To answer it, we must put ourselves in the minds of several individuals who would make the decision to initiate war. We must ask what their objectives are for themselves and their nation, what they value and what they fear. We must assess their proclivity to take risks, to bluff, or to be bluffed. We must guess at how they see us— our will and our capabilities—and determine what we can do to strengthen their belief in the sincerity of our threats and our promises.

But most difficult of all, we must evaluate all these factors in the context of an acute international crisis. Our problem is not to persuade the Soviets not to initiate war today. It is to cause them to reach the same decision at some future time when, for whatever reason—for example, an uprising in Eastern Europe that is getting out of control, or a U.S.-Soviet clash in Iran, or conflict in the Middle East— they may be tempted to gamble and try to end what they see as a great threat to their own security.

In such a crisis, perceptions of risks and stakes may change substantially. What may look like a reckless gamble in more tranquil times might then be seen merely as a reasonable risk. This will be the case particularly if the crisis deteriorates so that war begins to appear more and more likely. In such a situation, the advantages of achieving tactical surprise by going first can appear to be more and more important.

As I have indicated, the launch of strategic nuclear weapons against the Soviet homeland would lead almost certainly to a response in kind which would inflict unacceptable damage on Europe and the United States—it would be an act of suicide. The threat of such an action, therefore, has lost all credibility as a deterrent to Soviet conventional aggression, The ultimate sanction in the flexble response strategy is thus no longer operative. One cannot build a credible deterrent on an incredible action.

Many sophisticated observers in both the United States and Europe, however, believe that the threat to use tactical nuclear weapons in response to Warsaw Pact aggression increases the perceived likelihood of such an action, despite its absolute irrationality. They believe that by maintaining battlefield weapons near the front lines, along with the requisite plans and doctrines to implement the strategy that calls for their use, NATO confronts the Warsaw Pact with a dangerous possibility which cannot be ignored.

In contemplating the prospect of war, they argue, Soviet leaders must perceive a risk that NATO would implement its doctrine and use nuclear weapons on the battlefield, thus initiating an escalatory process which could easily get out of control, leading ultimately to a devastating strategic exchange between the two homelands. It is not that NATO would coolly and deliberately calculate that a strategic exchange made sense, they explain, but rather that the dynamics of the crisis would literally force such an action—or so Soviet leaders would have to fear.

Each step of the escalation would create a new reality, altering each side's calculation of the risks and benefits of alternative courses of action. Once U.S. and Soviet military units clashed, perceptions of the likelihood of more intense conflicts would be changed radically. Once any nuclear weapon had been used operationally, assessments of other potential nuclear attacks would be radically altered.

In short, those who assert that the nuclear first use threat serves to strengthen NATO's deterrent believe that, regardless of objective assessments of the irrationality of any such action, Soviet decisionmakers must pay attention to the realities of the battlefield and the dangers of the escalatory process. And, in so doing, they maintain, the Soviets will perceive a considerable risk that conventional conflict will lead to the use of battlefield weapons, which will lead in turn to theater-wide nuclear conflict, which will inevitably spread to the homelands of the superpowers.

In fact, it was a desire to strengthen the perception of such a likely escalation that led NATO to its December 1979 decision to deploy the new intermediate-range Pershing II and the nuclear-armed cruise missiles in Europe. The key element in that decision was that the new missiles would be capable of striking Soviet territory, thus presumably precipitating a Soviet attack on U.S, territory and a U.S. retaliation against the whole of the Soviet homeland. The new weapons thus "couple" U.S. strategic forces with the forces deployed in Europe, easing concerns that the Soviets might perceive a firebreak in the escalatory process. So long as the escalation is perceived to be likely to proceed smoothly, the logic continues, then the Warsaw Pact will be deterred from taking the first step—the conventional aggression—which might start the process.

But for the same reason that led Henry Kissinger to recognize that a U.S. President is unlikely to initiate the use of U.S.-based strategic nuclear weapons against the U.S.S.R., so a President would be unlikely to launch missiles from European soil against Soviet territory.

And, as I have indicated, more and more Western political and military leaders are coming to recognize, and publicly avowing, that even the use of battlefield nuclear weapons in Europe would bring greater destruction to NATO than any conceivable contribution they might make to NATO's defense.

There is less and less likelihood, therefore, that NATO would authorize the use of any nuclear weapons except in response to a Soviet nuclear attack. As this diminishing prospect becomes more and more widely perceived—and it will—whatever deterrent value still resides in NATO's nuclear strategy will diminish still further.

There are additional factors to be considered. Whether it contributes to deterrence or not, NATO's threat of "first use" is not without its costs: it is a most contentious policy, leading to divisive debates both within individual nations and between the members of the Alliance; it reduces NATO's preparedness for conventional war; and, as I have indicated, it increases the risk of nuclear war.

Preparing for tactical nuclear war limits NATO's ability to defend itself conventionally in several ways. Nuclear weapons are indeed "special" munitions. They require special command, control and communications arrangements. They require special security precautions. They limit the flexibility with which units can be deployed and military plans altered. Operations on a nuclear battlefield would be very different than those in a conventional conflict; NATO planning must take these differences into account.

Moreover, since most of the systems that would deliver NATO's nuclear munitions are dual-purpose, some number of aircraft and artillery must be reserved to be available for nuclear attacks early in a battle, if that became necessary, and are thus not available for delivering conventional munitions.

Most important, though, the reliance on NATO's nuclear threats for deterrence makes it more difficult to muster the political and financial support necessary to sustain an adequate conventional military force. Both publics and governments point to the nuclear force as the "real deterrent," thus explaining their reluctance to allocate even modest sums for greater conventional capabilities.

To the extent that the nuclear threat has deterrent value, it is because it in fact increases the risk of nuclear war. The location of nuclear weapons in what would be forward parts of the battlefield; the associated development of operational plans assuming the early use of nuclear weapons; the possibility that release authority would be delegated to field commanders prior to the outset of war—these factors and many others would lead to a higher probability that if war actually began in Europe, it would soon turn into a nuclear conflagration.

Soviet predictions of such a risk, in fact, could lead them to initiate nuclear war themselves. For one thing, preparing themselves for the possibility of NATO nuclear attacks means that they must avoid massing their offensive units. This would make it more difficult to mount a successful conventional attack, raising the incentives to initiate the war with a nuclear offensive. Moreover, if the Soviets believe that NATO would indeed carry out its nuclear threat once they decided to go to war—whether as a matter of deliberate choice or because the realities of the battlefield would give the Alliance no choice—the Soviets would have virtually no incentive not to initiate nuclear war themselves.

I repeat, this would only be the case if they had decided that war was imminent and believed there would be high risk that NATO's threats would be fulfilled. But if those two conditions were valid, the military advantages to the Warsaw Pact of preemptive nuclear strikes on NATO's nuclear storage sites, delivery systems, and support facilities could be compelling.

The costs of whatever deterrent value remains in NATO's nuclear strategy are, therefore, substantial. Could not equivalent deterrence be achieved at lesser "cost"? I believe the answer is yes. Compared to the huge risks which the Alliance now runs by relying on increasingly less credible nuclear threats, recent studies have pointed to ways by which the conventional forces may be strengthened at modest cost.

Writing in these pages only 15 months ago, General Bernard Rogers, the present Supreme Allied Commander in Europe, stated that major improvements in NATO's conventional forces were feasible at a modest price.[22] These improvements, he said, would permit a shift from the present strategy requiring the early use of nuclear weapons to a strategy of "no early use of nuclear weapons." General Rogers estimated the cost to be approximately one percent per year greater than the three percent annual increase (in real terms) which the members of NATO, meeting in Washington, had agreed to in 1978.

An experienced Pentagon consultant, MIT Professor William W. Kaufmann, has taken General Rogers' suggestions of four percent annual increases in NATO defense budgets and analyzed how those funds could best be allocated to improve the Alliance's conventional defenses. After an exhaustive analysis, he concluded that a conventional force could be acquired which would be sufficiently strong to give a high probability of deterring Soviet aggression without threatening the use of nuclear weapons.[23] Recently, an international study group also analyzed the possibilities for moving away from NATO's present nuclear reliance.[24] The steering committee of this "European Security Study" included among its members General Andrew Goodpaster, who once served as the Supreme Allied Commander in Europe; General Franz-Josef Schulze, a German officer, formerly Commander in Chief of Allied Forces in Central Europe; and Air Marshall Sir Alasdair

---

[22] General Bernard W. Rogers, "The Atlantic Alliance: Preceptions for a Difficult Decade," *Foreign Affairs*, Summer 1982, pp. 1145–56.
[23] Unpublished writings of Professor Kaufmann.
[24] *Strengthening Conventional Deterrence in Europe*, Report of the European Security Study, New York: St. Martin's Press, 1983.

Steedman, formerly the United Kingdom's military representative to NATO.

Their report concludes that NATO's conventional forces could be strengthened substantially at very modest cost—a total of approximately $20 billion which would be spent over a period of five or six years. For comparative purposes, note that the MX missile program is expected to cost $18 billion over the next five years.

The European Security Study stated that to constitute an effective deterrent, NATO's conventional forces did not have to match specific Soviet capabilities. Rather, these forces need only be strong enough to create serious concerns for Warsaw Pact planners whether or not their attack could succeed.

To accomplish this, the study concluded, NATO's conventional forces would have to be able to:

- stop the initial Warsaw Pact attack;
- erode the enemy's air power;
- interdict the follow-on and reinforcing armored formations which the Pact would attempt to bring up to the front-lines;
- disrupt the Pact's command, control, and communications network; and
- ensure its own secure, reliable, and effective communications.

The report outlines in detail how NATO could achieve these five objectives utilizing newly available technologies, and accomplishing with conventional weapons what previously had required nuclear munitions. These technological advances would permit the very accurate delivery of large numbers of conventional weapons, along with dramatic improvements in the ability to handle massive quantities of military information.

The effectiveness of the new technologies was testified to most recently by Senator Sam Nunn, a leading congressional expert on European defense issues:

We now have at hand new conventional technologies capable of destroying the momentum of a Soviet invasion by means of isolating the first echelon of attacking forces from reinforcing follow-on echelons. These technologies . . . capitalize on three major advances. The first is the substantially improved lethality of improved conventional munitions . . . . The second is the . . . growing capability of microelectronics to enhance the rapid collection, processing, distribution, and abilty to act upon infomation about the size, character, location, and movement of enemy units . . . . The third is improved ability to move and target quickly large quantities of improved conventional firepower against enemy force concentrations.[25]

The potential of these new conventional technologies is great. Unfortunately, they have not yet been accepted by any NATO nation for incorporation in its force structure and defense budget.

Moving from the present situation to revised strategic doctrines, war plans, and force structures to implement a conventional deterrent strategy could not be accomplished overnight. Still, over time NATO's basic strategy could be modified within realistic political and financial constraints.

The process should probably begin with a statement by the Alliance, at a summit meeting of its heads of government, of its intention to move to a policy of deterrence of Soviet conventional force aggression solely through the use of non-nuclear forces.

This statement of intention could then be followed by the drafting of detailed plans and programs. Conventional defense improvements would be set in motion; new doctrines debated and approved; parliaments tested as to their willingness to support the modestly larger expenditures necessary for strengthening the conventional forces.

In the meantime, immediate steps could be taken to reduce the risk of nuclear war. For example:

• Weapons modernization programs designed to support a strategy of early use of nuclear weapons—such as those to produce and deploy new generations of nuclear artillery shells—could be halted.

• The Alliance's tactical nuclear posture could be thoroughly overhauled, with an eye toward shifting to a posture intended solely to deter the first use of nuclear weapons by the Warsaw Pact. Such a shift would permit major reductions in the number of nuclear weapons now deployed with NATO's forces in Europe; no more, and probably less, than 3,000 weapons would be sufficient. Those weapons which raise the most serious problems of release authority and pressures for early use—atomic demolition munitions and nuclear air defense systems—could be withdrawn immediately. Nuclear artillery could be withdrawn as the program to improve the conventional posture was implemented.

 • The creation of a zone on both sides of the border in Europe, beginning in the Central Region, within which no nuclear munitions could be deployed, could be proposed to the Soviets.[26] The agreement to create such a zone could be verified by on-site inspections on a challenge basis. The Soviet Union has stated officially that it supports a nuclear-free zone, although it proposed that the width of the zone be far greater than is likely to be acceptable to NATO. If agreement could be reached on the size of the zone and adequate methods established to verify compliance with the agreement, such an agreement could build confidence on both sides that pressures for early use of nuclear weapons could be controlled. The January 1984 international conference in Stockholm on confidence-building measures in Europe would be a logical forum in which to discuss such an idea.

I now want to conclude this article by stating unequivocally my own views on the military role of nuclear weapons.

Having spent seven years as Secretary of Defense dealing with the problems unleashed by the initial nuclear chain reaction 40 years ago, I do not believe we can avoid serious and unacceptable risk of nuclear war until we recognize—and until we base all our military plans, defense budgets, weapon deployments, and arms negotiations on the recognition—that *nuclear weapons serve no military*

---

[26] Such a proposal was made in the Report of the International Commission on Disarmament and Security Issues, *Common Security: A Program for Disarmament*, London: Pan Books, 1982.

purpose whatsoever. They are totally useless—except only to deter one's opponent from using them.

This is my view today. It was my view in the early 1960s.

At that time, in long private conversations with successive Presidents—Kennedy and Johnson—I recommended, without qualification, that they never initiate, under any circumstances, the use of nuclear weapons. I believe they accepted my recommendation.

I am not suggesting that all U.S. Presidents would behave as I believe Presidents Kennedy and Johnson would have, although I hope they would. But I do wish to suggest that if we are to reach a consensus within the Alliance on the military role of nuclear weapons—an issue that is fundamental to the peace and security of both the West and the East—we must face squarely and answer the following questions.

- Can we conceive of ways to utilize nuclear weapons, in response to Soviet aggression with conventional forces, which would be beneficial to NATO?

- Would any U.S. President be likely to authorize such use of nuclear weapons?

- If we cannot conceive of a beneficial use of nuclear weapons, and if we believe it unlikely that a U.S. President would authorize their use in such a situation, should we continue to accept the risks associated with basing NATO's strategy, war plans and nuclear warhead deployment on the assumption that the weapons would be used in the early hours of an East-West conflict?

- Would the types of conventional forces recommended by General Rogers, Professor William Kaufmann and the European Security Study, serve as an adequate deterrent to non-nuclear aggression by the U.S.S.R.? If so, are we not acting irresponsibly by continuing to accept the increased risks of nuclear war associated with present NATO strategy in place of the modest expenditures necessary to acquire and sustain such forces?

• Do we favor a world free of nuclear weapons? If
so, should we not recognize that such a world would not
provide a "nuclear deterrent" to Soviet conventional aggression? If we could live without such a deterrent then, why
can't we do so now—thereby moving a step toward a non-
nuclear world?

1984

ARMS CONTROL AND THE PREVENTION OF WAR

Joseph S. Nye, Jr.

Joseph S. Nye, Jr. is professor of government at Harvard University. From 1977 to 1979 he served as Deputy to the Under Secretary of State for Security Assistance, Science and Technology, and chaired the National Security Council Group on Nonproliferation of Nuclear Weapons. His most recent books are *Living with Nuclear Weapons* and *The Making of America's Soviet Policy*.

The recent public upsurge of concern about nuclear weapons and nuclear war—the second such upsurge in the nuclear era—has rekindled interest in arms control. But the relationship between the prospect of nuclear war and the current talks on nuclear arms reductions is not that obvious. Some skeptics believe that the current arms reductions talks are more a palliative for public opinion than a serious means of reducing the risk of nuclear war. And the terminology "controlling arms" seems to focus on symtoms rather than the deeper causes of nuclear war.

Early formulations of nuclear arms control theory set three basic objectives: reducing the risk of nuclear war; reducing the damage done by nuclear war should it occur; and reducing the costs of arms races. Early theory stressed

Reprinted with permission. This essay originally appeared in the *Washington Quarterly*, Vol. 7, Number 4. Copyright © 1984 by The Center for Strategic and International Studies and the Massachusetts Institute of Technology Press.

informal reciprocity as much as formal treaties, and unilateral as much as bilateral measures.[1] Over the years, however, arms control has come to be associated with formal bilateral negotiation of treaties for reduction in numbers of arms. It is in this latter sense that there is uncertainty about the relationship between arms control and reducing the risks of nuclear war.

Risk of Nuclear War

What are the risks of nuclear war? No one knows; statistics are of little help and estimating the risk is fraught with danger. As Amos Tversky has pointed out, "People have no sensible mental model for dealing with very improbable events. So they either ignore them entirely and assume they will not happen, or, if forced to consider them, grossly overestimate their likelihood."[2] In recent years, public opinion polls have shown anything from one-third to one-half of the American public saying that they expected nuclear war with the Soviet Union within the next few years.[3] In contrast, my informal and unscientific polling of a few score of nuclear experts over the past year has produced a modal answer of expectations of nuclear war between the United States and the Soviet Union in the next decade of about one chance in one hundred. The range of answers among experts, however, stretched from one in five to one in a million. This compares with a known probability of being killed in a automobile accident in the same period of about one chance in four hundred. The point is not to prove that the public or the experts are wrong, but merely to remind us of the range of uncertainty in any estimates of the risks of nuclear war.

Despite the uncertainty, these subjective estimates do make a difference in terms of policy. It is now 24 years since C.P. Snow's prediction of nuclear war within a decade. Some have come to his defense by arguing that if Snow's prediction is correct within a century, he will have been justified. But the difference between a decade and a century makes all the difference in the world when one considers policy

---

[1] For example, see Thomas Schelling and Morton Halperin, *Strategy and Arms Control*, (New York, Twentieth Century Fund, 1961).
[2] Quoted in *New York Times*, December 6, 1983, p. 67.
[3] For example, *Time*, January 2, 1984, p. 51: *The Washington Post National Weekly Edition*, December 5, 1983, p. 12.

responses. If one lives with subjective estimates of the probability of nuclear war that are very high, one may be willing to accept policy responses that themselves involve higher degrees of risk or greater trade-offs of values. If, on the other hand, one believes that the experience of the last four decades proves that nuclear deterrence is extremely stable and nuclear war highly unlikely, one may be willing to bear more risks in one's policy responses. Yet, statistics from the past forty years could be misleading if conditions have changed. Even if one believes that the probabilities of a nuclear war are very low, it is hard to believe that they are zero if one also accepts Murphy's Law as the first principle of government, and fallability as inherent in human nature.

Not only is it difficult to agree on estimates of the absolute risk of nuclear war, it is also difficult to find agreement on trends in probability over time. For example, is the current situation more or less risky than the period of previous concern, 1958—1962? Those who argue that nuclear risk was higher in 1962 point to technical improvements such as permissive action links, improved command, control, and communication (C^3) national technical means of verification, and political factors such as U.S. and Soviet experience in managing crises. Those who argue that the risk is higher in the current period point to the loss of U.S. nuclear superiority; the greater Soviet capability to support forces in Third World areas; the deployment of vulnerable weapons and support systems that place a premium on preemption; doctrinal stress on protracted war-fighting and the deterioration of political dialogue.

In examining such arguments, it is interesting to note the mixture of technical and political factors, and the mixture of arguments which rely upon models which rest upon assumptions about rational actors and those which rest on models which stress bureaucratic and interpersonal politics.[4] Again, policy responses vary accordingly. Within a rational actor framework, the insanity of large-scale nuclear war (i.e., the extreme disproportion between political ends sought and the consequences of the military means used) suggests that nuclear war is very unlikely. At the same time political conflict will occur, and we will need to deter

---

[4] See Graham Allison, *Essence of Decision* (Boston Little Brown, 1971) for elaboration of these distinctions.

a variety of Soviet actions. The risk of nuclear war comes from a Soviet miscalculation of the credibility or capability of our commitment. One way to enhance deterrence is to add nuclear capability so that it is clear we cannot be beaten at the end of a multiple move game (or escalation ladder). Since the risk of deliberate war is low, one can afford to deploy systems (like MX missiles in silos) which are less than optimal in terms of crisis stability, but demonstrate commitment by responding in kind to a Soviet capability.

Another way to enhance deterrence is to demonstrate commitment by raising the stakes through alliances or stationing of various levels of conventional forces. In either case, the effort is to shift the burden of risk (and the uncertainty of escalation) onto the other side, and thereby deter political actions. The success of such a Model I policy of extended deterrence depends upon credibility which, in turn, is an uncertain function of stakes and capabilities. Policy disputes center on what types of capabilities prevent miscalculation in different geopolitical settings.

A Model II perspective gives rise to a very different set of policy concerns. There is no rational way that a nuclear war could start under Model I assumptions, but many ways that it could start through accidents involving men or machines. In Herman Kahn's metaphor about a proliferated world, nuclear deterrence is stable like a ball balanced in a cup until something jolts the cup. "It takes an improbable or implausible force to topple the ball. But some improbable and implausible events will occur and, barring a secular change in the situation, almost with certainty, the ball will eventually fall."[5] Even if the U.S. and Soviet systems are well designed to be accident free under normal circumstances, the risks of accident and malfunction may increase under alert conditions.[6] From this perspective, the critical policy issues are designing redundant, fail-safe, and better C^3 measures into nuclear systems as a means of reducing risks of nuclear war. Obviously, design of nuclear forces to avoid war depends on whether one thinks Model I (miscalculation) or Model II (organizational accident and malfunction) is the risk the more likely path to nuclear war.

---

[5] Herman Kahn, *On Thermonuclear War* (Princeton, Princeton University Press. 1961) p. 493.
[6] See Paul Bracken, *The Command and Control of Nuclear Forces* (New Haven, Yale University Press, 1983).

Paths to Nuclear War

One can imagine any number of specific scenarios for nuclear war with varying and debatable degrees of plausibility. The Harvard Project on "Avoiding Nuclear War" uses the simplifying device of generic paths to nuclear war. These paths are more general than scenarios. Indeed, a number of scenarios can be fitted to any particular path. They are also consistent with a variety of deeper causes or motivations. Essentially, they focus close to the point of precipitation of a nuclear war as a means of simplifying the inordinate complexities of scenarios and motivations, while allowing one to identify factors which affect the likelihood along any given path and actions which could reduce that likelihood (See Table 1.)[7] The five generic paths we have identified for nuclear war between the United States and the Soviet Union are: 1) *surprise attack*—a bolt from the blue attack on the nuclear forces of one of the superpowers; 2) *preemption in crisis*—an attack launched in desparation in time of crisis because one side believes (rightly or wrongly) the other intends soon to strike first; 3) *escalation of conventional war*—battlefield or tactical nuclear weapons are used after a clash of conventional forces; 4) *accidental or unauthorized use*—malfunction of men, machines or systems; 5) *catalytic use*—use of nuclear weapons by third nations or terrorist groups in a manner designed to involve the superpowers.

Surprise attack would probably be preceded by a period of extreme U.S.-Soviet hostility. But hostility alone would not be enough. One of the sides would have to believe that the objective nuclear balance had become sufficiently one-sided that it could expect a net positive advantage from a first strike. Such an advantage in turn would depend upon assumptions of some degree of ability to limit damage from retaliatory strike. Such a belief in turn might rest upon vulnerability of all legs of the strategic forces, belief in the effectiveness of defensive systems, belief that the enemy would not have the political will to retaliate, or belief in the effectiveness of a decapitating first strike.

Without some assumptions about the ability to limit damage, it is hard to envisage the conditions for a surprise

[7] This work is jointly developed with Graham T. Allison and Albert Carnesale as part of a multi-year project supported by the Carnegie Corporation at Harvard's Kennedy School of Government on "Avoiding Nuclear War."

TABLE 1

Generic Paths to Nuclear War	Factors Affecting Likelihood Along Path	Actions to Reduce Likelihood Along Path
Surprise Attack	• Extreme U.S.-Soviet hostility • Objective nuclear balance of U.S.-Soviet forces that allows leaders to expect net positive advantage from first strike (e.g. successful destruction or land-based ICBMs with no retaliation) • Objective C³I that allows leaders to expect net positive advantage from attack (e.g., "decapitation") • Misperceptions-misunderstandings of objective facts about forces or C³I in successful first strikes	• Strength incentives for peace and cooperation • Maintain objective conditions—robust, invulnerable, and redundant strategic nuclear forces—that make any first strike obviously crazy • Maintain objective C³I that is obviously robust, invulnerable, and redundant • Pursue arms control agreements that maintain confidence in retaliatory second strike capabilities while reducing confidence in successful first strike • Develop processes to limit misperceptions-misundestanding of objective conditions
Preemption in Crisis	• Perception that war is imminent and unavoidable • Objective nuclear balance of U.S.-Soviet forces (see above) • Objective C³I (see above) • Misperceptions-misunderstanding (see above)	• Crisis prevention and management • Maintain objective conditions... (see above) • Maintain objective C³I... (see above) • Pursue arms control agreements (see above) • Develop processes to limit misperceptions-missunderstanding... (see above)
Escalation of Conventional War	• Involvement of United States or USSR or both in conventional war • Objective or perceived balance of U.S. or Soviet conventional forces that tempts escalation • Involvement of United States or USSR client state in local war • Misperceptions-misunderstanding of objective factors • Vulnerability, doctrine, location of theater nuclear weapons • Misperceptions-misunderstanding in "fog of war"	• Crisis prevention and management • Objective balance of conventional forces that deters or provides adequate defense • Processes to limit misperceptions-misunderstanding • Reduce vulnerability or and reliance upon theater nuclear forces • Improve theater C³I. • Restrain nuclear proliferation, including particularly creation of nuclear free zones
Accidental or Unauthorized Use	• Numbers, location, devices, and processes for use of nuclear weapons • Communications systems	• Reduce numbers, locations, and improve devices and processes for use (e g., PAL) • Improve C³I
Catalytic Use	• Numbers of third parties with weapons and delivery systems • Sophistication of weapons and delivery systems	• Crisis prevention and management • Restrain nuclear proliferation • Crisis prevention and management • Improve intelligence capabilities

attack, particularly if projections about the climatic effects of a nuclear winter are correct. It is not true that surprise attack requires a belief in victory. The classic surprise attack at Pearl Harbor grew out of Japanese beliefs that it was the least bad alternative they faced rather than faith in victory.[8] In the nuclear age, however, some assumption about damage limitation is necessary for a nuclear attack not to prove to be the worst alternative. Thus if both sides maintain robust, invulnerable, and redundant strategic nuclear forces and C³I capabilities; if the offense maintains the advantage over the defense, and if there are processes of communication which limit any misperceptions about such objective conditions, surprise nuclear attack seems highly unlikely unless one or the other side succumbs to suicidal motivations. It might be argued that a declining Soviet empire faced with a growing U.S. military strength or an effective U.S. defense system might, like Germany facing a resurgent czarist Russia in 1914, decide upon a preventive war and implement it through a surprise attack. Even assuming such worse-case motivations, however, it is difficult to envisage a surprise attack unless the other conditions mentioned above were also present.

Preemption in a crisis might occur in a situation in which one or the other side believed that war was both imminent and unavoidable, and that in such circumstances it is better to go first than to go second. This might involve tactical but not strategic surprise since a crisis would already exist. Both sides would constantly be calculating the interaction effects, watching carefully for any sign of the other side moving to nuclear attack and acting to preempt before it did.

But like a surprise attack, a successful preemptive attack would depend both upon the vulnerability in the other side's strategic forces or C³I, and upon a belief that a retaliatory nuclear strike could be blunted to the point where the resulting damage was restricted below an acceptable level unless one believes that the impending nuclear attack was absolutely unavoidable. If such damage limitation is impossible, there will be strong temptation to believe that the nuclear war is avoidable and to seek last minute negotiations. Thus the preemptive path to nuclear war is

[8] See Scott Sagan, "The Failure of Deterrence: Pearl Harbor and Nuclear Strategy," Ph.D. Dessertation, Harvard University, 1983.

more plausible, the more vulnerable the forces and C³I of the other side, the more one is able to limit damage inflicted upon oneself and the poorer the processes for communication and negotiation in a point of deep crisis.

Nuclear escalation from conventional war would by definition occur in a setting of crisis but might not involve calculations of strategic incentives for or against preemption. On the contrary, it would more likely grow out of objective or perceived changes in the balance of conventional forces that one or the other side would be tempted to remedy through the use of tactical nuclear weapons, or from misperceptions and misunderstanding in the "fog of war" which would accompany such a conventional battle between the superpowers. Such an escalation might be deliberate or might arise from miscalculation or might occur by accident. Misperceptions of objective factors—questions of location, vulnerability and doctrine for the use of tactical nuclear weapons, and pressures from allies could all play a role in escalation from a conventional war. Given the incremental nature of the initial choices to use nuclear weapons and the already demonstrated high stakes proven by the conventional battle between the superpowers, escalation from a conventional war strikes me as the most likely path by which a nuclear war might begin.

Obviously, the likelihood of such an escalation depends upon the depth of hostility and existence of crisis in which both superpowers can become involved. The most dangerous crises are those where there is dispute or uncertainty between the superpowers about the symmetry of their stakes or where the instability of local actors can rapidly change preexisting perceptions of relative stakes. Such circumstances for miscalculations point to areas like the Persian Gulf or the Middle East rather than to areas like Europe, where both sides have high stakes which are relatively clearly perceived. Even in Europe, however, one can imagine internal instability in Eastern Europe spilling over into Western Europe in a manner which could lead to conventional confrontation. The prospects for reducing the risks associated with the path of escalation from a conventional war depend upon maintaining a sufficient balance of conventional forces to prevent any prospect of easy victory. Also important are invulnerability of theater nuclear forces to preemptive strikes, and maintaining processes for communication about crisis prevention and management.

Accidental nuclear war has received a good deal of public attention and many people believe that nuclear wars are likely to begin not through decisions of rational government leaders but because of mechanical or human accidents. Jonathan Schell, for example, has written that the "machinery of destruction is complete, poised on a hair trigger, waiting for the 'button' to be pushed by some misguided or deranged human being or for some faulty computer chip to send out the instruction to fire."[9] But this description of the hair-trigger nature of the system ignores the numerous precautions that have been taken to prevent accidents. A two-man rule requires parallel actions by two or more individuals at several stages in the process of communication and carrying out any order to use nuclear weapons. Permissive actions links (PALs) include a highly secure coded signal which must be inserted in the weapons before they can be used. Devices internal to the weapon are designed to insure that an attempt to bypass the PAL system will disarm the weapon. Moreover, the weapons themselves are designed to preclude accidental detonation as a result of exposure to heat blast or radiation. There is reason to believe that the Soviets share our concern with unauthorized and accidental war and there is reason to believe that they have taken measures to prevent it. Thus the prospects of accidental nuclear war are probably less than most dramatic accounts would lead one to believe.

Nonetheless it would be foolish to be complacent about accidents. Not only are all human systems subject to breakdown, but mechanical accidents and human frailties could become increasingly dangerous in times of deep crisis or conventional war during which time command centers would be threatened or destroyed. Moreover, there are certain inherent dilemmas in preventing accidental use of nuclear weapons which have thus far kept us from putting PALs on some systems such as submarines. There is always an uneasy balance between the degree of control required to insure that the weapons are not used accidentally and the degree of usability required to insure that the weapons would be used if needed. If it were certain that a weapon could never be used, the weapon would not contribute to deterrence. Because of the trade off between weapons that

---

[9] *The Fate of the Earth,* (New York, Knopf, 1982) p. 182.

are usable enough to provide credible deterrence but not so usable as to invite unintended use, there is always going to be some danger of accidental or unauthorized use. Nonetheless, procedures could be developed which reduce the numbers, locations and vulnerability of nuclear weapons and improve the devices and processes for controlling their use.

Catalytic nuclear war would occur if a third country or a terrorist group were to use nuclear weapons in a manner which deliberately or accidentally involved the superpowers. Unknown detonations or attacks by planes painted with colors of the opposing country or unexplained sinking of submarines at a time of deep crisis might serve as such triggers. The tendency to orient our intelligence collection primarily against the other superpower could reinforce the chances of a mistaken estimate at a time of crisis. In the next decade or two, one of the major contenders for playing such a catalytic role would have to be France, China or Israel. But looking further out into the future, if one imagined a rapid rate of proliferation of nuclear weapons, the number of candidates for attempts at catalytic action might increase. Restraints on nuclear proliferation and improvement in handling sensitive nuclear materials, broadened intelligence capabilities, and procedures for communication between the superpowers during crisis between the superpowers, all can help reduce the prospects of catalytic nuclear war. This path does not seem a major threat in the next decade, but it is a serious concern in a longer time horizon.

While nuclear war among the superpowers would have the most serious consequences, there is always the possibility of a nuclear war among minor powers or by a lesser nuclear power against a superpower. In principle, the overwhelming nuclear capability of the superpowers should deter any attack from a minor nuclear power as long as the rational assumptions underlying deterrence hold. But if one assumes that small or new nuclear powers may have weak command and control and communications systems, both politically and technically, then many of the restraints that help to reduce the risk of nuclear war between the superpowers may not hold in a situation involving minor nuclear powers. Indeed, the incentives to preempt among countries with weak and vulnerable new, nuclear weapons systems make them the most likely candidates for the first use of nuclear weapons since Nagasaki. Even if the overwhelming capabilities of the superpowers would deter any direct use by a smaller nuclear power against the superpower, it is quite possible that in areas such as the Middle East or the Persian Gulf, U.S. troops could be affected by the capabilities of new nuclear powers. While this path is not likely to lead to a major nuclear war, it might still lead to serious implications and damage inflicted on a superpower. Moreover, the United States, with its open political system, is far more vulnerable to terrorist attacks than the closed Soviet society.

The prospects of a nuclear war arising from new nuclear capabilities are not great in the short run of a decade (with the possible exception of South Asia). But the probabilities increase both with time and in the extent that there is relaxation in superpower efforts to restrain the rate of proliferation of nuclear capabilities. The risks of nuclear war along this path are strongly affected by the priority given to policies to restrain nuclear proliferation, policies for improved controls in the handling of special nuclear materials, and efforts to limit or resolve regional conflicts.

Levels of Causation and Types of Responses

With any complex event, we often distinguish precipitating, contributory, and deep causes. For example, the assassination of the Austrian archduke and rigidity of mobilization schedules were precipitating causes of World War I; the Austro-Russian competition in the Balkans and Serbian adventurism were contributory or intermediate causes; and the increased rigidity in European alliances was a deep cause. Or to use the simple metaphor of starting a fire: a match is precipitating cause; kindling is an intermediate cause; and the piling up of logs is a deep cause.

We can differentiate three dimensions of risk reduction measures in these terms. Crisis management refers to measures to deal with a crisis once it has begun, and to prevent the precipitating factors that could lead to war. Crisis prevention refers to efforts to deal with intermediate or contributory causes that give rise to crises in the first place. Long-range stability relates to efforts to deal with the basic causes of conflict inherent in the U.S.-Soviet relationship. All three levels are part of nuclear risk reduction. At each level, confidence building measures and stabilization devices can be designed to increase openness and predictability, provide warning and reassurance, and demonstrate a common interest. In other words, a nuclear risk reduction strategy can reach the deeper as well as the more immediate causes of nuclear war that are the focus of the generic paths discussed in Table 1.

For example, among the steps related to deeper causes are measures designed to remove some of the primary or most dangerous sources of potential U.S.-Soviet conflict. Peaceful settlement of regional disputes—with or without Soviet cooperation—can be of profound importance in reducing the risks of nuclear war. In a world where more than a hundred countries suffer from poverty, rapid social change, and fragile political institutions, this may seem an impossible task. Certainly one must establish priorities. Some Third World crises are more likely fuses to superpower conflict than others. Among the most dangerous are those where both sides have high stakes, but there is ambiguity or uncertainty about the relative interests. Policy devices that encourage effective communication about such issues can play a key role in the crisis prevention and management aspects of nuclear risk reduction.

Not all measures for crisis prevention need involve U.S. and Soviet discussions. Some measures to defuse situations with dangerous fuses will be unilateral—for example, U.S. economic aid in the Caribbean, or U.S. efforts to achieve peace in the Middle East, or more generally, U.S. prudence in the definition of our interests in Third World situations. Others may be multilateral, as with efforts to solve the Namibia conflict, or efforts to strengthen United Nations or regional organization peacekeeping capabilities.

The fact that some types of nuclear crisis prevention and management measures can be unilateral points to the importance of domestic political factors in a strategy for nuclear risk reduction. Indeed, some might say that in terms of susceptibility to policy intervention, domestic measures deserve the highest priority.

Domestic factors are included in all the paths to nuclear war listed in Table 1. The prospects of surprise attack would be heightened if domestic politics led to a "lulling effect" in which the prospective victim let its defenses atrophy and appeared vulnerable or if domestic politics in a potential aggressor nation were dominated by groups which felt they had "no acceptable alternatives." The possibility of preemption in a crisis might be increased by domestic debate that suggested the imminence of a first strike, or by psychological stress that led to a misreading of signals. Escalation of conventional war could be affected by domestic political pressures in the losing state; increased military demands and procedures during war, the simultaneous occurrence of a leadership struggle; or psychological breakdown under stress—just to name a few factors. Accidental war can similarly be affected by psychological stress or poor control procedures, and catalytic war might be affected by intelligence rigidly geared to bipolarity or inadequate procedures for dealing with terrorists. One way to categorize these types of domestic factors, and to direct attention to appropriate domestic policy responses is along the lines (political, bureaucratic, psychological) suggested in Table 2.

In short, many of the measures for reducing the risk of nuclear war do not require negotiation with the Soviet Union. They are susceptible to policy responses which are domestic and unilateral. As with the question or levels of causation, a sensible strategy for nuclear risk reduction must look at all types of possible actions, and give priority to those most susceptible to policy intervention. In fact, if one looks at a number of measures for nuclear risk reduction that are listed in Table 3, it is striking how many of them can be treated as unilateral initiatives.[10] This is not to belittle the arms control items in the second column of the table, but it does indicate that a dry spell for formal treaty arms control need not mean the end of efforts to reduce the risk of nuclear war.

Long-Run Stabilization and the Latent Roles of Arms Control

Stability can have several meanings in U.S.-Soviet relations. Political stability is difficult to agree upon because the two societies have different ideological perceptions of the legitimacy of the status quo over the long run. On the other hand, both sides may find common prudential interests in interim or specific situations of political stability in which

[10] Not all these measures are recommended. Many need detailed examination. For preliminary discussion, see Robert MacNamara. "What the U.S. Can Do," *Newsweek,* December 5,1983, pp. 48-55; and William Perry, "Measures to Reduce the Risk of Nuclear War," *Orbis,* Winter 1984.

TABLE 2
Avoiding Nuclear War: Domestic Factors

Domestic Factors	Policy Actions
1. *Political*	• Vigilant defense debate
• "Lulling effects"	
• Sense of desperation	• Provide alternatives
• Media war scares	• Presidential leadership
• Leadership challenge	• Be wary of assumption that opponent is acting in a unified manner
2. *Bureaucratic:*	• Examine and improve SOPs
• Standard operating procedures (SOPs)	
• Civil-military relations	• SOPs for civilian control in crisis
• Inadequate intelligence	• Improve intelligence capabilities
• Bureaucratic conflict	
• Presidential control	• Bureaucratic "filters"
• Redundant channels	
3. *Psychological:*	• Training and preparation
• Stress and assessment of risk	
• Crisis atmosphere and group think	• Multiple advocacy
• Insanity	• Screening, PALS, redundancy

TABLE 3
Nuclear Risk Reduction Measures

	Unilateral	Bilateral/Multilateral
Military Doctrine	No early use No decapitation No launch on warning No second use until communication	
Force Structure	PALs Improved C³I Improve conventional forces Reduce battlefield nuclear systems Clarify dual use systems De-MIRV ICBMs Deploy less vulnerable systems	START INF Space CTB
Communication	Test Notification	Upgrade hotline Crisis center Expand SCC "TAC Talks"
Political Stabilization	Regional crisis settlement Improve regional organizations Limit commitments to LDCs	Crisis prevention talks Revive UN peacekeeping

long-run questions of legitimacy can be begged. Moreover, both sides may also discover joint interests in crisis stability (the absence of incentive to preempt in a crisis), and a less vigorous arms race if economic constraints continue to grow.

Given the different nature of the two societies, explicit agreement on long-run stabilization will not be easy. But given also that there is some finite probability of nuclear deterrence failing by accident or miscalculation, a strategy for nuclear risk reduction cannot ignore the possibility of trying to ameliorate the basic conditions of conflict, however slow that may be. As argued above, the secretive nature of Soviet society and the disparate nature of the two societies enhances the dangers of miscalculation as a path to war. Thus one of the goals of long-run nuclear risk reduction measures is to increase the transparency and predictability in the U.S.-Soviet relationship as a means of reducing the chances of miscalculation. The aim is to poke holes in the black box.[11] A second goal of such measures is the canonical confidence building measures (CBM) goal of demonstrating the existence of common interests between the two rivals. The pursuit of such goals would involve strategies of increased contacts and exchanges, particularly those which develop in a climate of reciprocity. There are a variety of such exchanges and contacts; the following discussion deals with those in the military domain.

Viewed from this perspective, the process of arms control talks can be seen as a potentially significant CBM and stabilization measure. All too often, arms control efforts have been judged solely in terms of formal treaties and reductions in numbers of existing weapons. But arms control can also contribute to the enhancement of transparency and reciprocity in the relationship. When one compares the discussions in the 1950s with those of today, it is evident that the Soviet Union has gradually come to disclose more information. Provisions such as noninterference with national technical means; regular meetings of delegations and of the Standing Consultative Commission; acceptance of cooperative surveillance measures (such as in the Treaty on Peaceful Explosions); and provisions for exchange of

---

[11] For elaboration, see J. S. Nye (ed.), *The Making of America's Soviet Policy* (New Haven, Yale University Press, 1984).

information and establishment of common data bases are cases in point.

In fact, if one wished to enhance the role of arms control as a CBM or stabilization measure, one might supplement the existing negotiations by incorporating them in a broader framework of nuclear stabilization talks. Such an approach would have several tracks. Tactical air command talks would deliberately be designed to enhance transparency and communication rather than to reach reductions. They might include, for example, regular meetings between the Chairman of the Joint Chiefs of Staff and his Soviet counterpart. They would not necessarily seek a particular agreement but would discuss specific problems relating to stability- and confidence-building measures, such as occur in the context of current agreements for controlling naval incidents at sea. In fact, this might be a significant, if less obvious, role for a joint crisis-notification center. Officially, it would coordinate U.S. and Soviet reactions if a nuclear weapon were exploded by a terrorist group or a Third World country, but it might also involve the exchange of information more generally in relation to stabilization measures.

Another track would be regular force structure discussions that would not try to reach a negotiated outcome or agreement but would involve discussion of future defense plans. Yet another track in the nuclear-stabilization framework could consist of seeking limited agreement where possible. We have seen examples of this approach relating to physical areas: fencing off Antarctica from the arms race, for example, or fencing off the seabeds from nuclear weapons. We have also seen it in certain technologies. Whatever the merits of particular proposals—the list can be readily multiplied—the larger point is that formal arms reduction talks are only part of the repertoire of arms control when approached as a strategy for nuclear risk reduction.

Naturally, there are certain risks to approaching arms control as a CBM or stabilization measure. One danger is that public opinion in democracies would be lulled by the comforting existence of the process and would underinvest in defense. The effect of SALT in the 1970s is sometimes cited as an example. On the other hand, this lulling effect can be exaggerated. U.S. defense budgets declined in the 1970s as a result of changing domestic priorities and reaction to the Vietnam War, well before SALT I, and the debate over the SALT II probably accentuated attention to defense issues. In any case, overall Soviet political behavior was probably more important in its effects on U.S. opinion than the existence of arms control talks. Recent events have shown that arms control may be a domestic political necessity in democracies. If so, it can be better designed to fill its role as a nuclear risk reduction measure.

Conclusion

The basic conflict between the United States and Soviet Union has deep roots and will persist for a long time. During that time, there will be some danger of a breakdown of deterrence. The paths are outlined in Table 1. The most likely path is through miscalculation of intentions and escalation in an area of ambiguous interests in the Third World. A somewhat less probable, but still significant, path to breakdown would be through accident, mistake or chaos surrounding unforeseen events in situations where the two military forces confront each other. Further in the future, and somewhat lower in probability, is the prospect of catalytic nuclear war started by a third party. Least likely of the paths is a pure "bolt out of the blue" surprise attack.

A variety of measures can be taken to reduce the risk of nuclear war along each of these paths. Many of the confidence building measures that stress early warning (such as notification of multiple missile launches) are aimed at the lowest probability paths. Other measures such as improving physical communications (such as the hot line upgrade), or sharing and evaluating information about third party explosions (such as a joint crisis center) are useful in dealing with managing a crisis that has already begun, but are not very significant in preventing crises from arising in the first place. Because they often deal with less probable paths to nuclear war, or only with precipitating rather than deeper causes, CBMs are often treated as marginal in value and priority.

It would be a mistake to ignore even such modest improvements in lowering nuclear risks. But it would also be a mistake to constrain a strategy for nuclear risk reduction to measures that deal with the least likely paths (in Table 1) or only the precipitating rather than deeper causes. A serious strategy for nuclear risk reduction should work across the whole range of paths and proximity of causes. Those measures that deal with dangers of miscalculation between a closed and an open society should not be neglected simply because they are more political and less technical. On the other hand, particularly if there is a climate of deteriorating relations, it may be easier to start with more limited and technical measures. But such measures (e.g., the joint crisis control center) should be designed with an eye to their potential (perhaps subsequent) effect on broader and longer-term confidence building measures. Similarly, arms control and other negotiations should be designed to give long-term transparency and communication considerations as prominent a priority as the signing of formal arms reduction treaties. In the broad sense that includes informal discussions and unilateral measures, arms control can play a significant role in a strategy to reduce the risk of nuclear war.

1984

THE NUCLEAR DEBATE

Robert W. Tucker

Robert W. Tucker is a professor at the Johns Hopkins University School of Advanced International Studies and President of the Lehrman Institute. He wishes to thank Michael Mandelbaum, Josef Joffe and Paul Dyster for their help in the preparation of this essay.

In the almost four decades since the appearance of nuclear weapons, concern over the dangers these weapons raise has varied markedly. A preoccupation with nuclear weapons has characterized only a very few, and even among these few anxiety over the prospects of nuclear war has not been a constant. Beyond the nuclear strategists and a small entourage, the nuclear question has not evoked a steady level of attention, let alone of anxiety. On the contrary, the attention of foreign policy elites, and even more the general public, has swung from one extreme to the other and within a brief period of time.

Thus at the outset of the Kennedy Administration, a preoccupation with the prospect of nuclear war characterized a portion of the foreign policy elites, but hardly the public at large. That preoccupation, in part the product of high and sustained international tension and in part the response to Administration calls for measures of civil defense, quickly dissipated in the wake of the Cuban missile crisis. Within the period of scarcely a year it had virtually

---

Reprinted with permission of *Foreign Affairs*. Copyright © 1984 by *Foreign Affairs*.

disappeared. Yet there had been no significant change in the
strategic relationship between the United States and the
Soviet Union. Nor had the arms competition between the
two powers been significantly altered. Certainly the 1963
partial test ban did not alter this competition, whether by
making it less intense or less dangerous than it had been
earlier. But the test ban did signal that the political relationship between the two states had changed modestly for the
better and might register still further improvement. A
substantial and even dramatic change in outlook toward the
prospects of nuclear war went hand in hand with a changing political relationship.

A generation later, the same process, only now working in the opposite direction, marked the outset of the
Reagan Administration. On this occasion, an anti-nuclear
weapons movement developed that was unprecedented in
the breadth of support it appeared to enjoy. In this respect,
there is no real comparison between the anti-nuclear movement of a generation ago and that of today. Whereas the
movement of yesterday represented little more than the stir-
ring of a few, the movement of the 1980s assumed major
proportions. Even so, the appearance of the later movement
was almost as sudden as the disappearance of the earlier one.
As late as the winter of 1979-80 there was little to indicate
that nuclear weapons would become the critical issue of
public life and discourse they did become by the summer
of 1981.

The sudden rise of the anti-nuclear weapons movement and the attendant debate over nuclear strategy must
be attributed in the first place to a renewed fear of war with
the Soviet Union. By the same token, it also reflects a decline
in the faith by which we have come to live in the nuclear
age. For we are nearly all believers in deterrence, and this
despite the different ways in which this faith may be expressed. We are nearly all believers if only for the reason
that once we seriously admit nuclear war as a distinct
historical possibility, we not only conjure up a very dark
landscape but one in which our accepted categories of
political and moral thought no longer seem relevant. In the
still alien world of nuclear weapons, it is only a faith in deterrence that preserves continuity with a familiar past.

The idea of deterrence is, of course, as old as the
history of human conflict. But the functions that strategies

of nuclear deterrence are expected to serve and the expectations these strategies have raised are as novel as the weapons on which deterrence today rests. If nuclear deterrence is indeed something new under the sun, it is so not only because of the weapons but because of the expectations it has evoked. These expectations constitute the core of faith and their intensity has invested nuclear deterrence with a reliability that is tantamount, for all practical purposes, to certainty. In turn, faith in the effectiveness of deterrence is largely a function of the consequences generally expected to follow from the use of nuclear weapons. By a psychological mechanism as simple as it is pervasive, it is assumed that if the results of an act are inconceivable, the act itself must be inconceivable. The death of a nation is an event difficult to conceive, and the extinction of humanity far more so.

Nor is this all. It is faith in the effectiveness of deterrence that has enabled us to entertain what otherwise would prove to be irreconcilable convictions: a continued readiness to threaten the use—even the first use—of nuclear weapons to preserve interests deemed vital, but at the same time a conviction that nuclear war would in all likelihood destroy the ends for which it is waged; a belief, if not in the moral rectitude, then at least in the moral neutrality of a deterrence strategy, but also a disbelief that the use of nuclear weapons could ever be morally justified; these and other convictions can be reconciled if only the expectations placed in a deterrent strategy are strong enough. With enough faith in deterrence there is no need to torture oneself over the justification for ever employing nuclear weapons; the issues arising from the use of these weapons deal with a contingency that has been virtually excluded from our vision of the future.

The faith commonly placed in deterrence has never gone unquestioned. The history of strategic thought in the nuclear age is, after all, a history of the persisting controversy between the deterrence faithful and the deterrence skeptics, between those who believe that deterrence follows from the existence of nuclear weapons and those who believe a credible theory of use must be developed if deterrence is to be assured. The nature of that controversy is often misrepresented, not least of all by the participants themselves. It cannot properly be characterized simply as one "between those who wish to give nuclear weapons a war-deterring and those who want to give them a war-fighting role."[1] Those accused of wishing to give nuclear weapons a war-fighting role have not abandoned deterrence. At least, they have never admitted to doing so. Instead, they insist that the effort to fashion a war-fighting role for nuclear weapons, however precarious and even abortive that effort may ultimately prove, is undertaken in the first instance in order to enhance their role as a deterrent. The deterrence skeptics do not deny deterrence. They do deny a faith that is given, in the manner of all true believers, unconditional expression.

To the deterrence faithful, the position of the skeptics has always smacked of apostasy and perhaps never more so than today. To be sure, the faithful no less than the skeptics have regularly warned against the dangers of taking deterrence for granted. Still, there is a world of difference between what skeptics have understood taking deterrence for granted to mean and what true believers have understood it to mean. To the believer, deterrence is not only an inherent property of nuclear weapons, it is very nearly a self-sufficient property. "The strategy," one of them declares, "is determined by the weapon. The missiles have only to exist and deterrence is the law of their existence."[2] Deterrence is the law of their existence by virtue of their inordinate and uncontrollable destructiveness. Given this destructiveness, the failure of deterrence is not the beginning but the end of strategy. This being so, if deterrence fails, the only rational course is to end the conflict as quickly as possible and without regard to calculations of relative advantage. McGeorge Bundy, in a recent elaboration of the concept of "existential deterrence," echoes the well-known dictum of Bernard Brodie in declaring that if deterrence ever breaks down "the attention of both sides must be driven toward the literally vital need for *ending* the nuclear battle if possible, not winning it."[3]

[1] Theodore Draper, "Nuclear Temptations," *The New York Review of Books*, January 19, 1984, p. 45.

[2] Leon Wieseltier, *Nuclear War, Nuclear Peace*, New York: Holt, Rinehart & Winston, 1985, p. 38. This is, of course, the essential rationale for "existential deterrence." At the dawn of the nuclear age Bernard Brodie provided the first formulation of existential deterrence in observing that "everything about the atomic bomb is overshadowed by the twin facts that it exists and that its destructive power is fantastically great." Bernard Brodie, ed., *The Absolute Weapon*, New York: Harcourt Brace. 1945, p. 52.

[3] McGeorge Bundy, "The Bishops and the Bomb," *The New York Review of Books*, June 10, 1983, p. 4. In an essay written at the end of his life, Bernard Brodie declared that: "The main war goal upon the beginning of a strategic nuclear exchange would surely be to terminate it as quickly as possible and with the least amount of damage possible—on both sides." Bernard Brodie, "The Development of Nuclear Strategy," *International Security*, Spring 1978, p. 79.

The controversy over the necessary and sufficient conditions of deterrence is more intense today than it has ever been. This persisting debate does not, in the end, turn on technical considerations, though the disputants regularly foster that mistaken impression. Instead, what is ultimately at issue are varying judgements about the character and aspirations of the Soviet regime and, to a lesser extent, the American government. Whether asymmetries in strategic systems have political significance, whether some capacity for war-fighting is a necessary element of deterrence, are not issues that, at bottom, can be resolved by technical considerations but only by one's assessment of the two great adversaries. Among the priesthood of experts, the nuclear debate is not primarily a debate over nuclear weapons but a debate over politics. In this debate, both sides share a common faith; but how they interpret the conditions of faith depends on what they believe to be the truth about the Soviet-American conflict.

Thus, for all their differences, which are surely serious enough, the two sides to this familiar controversy not only believe in deterrence, they also believe broadly in the strategic status quo and are hostile to apocalyptic visions. By contrast, such visions are a hallmark of the anti-nuclear movement that has arisen in recent years. The view that nuclear war has become ever more likely, and that if we continue along our present course we will transform a possibility into a probability, is given frequent expression. Jonathan Schell has attributed the "collapse of deterrence" to nothing other than the buildup of nuclear stockpiles. "Possession inevitably implied use," he declares, "and use was irremediably senseless."[4] The crisis in deterrence stems, at bottom, from nothing more than the "continuing reliance on nuclear arms." George Kennan reaches a similar conclusion and attaches to it similar urgency. "The clock is ticking; the remaining ticks are numbered; the end of their number is already in sight."[5]

We may call this view that of "existential disaster." Nuclear weapons have only to exist in sufficient numbers and destructiveness to render disaster likely. Time is the great nemesis. It is so if only because no social contrivance—of

[4] Jonathan Schell. "Reflections: The Abolition," *The New Yorker*, January 2, 1984, pp. 64–5.

[5] George Kennan, *The Nuclear Delusion*, New York: Pantheon Books, 1983, p. 231.

which deterrence is one—can go on indefinitely without a breakdown. As is true of virtually all aspects of the nuclear debate today, this conviction was articulated a generation earlier. In 1961, the novelist and scientist C.P. Snow wrote: "Within, at the most, ten years, some of these bombs are going off. . . . *That* is the certainty. On the one side, therefore, we have a finite risk. On the other side we have a certainty of disaster. Between a risk and a certainty, a sane man does not hesitate."[6] Snow's forecast was made in the same spirit and on behalf of the same purpose—far-reaching measures of arms control—that today move Jonathan Schell and George Kennan. But whereas Snow's message could only be directed profitably to a quite restricted audience, Schell and Kennan have a potential audience that is far larger. And while Snow's prophecy was one of limited catastrophe, Schell and Kennan entertain a vision of a nuclear exchange that would "put an end to our own species."[7]

In retrospect, what seems remarkable is that for virtually a generation the issue of nuclear weapons had not been of central concern in public life. Certainly, the years between the Cuban missile crisis and the Soviet Union's invasion of Afghanistan had not been without portentous developments in the spheres that provoke so much anxiety today—changes in the strategic balance, the technology of nuclear weaponry and East-West crises. Yet these developments did not begin to provoke a comparable anxiety.

In one view, a heightened sensitivity to the dangers of nuclear weapons simply reflects the heightened perils of the competition in arms or the "arms race." In the 1983 pastoral letter of the American Catholic bishops, we read that "the dynamic of the arms race has intensified" and that one compelling reason for the letter is the growing dangers this dynamic holds out.[8] The nuclear freeze movement has been largely predicated on the belief that the danger of nuclear war in the late 1980s and 1990s will be greater than ever before because of weapons systems that, in the words of a movement leader, "will increase the pressure on both

---

[6] C. P. Snow, "The Moral Un-Neutrality of Science," *Science*, January 27, 1961, p. 259.

[7] Schell, *op. cit.*, p. 44.

[8] "The Challenge of Peace: God's Promise and Our Response," *Origins*, May 19, 1983, p. 1.

sides to use their nuclear weapons in a crisis, rather than risk losing them in a first strike."[9] *The New York Times'* national security correspondent expresses the concern that: "In 10 to 15 years, new technologies now being developed and tested could, if deployed, fundamentally and irretrievably undermine the basic philosophy that has been the center of both sides' nuclear strategy—mutual deterrence."[10] These technological developments promise to lead to ever greater "crisis instability." New weapons of greater accuracy and speed will at once sharpen the fear of preemptive attack while encouraging the hope of undertaking such an attack successfully should this prove necessary. And ever more complex command and control systems will, beyond a certain level of alert, make increasingly difficult the efforts of political leaders to retain effective control over their nuclear forces.[11]

What is crucial to this view is the contention that in certain circumstances the new technologies and the systems for controlling them will prove very dangerous. These circumstances are those of severe crises. In normal circumstances, by contrast, the dangers of the arms race have markedly diminished, when compared to a generation ago. The likelihood of accidental war is substantially lower today and the prospects of a preventive war, of a nuclear strike from out of the blue, are not seen by most expert observers as measurably enhanced. For the residual uncertainties that attend the use of nuclear weapons are such that a coldly planned attack appears almost certain to remain beyond the purview of rational policy choice. To contend otherwise in the case of the Soviet Union requires the assumption that Soviet leadership today is, or tomorrow will be, quite determined to impose its will on us in circumstances that cannot reasonably be interpreted as forcing it to do so and despite having to pay a price that is so high as to be without any real precedent. There is virtually no evidence to support such assumptions.

It is, then, only in periods of severe crisis that the effects of the arms race are properly seen as critical. The

---

[9] Randall Forsberg, "Call to Halt The Nuclear Arms Race," in Randall Forsberg *et al.*, *Seeds of Promise: The First Real Hearings on the Nuclear Arms Freeze,* Andover (Mass): Brick House Publishing, 1983, p. 197.

[10] Leslie H. Gelb, "Is the Nuclear Threat Manageable?", *The New York Times Magazine*, March 4. 1984, p. 26.

[11] The latter danger is examined at length in Paul Bracken, *The Command and Control of Nuclear Forces,* New Haven: Yale University Press, 1983.

case for considering these effects profoundly destabilizing can be summarized thus: when command systems that cannot be reliably controlled are joined to weapons systems that cannot be reliably protected, the stage is set for the breakdown of deterrence. This view rests on a truism that when it seems better to strike than to hold back, deterrence will in all likelihood break down. But what are the conditions in which it will be better to strike than to hold back? The critical condition would be the emerging conviction of one or both sides during a crisis that war is inevitable, but that something—perhaps even a great deal—can be gained by striking first. Another, though less than critical, condition is the existence of weapons that are believed to enhance the promise of preemption, but because of their vulnerability increase the risks of failing to preempt. We may call these weapons destabilizing. But what has brought the crisis to a point where the "destabilizing" weapons seem almost to "take over" and to undermine deterrence is a political process, a process out of which the conviction increasingly grows that war is inevitable.

Before weapons systems can impose a necessity of their own, statesmen must have created a situation that enables them to do so. Whatever their characteristics, weapons as such cannot undermine deterrence. To believe otherwise, as many appear to do, is to dissolve politics into technology. What weapons can do is to require a change in the operation of deterrence. They may do so chiefly by changing the point or the threshold beyond which deterrence breaks down and the conviction then emerges that war is inevitable.

It is the statesman who undermines deterrence. Moreover, he undermines deterrence not so much by permitting the development of the new technologies as by refusing to recognize that these technologies may require corresponding change in the operation of deterrence. If deterrence is in substantial part a function of technology, it must change as technology changes. The contention that the kind of crisis we could have a generation ago over missiles in Cuba would prove much more dangerous today does not mean that deterrence has been partially undermined. It means that the threshold beyond which deterrence is likely to break down has shifted. One of the tasks of the statesman in the nuclear age, and perhaps his most important task, is to adjust the definition of the nuclear threshold to the conditions that determine it and to bend all efforts to ensure that this threshold is neither crossed nor closely approached.

If these considerations have merit, an apparent obsession over the arms race is for the most part an obsession over the conflict that drives the arms race. An anxiety over technology is in reality largely an anxiety over politics. The great worry over deterrence being undermined by the new weapons is in fact a worry over the wisdom, or lack thereof, of political leaders who are today entrusted with the operation of deterrence.

Is the lapse of faith in deterrence to be laid largely at the doorstep of the Reagan Administration? A legion of critics insist that this Administration must bear a major responsibility for a movement and debate that might have been avoided by a government with a less ideological and less bellicose outlook. Whereas previous presidents were sobered by their tragic power to initiate nuclear war, this president is presumably different. He is different because he is in thrall to an ideology that blinds him to the terrible dangers of nuclear war.[12]

The evidence for this blindness consists, in part, of statements made about nuclear weapons and nuclear war by Mr. Reagan as a private citizen or as a candidate for office. Although betraying no particular sophistication about nuclear matters, none of these statements can reasonably be taken as grounds for coming to an apocalyptic view of the future. In the most quoted of his statements, the President responded to a question about whether he believed in the possibility of a limited nuclear war between this country and the Soviet Union in these words: ". . .I could see where you could have the exchange of tactical weapons against troops in the field without it bringing either one of the major powers to pushing the button."[13] Whatever one may think of this response, it scarcely demonstrates the power of ideology in blinding men to the dangers of nuclear war. No doubt, it must arouse those who take as an article of faith that any use of nuclear weapons can only lead to

---

[12] Arthur Schlesinger, Jr., "Foreign Policy and the American Character," *Foreign Affairs,* Fall 1983, p. 13.
[13] Bernard Gwertzman, "President Says U.S. Should Not Waver In Backing Saudi," *The New York Times,* October 18, 1981, p. 1.

an unlimited nuclear exchange. But there are many people who share Mr. Reagan's skepticism in this matter and who are not, by any reasonable definition, blind ideologues. Whether or not limited nuclear war in Europe is possible is not a matter to be settled by faith or ideology. Nor did the President in his reply indicate otherwise. If anything, his response was far less dogmatic than the vast majority of utterances on the subject.

One lesson to be drawn from the Reagan experience is simply the rising sensitivity to any statements about the possible use of nuclear weapons by high public officials, and particularly by the President. Such statements about nuclear weapons or strategy are likely to prove an invitation to trouble. For the public and its elites do not want to be reminded of the basis on which their security ultimately rests. The Reagan Administration badly erred by not taking this aversion sufficiently to heart. Instead of glossing over a subject that could only be dealt with at considerable risk, it responded to inquiries that were put to it, and occasionally even offered some gratuitous elaboration. The responses were neither startling for their novelty nor unreasonable in their substance. On balance, they preserved a striking continuity with positions taken by preceding administrations. Still, in the circumstances of the early 1980s, dominated as they have been by growing Soviet-American tension, responses that might otherwise have gone largely unremarked provoked a series of minor political storms.

The Reagan Administration not only tended to talk too much about nuclear matters, but to use an idiom that seemed to confirm the dark suspicions held by many about its intentions. Thus the dismayed and accusatory reaction to the 1982 Defense Guidance statement with its concept of "prevailing" in a protracted nuclear war. American nuclear forces, a critical passage reportedly read, "must prevail and be able to force the Soviet Union to seek earliest possible termination of hostilities on terms favorable to the United States."[14]

This document did not break new ground. Its essential features added up to little more than a refinement of the Carter Administration's 1980 Presidential Directive 59,

---

[14] Cited Richard Halloran, "Pentagon Draws Up First Strategy for Fighting a Long Nuclear War." *The New York Times*, May 30, 1982, p. 1.

which in turn built on strateglc concepts that may be traced back a generation. From Kennedy to Reagan, no administration has been able to disavow the prospect, however skeptically it may have viewed that prospect, of the controlled use of nuclear weapons. Equally, no administration has been able to disavow the prospect of emerging from a nuclear conflict with some kind of meaningful victory. Unable to disavow these prospects, no administration has been able to disavow the force structure that might make possible fighting a limited nuclear war. It was our least bellicose and most skeptical of recent presidents who declared during his first year in office that the American strategic arsenal "should be strong enough that a possible nuclear war would end on the most favorable terms possible to the U.S."[15] At the time, 1977, these words of Jimmy Carter did not provoke noticeable criticism. It is true that they do not go quite as far as the 1982 Defense Guidance paper. Still, the difference between ending a nuclear war "on terms favorable to the U.S." rather than "on the most favorable terms possible to the U.S." is scarcely great enough to account for the very different receptions given them.

The Reagan Administration has been repeatedly accused of breaking radically from its predecessors in being intent on recapturing the Golden Grail of strategic superiority. This is presumably the meaning of "prevailing," that is, of "concluding hostilities on terms favorable to the U.S.," just as it is the meaning of having a capability that "will insure that the Soviet leadership, by their own calculations, will determine that the price of aggression outweighs any potential benefits." These words of the Reagan-Weinberger Defense Guidance document do indeed suggest a kind of strategic superiority. But then so did the Carter-Brown PD59 "countervailing" strategy. The former Secretary of Defense, Harold Brown, has defined the countervailing strategy in these terms: ". . . to convince the Soviets that they will be successfully opposed at any level of aggression they choose, and that no plausible outcome at any level of conflict could represent 'success' for them by any reasonable definition of success."[16] The countervailing strategy does not

[15] Charles Mohr, "Carter Orders Steps To Increase Ability To Meet War Threats," The New York Times, August 26, 1977, p. A8.

[16] Secretary of Defense, *Annual Report to the Congress, FY 1982*, U.S. Department of Defence, January 19, 1981, Washington: GPO, 1981, p. 40.

posit an American victory. Instead, it promises a Soviet defeat. For it "seeks a situation in which the Soviets would always lose more than they could reasonably expect to gain from either beginning or escalating a military conflict."[17] Is this not, however, a definition of sorts of victory? Unless it is assumed that our losses, too, are always disproportionate to our gains, in which case there would scarcely be grounds for recommending it, the countervailing strategy does come close to a promise of victory.

The distinction between "countervailing" and "prevailing" is, accordingly, a very thin one. So too, is the difference with respect to the forces required to implement strategy. In fact, neither the Carter nor the Reagan Administration has pursued a procurement policy designed to achieve strategic superiority. Yet each has articulated a strategic doctrine that implies a kind of superiority. In part, this apparent anomaly is explained by the need to retain, if only for reasons of morale, some semblance of a claim to a theory of victory. In part, however, the explanation must be sought in the American strategic predicament. The root of that predicament is an asymmetry of interests that imposes more difficult and exacting deterrence requirements on the United States than on the Soviet Union. While in the Soviet case these requirements extend no further than to Eastern Europe, in the American case they extend, beyond this hemisphere, to Western Europe, Japan and the Persian Gulf. To an extent far greater than for the Soviet Union, deterrence for the United States has always been, and remains today, the extension of deterrence to others than the self. By its very nature, extended deterrence must have much less credibility than self deterrence. This liability of extended deterrence, moreover, cannot be fully compensated for by greater conventional forces. Greater conventional forces will raise the threshold of nuclear conflict but they cannot preclude nuclear conflict. Ultimately, compensation must be found either at the strategic nuclear level or nowhere. But it can only be found at the strategic level by forces that are more than simply the equivalent of the Soviet Union's forces. As we are now painfully aware, equivalence *and no more* must subject extended deterrence to pervasive and increasingly corrosive doubt.

---

[17] Harold Brown, *Thinking About National Security: Defense and Foreign Policy in a Dangerous World*, Boulder (Colo): Westview Press, 1983, p. 81.

Since the late 1960s, strategic doctrines have increasingly assumed the function of bridging the growing gap between the forces for extended deterrence and the forces in being. If the gap can no longer be bridged in fact, it can still be bridged in word. Without claiming strategic superiority—indeed, even while disavowing an interest in seeking superiority—the benefits of superiority are nevertheless salvaged in some measure. Thus the claim that we may still ensure that the Soviets would always lose more than they could expect to gain from resorting to any kind of armed aggression. Or the claim that in a nuclear conflict our forces will have the capability of imposing an early termination of the conflict on terms favorable to this country.

In proclaiming the strategy of prevailing, the Reagan Administration simply followed an established practice, though perhaps it did so too exuberantly. What is important is that it did so at a time when detente had clearly broken down and tension between the superpowers was rising to a level that had not been experienced since the years of the classic cold war. In these circumstances, the doctrine of prevailing was subject to a scrutiny it might not and probably would not have otherwise received. In these same circumstances, the earlier doctrine of countervailing power was subject to a criticism considerably harsher than the criticism that marked its appearance in 1980.

The real indictment made of the Reagan Administration is not of its military strategy but of its politics. It is not so much what Mr. Reagan has said about nuclear weapons and their possible use that has aroused opponents, but what he has said about the Soviet Union. In word and in spirit, though as yet much less so in action, this Administration has largely returned to the period of the classic cold war. It has done so, however, in strategic circumstances which are bleak by comparison with those of this earlier period.

The classic cold war began with an American monopoly of nuclear weapons. It ended, if we take the period immediately following the Cuban missile crisis as marking its end, with this country still enjoying a position of strategic superiority over the Soviet Union. A nuclear revisionism now contends that, contrary to what has been the conventional wisdom, strategic superiority is useless, in that it cannot be translated into diplomatic power or political advantage, and that this inutility was dramatically demonstrated at the time of the Cuban missile crisis. In turn, this view of strategic superiority is part of a larger assessment of the significance of nuclear weapons, an assessment in which these weapons are found to be "totally useless— except only to deter one's opponent from using them."[18] If nuclear weapons are useful only for deterring the use of nuclear weapons, if strategic superiority cannot be employed to any meaningful advantage, then clearly a good deal of the conventional wisdom respecting the history of the postwar period must be discounted. Neither the American monopoly of nuclear weapons at the start of this period, nor the subsequent American strategic superiority conferred any advantage on us. Indeed, if the revisionist view is to be literally credited, the existence of nuclear weapons and the fear of nuclear war had little to do with the maintenance of peace in Europe.

The consequences of nuclear revisionism, if once pursued to their logical conclusion, are quite startling. We are well advised to be skeptical of these efforts to recast our understanding of the history of the recent past, particularly when it is apparent that they are motivated by and put in the service of the disputes of the present.

Now that many have concluded that, in present circumstances, nuclear weapons are "useless," they apparently must persuade themselves, and others, that this has always been the case. But even if this were the case today, it was not the case in the past. Strategic superiority did confer advantages, even critical advantages, so long as we clearly enjoyed it. It did make extended deterrence quite credible, and it is on the credibility of extended deterrence that the structure of American interests and commitments ultimately rested yesterday and, in far more difficult circumstances, continues to rest today. The strategic superiority we once enjoyed also made it much easier for us to sustain a faith in deterrence.

In the decade or so following the Cuban missile crisis, the loss of strategic superiority had no more than a marginal impact on this nation's faith in deterrence. Although the

---

[18] Robert S. McNamara, "The Military Role of Nuclear Weapons: Perceptions and Misperceptions," *Foreign Affairs*, Fall 1983, p. 79.

Soviet achievement of strategic parity was an event of first-order importance, requiring a rethinking of the entire American security position, its effects on the structure of extended deterrence attracted only moderate attention and caused even less anxiety. In contrast to the early 1960s, the early 1970s gave rise to almost no agitation in the body politic over the nuclear issue, despite the momentous changes that had occurred.

Vietnam apart, the reason for this extraordinary unconcern was that we were in the floodtide of detente. Having developed slowly and unevenly in the course of the 1960s, by the early 1970s detente had become the centerpiece of the Nixon policy reformulation. In the context of detente, the loss of strategic superiority was generally seen as an event without great significance. Instead, far more attention was directed to the Strategic Arms Limitation Talks (SALT), though in retrospect the results of these negotiations, embodied in the 1972 Moscow accords, appear almost inconsequential in comparison with the Soviet Union's achievement of strategic parity. But the arms control negotiations were considered almost from the outset a litmus test of the overall relationship of the superpowers. If this relationship was relatively good, the possible consequences of the Soviet Union having achieved strategic parity might be taken in stride. Besides, the Soviet achievement did not challenge the regnant view that the preservation of mutual deterrence was best guaranteed by both sides maintaining a retaliatory force with the capability of assured destruction. The Moscow agreements were successfully defended as preserving mutual deterrence while stabilizing it by limiting the buildup of nuclear forces.

It was in this manner that public faith in deterrence was sustained during the 1970s, despite the continuing buildup of Soviet strategic forces. While detente lasted, faith in deterrence went unquestioned. It is in the fall of detente and the rise of a new cold war that we must find the simple but critical explanation for the prominence now given to nuclear weapons and the prospect of nuclear war.

The nuclear anxiety we have seen arise in recent years is not a response to mere atmospherics and cannot be exorcized by reassuring words. To argue otherwise is to trivialize the nuclear issue. While the Reagan Adiminstration could have moderated public reaction to the nuclear arms issue had it shown greater receptivity to arms control and greater discretion in its statements about nuclear war, it could not have escaped a substantial reaction. The Administration has learned a great deal about guarding its tongue, making pious gestures, and even playing the role of true believer in arms control. Still, the anti-nuclear arms movement and the nuclear debate persist. They persist because they are a response essentially to the breakdown of detente and to the dangers of war this breakdown is thought to raise.

What is immediately apparent in considering the present nuclear debate is its continuity with the past. Although a generation has elapsed since the last major debate over nuclear weapons, the questions raised today are largely the same questions that were raised then. What are the requirements of deterrence? Can these requirements be met indefinitely and, even if they can, at what political and moral cost? Are they compatible in the long run with the political institutions and moral foundations of a liberal-democratic society? What happens if deterrence fails? Can nuclear weapons be employed to achieve any of the traditional objectives of war? If they can, why has a plausible scenario of a nuclear conflict not been devised? If they cannot, must not the breakdown of deterrence be attended by the determination to stop the ensuing conflict and to do so without regard to considerations of relative advantage? But quite apart from the intrinsic difficulty of crediting a strategy—deterrence—that has only this response to the contingency of its breakdown, does not the quick termination of the conflict depend on the parallel behavior, if not the agreement, of both sides? If only one side moves to terminate the conflict, however, may it not be placed at a great and perhaps even fatal disadvantage? It is not only the questions that have remained by and large the same. The answers, too, have remained the same and they seem no more satisfactory than they did on an earlier occasion. None of this should prove surprising. All of our political and moral thought is predicated on the assumption of limits. Nuclear weapons challenge this assumption by virtue of their destructiveness and, of course, their rate of destruction. By introducing a new quantitative dimension into the conduct of war, by holding out the prospect of a war that might escape any meaningful limitation, nuclear weapons take the standards heretofore applied to force and threaten to make a hollow mockery of them.

Deterrence escapes these considerations only so long as the possibility of its breakdown is either denied or simply ignored. If the reliability of deterrence arrangements is believed to approach certainty, the only issues that can arise will concern deterrence and not nuclear war. These issues will not challenge the foundations of faith.

Even the champions of pure and simple deterrence have seldom been so indiscreet as to endow deterrent strategies with certainty. No social contrivance can be invested with certainty. All are flawed. All may fail, including deterrence. But once this is acknowledged, the difficulties that a faith in deterrence had managed to exorcize reappear, and in acute form. If a deterrent strategy may fail, it is absurd to refuse to consider seriously the possible consequences of failure beyond saying that all effort must be directed to bringing the conflict to an end as quickly as possible and without regard to any other considerations. Equally, if a deterrent strategy may fail, it is absurd to insist upon using and justifying the threat of nuclear war as an instrument of policy but to deny that any meaningful or just purpose could be served by such a war.

Yet, what are the alternatives to these absurdities? One, we have long been told, is frankly to acknowledge nuclear war as a distinct historical possibility. Having done so, though, what is the character of this possibility? We still cannot say with any real assurance. The actual character of nuclear war remains as obscure today as in the 1950's. It may well be, as Lawrence Freedman concludes in his history of nuclear strategy, that: "The question of what happens if deterrence fails is vital for the intellectual cohesion and credibility of nuclear strategy." Yet Freedman also concludes: "It now seems unlikely that such an answer can be found."[19]

Do any recent developments, however, promise to alter fundamentally the now familiar dimensions of the nuclear dilemma? Since the essence of that dilemma is one

---

[19] Lawrence Freedman, *The Evolution of Nuclear Strategy*, New York: St. Martin's Press, 1983, p. 395. Fred Kaplan, *The Wizards of Armageddon*, New York: Simon & Schuster, 1983, p. 391, reaches the same conclusion: "The nuclear strategists had come to impose order—but in the end chaos prevailed." See also Michael Mandelbaum, *The Nuclear Question: The United States and Nuclear Weapons, 1946-1976* New York: Cambridge University Press, 1979, p. 127.

of limits, a basic change might be effected by the conclusive demonstration either of no limits at all to the destructiveness of nuclear war or, conversely, of quite clear limits. In the one case the threat would arise of a nation's, if not humanity's, utter extinction. A global climatic catastrophe resulting from nuclear war has been offered in evidence of this position. In another case, the promise would be of a return to a warfare that could effectively distinguish between combatants and non-combatants. New weapons which are revolutionary in their accuracy have been offered in evidence of this position.

The prospect of a global climatic catastrophe consequent upon a nuclear war—a nuclear winter—recalls to mind Herman Kahn's Doomsday Machine. The Doomsday Machine was programmed to set off the Doomsday Bombs, thereby destroying civilization, should the Soviet Union commit an act of nuclear aggression that went above a certain threshold. Once set up, it was to be independent of human control. The Soviet Union was to be duly informed of its existence. The purpose of the machine was to perfect deterrence.

"Nuclear winter," as it is described, may be regarded as nature's equivalent of the Doomsday Machine. A nuclear war that goes beyond a certain threshold would result in a climatic catastrophe.[20] This prospect would at last compel men to do what their political and moral inventiveness have never been able to do. Once war holds out the certainty of mutual—indeed, of universal—destruction, it will be abandoned. Nuclear winter appears as the final confirmation of the very old idea that the institution of war contains within itself the means for achieving its own disappearance. All it needs do is become sufficiently destructive.

Provided that the nuclear winter findings are scientifically sound, they reinforce rather than transcend the familiar dimensions of the nuclear dilemma. We are unlikely, however, to find a reliable way by which the hypothesis of a climatic catastrophe might be tested other than by a way that risks the catastrophic event itself. As such, the nuclear winter danger seems likely to become another of the great unknowns surrounding nuclear weapons, and may yet fall

---

[20] For a review of these findings and possible policy implications, see Carl Sagan, "Nuclear war and Climatic Catastrophe," *Foreign Affairs*, Winter 1983/84, pp. 257-92.

victim to the politicization that claims almost any issue bearing on these weapons. Nuclear winter is an indication of how little we may yet know about the consequences of nuclear war. It points to the limited control, if control at all, we may have over those consequences.

The development of ever more accurate weapons appears to point in quite the opposite direction. It does so by promising a radical decrease in collateral damage, by permitting conventional weapons to replace nuclear weapons in many tasks, by dramatically raising the nuclear threshold and by markedly diminishing the prospect of escalation.[21] The advances in our ability to reduce collateral damage and to rely much more on conventional weapons is not found to blur the vital distinction between nuclear and conventional force. On the contrary, they make that distinction far more meaningful and effective. Most of all, the new weaponry, according to its champions, will give us choices we did not have before, provided they live up to advance expectations, the new weapons indeed give us choices we did not have before. They will extend the spectrum of violence. They will add a number of intermediate levels between the upper and lower extremes of this spectrum. But they will not solve the great dilemma created by nuclear weapons of finding reasonably clear and effective limits to force. The distinctive danger presented by nuclear weapons will persist, though now it may well be mitigated by the existence of weapons that afford a markedly greater opportunity to act in a restrained and discriminate manner.

The view that finds a salvation of sorts in the new weapons assumes that men have been indiscriminate in the conduct of war because they lacked the means to be discriminate—or, at any rate, more discriminate. This is a partial truth that, in the manner of all partial truths, becomes dangerous when taken as the whole truth. Indiscriminate or immoderate means decree immoderate ends. Yet discriminate

---

[21] Albert Wohlstetter has written of this revolution in precision that it is "in some ways more revolutionary than the transition from conventional to fission explosives or even fusion weapons." The reason is that an improvement in accuracy "by a factor of 100 improves blast effectiveness aginst a small, hard military target about as much as multiplying the energy released a million times." Once we can, in Wohlstetter's words, hit what we aim at and only what we aim at, we can also limit collateral damage. "It is the lack of technology smart enough, rather than the availability of large brute-force single weapons, that lies at the root of the problem of collateral damage." Albert Wohlstetter, "Bishops, Statesmen, and Other Strategists in the Bombing of Innocents," *Commentary*, June 1983, pp. 15-35.

or moderate means may also be used in the pursuit of immoderate ends. Men have been indiscriminate in the conduct of war, in part, because they have sought immoderate or unlimited ends. Should they continue to seek those ends, the threat of indiscriminate warfare must persist, few smart weapons notwithstanding.

It will not do, then, to assume that the advent of smart weapons will permit us to combine discriminating means with any of a wide variety of ends. That side against which the most accurate weapons are used in pursuit of immoderate ends may still be driven to threaten and to employ indiscriminate weapons. The new technology does not resolve the issue of limits. Nor could it be expected to do so.

The element of continuity in the present debate can be overdone. If from one perspective today's debate looks like nothing so much as a rerun of yesterday, from yet another perspective it appears quite different. Although the framework and essential terms of the present debate are the same as those of the past, its tenor has changed. In the course of a generation, there has been a considerable shift of position with respect to the legitimacy of nuclear weapons.

The significance of this shift cannot be found in the questions that are asked today; they are similar to a generation ago. Instead, it is in the choice of answers increasingly given to familiar questions. Thus, when the American Catholic bishops declare in their now famous pastoral letter on war and peace that "nuclear weapons particularly and nuclear warfare as it is planned today raise new moral questions," the reference point can only be the world of prenuclear weapons. The fashionably banal phrase that the world is now "wired for destruction" might just as truthfully have been uttered in the 1960s. It is not the essential predicament nuclear weapons have created for us that is novel but the new evaluations of that predicament. The bishops emphasize that: "What previously had been defined as a safe and stable system of deterrence is today viewed with political and moral skepticism." A predicament, they justly observe, that once had been widely accepted with little question, "is now being subjected to the sharpest criticism" and "evaluated with a new perspective."

The bishops' letter, with its criticism of American nuclear strategy, is a significant part of this new perspective.

A generation ago, in 1965, the Second Vatican Council expressed a quite different perspective.[22] It did so, in the first place, with respect to the possible use of nuclear weapons. The Council left the implication that the use of nuclear weapons in a war of legitimate defense would also be legitimate provided such weapons were used in a reasonably discriminating manner. What the Vatican Council condemned was "total war" and any acts of war "aimed indiscriminatly at the destruction of entire cities or extensive areas along with their population." What the American Catholic bishops condemn is nuclear war. The use of nuclear weapons is rejected, whether these weapons are used against military targets or against civilian centers of population, whether first strike or in a retaliatory second strike, whether in a strategic or theater nuclear war. The rejection is complete. Nor does it matter that the bishops' position is based on the conviction that the use of nuclear weapons cannot be controlled and that the effects cannot be limited, considerations that are not, after all, very different from those emphasized by Vatican Council II. What does matter is that the bishops invoke these considerations to condemn nuclear war unqualifiedly, while Vatican II invoked them to form only a carefully qualified statement about the circumstances in which the use of nuclear weapons would be illegitimate.

This is an interpretation of the bishops' letter, let it be emphsized. Nowhere do the bishops expressly condemn any and all use of nuclear weapons. What they do expressly and unequivocably condemn is indescriminate warfare. But that is all. On the first use of nuclear weapons, they "do not perceive any situation" in whch initiation "can be morally justified." On limited nuclear war, they want to be assured that a series of conditions can be satisified before condoning the limited use of nuclear weapons. Unless these conditions can be satisfied, and clearly they cannot, the bishops remain "highly skeptical" about the real meaning of "limited." Does all this amount to the complete rejection of nuclear weapons? Some argue that it does not, that it permits the bare possibility of the most restricted use of

[22] Cf. Second Vatican Council, *"Pastoral Constituiton on the Church in the Modern World*, December 7, 1965, National Catholic Welfare Conference, 1965. The statement on war appears in Part II, Chap. V.

nuclear weapons.[23] But even if this view is credited and, in Father Bryan Hehir's words, the letter leaves "a centimeter of ambiguity" on use, we have come very close to total rejection. There is no way by which American nuclear policy—past, present or probable future—can be reconciled with the bishops' position.

The position taken by the Catholic bishops toward nuclear war is quite close to the position of many who make up the deterrence faithful. "Of course," Leon Wieseltier writes, "there can be no nuclear war that is just. There is no moral standard that can sanction it."[24] Of course, there can never be a just nuclear war, it it is assumed that no meaningful limits can or will be set to the conduct of such war. Given that assumption, nuclear war must either destroy the ends for which it is presumably fought or result in destruction that is disproportionate to those ends. In either case—or, what is generally held as more likely, in both cases—nuclear war must prove unjust.

This absolute condemnation of any and every nuclear war cannot but have a bearing on the moral assessment of deterrence. As long as nuclear war is not condemned without qualification, as long as the prospect is held out that a nuclear conflict may satisfy the minimal standards of justice, deterrence structures may be maintained without corrosive moral anxiety and defensiveness. Once this prospect is excluded, however, deterrence must become more difficult to sustain. If nuclear weapons are by their very nature illegitimate, because their use cannot be controlled or their effects limited, deterrence structures that rest on the threat to use these weapons are also likely to be seen as illegitimate. What gives these structures their one and only saving grace is the promise that they will never have to be put to active use. Even then, the justification of deterrence will largely rest on the grounds of necessity. Yet the plea of necessity, taken alone, can never prove very satisfactory. If deterrent structures are to be given the requisite support for sustained periods, they must be seen as responding to something more than necessity. That plea might alone suffice if these structures were securely endowed with the quality of certainty. Since they cannot be so endowed, the slightest lapse of faith

---

[23] Cf. Bruce M. Russett, "Ethical Dilemmas of Nuclear Deterrence," *International Security*, Spring 1984, pp. 52-3.
[24] Wieseltier, *op. cit.*, p. 28.

in the reliability of deterrence must give rise to a growing sense of despair—moral and otherwise.

It must also give rise to a growing disposition to refuse to endow deterrence with moral legitimacy. This disposition, in the view of some critics, is already apparent in the position taken by the Catholic bishops. Despite their "strictly conditioned moral acceptance of nuclear deterrence," these critics argue that the logic of the bishops' position is to undermine deterrence. By insisting on the doctrine of "no use—ever," the bishops would strip deterrence of one of the elements indispensible to its effectiveness. "Deterrence," one critic notes, "is not inherent in the weapons. It results from a combination of possession and the will to use them. If one side renounces, for moral or other reasons, the intent of ever actually using nuclear weapons, deterrence ceases to exist."[25] Does it? If one possesses nuclear weapons and foreswears using them, is it reasonable to conclude that their deterrent role "ceases to exist"? It would not seem so. In some measure deterrence *is* inherent in the weapon and its possession. This is true even of far less awesome weapons. It is certainly true of weapons that are as destructive as those on which deterrence rests today, weapons that have been used only twice, and about which there is happily little hard evidence on the will to use them. There is, after all, some merit in doctrines of existential deterrence. The bishops, it is true, would put these doctrines to a rather exacting test by a policy of retaining possession of nuclear weapons while renouncing any use of them. But it was only in this manner that the bishops could counsel a course of action that in their judgment conforms to just war criteria while also managing to retain political relevance.[26]

A less severe though far more persuasive criticism is that the bishops' effort serves to weaken deterrence. It does so not only by insisting on "no use—ever" but by undermining the legitimacy of deterrence even while giving deterrence a "strictly conditioned moral acceptance." Yet it is not only bishops' letters and the like that undermine deterrence. In a way that is less apparent, though perhaps no less

[25] Charles Krauthammer, "On Nuclear Morality," *Commentary*, October 1983, p. 49.
[26] For the argument that the bishops successfully combined moral purity and political relevance, cf. Frances X. Winters, S.J., "The American Bishops on Deterrence—Wise as Serpents: Innocent as Doves," *Science, Technology, and Human Values*, Summer 1983, pp. 23-29.

effective, so do the champions of minimum deterrence. For their position, too, comes very close to one of "no use—ever"; certainly it does so in spirit. What else can be the meaning of their counsel that in the event deterrence fails, the overriding duty of the statesman is to try to bring the war to an end as quickly as possible and without regard to other considerations? If this is the great goal of the statesman, to which all else must be subordinated, the question arises: why should the side made the object of a preemptive strike—presumably this country—respond at all? To do nothing in response to a nuclear attack would likely hold out the best prospect of bringing the conflict to an end in the quickest and least destructive way.

The combination of renouncing a preemptive attack and of committing oneself to terminating a nuclear war "as quickly as possible" is very close to the bishops' "no use—ever." The threat of a second strike may serve a deterrent purpose. But even that purpose may be substantially negated by the commitment, if it is generally known, to war termination as quickly as possible. Indeed, as between the bishops' commitment to "no use—ever" and a minimum deterrence plus quick termination, the difference appears quite negligible. Given the assumptions of minimum deterrence, a second strike must in all likeliliood prove strategically pointless and morally perverse.

The bishops' position, then, is the moral analogue of the strategic position of minimum deterrence. What to the former is morally proscribed, to the latter is strategically absurd. To both, deterrence is justified only if it need never be "acted out." Given this similarity, it is less important that what the bishops may not "intend" doing, the supporters of minimum deterrence may intend to their hearts' content. Far more important is the agreement on the illegitimacy of any and all nuclear war.

How may we account for the change that has occurred with respect to the legitimacy of nuclear weapons? Is it that the public has simply awakened at last to the dangers, has become aware of the nature of the catastrophe that would ensue if these weapons were ever to be used? If so, all that needs explaining is why the public took so long to awaken to the dangers. But once it had done so, it was only to be expected that the condemnation of nuclear weapons would follow. Thus George Ball, writing of the "long overdue" awakening of public interest in, and concern for the military use of, the atom, takes it as self-evident that this interest must lead, as in Ball's judgment it already has led, to enveloping nuclear weapons in a "rigid taboo."[27] To understand these weapons—to know that they cannot be controlled in use and effect, and therefore cannot in fact be employed to achieve a political objective—is to condemn them. The sense that nuclear weapons; are illegitimate is synonymous with a growing awareness of them.

It is an appealing view if only because of the role and motive it imputes to the great public. Until quite recently, we are asked to believe, the public regarded the esoteric realm of nuclear weapons and strategy with a detachment bordering on indifference. It did so presumably because it largely dismissed the prospect of nuclear war. "So long as Americans regarded the danger of nuclear war as remote and unreal," George Ball notes, "most were content to leave nuclear weapons to academic experts, military theorists, and science fiction writers." But once the Soviet-American relationship began to deteriorate badly at the end of the 1970s, the veil was suddenly torn from before the public's eyes. The danger of nuclear war was no longer seen as remote and unreal. The sudden appreciation of the danger led to the anti-nuclear weapons movement and, synonymous with the movement, to the growing sense that nuclear weapons are illegitimate.

In part a plausible account, it nevertheless distorts the history of the past few decades. The development of nuclear weapons and strategy is seen as taking place almost on a different planet as far as the public is concerned. One would never know from this account that America's nuclear monopoly in the late 1940s was widely credited, whether rightly or wrongly, with deterring a Soviet attack on Western Europe; that a strategy of massive retaliation formed a mainstay of American policy in the 1950s; that the great crisis of the early 1960s over Cuba was provoked by placing nuclear missiles on the island and was resolved only at the risk of a war between the superpowers that might have led in turn to the use of nuclear weapons; and that a decade of much publicized arms control negotiations had occurred

[27] George Ball, "The Cosmic Bluff," *The New York Review of Books*, July 21, 1983, p. 37.

during the 1970s, which at the least maintained public awareness of the nuclear weapons issue, and at the most, by constant repetition of the need to control the dangers of the arms race, prepared the ground for the movement that sprang up once these negotiations—and the superpower relationship so closely identified with them—began to collapse.

It is scarcely credible to picture the past several years as the period of a great awakening of the public to the physical and moral perils of nuclear weapons. No one was oblivious to the perils of nuclear war. The destructiveness of nuclear weapons has long been an integral part of the informal educational curriculum of this society. The change in attitude that has undoubtedly occurred in the past generation toward nuclear weapons is not so much the result of a heightened understanding of the characteristics of these weapons and the dangers of nuclear war as it is of a heightened appreciation of the increasing power at the disposal of the Soviet Union. There are, of course, other reasons for this change. Nuclear weapons are increasingly seen as illegitimate, in part because force in general is increasingly seen as illegitimate. In turn, a changed attitude toward the use of armed force must be attributed in part to the continuing impact of Vietnam. In part it also reflects deeper changes occurring in American society that militate against this most ancient activity of collectives. In time, the deeper explanation of the reaction to Vietnam may well be found in the transformation of American society in directions prophesied long ago by some of the great nineteenth-century sociologists. Derided earlier in this century, the view that liberal-capitalist societies are inherently pacific—and even pacifist—is one that can no longer be readily dismissed.

These considerations are necessarily speculative, but the significance of the increased power of the Soviet Union in effecting a changed attitude toward nuclear weapons in this country seems much less so. The visible ability of the Soviet Union effectively to match any threat of nuclear force on our part clearly has played a considerable role in prompting the reevaluation, moral and otherwise, of nuclear weapons. It is not the first time that the fear of retaliation in kind has led to a display of heightened moral sensitivity. Moralists are understandably reluctant to acknowledge the effect that considerations of reciprocity have in these matters. Their reluctance does not diminish the significance of reciprocity. In placing restraints on behavior, and particularly collective behavior.

Unless we are to assume a moral transformation of sorts, never a very promising assumption, an altered view of the legitimacy of nuclear weapons reflects an altered distribution of this form of power. The marked growth of Soviet strategic power in the past generation accounts for the hardening of the conviction that nuclear weapons, any and all nuclear weapons, must prove indiscriminate in their effects, when in practice weapons developments for the first time hold out the solid promise of introducing an appreciable element of discrimination. From a broader perspective, the growth of Soviet military power is reflected in the widespread disposition to minimize, if not almost dismiss, the importance of other differences in accounting for the persistence of the conflict between the Soviet Union and this country. A generation ago, differences in ideology, values and political structures were still accorded a prime importance. Today, their role in explaining the persistence of the conflict is much reduced. Yet an image of the Soviet Union that has changed substantialy for the better since the mid-1960s contrasts strikingly with the reality of the Soviet government's conduct at home and abroad—a reality that scarcely bears out this optimistic image.

Whatever the precise explanation of the change in attitude toward nuclear weapons, it seems very likely that the change will persist. For the circumstances that must roughly account for it are not of a transient character. The unrest and disaffection that is the result of this change can only be kept at tolerable levels by a restoration of faith in deterrence. How such restoration may be effected is the issue around which the nuclear debate has increasingly centered.

There are, in principle, three ways by which a faith in deterrence might be restored. In one, restoration would take the path of attempting to re-create the circumstances that once conditioned the operation of faith. The critical circumstance, of course, was strategic superiority over the Soviet Union. In retrospect, there is now a tendency to discount the view that strategic superiority once conferred real and significant advantages. The increasingly fashionable theme of the inherent inutility of nuclear weapons is applied to a recent past in order to correct the presumably mistaken view that our strategic position ever operated to our advantage. If it did not, then the attempt today to recapture some semblance of strategic advantage must be regarded as at best a vain enterprise, and this even if there were a reasonable prospect that the effort might one day succeed.

Today's nuclear revisionism notwithstanding, the strategic superiority of yesterday did confer advantages. Not the least of these advantages was a degree of faith in the operation of deterrence that has since declined. Whether this faith might be restored to a former level, even if a measure of strategic superiority were once regained, is surely a legitimate question. But it cannot be answered simply by tendentious readings of the past that are sharply at variance with common-sense interpretations. Nor can it be fairly responded to by intimations to the effect that the very attempt to regain a measure of strategic advantage over the Soviet Union must be regarded as inherently undesirable and even illegitimate. The attempt may prove impossible of achievement, but that is another matter. To judge it as inherently undesirable and even as illegitimate, largely for the reason that the Soviet Union might consider the effort synonymous with a policy of confrontation, is to sanction the disadvantages under which our position of extended deterrence must operate in conditions approximating strategic parity.

The promise of technology has once again stimulated hopes of regaining some semblance of strategic advantage. It has done so with respect to the precision-guided munitions. To a still greater extent, it has done so with respect to weapons of defense against ballistic missiles.

The advent of offensive weapons of great accuracy would evidently confer a substantial measure of strategic advantage if, being largely in the possession of one side, they had a highly effective counterforce capability. But the history of the past three decades does not afford much reason for assuming that the lead we may presently enjoy in "smart" weapons will be kept for more than a brief period. Nor is there much reason to assume that the effectiveness of these weapons as a counterforce system will be greater in our hands than in Soviet hands. If anything, it is the contrary assumption that seems more reasonable. For the differences between the two societies must make the concealment of targets appropriate to the new weapons far more difficult

for the United States than for the Soviet Union. The openness of American society almost ensures that, as between
the two, we would be the disadvantaged party.

In the case of the precision-guided munitions, we are
considering weapons that are either operational today or
close to becoming so. By contrast, in the case of weapons
to defend against ballistic missiles, we are dealing for the
most part with technological prospects that cannot be
transformed into operational weapons systems for at least
20 years, if indeed these prospects can ever be realized.

It is only with respect to a certain type of ground-
based defense—terminal-phase defense of point targets—
that an effective operational system might be put in place
by the end of the 1980s. A terminal-phase defense would
proceed on the basis of a technology that goes back to the
1960s. Forbidden by the Anti-Ballistic Missile Treaty in
1972, except for one limited site, terminal defense is
restricted to the most accessible or vulnerable phase of an
attacking missile's trajectory. To be successful in the defense
of missile emplacements, the effectiveness of terminal
defense need be no more than modest, since all that is
required is that a substantial portion of the missiles be saved.
This is in sharp contrast to the requirement of a defense of
cities.

A comprehensive system of defense against ballistic
missiles—a Star Wars system that would extend its reach
into space—could become a reality in the next century. But
the problem of restoring faith in deterrence is one for today,
not for the next century. It cannot be met by a prospect
that is so far removed and so attended by uncertainty. A
Star Wars defense is not only a very complex and difficult
undertaking; even if once constructed its operational effectiveness would remain quite uncertain, assumming that any
of the present schemes were implemented.

The central difficulty in devising a comprehensive
system of defense against ballistic missiles is rooted in the
very great destructiveness of nuclear weapons and the very
great speed of ballistic missiles. These characteristics have
given the offense a predominance that it has never before
achieved. That predominance, moreover, seems assured by
the relative ease with which simple and cheap countermeasures may be taken to defeat defensive efforts. Then,
too, the requirements for success in the case of defensive

systems are far more exacting than those for offensive
systems. Once again, this striking disproportionality is due
to the very great destructiveness of nuclear weapons.

Whatever the prospects of strategic defense, we can
gain advantage from them only if we can remain well ahead
of the Soviet Union in the competition to develop a missile
defense. The assumption that we can remain well ahead is
rooted in the belief that is as old as the postwar competition in arms between the United States and the Soviet Union.
In this view, the Soviet Union is, and will remain, the
technological inferior of this country. Yet our superiority
has not prevented the inferior party from duplicating our
technological achievements in weapons, often within a very
brief period. On more than one occasion, this duplication
has also been carried out with a vengeance. There is no
apparent reason to conclude that on this occasion the Soviet
Union would prove unable to do what it has done with
regularity in the past. Having sacrificed so much to reach
its present position of strategic eminence, it may be expected
to remain willing to make the necessary effort and sacrifice
to keep this position.

It would be ironic if the principal consequence of Star
Wars efforts, rather than to confer a measure of strategic
advantage, was instead to subject our principal alliance to
new and serious strain. The layered defense that might just
possibly work one day for the United States either would
not work at all for Western Europe or would work only
imperfectly. The time that is the vital ingredient for such
a defense is too compressed in the case of Western Europe.
The view has been expressed that, in these circumstances
of a two-class system of defense, Europe would intensify
its perennial fear of the United States decoupling from its
allies. But surely it would not be our growing invulnerability
to Soviet missile attack that heightened this fear. A growing invulnerability, however modest, should instead reassure
our allies, on the reasoning that what promotes American
strategic invulnerability strengthens extended deterrence. On
this reasoning, the Europeans should welcome America's
growing invulnerability. Admittedly, a growing Soviet
invulnerability as well must partly offset this reassurance
to Western Europe. Still, the net result, one might think,
would still point to West Eurpopean reassurance.

In all likelihood, though, the reality would be otherwise and would result from Western Europe's perception that it was now more exposed than ever. The fact that the two great nuclear adversaries were increasingly protected, while Europe was not, would heighten fears that the risks of nuclear war *in Europe* had increased that in the words of a former mayor of West Berlin, Heinrich Albertz, Europe was now being turned into a "shooting gallery of the superpowers." However unfounded the perception, it might nevertheless be broadly shared. For it would reflect the familiar "logic" of the protected that their security consists in there being no sanctuaries.

The preceding considerations suggest that the disadvantages attending our position of extended deterrence are unlikely to be compensated for by technological advances. Those disadvantages may one day create sufficient support for prompting a general withdrawal from our major postwar commitments. A policy of withdrawal represents the second way by which a faith in deterrence might be restored. If the interests in defense of which we were prepared to risk not only nuclear war but any serious use of force did not extend beyond the North American continent, the prospect of our future involvement in a nuclear conflict would sharply decline. It would sharply decline because deterrence, having now become synonymous with the prevention of a direct attack by the Soviet Union upon the United States, would possess maximum credibility. It would do so even assuming that the Soviet Union's strategic forces enjoyed a substantial advantage over our own forces. For the Soviet Union would still have to incur terrible risks in attacking this country. In a world where we would no longer contest them, what incentive would the Soviets have to take such risks? An America, then, that defined its vital interests in terms that did not extend beyond this continent would be an America that placed its physical security in least jeopardy. By the same token, at would also be an America that provided a favorable context for the restoration of faith in deterrence.

This, at least, is the principal thrust the argument on behalf of a policy of withdrawal must take. It remains the case, however, that the argument on behalf of withdrawal is one that has yet to receive much open support. Even among those who are most adamant about the dangers of

our present nuclear strategy and most insistent upon changing that strategy, there is an unwillingness to draw the connection, or even to acknowledge a connection, between a
policy of withdrawal and a radical change in nuclear strategy.
It may be that withdrawal is nevertheless the unavowed
agenda of much of the anti-nuclear weapons movement. Certainly this is the conclusion one is almost driven to make
in the case of some of its most articulate supporters. It may
also be, however, that in the case of many—perhaps the
majority—we have the not unfamiliar situation of a movement that entertains contradictory goals, that see substantially, and in time even radically, the nation's nuclear strategy, while not changing in any significant way the nation's
interests and commitments. In this instance, moreover, the
ground for entertaining goals all too likely to prove incompatible has been well prepared by arguments on behalf of
the compatibility between radical change in nuclear strategy
and continuity in major interests of postwar policy.

The infrequency with which a policy of withdrawal
is given serious consideration today must no doubt be found
in the legacy of our interwar experience. Then, a policy of
withdrawal—of isolation, principally from Europe—
threatened in the end to lead to the worst of outcomes. The
persisting fear that it would do so again must in large
measure account for the near unanimity with which the
undesirability of withdrawal is still considered to keep it
beyond the pale of serious discussion.

If withdrawal is unthinkable, though, the reasons for
this ought at least to be made clear. Certainly, it will not
do to respond that the unthinkable may not be thought else
it become thinkable. Walter Lippmann once pointed out that
this reasoning was part of the case made against alliances
and he argued that an objection which men would not
examine and debate was a mere prejudice. In part, the case
against withdrawal is also little more than a prejudice.

In part, however, this case rests on the assumption
that even if we were once to decide upon a policy of
withdrawal, we would do so only subsequently to find
ourselves forced to try to retrace our steps in circumstances
more dangerous to our security than ever. Suppose, it may
be argued, that we were to withdraw from Europe only to
attempt to return in circumstances of great instability,
brought on by Soviet threats to forestall nuclear arming by

West Germany. Clearly, this would be a very dangerous situation and it would have been largely brought on by our withdrawal.

It may well be objected that this argument succeeds by juxtaposing very nearly the worst of possible worlds, resulting from our decision to withdraw, with something resembling if not the best then a very tolerable world, resulting from our determination to retain the present policy. Still, it is not unreasonable to put a greater burden on those moving for radical change in policy. An American withdrawal, however staged, would be a momentous event. The uncertainties that it would open up are considerably greater than the uncertainties attendant upon a policy of the status quo.

The relevant question here, however, is whether the instability arising from our withdrawal would represent a greater threat to our core security than the continued pursuit of the policy of extended deterrence. The argument that withdrawal would represent a greater threat rests on the assumption that we would not—indeed, could not—accept the consequences of withdrawal. This unwillingness—and inability—to accept the consequences of our decision, it is argued, could easily result in something near the worst of possible worlds. And well it could. But this world would threaten our physical security only if, having decided for other reasons that we could not live with the consequences, we determined to retrace our steps.

What are these other reasons what would presumably drive us to retrace our steps? One, many would insist, is the very prospect of a war again occurring in Europe, a war we could not escape involvement in, just as we could not escape involvement in World Wars I and II. But one compelling reason why we could not avoid intervening in previous wars was because of balance-of-power considerations. A hostile power in control of Europe, we calculated, might ultimately pose a threat to our physical security. The calculation may have involved an element of exaggeration. Still, it was not unreasonable, resting as it did on the assumption that the power of this nation might prove insufficient to deter attack by a hostile power in control of Europe or, even worse, Eurasia.

This reasoning, though, seems no longer relevant. It applied to a pre-nuclear world and to a balance-of-power system. In such a system a surfeit of defensive and deterrent power was practically unachievable. This being so, a great object of diplomacy was to avoid isolation. In this respect, as in so many others, nuclear-missile weapons have effected a revolution in international politics. A great nuclear state, able to destroy any other state or combination of states, is no longer dependent on balance-of-power considerations for its core security. It possesses what was heretofore considered unachievable: a surfeit of deterrent power. And although in the extreme situation it is absolutely vulnerable with respect to its great nuclear adversary, this vulnerability cannot be significantly affected by alliances and allies. On the contrary, while allies cannot improve one's core security, they may threaten it, since the prospect of using nuclear weapons is most likely to arise as a result of threats to their security.

These considerations do not address the argument that a nuclear peace is indivisible and that we cannot escape our present involvement in Europe, if only for the simple yet compelling reason that nuclear conflict in Europe would inevitably become a global nuclear conflict. This argument is of a piece with the view, also put forth with utter assurance, that any use of nuclear weapons between the great powers must result in the unlimited use of nuclear weapons between them. Still, the latter view has at least something more to support it than mere assertion, although ultimately it too is necessarily speculative. The former view, however, seems no more than mere assertion. Far from being of necessity indivisible, a nuclear peace may be more divisible than any peace we have known for a very long time.

Why must a policy of involvement that requires extended deterrence be defended by arguments that no longer carry persuasion? It is as though those making them fear that if the truth were known about why we persist in such a policy it might prove insufficient to command the necessary support. The truth is scarcely startling. If we refuse to equate our vital interests simply with our physical security, it is because great nations have almost always refused to make this equation. They have always insisted that their identity consists of more than physical attributes and that it encompasses the preservation of certain values and of the institutions—political, economic, and social—

that embody these values. Nations require allies and friends not only for reasons of physical security but in order to ensure an environment that will be receptive to these values. In the end, this is why we have refused to entertain a policy of withdrawal, even though this continued refusal may one day exact a terrible price.

The effort to regain strategic superiority, or some semblance thereof, and a policy of withdrawal are two radically different ways to attempt a restoration of faith in deterrence. Either way may be pursued largely independent of the will and desire of the Soviet Union. This is one of their undoubted attractions and is to be sharply contrasted with the third course, detente, which is evidently dependent on the cooperation of the Soviet government. The attraction of detente, on the other hand, is that it is easier to pursue than strategic superiority while less likely to result in the sacrifice that withdrawal probably entails.

There is little that needs here to be said in a general vein about the third way of restoring faith in deterrence. If the view taken in previous pages is correct, the immediate and decisive reason for the lapse of faith in deterrence was the breakdown of detente.

Unquestionably, the loss of strategic superiority affords the deeper explanation of this lapse. Yet it is remarkable that the passing of our strategic superiority had so limited an effect on both the general public and, more impressively, on the bulk of the foreign policy elites. The fact that it did not shake the faith that had been formed in an earlier period must be attributed largely to the relationship of detente that arose in the course of the middle to late 1960s, reached a high point in the early 1970s, and was already in marked decline by the middle 1970s.

In retrospect, what must also impress the observer is how so modest an improvement in the Soviet-American relationship had so reassuring an effect on the public and elites alike. Whatever one's appreciation of the detente of the early 1970s, the tangible achievements of that relationship were on almost any reckoning modest. This is as true of the arms control measures, the centerpiece of the detente, as it is of the other achievements attributed to the relationship. The earlier experience suggests that it may take surprisingly little in the way of an improved Soviet-American

relationship in order to still present anxiety and unrest and
to restore a lapsed faith.

An improved relationship between the two great
nuclear powers is the precondition of virtually any significant measures of arms control. More than this, there is a
rough proportionality that may be expected to obtain between the state of this relationship and the prospects for arms
control measures. A modestly improved relationship may
create the prospect for modest measures of arms control.
This being the case, ambitious arms control schemes are
either purely imaginary undertakings or they are predicated
on a relationship between the United States and the Soviet
Union that goes far beyond even a rather loose definition
of detente. Thus proposals for very deep cuts in nuclear
arms—let alone for the abolition of these weapons—are idle
unless they assume a relationship that has in all likelihood
passed beyond the stage of a mere detente and has become
something more intimate and promising. The prospects for
this are such that they seem scarcely worth pausing over.

It may seem quixotic at this time even to speculate
on the prospects of detente. Yet unless we are to assume that
the future of the Soviet-American relationship holds no place
for any real improvement and that we can only look forward to unrelievedly grim years, such speculation does not
seem out of place. One thing is clear. If it is out of place,
not only will the attempt to restore faith in deterrence likely
prove a futile enterprise but the nuclear anxiety we have
recently experienced can be expected to persist.

1984

ARMS CONTROL
WITH AND WITHOUT AGREEMENTS

Kenneth L. Adelman

Kenneth L. Adelman is Director of the U.S. Arms Control and Disarmament Agency. He is a former Senior Political Scientist at the Strategic Studies Center of SRI International and Adjunct Professor at the Defense Intelligence School. He is a member of the International Institute for Strategic Studies and the author of numerous articles on U. S. intelligence and foreign policy.

Of all the emotions arising from strategic arms control today, the most profound is disappointment. In this, as in little else in the vast realm of arms control, conservatives and liberals concur—conservatives for the failure of arms control to diminish the ever more ominous Soviet strategic buildup, liberals for its failure to diminish the ever more wasteful strategic "arms race."[1]

Few fields of human endeavor display as great a gap between what is hoped for and what has been realized as

---

[1] The Senate Foreign Relations Committee's November 1979 report on SALT II was quite perceptive in this regard: "...while giving due weight to these modest though useful steps, the Committee is disappointed that more could not be achieved from the arms control point of view. The permitted aggregates are very large...but the most important reason for the committee's sense of disappointment is the large increase in warheads expected on both sides, despite the modest reduction in the numbers of permitted launchers. Thus, paradoxically, a vast increase in the quantity and destructiveness of each side's strategic power will occur during the period of a treaty that seeks to limit strategic offensive arms." *The SALT II Treaty*, Senate Executive Report 96-14, November 19, 1979, pp. 316-317.

Reprinted by permission of *Foreign Affairs*. Copyright © 1984 by *Foreign Affairs*.

strategic arms control. Former Secretary of Defense Harold Brown said it best: "Measured against these glittering possibilities, the achievements of arms negotiations to date have been modest indeed, as are their immediate prospects.... In all, not much to show for 35 years of negotiations and 20 years of treaties."[2]

People of all ideological stripes bemoan this state of affairs. They long for a breath of fresh air in this all too stagnant endeavor. "Arms control theory is now at a dead end," Henry Kissinger recently observed. "The stalemate in negotiations reflects an impasse in thought."[3] We should not have an impasse in thought. With a half-generation of experience, we should now have enough data to judge what in strategic arms control works and what does not. We ought to be able to glean what new approaches might offer. We should, for instance, complement traditional arms control with a new or refurbished approach: arms control without agreements. But first, four basic questions: What is the problem? What did we expect? What should we expect? How do we get there?

At first glance, the problem seems clear: we have ratified no nuclear arms control agreement for more than a decade, and Moscow has furnished scant evidence that we can do so anytime soon.

But is this really the problem? Thinking it is stresses the *existence* of an arms agreement rather than its effect, a misplaced emphasis. For the objective is not an agreement for its own sake; were it so, an agreement could be readily obtained (most easily by signing up to the Soviet proposal). Any nation can conclude an agreement with another if it yields to terms sufficiently favorable to that other state.

Arms control agreements are neither good nor bad in the abstract. Their value depends upon their terms, and even more, on their effects. If an agreement reduces the risks of war, strengthens sound international norms, and contributes to world stability, as has the Non-Proliferation Treaty of 1968, then it is worthy. But if an agreement inflates expectations without much, if any, concrete benefit, as did the interwar arms pacts and especially the Kellogg-Briand

---

[2] Harold Brown, *Thinking about National Security: Defense and Foreign Policy in, a Dangerous World,* Boulder (Colo.): Westview Press, 1983, p. 185.
[3] Henry A. Kissinger, "Should We Try to Defend Against Russia's Missiles?" *The Washington Post,* September 23, 1984, p. C8:

Pact, then it is not of much value and can even have adverse effects.

While the logic here is irrefutable, the passion for "an agreement" is barely resistible. American society is result-oriented. To be without any agreement is to invite serious criticism—witness the cry against Ronald Reagan during the recent campaign. To achieve an agreement, even one that leaves the strategic plans of both sides relatively unaffected, is to earn acclaim. Such a standard invariably proves counterproductive. As Dean Acheson said, we can never get a good arms control agreement unless we are fully prepared to live without one.

What are the problems with getting a good agreement? Some are on our side, many on the Soviet side.

Alexis de Tocqueville was on key 150 years ago when he wrote in *Democracy in America* that our system "can only with great difficulty regulate the details of an important undertaking, persevere in a fixed design, and work out its executions in secrecy or await their consequences with patience."[4] Persevering in a fixed design is much more difficult in our democratic, free-enterprise system—which rewards risk-taking, thrives on innovation, and equates success with action—than in the Soviets' totalitarian, centralized system—which rewards risk-aversion and thrives on predictable control.

Surely the Soviets watch the dizzying pace of changes in U.S. arms control proposals—the 1983 "build-down" concept constituting at least the fourth U.S. strategic arms approach in seven years—with wonder and with pleasure. While critics of the Administration in 1983 derided what they saw as a lack of U.S. flexibility in the Strategic Arms Reductions Talks (START) and intermediate-range nuclear forces (INF) negotiations, the Soviets may have wondered about the half-dozen or more significant modifications in our START and INF proposals which we made in fairly rapid order. In any case, the Soviets can take pleasure in the expectation that if they stand pat, we will meanwhile negotiate with ourselves and probably change our position as a result.

---

[4] Alexis de Tocqueville, *Democracy in America*, Vol: 1, New York: Alfred A. Knopf, 1946, p. 235.

To lurch from one objective, or fresh approach, to another—buffeted by the pressures of impatient groups seeking a prompt agreement—is to be playful with arms control. It is not to be serious about arms control. Indeed, the surest method to assure that we never conclude a significant agreement with the Soviets would be for us to propose each new notion that moves some American faction—a nuclear freeze one day, a MIRVed ICBM test ban a second day, build-down or a cruise missile deployment moratorium the next, and so on.

We must curb some of our instinctive impatience. Arms control lends itself to speedy results no more so than do negotiations on other complicated political or economic matters. The Austrian State Treaty of 1955 took more than ten years of hard negotiations. Impatience there could well have doomed Austria to less than the complete removal of Soviet occupation troops and less than the establishment of a fully democratic, neutral state in the heart of Europe. The Limited Test Ban Treaty (1963) came after eight years of effort, the Non-Proliferation Treaty (1968) took more than three years, the first Strategic Arms Limitation Talks agreement (1972) two-and-a-half years, and SALT II (1979) almost seven years.

As endemic as impatience is our inability to keep a secret, for long anyway. Leaks about arms control preparations and negotiations sabotage their chances for success. The likely prospect that any new offering will be leaked spurs any President to announce it himself. Such, sadly, has become standard fare. While admittedly adding dramatic flare, this is precisely what arms control does *not* need. Public fanfare invariably leads to dashed hopes and deepening suspicions that the endeavor is being transformed from one primarily of strategic significance to one primarily of public relations.

The problem here is colossal. A glaring deficiency in our system is the unavoidable urge, nay necessity, to exaggerate in order to make an impact. Flamboyant rhetoric and stark conclusions are used where subtlety and ambiguity should be. Even before President Kennedy called the Limited Test Ban Treaty of 1963 a key step in "man's effort to escape from the darkening prospects of more destruction," agreements have been adorned with rich superlatives. In the arms control realm, the Hawthorne effect holds in spades, namely, that that which is observed changes by the very act of observation. It is not so much the *fact* of being observed that so alters arms control as it is the overwhelming *amount* of observation it attracts. Should arms control ever approach the public inattentiveness with which trade negotiations or civil aviation talks have been met, it would yield richer results. But this, certainly, is not to be.

Our flamboyance and openness contrast with Soviet stodginess and secrecy. Looking at us, the Soviets face a cacophony of voices, of facts and views, a veritable information overload. Looking at the Soviets, we face an unsettling paucity of inside knowledge and hard data. Hence verification is a problem primarily for the United States.

The question "How much is enough?" must be posed concerning the terms of verification, as it must be asked of defense spending. That no significant arms control treaty is perfectly verifiable has become better known of late. An acceptable degree of verifiability depends upon the judgment of the President and the Congress, which must take into account (a) the precision of treaty language and the technical capabilities for monitoring treaty compliance with an adversary who may try to cheat clandestinely; (b) the military risks of undetected violations or ones that are detected in a late stage; (c) the adversary's record of past compliance; and (d) the overall benefits that will accrue from the treaty in security or political terms. This standard is as demanding as the judges make it, though it should be stringent.

Meanwhile, tough choices must be made between high-confidence verifiability and strategic significance. Elements easiest to verify, such as fixed launchers for intercontinental ballistic missiles (ICBMs) and sea-launched ballistic missile (SLBM) platforms in SALT I and II, are not necessarily the most important or useful measures of strategic strength. Indeed, their limitation may even be detrimental to strategic stability: limiting launchers without limiting warheads encourages MIRVing (multiple independently targetable reentry vehicles) which increases the value of each launcher to an attacker and, in essence, raises pressures to strike first in a crisis. Those elements having the most strategic significance—such as warheads, throw-weight, and non-deployed missiles, all included in our START proposal—are much harder to verify.

Moreover, new systems coming along, such as cruise missiles and mobile ICBMs, are both more stabilizing and less verifiable. The very traits that make them less vulnerable, and hence which discourage pressures for a first strike, are precisely those which thwart verification.

Even more troublesome is verification's twin, compliance. Verification involves the means to detect an opponent's adherence, and compliance involves the adherence itself, whether detected or not. Both are critical. Arms control is empty without compliance, and compliance is impossible to know in a closed society like the U.S.S.R. without verification. Distrust of Soviet adherence to agreements runs consistently high among Americans, with polls indicating that some 70 percent of the public believe the Soviets are cheating on existing agreements and *would*, cheat on future agreements.[5] In January 1984, responding to a congressional mandate, President Reagan documented seven cases of Soviet violations and probable violations of arms control undertakings. The most important are the high degree of Soviet encryption (scrambling) of its telemetry (radio signals from missile tests) and the construction of a radar near Krasnoyarsk. These two foreshadow ominous developments: encryption of missile telemetry portends the increasing concealment and deception of all U.S.S.R. strategic programs, and the new radar bespeaks a possibly significant step toward a nationwide anti-ballistic missile (ABM) capability. Both indicate brazen Soviet disregard for arms control commitments. For the Soviets certainly knew we would detect such a massive structure as the new radar, several football fields large, whose existence could not reasonably be reconciled with the ABM Treaty. Even more disturbing is that the construction must have been planned in the 1970s—the very heyday of detente and of high and rising expectations for arms control.

What to do about Soviet violations remains most confounding of all. The usual deliberations in the Standing Consultative Committee and higher level diplomatic protests are necessary but not sufficient. Military countermeasures may be appropriate, but unless begun as a "safeguard," and incorporated in a treaty's ratification process, they may be too little, too late.

[5] Poll for the Committee on the Present Danger, conducted by Penn and Schoen, April 1984.

What might be labeled the "massive retaliation" theory of verification formerly prevailed, namely that the domestic and international reactions stemming from a Soviet violation would deter or at least end it. But the muffled public and world response to President Reagan's January report belies this "massive retaliation" theory of compliance.

Cancellation of our obligations in treaties that the Soviets violate is one legal recourse, but one politically painful and at times even unwise. It does not seem wise for the United States to respond to Soviet, Vietnamese or Iraqi use of chemical weapons, in stark violation of the 1925 Geneva Protocol and the 1972 Biological Weapons Convention, by abrogating these treaties. We have no intention of ever initiating the use of chemical weapons, and our abrogation would diminish the accords' salience for the violating state and for scores of other states adhering to them.

Nonetheless, some effective response must be found if Soviet violations are not corrected. Otherwise arms control is doomed. For a treaty prohibition adhered to by open societies and violated by closed societies is no prohibition at all. Rather, it is unintended unilateral disarmament in the guise of bilateral or multilateral arms control.

Another major problem in strategic arms control, one of the most complicated, stems from the different force structures and approaches of the United States and U.S.S.R. The U.S. strategic force and doctrine evolved from the Air Force and its strategic bombing concepts of World War II. We stressed high technology and placed a premium on strategic bombers and later, ballistic missile submarines. From the earliest period in the nuclear era, we emphasized a deterrent doctrine and a retaliatory strategy.

The Soviet strategic force and doctrine arose from its army, its artillery actually, and stressed size and sheer firepower. In evolving their strategic systems, the Soviets compensated for their lack of technological sophistication with a brute-force design, which now furnishes them with tremendous growth potential as they have become more technologically sophisticated. Their strong, almost paranoid urge for greater and greater military power, lack of air and naval traditions, and keen intent upon the strictest command and control restrictions—all these pushed them into a far greater reliance on air defense and civil defense and land-based missiles. Although the Soviet Union is deploying a dynamic triad of its own, the two sides' approaches and forces are not the same in major respects. Thus, even with good faith and Herculean efforts on both sides, it will be difficult to bridge the wide disparities—to balance systems that are comparable and to make trade-offs between systems that are not. This difference exacerbates substantial differences between U.S. and Soviet goals in arms control.

Last is the problem of frequent leadership changes. This debilitates arms control. It breaks continuity and makes it difficult to make tough decisions essential for a balanced agreement. Usually these changes arise on the American side. In the initial decade and a half of strategic arms discussions, five different U.S. Presidents faced the same General Secretary heading the Soviet Union (Leonid Brezhnev). This proved most disruptive in the past three presidential elections, when challengers opposed the incumbents' arms control approach. And new administrations inevitably feel an obligation to reinvent the wheel of arms control.

Of late there has been a reversal of roles: President Reagan faced three different Soviet leaders in his first three years in office (Brezhnev, Yuri Andropov, and Konstantin Chernenko). The problem here is not so much newcomers opposing their predecessors as it is stagnation in Soviet policy. This is not surprising, given the health of the Soviet leaders. Besides, in the Soviet system a new leader needs considerable time to consolidate his hold (witness Josef Stalin from approximately 1924 to 1934 and Nikita Khrushchev from around 1953 to 1957). The President's meetings with Foreign Minister Andrei Gromyko in September 1984 will, we hope, lead to a reinvigoration of our dialogue with the Soviets; but we have yet to see whether or when the Soviet leadership will be both willing and able to bargain on tough issues.

These obstacles we know now, far better than we did at the dawn of strategic arms control. Still, it is worth asking: What did we expect? And, has it come about? In a nutshell we expected an end, or at least a tempering, of both the strategic buildup and of Soviet aggressive actions around the world. Neither has come about.

Even though both sides have now signed three strategic arms agreements, both have increased their strategic offensive capabilities, the Soviets far more than we; the number of U.S. missile warheads has doubled and that of the Soviet Union has quadrupled. Since the strategic arms talks began in 1969, the Soviets have introduced four new classes of land-based missiles, upgraded them several times, and launched at least five new or improved classes of ballistic missile submarines. They are currently flight testing yet another new type of ICBM, contrary to the terms of SALT II. Since the first strategic arms accord was signed, the Soviets have added more than 6,000 nuclear warheads; just from the time the second was signed (1979), they have added 3,850. The existence of the massive Soviet strategic buildup has become a matter of fact, not debate. Current controversy instead revolves around its durability and its consequences.

While the Soviet Union marched ahead in its strategic capabilities, the United States dawdled. Our defense spending, by the mid-1970s, had for seven years been in real decline. When Ronald Reagan assumed office in 1981, the United States had an open production line in only one leg (i.e., sea-based) of the strategic triad, whereas the Soviet Union had open and active production lines in all three.

Arms control has impeded the Soviet buildup little, if at all. No one can reasonably argue that the strategic balance is more stable or more favorable to the United States today than it was when the strategic arms talks began. For it palpably is not. Those who most fervently championed SALT I and II for the accords' reputed ability to help stop the strategic arms race are those who now most fervently decry the staggering growth in strategic weapons within the terms of those very treaties. We may have created our own illusions—and the folly here has been bipartisan—but the Soviets never misled us in this regard. Given a choice between constraining U.S. strategic forces or protecting their own strategic buildup, they have consistently chosen the latter. They continue to do so in their proposals offered in START.

Second, we expected arms control negotiations at least to temper Soviet misbehavior in regional crises. Again, the outcome has been different. Between 1970 and 1976—the time of arms control "breakthroughs" and intensive U.S.-Soviet dialogue, including *five* summits—the Soviets (*a*) furnished considerable arms and ammunition to back North Vietnam's war against South Vietnam, which subverted and finally destroyed the peace accords; (*b*) threatened to

intervene militarily in the Yom Kippur War, which caused
the United States to go on strategic alert, despite a recently
signed U.S.-Soviet agreement to warn each other about just
such instances; and (c) expanded involvement in sundry
African countries by dispatching significant arms, Cuban
soldiers, and Soviet officers.

During these very years, five countries became
Marxist—South Vietnam, Laos, Cambodia, Mozambique
and Angola—nearly all with substantial help from the Soviet
Union. Two more—Ethiopia and Afghanistan—went com-
munist during 1977 and 1978, again with considerable Soviet
assistance. And these were the same two years in which the
SALT II negotiations intensified, Mutual and Balanced Force
Reduction (MBFR) talks continued, and *four* new arms control channels were opened up.[6] In 1979 after Secretary of
State Cyrus Vance met Soviet Ambassador Anatoly
Dobrynin more than 20 times and after the Carter-Brezhnev
Summit to sign SALT II, Soviet propaganda still blared out
false statements designed to further inflame Iranians during the hostage crisis and, even worse, the Soviets began
their massive invasion of Afghanistan.

In marked contrast, over the past four years, Soviet
global behavior has been most inhibited while arms control and high-level diplomatic negotiations have unfortunately been most stalemated. Of the three major wars in
this era—those in Lebanon, the Falklands, and Iran/Iraq—
none was at its core an East-West conflict. Since leaving the
arms negotiations in late 1983, Soviet words have become
harsher but their actions have remained tepid.

Given such a clear historical record, should we give
up the goal that arms control negotiations should at least
temper Soviet expansionism in regional crises? The answer,
in a word, is yes.

To assign arms talks responsibility for eliminating or
even diminishing geostrategic competition is to burden them
with much more than they can conceivably carry. To laden
arms control with such unrealistic expectations is inevitably
to cause it to break down. Arms control can best be considered one single element in a full panoply of political,
economic and defense efforts. But, frankly, such modesty

---

[6] These included negotiations on a comprehensive test ban, Indian Ocean naval
demilitarization, banning anti-satellite weapons, and conventional arms transfers.

has been lost since arms control has been thrust forward as the barometer by which superpower relations (indeed, global tranquility) are gauged.

What *should* we expect from arms control? We should expect an arms control accord to increase strategic stability and thereby reduce the risk of war (the most vital goal of all), to reduce nuclear weapons to equal and substantially lower levels, and to be effectively verifiable. These goals, while simple to state, are of course exceedingly difficult to attain.

Critics of the Reagan Administration who argue that we are much too ambitious correctly grasp the difficulties of achieving deep reductions, particularly in the most destabilizing strategic weapons. These critics advocate more modest goals, with more significant limits on arms coming somewhere down the road. Such was the promissory nature of SALT I and II, agreements advanced not so much for what they themselves delivered as for what they promised future agreements would deliver.

If we should eventually have to settle for something less than the level of deep reductions we now propose, it should only be after a most valiant try and only with extreme reluctance. This does not mean that we should *ask* for less. Unless we seek arms control with a real military bite—an agreement that reduces destabilizing weapons and increases strategic stability—we relinquish any chance of ever achieving these goals. Moreover, proposing an arms control approach that does not even attempt to slow down, much less halt, strategic competition may so undercut public support as to bankrupt the entire process.[7]

Herein lies the core set of questions: whether the Soviet Union will *ever* accept an arms control regime that significantly reduces its strategic forces; whether our strategic concepts will *ever* become so compatible as to agree on how to distinguish stabilizing from destabilizing weapons; and whether the Soviets will *ever* accept true equality between strategic forces. Will they instead continue to mask their

---

[7] Again the Senate Foreign Relations Committee report in November 1979 on SALT II was on key: "...to be worthwhile, and to preserve the base of support in the U.S. for the arms control process, SALT III must achieve much greater progress in reductions and qualitative limits." Senate Executive Report, *op. cit.*, p. 317.

demand for strategic superiority in the guise of "equal security"? We do not know.

But we do know that we cannot find out unless we try. If, after enough time and with enough incentives, the anwers to these core questions are no, then we will have learned something rather important: that arms control cannot be justified on military/security grounds. If the answers turn out to be yes, we will have taken, together with the Soviets, a big step forward in making the world a much better place.

We will not have the answer unless we negotiate with most modest publicity and most vigorous diligence, all the while providing for an adequate defense. Doing so is much trickier than it sounds. For the arms control process has become handicapped by constant carping from both ends of the political spectrum.

To many conservatives, the very act of arms negotiations inevitably saps the will of the West and erodes support for essential defense programs. This concern predates the onset of strategic talks. While the point may have been especially valid in the 1970s, it is less so now. Americans have come to realize that talking does not make it so, that no amount of arms talks can substitute for defense programs. Only an effective treaty that is adhered to can help our security. The converse of earlier fears may be truer today, namely that a president unfortunately must depend upon ongoing arms control talks to build the necessary congressional support for controversial defense programs.

To many liberals, defense programs are frequently seen to be so provocative to the Soviets as to squander chances for successful arms control. Time after time the cry goes forth for us unilaterally to halt tests or deployments of systems—be they the B-1, the MX, sea-launched cruise missiles (SLCMs), the Pershing II, or anti-satellite interceptors—quite irrespective of what the Soviets do, so as to "give arms control a chance." Sadly, this is not the way the world works. No labor union would ever scrap its strike fund, pledge never to have its workers walk off the job, and then one-by-one relinquish demands to management in order to set a climate conducive to successful negotiations. Nor should we. The Soviets never would; they are no different in this respect from other tough negotiators, only tougher than most. If they can realize their goals without giving up anything in return, they will. If we hand them strategic superiority by neglecting to modernize our forces, we cannot hope to attain strategic stability or parity through arms control. But if we pursue programs that redress the imbalances that have arisen from the unparalleled Soviet military buildup, the Soviets will have a strong incentive to negotiate genuine arms reductions.

How do we get there? How do we move toward our goals, particularly that of furthering strategic stability?

Given the staggering obstacles set forth above, the temptation is strong in some quarters to step aside from nuclear arms control, at least until more favorable conditions materialize. The Soviets have of late sought to do something on this order, for their own reasons. But there is no walking away from the nuclear dilemma. Nor should there be. People in the United States and around the world expect Washington and Moscow to address and redress the nuclear buildup.

Recently, the Soviets have sought to switch the spotlight from nuclear arms talks to those on "preventing the militarization of space," as they first publicized in June and as President Chernenko reinforced in mid-October. While they no doubt wish to play down their walkout from the nuclear arms talks, surely their prime purpose here is to help abort research for the President's Strategic Defense Initiative (SDI), or "Star Wars" in the vernacular.

The Soviets, posing the issue in this way in public, neatly slide over the fact that both the United States and the U.S.S.R. have long relied on using space for such important military functions as communications, early warning of attack, navigational assistance, and monitoring of the others' forces. Furthermore, space systems are essential for verifying strategic arms accords. The Soviets also slide over their possession of an operational, dedicated anti-satellite (ASAT) interceptor, while ours is in the early phase of testing. Finally, the Soviet formulation lumps together two programs with quite distinct goals: ASAT a near-term development program for us, designed to destroy orbiting satellites and to redress a specific military imbalance; and SDI, a long-term research program designed to explore the potential for defense against ballistic missiles.

A Soviet-American discourse on such matters is long overdue. The ABM Treaty explicitly recognizes a continuing and intrinsic relationship between offensive and defensive strategic forces. Opening a dialogue on this relationship would bring both of us "back to basics" on matters critical to future arms control, matters last pursued seriously a decade and a half ago. Such a dialogue could be conducted within the "umbrella talks" the President proposed in his U.N. speech of September 1984. Besides enabling spin-offs of actual negotiations—for example, on nuclear arms and on space— umbrella talks could continue for jointly exploring overall security/arms control matters and discussing the host of ongoing multilateral arms talks (MBFR, Committee on Disarmament, and Conference on Disarmament in Europe).

U.S.-Soviet discussions on offense-defense would revive the conceptual approach underlying the ABM Treaty. Research on defensive systems, as embodied in SDI, is not only permitted under the ABM Treaty but was actively advocated by the Nixon Administration when the treaty stood before the Senate. Defense Secretary Melvin Laird advocated that we "vigorously pursue a comprehensive ABM technology program."[8] The research itself may eventually furnish possibilities for deterrence to be based more upon defense against missiles that could strike either the United States or our allies, rather than relying solely upon the threat of annihilation. The results of SDI are years away, and naturally we do not know what they will be. Estimates vary wildly. We can surmise now, however, that even a less than perfect or less than comprehensive defense could markedly increase the uncertainty of success to a potential attacker. And this, after all, is the quintessence of deterrence. Should the technology prove attainable and affordable, defensive systems would clearly be most effective and stabilizing in a world of markedly reduced offensive forces on both sides. We must, meanwhile, scrupulously guard against the vicious circle of defensive efforts spurring the other side to add yet more offensive weapons, in order to saturate the prospective defenses. Again, this could best be done in frank discourse with the Soviets.

[8] Testimony by Secretary of Defense Melvin R. Laird, June 6, 1972, U.S. Congress, Senate Committee on Armed Services, *Military Implications of the Treaty on the Limitations of Anti-Ballistic Missile Systems and the Interim Agreement on Limitation of Strategic Offensive Arms*, Hearing 92:2, p. 5.

There is much to learn in the research on SDI; yet it is valuable on its own merits and as a prudent hedge against the Soviets' active defense programs and research. For they have not only constructed the permitted ABM defensive system around Moscow but also taken some steps toward fashioning a nationwide ABM capacity. They are also engaged in vigorous research in such SDI areas as lasers and neutral particle beams. Surely the worst outcome of all would be one in which our hands were somehow tied on defensive systems while the Soviets gained substantial further advantages in this realm. Admittedly, SDI and the offense-defense relationship need the most careful deliberations within our government, with the allies, and with the Soviets. The first two are under way; the last lamentably is not.

We do have a firmer historical and technological base on the offensive part of this equation. Indeed, we can learn from experience which previous offensive arms control approaches have been successful and which have not. For one, designing ways to stop modernization of weapons has been consistently unsuccessful even though it has become more popular. Long a theme in arms control, the ban on modernization has been played out in the prohibition on flight-testing or deploying more than one new type of ICBM, as provided in SALT II; the nuclear freeze movement; and in testing bans and moratoria conceived for ASATs, nuclear explosions, testing or producing MIRVed ICBMs, and so forth.

This approach has proven rather futile, as could have been anticipated. Types of progress can no more be stemmed in weapons development than in industry, sports, or any other human endeavor. Nor should it be. Through modernization of weapons, we keep deterrence strong today with one-fourth fewer nuclear weapons than in 1967 and a startling 75 percent less megatonnage than in 1960. Moreover, modernization has of late concentrated on making nuclear weapons smaller, safer, more reliable, and more survivable—in stark contrast to research in the late 1940s on hydrogen bombs which strived to create ever more enormous blasts.

By and large, the newer strategic systems (the SS-25 ICBM on the Soviet side, the Midgetman ICBM on ours, SLCMs on both) increase the survivability of forces and

thereby reduce the pressure to "use or lose" them. The dispersion of firepower makes each weapon a less inviting target,
thus less likely to be fired upon or to be fired early in a crisis.
Marked improvements in command, control, communications, intelligence ($C^3$1)—the top strategic priority of the
Reagan Administration—make the chances of accidental war
yet less likely and the President's grip on our nuclear forces
yet more firm. This, too, is all to the good.

Moreover, defining what constitutes modernization
for effective arms limitations can be nigh unto impossible.
It is no easier to set criteria to determine (as in SALT II) when
a missile becomes a "new" one with new components or a
renovation than it is for an automobile or an appliance. By
concocting a phalanx of cumbersome definitional difficulties
which in the end are of scant utility, provisions to retard
or rule out modernization open the door to endless doubts
over Soviet compliance (witness the SS-25 as a second "new
type" missile in SALT II terms). This only harms U.S.-Soviet
relations rather than improving them.

Another approach which grows in popularity as it
declines in utility is that of tying the deployment of
individual weapons systems to the vicissitudes of arms
negotiations. This approach has grown remarkably popular
in Congress, but it sprang forth in NATO's INF dual track
decision of 1979, which linked the deployment of missiles
in Europe explicitly to negotiations with the Soviet Union.
This NATO plan arose in part from European fears that the
United States would give away too much in strategic arms
control.

However successful the final result—and it was successful, thwarting the Soviets' number-one foreign policy
goal of splitting the Alliance by stopping the deployments—
the dual-track formulation itself created far more problems
than solutions. That formulation practically invited the
Soviet Union into NATO's councils, bestowing upon Moscow
power over the Alliance's ability to redress an imbalance the
Soviets had created in the first place. It also stirred European public opposition to their governments, which the
Soviets could and did handily exacerbate. Nonetheless,
political parties which supported the NATO decision were
favored by voters in the key European countries quite consistently during the four years between the NATO decision
and the initial deployments.

Despite NATO's recent tumultuous experience with the dual-track formulation, the concept is being more widely advocated, and even bastardized at that. An extreme extension of this approach was embodied in a House amendment to the Defense Authorization Bill in May 1984. It provided the Soviet Union an opportunity in effect to kill a strategic system, the MX missile, that four presidents and a distinguished bipartisan panel (the Scowcroft Commission) deemed critical to our national defense. All Moscow would have to do is to send a delegation to Geneva to resume a negotiation which it had no business to interrupt. The MX would then almost certainly be killed, not as part of a trade-off encompassing concessions on their part, but merely by Soviet diplomats showing up where they should have been all the while.

Congressional politics is marked by a member differentiating himself or herself from the party or administration, particularly on such a high-profile matter as arms control. A president must negotiate with congressional leaders, as well as with the Soviets, on sundry strategic programs. But, as is often quipped, we need to stop spending so much time negotiating with ourselves and start spending more time negotiating with the Soviets.

Pressure has developed for a given amount of arms negotiations at any one time. This new "zero sum theory of arms control" goes: if negotiations are proceeding with the Soviets (as in 1982 and 1983 on both INF and START), then the need for vigorous negotiations with the Congress recedes; if negotiations stall with the Soviets (as in 1984), however, then they are replaced by more extensive and intensive negotiations with Congressmen and Senators in order to retain controversial weapons systems needed for our security and for incentives in ensuing arms talks.

But there is a price paid for this state of affairs. Presidential control over both arms control and strategic planning slowly, yet detectably, ebbs. Both are thus deprived of needed coherence and continuity, characteristics which are not notable hallmarks of the legislative process.

No arms control negotiation can be successful without central management; no negotiation of any kind can. The same holds for strategic planning. This has been recognized and practiced. In the postwar era, Congress has never deprived a president of a strategic program he deemed necessary (though it has funded a few which presidents have considered unnecessary). Hence the MX affair takes on a grander dimension and may set a more ominous precedent. Canceling the MX could damage prospects for arms control and strategic coherence. If the President fails to gain congressional approval of basic strategic programs involved in arms control negotiation, the Soviets are encouraged to be obstinate even longer. Hence the crying need for more bipartisanship in these matters, a subject about which so much has been written and so much more needs to be done.

Congress, of course, has a critical role to play in these matters, and a great service to perform. Members of Congress provide essential continuity between administrations. As such, they are the trustees of the long-term national interest; clearly this was the Founding Fathers' intention. But Congress best performs this role not by haggling over minor matters but by taking the wider and longer perspective. In particular, it should scrap the notion of a "dual track" approach altogether. Defense programs, whether the Pershing II, MX or ASAT, should be designed to meet U.S. security needs and should be funded or discarded solely on that basis. Should arms control accords be concluded and implemented that actually alter those security needs, the relevant defense programs can then be altered accordingly.

Above all else, Congress and the public must grasp that arms control demands patience. President Eisenhower was right when he stated (On January 25, 1956, at a press conference) that "as everybody has always known, any move for disarmament is going to be slow, tortuous, and certainly gradual, even at the best." No American exhortation or unilateral concessions, such as sinking the MX or holding up SLCM deployments, are likely to get the Soviets back to the table and into serious negotiations. That is a decision only Moscow can make, for its own internal and other reasons.

It is well to remember that the Soviets left the arms talks not because of the Reagan Administration's overall handling of the relationship, not because of past rhetoric, and not because of the "deep cuts" we proposed on strategic arms. They left, quite simply, because NATO carried through the 1979 decision to redress the European imbalance arising from the Soviets' extensive SS-20 deployments, averaging one a week. It is hard to imagine any president proceeding differently on INF deployments in response to the Soviet insistence on its "half-zero" option—hundreds of INF warheads on their side and zero on ours. And it is equally hard to imagine any Senator or Representative favoring such a lopsided arrangement as the Soviets proposed.

Congress is to be applauded for its rejection of "bargaining chips" as justifications of weapons systems. Again, each system should rise or fall on its own merits; none should be constructed solely in order to be discarded. They seldom are so discarded. Meanwhile, defense dollars have been wasted and, even more important, precious defense credibility has been squandered.

What specifically should our approach to arms control look like?

We can and must be ready for tough bargaining and equally tough trade-offs once the Soviets seriously reengage. Even under the best of circumstances, a relatively comprehensive START agreement will require extensive hammering out given the two sides' different doctrines, force postures, goals, etc. noted earlier. This preparation has, in fact, been under way in the Reagan Administration for some time. When the President said his team was ready any time, he meant it substantively, not just logistically.

Such preparations, however critical, constitute just the first of several elements that furnish greater hope for progress in strategic arms control beginning in 1985:

—The absence of such a momentous event as NATO redressing the balance in Europe with the initial Euromissile deployments sets a better stage for success. It was, after all, the Soviet fixation on INF which provided such an ominous setting for arms control these past four years.

—One can safely presume that no matter how long the stagnation in Moscow persists, the Soviets will at least not change leadership as often as they did over the past four years. Again, this was debilitating since arms control inevitably involves tough trade-offs within each government as well as between them. Seldom over the past years was there much evidence that trade-offs were taking place behind those thick Kremlin walls.

—The strategic modernization program begun in 1981, based on a much stronger U.S. economy, offers the Soviets considerably more incentives to come to terms than previously existed. SDI adds measurably in this regard.

—Last is the simple fact of continuity of the Reagan Administration, with the expertise it has accumulated and the lessons it has learned about arms control in particular and dealing with the Soviet Union in general.

While we are ready and willing to achieve a broad agreement on nuclear weapons, the suggestion is sometimes made that we should limit the scope of strategic arms control to a few critical elements, e.g., warheads and launchers on ICBMs and SLBMs, and heavy bombers. Certainly, prospects of success in negotiation can rise as the number of items under negotiation falls—this approach has been advanced as a "quick fix"—and some of the toughest verification problems fade away as well.

This notion is novel only in degree, not in kind. For despite the label of "comprehensive" strategic arms accords, past agreements have not even attempted to limit all key measures of strategic power. Such critical measures as accuracy, reliability, and C^3I simply cannot be controlled directly. But further trimming down the number of elements to be limited poses two difficulties. Deciding what to include and what to exclude becomes a nexus of disagreement between the two sides, each seeking to limit areas of the other's relative strength. Even graver a problem is the limited effectiveness of such an accord. In arms control—as in wage-price controls, pollution controls, or any type of controls—to limit only a few select elements is to let other elements run free. This can thwart, if not nullify, the whole enterprise. As with a balloon, when parts are pressed down, other areas bulge out.

Yet another approach to bring speedier, easier results is to limit an arms control agreement to broad principles rather than specific weapons systems or their characteristics. This approach contains all the strengths and deficiencies of the 1974 Vladivostok understanding. It can be more readily negotiated, with disagreements put aside or elevated to a common level of abstraction. Such accords, however, may be so abstract as to leave the two sides squabbling over just what the principles mean, and how they are to be applied. The United States and Soviet Union disagreed, *after* Vladivostok was signed, over whether the Backfire bombers and cruise missiles were or were not included. This is most unfortunate as, at the bare minimum, arms control is meant to reduce tensions between the United States and U.S.S.R., not to exacerbate them.

Focusing on arms control through agreements-in-principle could detract attention and energy from the need for real reductions of weapons. Moreover, a long line of broad "principles agreements" involving the United States and U.S.S.R. already exists, including the U.N. Charter, the 1972 Basic Principles Agreement, the 1973 Agreement on the Prevention of Nuclear War, and the 1975 Helsinki Accords, as well as the Vladivostok Accord. The most charitable thing that can be said about this panoply of signed documents is that strategic stability has not palpably improved because of them. George Marshall once said: "Don't ask me to agree in principle; that just means that we haven't agreed yet." Another approach, and to me the most promising of innovative thoughts, is arms control through individual but (where possible) parallel policies: i.e., arms control without agreements (treaties, in particular). In simple terms, each side would take measures which enhance strategic stability and reduce nuclear weapons in consultation with each other—but not necessarily in a formalized, signed agreement. Those measures could be enunciated as national policies and could be confirmed in exchanges, ideally after some understandings or at least discussions with the Soviets. Not all aspects of arms control could or should be so fashioned. But some areas may benefit from less emphasis on the formal process—whether negotiations are on or off, whether one side puts forward a new proposal or another—and far more on the results—whether there is greater stability and fewer nuclear weapons on either or both sides. If the Soviets are willing, we can attain these results together in evolving parallel policies.

Adopting this approach of individual, parallel restraint could help avoid endless problems over what programs to exclude, which to include, and how to verify them. The focus should be on areas or strategic systems of greatest military importance. Arms control without agreements could be easier to discuss with the Soviets and quicker to yield concrete results. Being less formal, such arrangements could be more easily modified if circumstances change than could legally binding treaties.

While appearing novel, this approach of arms control without agreements is by no means new. Winston Churchill, in a March 1933 speech before Parliament, contrasted what he deemed the glaring deficiencies of formalized disarmament negotiations with the oft-hidden benefits of "private interchanges" in normal diplomatic discourse, such as: " 'If you will not do this, we shall not have to do that,' 'If your program did not start so early ours would begin even later,' and so on." Churchill believed "a greater advance and progress towards a diminution of expenditure on armaments might have been achieved by these methods than by the conferences and schemes of disarmament which have been put forward at Geneva."[9] At the dawn of strategic arms talks, others advocated a similar approach.[10] And, in a way, it has been practiced ever since. Today we have a policy of not undercutting SALT I and SALT II, as long as the Soviets show equal restraint, and a policy of reaffirming adherence to the obligations of the unratified Threshold Test Ban Treaty and the Peaceful Nuclear Explosions Treaty. The Soviets state similar policies. At times, a treaty has followed a period of unilateral restraint, as the 1962 unilateral U.S. renunciation of nuclear weapons in space helped lead five years later to the Outer Space Treaty, and as the 1969 unilateral U.S. renunciation of biological and toxin weapons helped lead three years later to the Biological Weapons Convention.

But such practices need not lead to full-blown treaties. The United States and U.S.S.R. hold discussions on nonproliferation—instituted on a regular, twice-yearly basis during the Reagan Administration—which are helpful to both sides and to world stability. The two countries talk, not about what they might talk about or when or where, but about the *real* difficulties of preventing problem countries from

---

[9] Winston S. Churchill, *While England Slept*, New York: G.P. Putnam, 1938, p. 48. Churchill went so far as to deem the Geneva disarmament process harmful, in the same speech to the Parliament: "The elaborate process of measuring swords around the table at Geneva...stirs all the deepest suspicions and anxieties of the various powers, and forces all the statesmen to consider many hypothetical contingencies which but for this prolonged process perhaps would not have crossed their minds."

[10] Thomas C. Schelling and Morton Halperin, *Strategy and Arms Control*, New York: Twentieth Century Fund, 1961, p. 5; for full discussion see chapter 8, pp. 77-90.

acquiring the bomb. Receiving less publicity enables them to work more productively, and continuously. When the Soviets suspended START, INF and MBFR at the close of 1983, they informed us that the nonproliferation dialogue would continue on schedule.

Strategic stability can be enhanced by making our forces less inviting to a Soviet first strike and less threatening in terms of a dangerous first strike potential. We need to communicate with the Soviets—explicitly through discussion, but if they refuse, then implicitly through example—on how to lower the incentives to launch nuclear weapons preemptively. We need to talk about how some systems are inherently more destabilizing in this regard, such as ICBMs, which provide scant warning time, are highly accurate, concentrated in firepower, and difficult to defend against. Other systems, such as strategic bombers, are inherently more stabilizing because they are slower, can be recalled before they release their nuclear weapons, and are easier to defend against.

Finally, a fruitful dialogue could evolve into U.S.-Soviet discussions—without expectations of a legal document or even full agreement as a result—on crisis prevention, crisis management, increasing openness, and sharing more and accurate information. This could be done through discussions between U.S. cabinet officers and Soviet counterparts, or U.S. and Soviet regional experts or, best of all, under the arms control umbrella—all proposed by the President at the United Nations in September 1984. One can also envision a similar but wider dialogue between NATO and the Warsaw Pact, which might profitably evolve from or even within the MBFR forum.

The second prime goal, reduction of nuclear weapons, can likewise be pursued by way of individual, or, better yet, reciprocal restraint. The United States has unilaterally reduced its own nuclear arsenal quite markedly over the past two decades, and many of these reductions took place before the beginning of the SALT process. At times, the arms control process itself has contributed to keeping obsolete and even dangerous nuclear weapons in the arsenal in order to bolster bargaining leverage for ongoing or prospective negotiations. NATO also unilaterally decided over the past half-decade to withdraw 2,400 nuclear weapons from its total arsenal. Both sets of reductions have been quite beneficial; having the effect of raising stability and lowering reliance on nuclear weapons, they constitute moves toward arms control without agreements. One can safely postulate that neither would have happened had it depended upon an arms control treaty.

While the trend in nuclear weaponry generally is toward smaller and safer devices, the trend in military strategy generally is to move away from our present heavy reliance upon nuclear weapons. SDI research, if productive, may eventually favor a non-nuclear defense over a nuclear offense, leading to a stable balance at much lower levels of nuclear weapons. Far closer to being realized are dramatic improvements in conventional weapons which could help us to raise the nuclear threshold; these weapons could reduce the chances of conventional wars which could then become nuclear, and they could assume military roles which, until now, could be filled only by nuclear weapons. With more accurate guidance systems and more effective conventional munitions ("smart weapons"), for exhardened point targets such as bunkers, bridge pylons and other targets behind enemy lines. New submunitions could delay and defeat massed Soviet armor with the effectiveness of nuclear weapons.

We need to swim with this technological tide. President Reagan is personally committed to working toward radically reducing the numbers and degree of reliance upon nuclear weapons. This goal can best be furthered by planning, along with our NATO allies, to build up our conventional forces in order to raise overall deterrence and to eliminate the need to use nuclear weapons early in response to a massive Soviet conventional attack on Western Europe.

All such steps must be carefully managed. We need to work closely with our allies and communicate precisely with the Soviets so that there would be no misunderstanding about our continuing deep commitment to NATO and its doctrine of flexible response. In particular, we in no way wish to make Western Europe "safe" for a conventional attack. The Alliance has depended upon nuclear deterrence to compensate for the Warsaw Pact's conventional superiority since 1949, and will continue to do so in the future.

Our nuclear forces must serve the additional role— beyond deterring a Soviet nuclear attack on the United States—of "extended deterrence," helping to protect our friends and allies abroad against any type of armed attack from the Soviet bloc. In this endeavor we have reaped sweeping success; Europe is approaching a modern-day record, 40 years without war. No mean accomplishment.

Despite the possibilities of this approach—arms control without agreements—it could encounter stiff resistance here at home. Some conservatives could justifiably fear more unilateral than reciprocal or parallel restraint from this approach. But if that happened, if this approach created great pressures for harmful unilateral concessions, then it would and should readily lose support; it would soon be rendered ineffective. Moreover, conservative opponents could claim that the objective of arms control is to control Soviet forces, not ours. But arms control is not one-sided. It is not a zero-sum game. Both sides can gain by taking the right strategic steps on their own and in collaboration with each other, even while realizing that their strategic doctrines and tasks for strategic forces diverge substantially.

Some liberals may be even more bothered, detecting here a devious way to kill arms control as practiced over the past half-generation. As stated, however, this approach would supplement, not supplant, the traditional track. Besides, they should see that, if successful, this manner of proceeding could result in fewer nuclear weapons and greater global stability, issues which should be of deepest concern to them. In addition, this approach could be applicable across many areas of arms control to supplement the traditional track.

In its greatest asset lies its greatest liability: blandness. Useful measures of restraint, even if reciprocal, constitute scant material for a media event, furnish no soaring political lift. Such moves are far more likely to further strategic stability and reduce nuclear weapons than they are to fill peoples' deep longing for an arms control treaty (sometimes used in the media interchangeably with "a peace treaty").

Certainly a primary role filled by the arms control process is to reassure the public that somehow, some way, its government is grappling with The Nuclear Issue. Pope John Paul II wrote the United Nations in June 1982 that the world should not be condemned to be "always susceptible to the real danger of explosion." It is painfully depressing to face up to the fact that the world is so poised, and may be condemned to remain so.

Throughout human history, hope has been as powerful and deep an emotion as fear, lust, aggression and love. Free people have rightly asked their governments to contend with the greatest of all human dilemmas involving the most awesome of all human weapons. Governments have a solemn obligation to do their very best. Arms control should not be allowed to degenerate. Rather, it should be molded into the most effective instrument we know how to fashion. Then the sweeping hopes long associated with arms control can be justified.

1985

WHAT WENT WRONG
WITH ARMS CONTROL?

Thomas C. Schelling

Thomas C. Schelling is the Lucius N. Littauer Professor of Political Economy at Harvard University's John F. Kennedy School of Government. He is the author of *The Strategy of Conflict, Arms and Influence* and the coauthor of *Strategy and Arms Control*.

Arms control has certainly gone off the tracks. For several years what are called arms negotiations have been mostly a public exchange of accusations; and it often looks as if it is the arms negotiations that are driving the arms race. It is hard to escape the impression that the planned procurement of 50 MX missiles (at latest count) has been an obligation imposed by a doctrine that the end justifies the means—the end something called arms control, and the means a demonstration that the United States does not lack the determination to match or exceed the Soviets in every category of weapons.

Despite the inflamed rhetoric on strategic weapons, there has not been much substance behind the ill will that followed détente. Nobody seriously believes that either side's capacity to retaliate after receiving a nuclear attack is, or is going to be, in sufficient doubt to make preemption a preferred choice in any imaginable crisis. Détente survived

Reprinted with permission of *Foreign Affairs.* Copyright © 1985 by *Foreign Affairs.*

a U.S. war against an ally of the Soviet Union in Southeast Asia; it did not survive the Soviet war against Afghanistan. But the reprisals were mostly attempts to deny athletes, bread grains and pipeline equipment to the Soviet Union; one attempt failed and a second was reversed for the benefit of American farmers.

Poland became an issue, but of all the possible Soviet responses to an unacceptable condition in Poland the one that ensued was the gentlest that anyone could have seriously contemplated.

Furthermore, we have what ought to be an important source of reassurance, a "confidence-building" experience: 40 years of nuclear weapons without nuclear war. That certainly challenges any notion that nuclear war is inevitable. This is a reassurance that some advocates of disarmament do not like to have voiced, fearful that it might lead to complacency. But I want national leaders in a crisis to be complacent in the knowledge that nuclear war is so unlikely that initiating it is never prudent.

I see no reason to believe, as the Palme Commission concluded two years ago, that the threat of nuclear war is more ominous today than it has been for many years. I know of no way to reassure people who disagree, but there is no prudential wisdom in exaggerating the danger of nuclear war by an order of magnitude, as both sides of the political spectrum in this country have been doing for half a dozen years.

With those remarks as prelude, what follows is my interpretation of what has happened to strategic arms control over the past 30 years. I shall argue that the thinking on arms control was on the right track, and was effective, from the late 1950s to the early 1970s, culminating in the Anti-Ballistic Missile Treaty of 1972, but that things have derailed since. Maybe that loss of direction was natural and expectable, even inevitable. Even so, it is worth examining what went wrong.

The modern era of strategic arms control dates from the late 1950s. In 1957 the Gaither Committee examined the adequacy of U.S. strategic weapons and their deployment, and became alarmed at the vulnerability of the retaliatory force to surprise attack. Bombers were clustered, unprotected, on a few bases. Studies showed that Soviet bombers, too few to be identified by the Distant Early Warning Line, might be sufficient to destroy or disable our fragile aircraft, eliminating the prospect of the reprisal that was supposed to deter the attack in the first place. Announcement in 1957 of a Soviet flight test of an ICBM precursor further dramatized the vulnerability of a retaliatory force that offered only a small number of soft targets. The seriousness of bomber vulnerability was evidenced by the limited airborne alert during the last years of the Eisenhower Administration maintained to keep at least a small force safely in the air at all times.

It was agreed by President Eisenhower and Secretary Khrushchev that East-West talks on "measures to safeguard against surprise attack" should take place in the fall of 1958. It was not clear what they had in mind, but with a commitment to negotiations, the U.S. government had to collect its thoughts. A high-level group of officials met regularly and ultimately educated itself that a surprise attack was the central problem of strategic-force vulnerability.

The Geneva negotiations were to involve five participants from the West and five from the East; representatives of Canada, Great Britain, France and the Federal Republic of Germany gathered in Washington in the fall of 1958. By the time the team went to Geneva, after a few weeks of discussion in Washington, strategic-retaliatory-force vulnerability had been identified as the surprise-attack problem, and indeed as *the* problem of nuclear war.[1] Nothing came of the negotiations on surprise attack (November-December 1958). But the occasion was crucial in identifying what was to become pivotal in arms negotiations for the next decade and, more important, in the design of strategic forces.

The large, above-ground, soft, slow-to-fuel Atlas missile was abandoned in favor of a new ICBM (intercontinental ballistic missile), dubbed Minuteman for its ability to fly instantly on warning. The navy's strategic future was assured with the development of the untargetable Polaris submarine. Secure, survivable forces were identified with what came to be called "strategic stability." Thus, in the event,

---

[1] An intellectual milestone was the publication of Albert Wohlstetter's "The Delicate Balance of Terror" in *Foreign Affairs*, January 1959. It had been available in manuscript to the Surprise Attack Team. My own "Surprise Attack and Disarmament," published in December in the *Bulletin of the Atomic Scientists* that same year, explicitly identifying arms control with reciprocally reduced strategic-force vulnerability, came out of those preparations for the Geneva negotiations.

the vulnerability problem was temporarily solved by unilateral action without any boost from arms control.

The idea that both sides could favor each other's strategic force security was dramatized by Secretary of Defense Robert McNamara's testimony to Congress that he would prefer the Soviet Union to invest in secure, hardened underground missile silos, rather than soft sites above ground, because the latter both invited and threatened preemptive attack while the former would encourage patience in a crisis.

Two technological developments of the 1960s came to endanger this strategic-force stability: one was ABM, the other MIRV. Antiballistic missiles at that time were thought of primarily as for area defense of populations, not for point defense of military targets, and were seen as potentially destabilizing. What was worrisome was that ABMs might offer a strong advantage to a first strike. The idea was that ABMs might work better when alert than when taken by surprise, might work poorly against a prepared attack but well against a damaged retaliatory force.

There was also the prospect that burgeoning defenses would require indefinite enlargement of the retaliatory force. Thus ABM systems deployed in both countries would make preemptive war more likely and the arms race more expensive. It was this conviction that led the Johnson Administration in 1966 to propose negotiations to forestall deployment of ballistic missile defenses.

The ABM treaty signed in 1972 had one characteristic that was incompatible with its philosophy but was probably a political necessity. The treaty was intended to preserve the efficacy of retaliatory forces by keeping them from being degraded by enemy defenses. Human and economic resources were hostages to be left unprotected. But ballistic missile defenses could also be used to protect military hard targets, indeed were generally thought superior in that mode of deployment. Land-based, fixed-site missiles were difficult and expensive to protect passively, by hardening or dispersing silos, while active defenses might have been cost-effective and compatible with the philosophy of the treaty, as long as there was a clear distinction between the technology of defending military targets and that of the forbidden defense of human resources. (This was acknowledged in the treaty provision allowing a very limited local active defense, a provision that in the end the United States chose not to take advantage of.) I have always supposed that the disallowance of local hardpoint defense was partly due to the difficulty of guarding against upgrading, either surreptitiously or upon abrogation of the treaty, but also partly for political simplicity. It might have been hard to convince the American public, which had its own reasons for disliking an ABM system, that exceptions should be made for air force assets but not for people.

The other development of the 1960s that threatened stability was the multiple independently targetable reentry vehicle (MIRV). A missile with ten independently targetable warheads is a replica of an air base with ten aircraft. If it takes one weapon to destroy ten weapons (or two or three to destroy them with confidence), MIRVed but targetable forces equal in size are reciprocally vulnerable to an attack by only a fraction of an enemy's force. (For retaliatory forces that cannot be targeted, things that are hidden or mobile and cannot be found on short notice, the MIRV is merely an economical way of packaging warheads.) There was no serious effort to constrain MIRVs until many years after a ban on ABMs became an objective in the Johnson Administration. The SALT II treaty signed in 1979 attempted to limit not only numbers of missiles but numbers allowed to be MIRVed.

That 15-year period from 1957 to 1972 is a remarkable story of intellectual achievement transformed into policy. Three books appeared in 1961 that epitomized an emerging consensus on what strategic arms control should be about. Each was a group effort, and each stimulated discussion even while being written. During the summer of 1960, Hedley Bull's manuscript, *The Control of the Arms Race*,[2] was circulated by the Institute for Strategic Studies in preparation for that institute's second annual conference. That same summer a study group met on the outskirts of Boston, and Morton H. Halperin and I produced a little book, discussed at numerous meetings of the Harvard-MIT Faculty Seminar on Arms Control during the fall of 1960, reflecting what we took to be a consensus, one that was wholly consistent with the ideas that

---

[2] London: The Bradbury Agnew Press Ltd., 1961.

developed around Hedley Bull's manuscript at the ISS.[3]
And in the spring of 1960, Donald G. Brennan organized
a conference that generated *Arms Control, Disarmament,
and National Security*.[4] Together those efforts were an
intellectual achievement; a number of participants in the
Harvard-MIT seminar took positions in the Kennedy White
House, Department of State and Department of Defense;
others from RAND and elsewhere, who had been part of
this intellectual movement, moved into the government as
well. So it is not completely surprising that those ideas
became the basis for U.S. policy and were ultimately
implemented in the ABM treaty. I consider that culmina-
tion of 15 years of progress not merely the high point but
the end point of successful arms control.[5]

Since 1972, the control of strategic weapons has made
little or no progress, and the effort on our side has not
seemed to be informed by any coherent theory of what arms
control is supposed to accomplish. Maybe right now there
is nothing it can accomplish. But there has been retrogres-
sion in the doctrine.

A qualification needs to be added to this judgment
that nothing constructive has happened. The five-year
interim agreement governing offensive weapons that was
part of the 1972 SALT I package was succeeded by the SALT
II treaty of 1979, which was still unratified at the invasion
of Afghanistan and never had a chance after that. Both sides
have so far avoided going expressly beyond the limits contained in that treaty even though it has no formal standing.
This is a powerful demonstration that restraints can be
reciprocated without formal obligation.

One development since 1972 has been a hardening
of the belief among diplomats and the public that arms control has to be embedded in treaties. In the 1960s, I used to
believe that a tacit understanding might be arrived at regarding ballistic missile defenses: namely, that the United States
would have to proceed at full speed unless the Soviets

---

[3] Thomas C. Schelling and Morton H. Halperin, *Strategy and Arms Control*, New
York: The Twentieth Century Fund, Inc., 1961, and reissued as a Pergamon-Brassey Classic,
1985.
[4] New York: George Braziller, 1961.
[5] Others would tell the story with more attention to the nuclear test treaty in 1963
or the nuclear nonproliferation treaty signed in 1969 and ratified in 1970. They were indeed
important achievements but independent of strategic-forces development.

stopped in their tracks, but the United States would happily forego the cost of building an ABM system if the Russians put a stop to theirs. I saw no advantage in a treaty. I later came to believe that the advantage of the treaty was to put the quietus on ABM in this country, especially in the Congress. But reciprocated restraint may often be as good as formal negotiations and treaties, sometimes better. This idea was better understood up until a dozen years ago than it has been since.[6] Let me illustrate how something that deserves to be identified as arms control can come about informally and even without being recognized as arms control by the participants. This is the apparent understanding that a war in Europe should be kept nonnuclear if possible, and that reciprocated efforts should be made to ensure this. Secretary McNamara began an aggressive campaign for building up conventional defenses in Europe on the grounds that nuclear weapons certainly should not be used and possibly would not be used. (The no-first-use idea emerged later as a reflection of this same principle.) Throughout the 1960s, however, the official Soviet line was to deny the possibility of a non-nuclear engagement in Europe, even to deny that any nuclear war could be kept limited.

Yet the Soviets have spent enormous amounts of money developing non-nuclear capabilities in Europe, especially aircraft capable of delivering conventional weapons. This capability is not only expensive but utterly useless in the event of any war that is nuclear from the outset. It can only reflect a tacit Soviet acknowledgment that both sides are capable of non-nuclear war and interested in keeping war non-nuclear.

If "arms control" includes expensive restraints on the potential *use* of weapons as well as on their deployment, this reciprocated investment in non-nuclear capability has to be considered a remarkable instance of unacknowledged but reciprocated arms restraint. And it reminds us that the inhibitions on "first use" may be just as strong without declarations as with them.

---

[6] Kenneth L. Adelman, Director of the Arms Control and Disarmament Agency, has resurrected the notion that not all arms restraint has to be formalized. "Arms Control With and Without Agreements," *Foreign Affairs*, Winter 1984/85, pp. 240-263.

Until the emergence of a Strategic Defense Initiative (SDI) in 1983, for the last 13 years the focus of arms control has been on offensive weapons. I judge the proposals and negotiations on offensive weapons to have been mostly mindless, without a guiding philosophy. What guiding philosophy there used to be has got lost along the way.

The main difference between pre-1971 and post-1972 arms negotiations has been the shift of interest from the *character* of weapons to their *numbers*. In the United States this is the common interest that has joined left and right, leaving almost no room in between. The proposals of the Carter and Reagan Administrations have been for reduced numbers of offensive weapons. Simultaneously, the *programs* of the Carter and Reagan Administrations have been to match numbers. (This is matching in each category of weapons, not merely in some aggregate index of firepower.) Sophisticates in the freeze movement might talk privately about first-strike or second-strike weapons, about vulnerability and survivability, but the simple public goal has been freezing numbers and looking toward reduction. The last two administrations have been intent on matching hard-target capabilities, number for number, almost without regard to whether denying strategic-weapon targets to the enemy—such as deploying untargetable weapons—was a superior alternative to matching hard-target capability.

Thus there are two points to discuss: the interest that everybody claims in ultimately reducing numbers through arms control, and the interest in matching enemy capabilities whether we like them or not.

On the "arms control" interest in reducing numbers, nobody ever offers a convincing reason for preferring smaller numbers. (I may exaggerate: saving money is a legitimate reason, and whether or not smaller numbers would cost less, people may be excused for thinking so.) And some people think that with fewer weapons there is less likelihood that one will fall into mischievous hands or be launched by mechanical error; this I think is incorrect, but may not be worth refuting because it is no one's main motivation. For the most part, people simply think that smaller numbers are better than bigger ones. Those who believe we already have ten times what we need never explain why having merely five times as many should look better. If people really believe that zero is the ultimate goal it is easy to see that downward is the direction they should go. But hardly anyone who takes arms control seriously believes that zero is the goal.

Furthermore, political and even professional discussion, to say nothing of editorial and popular discussion, has great difficulty in deciding which numbers matter. It is surprising how few people who concern themselves seriously with arms control are aware that the sheer explosive energy in American strategic weapons, the megatonnage of alert warheads, was several times greater 20 years ago than it is now. Not that gross megatonnage is the important measure; my point is merely that this is not an uninteresting fact, and people who are unacquainted with it may be people who really do not know (or do not care) what numbers they ought to be interested in.

In 1963 Lieutenant-General (then Colonel) Glenn Kent, of the United States Air Force, published an Occasional Paper of the Harvard Center for International Affairs in which he looked at the following question: if we were to have a limit of some kind on strategic missiles, what would be the most sensible limit?[7] He argued that we should want both sides to be free to proliferate weapons in whatever dimension would reduce their own vulnerability, but without increasing the other side's vulnerability. In those days missile accuracies were poor and megatonnage mattered more than today; big explosives, however, were less efficient than small ones because the lethal area was less than proportionate to the yield of the individual bomb or warhead. Kent concluded that the correct magnitude to limit was the sum of the lethal areas covered by all the warheads in the inventory; this would be calculated by using the two-thirds power of the yield of each weapon. In this formula, each party would then be free to proliferate smaller and smaller warheads on more and more missiles, thus becoming less and less vulnerable without acquiring any more preemptive attack capability. He further calculated that the weight-to-yield ratio went up as warheads got smaller, that the weight of the warheads would be roughly proportionate to the two-thirds power of the yields, and that no matter how many warheads were on a given missile, the physical volume of the missile

---

[7] *On the Interaction of Opposing Forces Under Possible Arms Agreements*, Cambridge: Harvard University Center for International Affairs, 1963.

would be approximately proportionate to that calculated index of lethality. And you could calculate the volume by looking at a missile from a distance, so monitoring would be easy.

Kent's specific formula may be somewhat obsolete technologically, but its virtue remains relevant; it attempts to answer the question, if you were to limit something, what would you want to limit? The point of recalling Kent's investigation is that his question does not get the attention it deserves. In a very crude way, drawing a distinction between multiple- and single-warhead weapons moves in that direction; the Scowcroft Commission's advertisement for a single-warhead missile (Midgetman) to substitute ultimately for the MlRVed MX reflects a tardy and halting return to some inexplicit criterion in the spirit of Kent's proposal.

The SALT process tends to deal not only with numbers but with numbers in fixed categories. And the categories relate to things like land, sea and air, not strategic characteristics like susceptibility to preemption or capability for preemption, nor even relevant ingredients like warheads per target point, readiness, speed of delivery, accuracy or recallability after launch. The result has been that as fixed-site ground-based missiles have become more and more susceptible to successful attack (unless fired on warning), and as the SALT limits on MIRVed missiles invite building up to those limits, the process has moved exactly opposite to the direction that Kent pointed to.

What has been lost is the earlier emphasis on the *character* of weapons, and what has taken its place is emphasis on *numbers*, and specifically numbers within *fixed categories*, categories having nothing to do with the weapon characteristics that most deserve attention.

The rigidity of the emphasis on categories is illustrated by the MX controversy. The Scowcroft Commission was in a quandary: it apparently found little or no military virtue in the MX but felt it necessary to demonstrate, to the Soviet government and to allied governments, that the United States was determined to spend money to overcome any strategic-weapon deficiency vis-a-vis the Soviet Union, and specifically an apparent deficiency in large land-based missiles. The MX was alleged to be the only missile ready for procurement; and since quick procurement was essential, the commission recommended 100 MX, with a longing glance at an economical single-warhead missile (Midgetman) that was not even under development. Bemused by the SALT tradition, their horizon in searching for appropriate weapons was short of the oceans; they appear not to have considered as an alternative the scheduling of some equivalent number of Trident submarines. Perhaps Tridents were not considered quite equivalent militarily to the MX; but since the object was a demonstration of resolve to procure, and not the particular characteristics of the MX, and because the Trident solved the basing problem that had vexed the Carter and Reagan Administrations for most of eight years, the Trident solution at least ought to have been considered. (If it was, it does not show in the commission report.)

What a strange product of an arms-control mentality—to constrain the United States to purchase one of the least attractive weapons (in terms of what arms control is intended to bring about) and to preclude the procurement of a secure, non-targetable undersea system instead. What a lost opportunity to announce that the United States would compete by procuring weapons of its own choosing, not by matching, category by category, whatever the Soviets chose to deploy. Instead, we have "arms control" for its own sake, not for the sake of peace and confidence.

Arms control for its own sake is similarly implicated in the widespread abhorrence of submarine-based cruise missiles. The cruise missile, as advertised, is an economical retaliatory weapon, too slow for preemptive attack, yet difficult to defend against as it penetrates Soviet air space, impossible to locate on station because it can be based on submarines. It ought to seem a splendid answer to the problem of vulnerability in the retaliatory force. The widely voiced objection is a simple one. It is easy to hide; it can be got surreptitiously on board submarines. Because it can be fired from a torpedo tube and each submarine can have a reload capability, and because there are more attack submarines capable of carrying cruise missiles than any treaty limitation on the missiles would allow, there is no way to monitor a limitation on numbers of cruise missiles. The logic is that if you cannot find them you cannot count them; if you cannot count them you cannot have verifiable limits; if limits cannot be verified you cannot have arms control.

But who needs arms control if economical and reliable retaliatory weapons are available that are neither susceptible to preemption nor capable of preemption? There may be an answer to this question, but it has not been given. Again, arms control appears to get in the way of pursuing its own objective. Possibly there is some imperative in arms control to do something about offensive weapons, even when there is nothing constructive to be done; so something was done that could not be constructive and the result is confusion or worse. Possibly the first SALT agreement became a compelling model: Secretary of Defense Melvin Laird, after the signing of the SALT agreement, referred to it immediately as "SALT I," and looked forward to SALT II, freezing a procedural pattern with roman numerals. Perhaps the arms control bureaucracy nurtures itself on formal negotiations and ratified treaties, and has lost any subtlety it might have had. (Adelman's *Foreign Affairs* article is at least a hint at a less heavy-handed approach.) Perhaps an administration with no genuine interest in arms limitation finds in arms control the best pulpit from which to preach arms competition.

There is a separate development to weave into this story. Ten years ago, late in the Nixon Administration, secretaries of defense began to pronounce a new doctrine for the selection of strategic weapons. This doctrine entailed a more comprehensive target system than anything compatible with the McNamara doctrine. Its philosophical basis was that, if a war occurred, the president should have some alternative to mutual destruction, and the alternative proposed was a counterforce capability that could be operated purposively in a wartime environment, susceptible to control.

And there was a new strategic element: the threat of destroying a large part of the Soviet population and industrial capacity might no longer deter Soviet leaders, whose affection was for their own leadership and not for the people they served. The only effective deterrent threat might be the destruction of their entire military power base, including ground and naval forces. This required, of course, much larger and more versatile weapon capabilities for our forces.

The philosophy underlying the ABM agreement came under attack because it represented the mad notion that the only alternative to peace was mutual obliteration. The name of the strategy was abbreviated, and the acronym, MAD— Mutual Assured Destruction—has been brandished as a derisive slogan. Since 1964 the correct name of the strategy is not "assured mutual destruction," but "assured *capability* for mutual destruction," the difference being that the capability does not have to be ineluctably exercised at the outbreak of even an intercontinental nuclear war. The three crucial elements are an assured capability, restrained targeting and some capacity for war termination.

What has happened is that a capacity to maintain *control* over the course of war has come to be identified with a vigorous and extended *counterforce* campaign, while *retaliatory targeting* has been identified with what Herman Kahn used to call "spasm." The choice is presented as one between a counterforce campaign that is subject to control and a purely retaliatory campaign that is a total spasmodic response. I find it more plausible that the actual choice is between the two opposite alternatives. A controlled retaliatory capability seems to me supremely important, as these things go, and probably achievable, at least if somewhat reciprocated on the other side. But it is unlikely that "controlled" counterforce warfare on the scale typically envisioned could be sustained all the way to a termination that left populations and their economic assets substantially intact; indeed *uncontrolled* counterforce is probably what you would get.

But as long as the counterforce doctrine is governing, it will be hard to impose a reciprocal denial of substantial preemptive capabilities, since the capability to destroy hard targets, publicly eschewed by McNamara, has now become central to the doctrine. How this doctrine might be squared with arms control has never been clear to me, but it probably explains why the current arms control framework has become the one within which the numerical arms race is driven.

I should note briefly that the bargaining chip idea has again become transparent. The Administration, the Scowcroft Commission, and even Congressman Les Aspin have all publicly averred that an initial MX program was essential to drive the Soviets to the bargaining table. No one has given an estimate of the likelihoods of successful disarmament negotiations with and without MX: if the prospect were ten percent without MX and 30 percent with

it—a differential I find implausibly large—it could still be
a bad bargain if it is not the weapon we want. The
Administration has never been altogether clear whether the
MX itself is a definitive program whose completion will lead
to arms control, or is a contingent program whose abandonment is up for discussion. Publicly acknowledging that
Soviet intransigence can oblige the United States to procure
an expensive weapon of admittedly little or negative military
utility is embarrassing.

Another debating strategy that attempts to make
things better by first making them worse is publicizing the
argument that any perceived inadequacy of U.S. strategic
weaponry visa-vis the Soviet Union, or even a perceived lack
of competitive determination on the part of the United States,
would invite the Soviets to press hard in the next confrontation in the confident belief that the United States must back
down, much as Khrushchev did in 1962. In the face of Soviet
hubris over strategic superiority, the United States will have
no choice but to back down—a situation that invites confrontation. This may be a good argument for more armament if Americans believe it and Russians do not. It is a
dangerous one if Russians believe it and believe that
Americans do too. I find no logic in the argument, but it
is one of those that could be self-fulfilling in a dangerous
way. The argument could easily have been neutered by an
administration that saw the danger in it and did not itself
rely on such arguments to bolster support for its programs.
One hopes that the Russians know better.

Finally we come to the Strategic Defense Initiative—
President Reagan's dream of harnessing technology to provide impregnable defenses against ballistic missiles sometime
in the future, making nuclear weapons obsolete and permitting nuclear disarmament. How it can be thought that
space-based defenses against ballistic missiles can completely
deny the delivery of nuclear explosives to the proximity of
U.S. population centers by land, sea and air, I do not know;
but excusing the idea as an extravagance, let us try to see
how the concept fits into arms control.

There is an easy way to fit it, even into the philosophy
of the ABM treaty, but it is an interpretation that denigrates
the President's dream and is nowhere near commensurate
with the attention SDI gets. That is to argue that defending

targetable U.S. missiles, like the MX, against preemptive attack through high-technology ABM is attractive and unobjectionable. It was a flaw in the ABM treaty that "good" ABM (protecting missiles) was disallowed along with "bad" (protecting cities). In consequence there is no way to protect the MX. A partial reversal of the ABM ban to permit defense of retaliatory weapons would bring us back to the McNamara spirit. This is a line taken by many defenders of SDI, although it is not clear to me whether it is an opportunistic rescue of ground-based missiles under the SDI umbrella, a minimally defensible foot in the door for SDI, a fillip to advanced research, or merely an attempt to rescue the President's image by showing that the concept of SDI, though overblown and oversold, is not quite empty.

There is, of course, the technical question of whether defenses good at protecting ground-based missiles are sufficiently distinguishable from defenses for population centers, so that rather than repairing the ABM treaty by inserting an exception we should be deciding whether or not to abandon it. There are so many interested parties with different interests that it is hard to find common ground even among those who share the same enthusiasm.

Let us leave aside the fact that cities are soft, unconcealable, and almost certainly unprotectable no matter how successfully ballistic missiles may be fended off, there being such a multitude of alternative means of wartime delivery or prewar positioning. There remains the question whether the President's dream is a good one.

He speaks of no longer depending on deterrence but of being unilaterally able to nullify any Soviet nuclear attack. Would we prefer to rely on defense, which is unilateral, or on deterrence, which is contingent and reciprocal? My question is whether we should wish away deterrence as the foundation of peace.

Those 40 years of living with nuclear weapons without warfare are not only evidence that war can be avoided but are themselves part of the reason why it can be; namely, increasing experience in living with the weapons without precipitating a war, increasing confidence on both sides that neither wishes to risk nuclear war, diminishing necessity to react to every untoward event as though it were a mortal challenge. I go further than that: a prudent restraint from aggressive violence that is based on acknowledgment that the world is too small to support a nuclear war is a healthier basis for peace than unilateral efforts to build defenses. I like the notion that East and West have exchanged hostages on a massive scale and that as long as they are unprotected, civilization depends on the avoidance of military aggression that could escalate to nuclear war.

Most of what we call civilization depends on reciprocal vulnerability. I am defenseless against almost everybody that I know, and while most of them would have no interest in harming me there must be some that would. I feel safer in an environment of deterrence than I would in an environment of defense. It is often said that terror is a poor basis for civilization, and the balance of terror is not a permanently viable foundation for the avoidance of war. Fear can promote hostility, and fear can lead to impetuosity in a crisis. I agree, but I do not equate a balance of deterrence with a balance of terror, even though the roots of "deterrence" and "terror" are the same. Twenty years ago I wrote and still believe:

The extent of the "fear" involved in any arrangement—total disarmament, negotiated mutual deterrence, or stable weaponry achieved unilaterally by conscious design—is a function of confidence. If the consequences of transgression are plainly bad—bad for all parties, little dependent on who transgresses first, and not helped by rapid mobilization—we can take the consequences for granted and call it a "balance of prudence."[8]

People regularly stand at the curb watching trucks, buses and cars hurtle past at speeds that guarantee injury and threaten death if they so much as attempt to cross against the traffic. They are absolutely deterred. But there is no fear. They just know better.

[8] Thomas C. Schelling, *Arms and Influence*, New Haven: Yale University Press, 1966, p. 259.

1985

BETWEEN AN UNFREE WORLD AND NONE: INCREASING OUR CHOICES

Albert Wohlstetter

Albert Wohlstetter is President of the European American Institute for Security Research and Director of Research at Pan Heuristics. The author is deeply indebted to his colleagues Richard Brody, Gregory Jones, Paul Kozemchak, Stephen Prowse and Arthur Steiner. This essay is based in part on a paper presented at a conference on "Nuclear Weapons and the Nature of Politics" held by the John M. Olin School of International Politics at the University of Chicago.

Would nuclear war endanger civilization or even the human species? Does that possibility require us to subordinate all considerations of freedom to survival and to dismiss any possibility of responding justly to a nuclear attack—or at least to anyone whose memory stretches back as far as 1958 to the Campaign for Nuclear Disarmament, and the famous controversy between the philosophers Bertrand Russell and Sidney Hook over whether it was better to be "Red or Dead." The question, at any rate, is not dead. It is implicit in nightmare visions like "The Day After" that continue to flood our television and movie screens, and it appears in even more gruesome form in the cold and dark post-nuclear world described by some scientists. The horrors revealed by science can exceed, it seems, those of science fiction: the sense of one meeting, in 1983, was that there

Reprinted with permission of *Foreign Affairs.* Copyright © 1985 by *Foreign Affairs.*

may not be any world after nuclear war. As biologist Anne Ehrlich summarized it:

In the northern target regions, it is unlikely that more than a tiny fraction of the original population could survive the first few months after a nuclear war of appreciable scale. . . . Nuclear war would render all but uninhabitable the only known habitable planet in the universe. Nothing of value to anyone alive today is likely to survive such a catastrophe—and least of all, the ideologies that supposedly motivated it. The virtues of freedom—or communism—pale when survival is not an available option and there may be no future generations to whom it can be bequeathed.[1]

This particular meeting was based in good part on a draft study by the scientists Richard Turco, Brian Toon, Thomas Ackerman, James Pollack and Carl Sagan (now generally called "TTAPS, an acronym of the authors' last names).[2] Though they have greatly overstated the scientific consensus, TTAPS does have prestigious support. It extended the results of an international study in 1982 sponsored by the Royal Swedish Academy of Sciences (published in its magazine, *Ambio*) which indicated that smoke from fires ignited by a nuclear war might bring about a world of "twilight at noon."[3] It seems to be confirmed by the conclusion of our own National Academy of Sciences at the end of 1984 (NAS 85) that there is a "clear possibility" a major nuclear exchange would obscure the sun for an extended period and bring on freezing temperatures with catastrophic long-term effects in the northern hemisphere. To this formidable international array of scientists Admiral Noel Gayler, former deputy director of the Joint Strategic Targeting and Planning Staff, has added some American military authority. Such massive scenarios, he has said, are "quite reasonable":

Whatever our rhetoric or theirs, in a general nuclear war cities will be struck, and they will burn. Will not at least some of the smaller cities be spared? Not likely.[4]

[1] Anne Ehrilich, "Nuclear Winter," *The Bulletin of the Atomic Scientists*, April 1984, p. 145.
[2] The basic paper went through several drafts in 1983 before publication in *Science*, December 23, 1983, pp. 1283-1292.
[3] Paul Grutzen, J.W. Birks, "The Atmosphere after a Nuclear War: Twilight at Noon," *Ambio*, 1982, Vol. II, Nos. 2-3, pp. 114-125.
[4] Statement of Admiral Noel Gayler before the Joint Committee of the U.S. Congress, "Consequences of a Nuclear War," July 11, 1984.

The idea that any major nuclear conflict would mean the destruction by each side of the other's cities dominates the European and American political establishment, including the press. And apparently the concern goes beyond that of major nuclear attacks or responses. In fact, TTAPS has estimated that even a *"small"* nuclear war burning 100 cities might trigger a global climatic disaster. And the editors of *The New York Times* have taken that to mean that *any* nuclear conflict on an appreciable scale would leave no survivors. The *Times* concludes that, so long as there are "those in the United States or the Soviet Union who believe there is any point in ever risking nuclear war, defining degrees of destruction is not an empty exercise."[5]

Like most of our political establishment for the last 20 years, the *Times* firmly believes that "deterrence works because it is based on horror"; and apparently the less restraint and the more horror the better. Hence the enthusiasm for the latest flurry of calculations and TV spectaculars on the nuclear apocalypse which indicate that the horror would be total; and hence the drift of the Western establishment toward threatening to use, but resolving never actually to use, nuclear weapons first or second, early or late. "Deterrence Only" means giving up if deterrence fails; it assumes, as some make explicit, that to acquire weapons in order to be able to respond to such attacks discriminately is wrong and hopeless, but that even "under communist rule... as long as life exists, there is hope. A nuclear holocaust would wipe out that hope."[6]

It appears then that we may be faced with a choice between darkness at noon in the political sense of Koestler or darkness at noon in the literal sense.

Recent calculations of the possible global effects of a nuclear war are not the first. They are only the latest in a long line, though they may be the grimmest since the early 1940s.

The possibilty of a total nuclear cataclysm came up even before the formal start in August 1942 of the Manhattan Project. Two months earlier, Edward Teller had expressed concern that the enormous heat he had calculated would

---

[5] "The Winter after the Bomb," *The New York Times*, November 6, 1983.
[6] John Cardinal Krol, Hearings before the Committee on Foreign Relations, U.S. Senate, 96th Congress, First Session, September 14, 1979; and "The Churches and Nuclear War" in *Origins*, Vol. 9. No. 15, September 27, 1979.

build up in an atomic bomb might be enough to "melt" the
Coulomb barrier between light nuclei. Robert Oppenheimer
suggested that, if so, a single explosion of an A-bomb might
ignite and destroy the atmosphere of the entire planet. A
detailed theoretical investigation of the basic theory of thermonuclear reactions disposed of this appalling possibility
before Trinity, the first test. It showed that there was virtually no danger that the test would set the atmosphere on
fire. Definitive theoretical work on this point must have been
quite a relief.

Nonetheless, in the immediate aftermath of
Hiroshima, Manhattan Project scientists talked in apocalyptic terms of the alternatives as being "One World or None."[7]
They argued typically and without equivocation that "if war
breaks out, atomic bombs will be used and they will surely
destroy our civilization." It was this catastrophic early prospect of "no world" that lent urgency to the pursuit of "one
world." Literally hundreds of other statements by Manhattan Project scientists issued shortly after Hiroshima were
very similar. Though few conjured up a disastrous global
change in climate, Edward Teller did caution that "it was
not even impossible to imagine that the effects of an atomic
war fought with greatly perfected weapons and pushed by
utmost determination will endanger the survival of man."[8]

A basic assumption of that period was that in an
atomic war both the attacker and his victims would aim their
atomic bombs primarily or exclusively against the other's
cities. Scientists asserted typically that "atomic bombs are
weapons used only against large cities and industrial
centers."[9] This was a natural, though mistaken, inference
from the circumstances in which thse first two A-bombs were
used and from the experience of strategic bombing in World
War II when thousands of non-nuclear weapons were
delivered in single raids, some of which destroyed more
civilians than the Hiroshima or Nagasaki bombs.

The alternative of "no world," then, contemplated a
war that began with the destruction of the major cities of
one side, followed a few hours later by the destruction of

---

[7] Dexter Master and Katherine Way, eds., *One World or None; A Report to the
Public on the Full Meaning of the Atomic Bomb*, New York: McGraw Hill, 1946.
[8] Edward Teller, "How Dangerous Are Atomic Weapons?" *The Bulletin of the Atomic
Scientist*, January 1947, p. 36.
[9] "The Atomic Scientists Speak Up," *Life*, October 29, 1945, p. 46.

the cities on the attacker's side. This is the way an atomic war appeared in the writings of the eminent scientists associated with the Metallurgical Laboratory (Met Lab) at the University of Chicago. Met Lab scientists, like James Frank and Leo Szilard, recognized that if the attacker expected his own cities to be destroyed only a few hours latter than his victim's, this might act as a deterrent to attacking the victim's cities. However, they did not give much weight to the stability of such a deterrent. They thought that nuclear war was sure to break out through some irrational or unauthorized act or accident, "sooner or later." This lent great urgency to making drastic changes in the international system.

Events soon indicated that "one world" was not a realistic alternative. The Soviets turned down the Baruch-Acheson-Lilienthal plan for international control or atomic energy at the end of 1946. A series of crises followed over Berlin, Czechoslovakia and other key points, culminating in the first Soviet explosion of a nuclear weapon in August 1949. In the course of these crises, and later in debating the hydrogen bomb, the major Manhattan Project scientists began to reexamine their insistence that unless there was one world there would be none at all. They reviewed the possibilities for limiting the catastrophic effects of a nuclear war and devoted about a decade to the intense pursuit of programs of defense that might preserve Western civilization. These efforts included programs for the large-scale use of small tactical nuclear weapons in Europe rather than large strategic warheads (Project Vista at California Institute of Technology); for the fleet defense of the sea lines of communication (Project Hartwell at Massachusetts Institute of Technology); for extensive shelters and other "passive" civil defense measures in the United States (Project Charles and its sequels, leading to the Gaither report); for the interception of Soviet bombers on their way to target and other measures of "active defense" of the continental United States (The Lincoln Summer Study, Project Lincoln at MIT and others).

A consensus of such studies, embodied in a 1953 report by the Panel of Consultants on Disarmament of the Department of State entitled "Armaments and American Policy," was that our preoccupation with a major offensive capacity against the Soviet Union should be, but was not,

matched by any corresponding concern for defending the
United States against a Soviet atomic attack.[10] The report
concluded that the interception of a high percentage (though
not all) of enemy bombers on their way to the United States
was feasible and important. Civil defense measures could
further contain the damage done by those Soviet bombers
that got through the defense. Defenses would improve the
position of the United States by reducing the damage the
Russians could do on any one given date, and by making
it more difficult and expensive for the Soviets to achieve a
specified result. Defenses would help develop a healthy (but
not yet excessive) sense of the dangers of the atom. Such
a continental defense would help the United States in
negotiating for the regulation of atomic weapons. It could
not be read by the Soviets as an aggressive move. And, while
geography made such a defense of Europe less practicable,
given the state of the art then current, "if the United States
can maintain some immunity to a knockout, the American
connection may yet serve to protect the Western Europeans
and so to quite their fears."[11] Moreover, research and development were likely to yield still more impressive gains, and
might eventually give increased hope for the air defense of
Europe.

    In brief then, the consensus in 1953 of the major
figures of the Manhattan Project, such as Robert Oppenheimer and Hans Bethe, not only reversed their 1945 views,
but contrasts even more with almost every stereotype of the
Mutual Assured Destruction (MAD) dogma which has
dominated our elites, including our scientists, in the decades
after the Cuban missile crisis.

    Such views on the vital importance of limiting the
catastrophe of a nuclear war strongly influenced high
officials in the Truman as well as the Eisenhower Administrations, as National Security Council documents of that time
show. Indeed, the belief in the importance of assuring the
survival of civil society in a nuclear war was a basic tenet
of elite opinion outside the government, as common in *The*

    [10] See "Report by the Panel of Consultants of the Department of State to the
Secretary of State," for the report entitled "Armaments and American Policy" in *Foreign
Relations of the United States, 1952-54, Vol. II, National Security Affairs*, Part 2, Department of State Publication, 9392, pp. 1056-1091. Referred to hereafter as Consultant Report
1953.
    [11] Ibid., pp. 1083-1084.

New York Times and the rest of the media as its opposite
is today. The present notion that we should avoid any element of defense or restraint in offense and should try to
assure mutual destruction is the anomaly—comparatively
recent and perverse innovation. It was *not*, as is widely
assumed, the basis for the second-strike theory of stable
deterrence from the beginning.[12]

In the intense emotions generated by the dispute over
the H-bomb, both the majority faction of the scientists who
opposed it and the important minority who favored the H-
bomb tended to caricature each other's views: one side
accused the other of being for offense only, and in turn was
said to be for defense only. The Panel of Consultants to the
State Department rejected the arguments that giving attention to continental defense was dangerous because "such a
change would require a lessening of our attention to the
development of our strategic air capability"; the panel said
this argument was "based on the mistaken notion that we
must have one or the other and cannot have both."[13] The
offense favored by scientists like Hans Bethe would "fit the
weapon to the target and . . . attempt the best accuracy . . .
to avoid unnecessary destruction."[14]

It was the Soviet intercontinental ballistic missile
(ICBM) tests and the Sputnik in 1957 which brought to an
end this decade of effort by the Manhattan Project physicists
to limit the catastrophic effects of nuclear war. The views
they then adopted, reversing their position 180 degrees,
paralleled a reversal in the views of the U.S. Navy and
followed the development of similar European views which
rationalized the spread of small nuclear forces to be aimed
exclusively at population centers. These views helped shape
the declaratory policy of Mutual Assured Destruction
adopted with substantial incoherence by the U.S. government five or six years later. They have persisted as the prospects for discriminating military from civilian targets
changed drastically for the better. The average yield of the
nuclear weapons we might "fit to targets" was 15 times larger
in 1957 than in 1982, and "the best accuracy" we expected

[12] Rand Reports R244S, *Selection of Strategic Base Systems*, March 1953, and R266,
Selection and Use of Strategic Air Bases, by A. Wohlstetter, F. Hoffman, R.J. Lutz and
H.S. Rowen (April 1954) June 1962, especially pp. 15–21, Santa Monica: Rand Corporation.
[13] Consultant Report 1953, *op. cit.*, p. 1085.
[14] Testimony of Dr. Hans Bethe, April 19, 1954, at the Atomic Energy Commission
Personnel Security Board Hearing, *In the Matter of J. Robert Oppenheimer*, Cambridge:
MIT Press, 1971, p. 329.

then has seen revolutionary improvement. It is ironic that for about a decade, when discrimination among targets was most difficult, major figures of the Manhattan Project called for it most intensely, and now that it is more possible than ever, many oppose it.

Early in this period of emphasis on defending and sparing civilians rather than killing them, the decision to go ahead with the H-bomb briefly generated a new and rather different discussion of a global catastrophe leaving no survivors. For some, the possibility of an ultimate nuclear catastrophic came up in a more ambiguous and, in fact, more ambivalent form: it appeared that one might actually want to rig the possiblity of a total nuclear catastrophe on purpose. Opponents of the H-bomb opposed it because of its enormous expected yields which made it possible for one warhead to destroy an entire large city, and which made it seem only for that purpose. Multi-megaton weapons seemed bad enough for the direct harm they might do, but Hans Bethe in 1950 raised the possibility that carbon-14 from exploding H-bombs might poison the air for 5,000 years and so make life impossible.

Bethe's calculations did not satisfy Leo Szilard because "it would take a very large number of bombs before life would be in danger from ordinary H-bombs." Szilard had something else in mind:

What I had in mind is this: the H-bomb, as it would be made, would not cause greater radioactivity than that which is due to the carbon; but it is very easy to arrange an H-bomb, *on purpose* [my emphasis], so that it should produce very dangerous radioactivity.[15]

Szilard did not estimate how many megatons of TNT equivalent yield the total number of H-bombs exploded might require in order to produce enough cobalt-60. (My colleague, Gregory Jones, has estimated roughly that it might come to 100,000 megatons—much more than all the megatons in the world's nuclear arsenals and, therefore, not really very cheap.) I have stressed Szilard's phrase "on purpose" because his concern was very different from the first scare about the A-bomb burning up the atmosphere, and

---

[15] "The Facts about the Hydrogen Bomb," The University of Chicago Round Table, *The H-Bomb*, New York: Didier, 1950, p. 113.

very different from Bethe's concern about the H-bombs. Szilard said that his Doomsday Machine (to anticipate Herman Kahn's name for a similar conceptual device) had a practical utility and was likely to be adopted by both the superpowers:

You may ask . . . who would want to kill everybody on earth? Let us suppose that we have a war and let us suppose that we are on the point of winning the war against Russia . . . . The Russians and others can say: 'You come no farther. You do not invade Europe, and you do not drop ordinary atom bombs on us, or else we will detonate our H-bombs and kill everybody.'

Faced with such a threat, I do not think that we could go forward.[16]

Asked whether any nation would really be willing to kill all people on earth rather than suffer defeat, and specifically whether we would be willing to do it, Szilard answered:

I do not know whether we would be willing to do it, and I do not know whether the Russians would be willing to do it. But I think that we may *threaten* to do it, and I think that the Russians might *threaten* to do it. And who will take the risk then not to take that threat seriously?[17]

Always a pioneer, Szilard in this response clearly foreshadowed the argument that was to become common among proponents of mutual destruction and even the end of the world (even though we would be unwilling to execute the threats), and that the threat would be enough for purposes of deterence. This was the line of argument that eventually culminated in the "Deterence Only" school of strategic thought.

When Herman Kahn invented a conceptual device he called the Doomsday Machine in 1960, he intended it as a reduction to absurdity of the view—increasingly popular in the academy after Sputnik—that targeting population was the cheapest and best way to deter nuclear attack. However, as was frequently the case with Szilard, it was not easy to tell whether his modest 1950 proposal for destroying everybody inexpensively was not also tongue-in-cheek.

---

[16] *Ibid.*, p. 114.
[17] *Ibid.*

Szilard pointed out that his Doomsday Machine would make it cheaper to kill everybody in the world rather than only in enemy territory. The global apocalypse, in short, would come at bargain prices.

Here again, Szilard was ahead of his time. The perverse arguments that began to pop up in academia after 1958 for avoiding military targets and focusing on cities took the implausible line that threats against military targets led to exponential increases in spending on both sides, since military targets could be more cheaply multiplied than cities. Targeting cities, therefore, was the only way to escape an arms race.

Today many theorists of global disaster seem unable to decide whether threatening cities and assuring mutual destruction is an evil or a good thing. Carl Sagan, for example, at one point in his recent essay on the implications for policy of nuclear winter, seems to express my own concerns about apocalyptic threats: "To the extent that these are not credible, they undermine deterrence; to the extent that they are credible, they set in motion events that tend toward apocalyptic conclusions." Sagan, however rejects weapons like "burrowing low-yield warheads," even though they would be much less likely to cause a climatic disaster, as "provocative". "They are the perfect post-TTAPS first-strike weapon."[18]

The jargon about "provocation" and "first strike" casually misuses the second-strike theory of deterrence. No single performance characteristic of a weapon, whether precision or warhead yield or speed of delivery, establishes whether a nuclear force has the capability for credibly performing a second strike, or a preclusive first strike, or both, or neither. In this context, such casual labels are merely code words for preferring large-yield warheads that do enormous collateral harm. Both low-yield, deep penetrating warheads and large-yield warheads exploding at the surface of the earth can destroy underground military targets. The difference is that the small penetrating warhead will do much less collatral harm, perhaps two orders of magnitude less.

---

[18] Carl Sagan, "Nuclear War and Climatic Catastrophe," *Foreign Affairs*, Winter 1983/84, pp. 284, 280.

In the intellectual confusion of contemporary MAD doctrine, it is the reduced risk of collateral damage, local and global, that is regarded as evil. And in spite of a welcome bow in the direction of abandoning apocalyptic threats, the basic thrust of many nuclear winter theorists is exactly the opposite of the earlier rejection of large H-bombs because of the enormous collateral harm they might do. The thrust, as foreshadowed by Szilard, is toward rigging things to make sure the harm would be global. On the other hand, the possibility of a global climatic disaster has recently made even some supporters of MAD threats doubtful about strikes against population centers. Now even they contemplate the need to avoid cities—or at least some cities.

But on the whole, theorists of nuclear winter, like supporters of MAD in general, continue to oppose the development of more discriminately effective offense and defense weapons or any preparations to respond to attack in ways that would confine destruction to military targets. That has influenced their choice of cases to investigate in ways that cloud their conclusions even more than the numerous uncertainties about the density of fuel near specific targets and the like in models of nuclear winter. They have selected cases calculated to create enormous collateral damage both local and global.

The many uncertainties that shroud nuclear winter come in several distinct kinds. The first has to do with whether, when and how an attacker, such as a Soviet planner, might choose to use nuclear weapons, and how many and what types of weapons he would use. He might choose to attack in the summer when concentrations of fuel are dry and most easily ignited and when his own crops are in their growing season and therefore likely to be affected most drastically. He may include in his initial attack many targets like steel mills that have no time urgency since they could not affect the course of a war for months or even a year, and do this even though their rapid initial destruction along with urgent targets would greatly increase the amount of smoke generated in an interval short enough to make nuclear winter effects far more likely.

He might decide to attack cities and other targets with high densities of fuel, such as oil refineries outside cities, and he may explode high-yield weapons at altitudes that would maximize the thermal pulse over combustible areas and so send smoke in huge quantities into the atmosphere. He may blindly barrage mobile or concealed military targets with little military but large environmental effect. And he may use multi-megaton weapons at or near the surface of the earth in ways that would maximize the chance of sending submicron dust in large quantities into the stratosphere.

On the other hand—far more likely—a Soviet planner might use nuclear weapons to accomplish some military purpose in the course of a war, and do it in a way that takes account of the fact that destruction extraneous to that purpose could cause a nuclear winter and make that military purpose idle. He could try to avoid these self-defeating effects. If he is involved, for example, in a conventional war on the critical northern or southeastern flanks of NATO, or in the Persian Gulf or in the center of NATO, and has suffered unexpected reverses, he might use nuclear weapons against selected targets whose destruction or paralysis could turn the tide of battle. He could do this perhaps by destroying or putting out of action, for the duration of the battle or the war, most aircraft and the maintenance facilities on main operating bases, munition stockpiles, defense radar and communications and the like; and he could block reinforcements from inside or outside the theater. Moreover, he could do this in a way that would least interfere with the movements of his own military forces and his other military efforts, and would also confine the generation of smoke or dust to levels well below the diffuse zone of uncertainty for severe global effects. Most precautionary measures taken to prevent harm locally to his military effort would also be useful in staying well below that zone.

A second sort of uncertainty concerns how the victim of an attack, such as NATO, might respond. If a Soviet attacker had used nuclear weapons with effects largely confined to military targets in a local theater of war, and if NATO had prepared no response except for devastating cities and risking a nuclear winter, it might not respond at all. Or, conceivably, it might respond in a way deliberately to assure mutual destruction and, incidentally, the ruin of the hemisphere. Or, far more likely, it would follow the Soviet attacker in restricting itself to measures that stopped key military operations but kept things from getting out of hand and destroying the planet.

There is the other case, in which the Soviets had launched an attack generating enough smoke and dust to have a substantial probability of bringing on severe global effects; NATO might then respond by generating still more smoke and dust and increasing the likelihood of even more severe effects and danger to the species. This would differ from the "tit-for-tat" response in the stereotype of mutual escalation. It would be tat-for-tat, NATO bombing itself in response to Soviet bombing of NATO. Or—again more likely—it might choose a form of response that would serve a military purpose but did not substantially further increase the probability of a ruin that would encompass the West as well as the East. Here too, boomerang effects may influence choice.

A third type of uncertainty has to do not with choice but with matters of fact. Some of these have been deplorably neglected but should yield to further empirical study, such as the density of fuel at various locations; related issues as to how the fuel would burn and generate various kinds of smoke and soot in varied circumstances may be harder to resolve.

All of these first three sorts of uncertainty, those that involve the choices of the two sides and those that have to do with the local concentrations of fuel of various sorts, have to do with the amount of smoke and submicron dust which would be generated and lofted into the troposphere and stratosphere during a nuclear conflict.

A fourth sort of uncertainty—one which will be under investigation for many years—is more complex than the third category. It has to do with how the smoke and dust are likely to be transported vertically and horizontally in the troposphere and stratosphere, how clouds of smoke particles might form and be reduced by rain-out, how much solar radiation would reach the earth through the smoke clouds, and how much infrared radiation would escape and the resulting light and heat at the earth's surface. The first-generation models of the atmosphere after a nuclear war were designed by experts on planetary atmospheres. They were more appropriate for studying nuclear war on desert planets like Mars than on the earth, most of whose surface is ocean. Current models indicate considerably smaller, though still substantial, effects for the huge exchanges.

Finally, there are the biological effects of possible patterns of change in temperature and light at the earth's surface. Biologists and physicians have been among the most prominent prophets of a global nuclear winter. Their work on global effects, however, has focused only on cases even more extreme than the enormous baseline cases looked at by the Swedish study in *Ambio*, TTAPS and NAS 85, and so far has been supported by less evidence than the work on climatic changes.

Of these five types of uncertainty, the first and second—those that involve choice—have been least satisfactorily addressed. Yet they are of immense importance and can dominate the rest. The weapons and strategies that adversaries choose make quite a difference. And alternatives that can reduce smoke and dust even more drastically have not been much explored. These first two sorts of uncertainties differ greatly from the others precisely in that they are a matter of choice. They are choices—partly independent and partly interlocking—made by the antagonists.

Nuclear winter theorists, however, tend to treat these uncertainties as if they were simply matters of chance uninfluenced by choice, like the collision of an asteroid with the earth or the impact of a comet that lofted devastating dust. Nuclear winter theorists treat antagonists as rather like asteroids and comets, or, at least so far as the application of intelligence is concerned, like the dinosaur that may have become extinct as the result of such a collision. They presume explicitly, at any rate, that the antagonists will make their choices of targets, methods of attack and timing without any intelligent considerations as to the likely implications of such choices for their own destruction by a nuclear winter. The NAS 85 study, for example, assumed that neither side would refrain from attacking military or economic targets located in cities in spite of the dangers of igniting their dense fuel. And, in fact, its baseline case involved explosions over 1,000 cities in proportion to their population—attacks in which each side's explosions are well designed to contribute to its own destruction.

Attacks on populations, or attacks which ignore collateral harm to population, of course, have had many advocates in the Western establishment. And even more members of the establishment consider that any use of nuclear weapons will end in devastating cities on both sides even if we try to avoid it. Nuclear winter theorists cite as justification for their assumptions statements not only by some Western strategists but by a good many former high officials—defense secretaries, chairmen of the Joint Chiefs of Staff and deputy directors of the Joint Strategic Targeting and Planning Staff.

What is novel in nuclear winter theory, what makes it capable of exhibiting with a particular clarity the incoherence and implausibility of much establishment doctrine, is that it assumes that each side will use weapons to bring about its own destruction not merely as part of a process of mutual "escalation," but directly with its own weapons. The rebound of one's own weapons eliminates the middleman in self-deterrence. Even if nuclear winter should ultimately turn out to be a less substantial danger, it will nonetheless have served a useful function. Its proponents carry one step further the assumption widespread in Western elites that in a nuclear conflict neither side would persist in choosing to keep the destruction done by its own weapons within bounds short of self-destruction.

Nuclear winter theorists also make clearer some of the absurdities in the Western view of Soviet behavior. Even apart from nuclear winter, one need not support, as some members of our foreign policy establishment assume, that only "gallantry" or some courtly interest in Western welfare would lead the Soviets to place limits on their use of nuclear weapons. The Soviets have always had strong reasons of self-interest not only to be wary about using nuclear weapons at all, but to try, if they should feel that the risks of using them in the course of a war are less than the risks of not using them, to keep the risks from getting completely out of hand. It is absurd to suppose that the Soviets would totally disregard the risk of disaster to themselves. Yet that may be a canonical assumption about Soviet attacks.

Moreover, it is one thing to say that political and military leaders sometimes mindlessly take the most self-destructive course. It is quite another thing to suppose that one's adversary will always either do nothing or mindlessly attack in a way that will do himself the most harm; and it is still another thing to recommend mindlessly suicidal behavior on our side, and to rig our preparations so that we could not respond against the source of attack without killing ourselves. When strategists rely on Mutual Assured Destruction, they assume intelligence can have essentially no influence at all.

Recent studies of a potential global nuclear disaster seem to generalize about the outcome of nuclear conflict— whether fought in a theater of operation in Europe or Asia; between the superpower homelands; with past, current or future weapons, of small or large yield, in modest or huge numbers; in accordance with present secret war plans or any future plans developed with the knowledge of these new global effects—and independently of whether the antagonists have prepared and try to restrict the damage done to each other or to themseles. In fact, the principal studies starting with a National Academy of Sciences report in 1975 (NAS 75) of the effect of nuclear war on the ozone, to the recent NAS 85 study on nuclear winter, take as their baseline case a conflict in which each adversary directs thousands or tens of thousands of weapons, many of very large yield, at locations and at burst altitudes calculated to do immense direct damage to the civil society of its antagonist; each thus also helps to bring on a global disaster destroying itself. The studies do not consider cases where either antagonist tries to confine damage to military targets or in any way tries to prevent damage to his own political, military or civilian resources.

The TTAPS baseline case assumed 5,000 total megatons, and 10,400 warheads with a yield between 0.1 and 10 mt. It assumed 1,000 mt would explode over urban or industrial areas, generating over 130 million tons of smoke. The remaining 4,000 mt exploding over non-urban land areas was calculated to generate an additional 95 million tons of smoke and to loft 65 million tons of submicron dust into the stratosphere.

NAS 85 assumed 6,500 mt and 25,000 nuclear explosions (the largest number of nuclear explosions in any of the studies); 3,500 of these, with a total yield of 1,500 mt, were assumed to be detonated over the largest 1,000 cities in NATO and the Warsaw Pact, generating 150 million tons of smoke. Explosions outside of cities were calculated to generate 30 million tons of smoke and to loft about 15 million tons of submicron dust into the stratosphere.

Are these "scenarios" of nuclear winter "reasonable" as is claimed? Not really. Neither the baseline cases nor the smaller excursions are. I have never been an enthusiast for the scenarios favored by many strategists and planners. They seldom have much relevance to the uncertain evolution of sequences of events likely in real contingencies. They seem more closely related to the movies or TV dramas that have given them their name. But the cases on which nuclear winter calculations have been based make little consistent sense even as scripts for movies. They hardly describe a sequence of events at all. Rather they list a collection of simultaneous explosions by the two antagonists well-designed to bring on a global disaster. In particular, such sets of explosions seem dubious as aspects of conflicts fought under the shadow of a nuclear winter.

The baseline cases are, first of all, huge. In fact, some may be infeasibly huge even if the contestants used the entire world arsenal and cooperated to detonate as many weapons as possible. The authors of these calculations seem only intermittently aware that in the normal course of a conflict some weapons would be duds or carried on vehicles that had some mechanical or operational failure preventing them from getting off the ground; some weapons would destroy other weapons (for example, weapons in stockpiles or weapons placed in vehicles that were hit on the ground or on their way to target), or both the attacking weapon and the weapons destroyed might explode at sea where they could do damage to naval targets without any substantial global effect on climate, and so on. The chairman of the panel that produced NAS 85 has suggested that, in assuming the explosing of 25,000 nuclear weapons (about half the world's arsenal), the panel "didn't want to take an extreme position," that it wanted to leave "planty of room on either side" of the estimate.[19] But it is more than doubtful that the two antagonists, even with much collaboration, using the entire world's stockpile, could arrange to explode that many nuclear warheads of the required range and distribution of yields.

Second, the explosions do seem to require a collaboration of the antatonists. Take the countersilo part of the NAS 85 baseline: the United States and the Soviet Union

---

[19] George Carrier, CBS transcript, *Face the Nation*, December 16, 1984, p. 2.

explode two bursts in the megaton range at the surface of the earth near each silo of the other side in order to assure that the missiles in silos will be destroyed. But with singular lack of success—since each side launches its missiles at the other side. In fact, this example illustrates a characteristic of these odd scenarios: attacks which are nominally directed at military targets seem to do very little direct harm to their military targets, but do manage a large contribution to global disaster.

Third, even if one were to assume that it is reasonable to direct a great many large-yield weapons at highly combustible cities, the choice of targets made by the pair of superpowers acting in unison seems rather bizarre. The Swedish Academy, for example, presumes that 15 nuclear explosions with a total yield of ten megatons will occur over each one of such cities as Manila, Jakarta, Bombay, Calcutta, New Delhi, Madras, Dacca, Sydney and Hong Kong. In a war between the United States and the Soviet Union? The Swedish Academy study in fact presumed that the two superpowers together would explode 173 mt in the southern hemisphere. The World Health Organization (WHO) topped that in its 1982 study on the biological effects of nuclear war: it assumed 1,000 mt would explode in the southern hemisphere.

Fourth, these baseline scenarios involve attacks on population centers on such an enormous scale that the direct destruction done locally seems almost imaginably large. The Swedish Academy scenario would directly kill or maim over a billion persons; WHO's scenario, over two billion. Professor Sagan makes much of the fact that these two billion casualties would be just the beginning: the global effects of smoke and soot might take care of the other half of the world's population.

Moreover, the "small" or "limited" scenarios may be even more absurd than the baseline cases. The TTAPS 100-mt exchange is the one most widely referred to as showing that any nuclear conflict, even a "limited" nuclear war, would trigger a devastating global change in climate. The 100-mt exchange is also the basis for estimates of the "threshold" number of missiles that would trigger a drastic climatic change, and therefore the maximum number of nuclear weapons that could safely be left undestroyed and replaced out of the world's stock of about 50,000 nuclear weapons—if we were to be sure that no combination of powers, no matter how mindless their behavior, could bring about a nuclear winter. But TTAP's 100-mt case, which involves one thousand 100-kiloton weapons exploding over the 100 most populated cities in NATO and the Warsaw Pact, is not "small." And it is certainly not "limited" in the relevant sense of illustrating the results of attempts to confine collateral damage to military targets.

Both sides, including whichever side may be thought of as striking first in this odd collaboration, ignore military targets—which makes this "limited" case even more absurd than the massive baseline scenarios. My colleague, Richard Brody, calculates that this 100-mt attack might cause as many as 300 million casualties directly and locally. This does not count the global effects which are worse for this 100-mt countercity attack, as TTAPS itself points out, then those of their 3,000-mt countersilo war. In fact, by changing the value of its fuel parameters, TTAPS derived about the same amount of smoke and soot (130 million tons) from this 100-mt case as from the 1,000 mt exploded over cities in its huge baseline case.

Professor Sagan has indicated the threshold suggested by the TTAPS 100-mt case in several ways: from 500 to 2,000 weapons or one percent of the world's nuclear arsenal (about 500 weapons); or one percent of the strategic offense warheads (about 180 weapons). However, the notion of a "threshold" here is quite deceptive—and not merely because there is no fine line nor even a well-defined band of uncertainty about the number of weapons that might trigger a global disaster. More important, the location of the diffused zones separating safety and disaster would depend on whether the weapon exploded were of high yield, detonated over cities or other dense concentratons of fuel, burst at high altitude or on the surface of the earth or well beneath it, and so on. So long as one assumes that nuclear weapons will be used mindlessly or deliberately to maximize the likelihood of disastrous global effects, the number of explosions would have to be extremely small to stay below the zone of uncertainty. The threshold numbers named by Professor Sagan *are* extremely small. No enforceable arms agreement is ever likely to reduce the world's arsenal by the required 99 or more percent. (The superpower agreement that Sagan suggests would beat swords into plowshares by

using the fissionable material in bombs for nuclear electric
power and would actually quickly *spread* plutonium useable
in bombs.[20]
    Nuclear disarmament will never be 99 and 44/100
percent pure. The most extensive nuclear disarmament feasible will not permit the luxury of the mindless use of those
nuclear weapons that may remain hidden. And disarmament
far short of 99 percent is a long way off. Nuclear winter
theorists propose such Utopian solutions because they reject
the idea that an attacker could use nuclear weapons for some
military purpose and yet confine the effects substantially
to military targets. They do not calculate the outcome for
the global environment of such a selective attack.
    In fact, the critical unexamined claim made by
nuclear winter theorists in drawing implications for policy
is that a Soviet or other prospective attacker would deter
himself without any need for a suicidal decision to respond
on the part of his victim; that the attack itself would cause
global harm engulfing the attacker even if the victim did
not respond. If the claim were true it would fill a void at
the very center of MAD doctrine.

    Since the dogma of Mutual Assured Destruction per-
sists in the West, it is worth spelling out clearly what makes
it hollow:
    (1) If a responsible political leader, contemplating a
strike in aggression, expects that he (and his political and
social order or his military force or whatever he values most)
will be harmed vastly more than if he does not strike, he
is unlikely to strike.
    (2) That is the basic theorem of the second-strike
theory of deterrence, phrased as it should be in terms of
comparing the risks of striking and not striking rather
than in terms of "acceptable damage." Where the harm
he might suffer in striking is at the extreme, we say the
aggressor will not attack because he does not want to commit suicide.

---

[20] Such an agreement has been proposed once again by George Kennan and Admiral
Gayler. It ignores the fact, public since 1976, that plutonium is not "denatured" by irradia-
tion in power reactors. Such plowshares make effective swords. Albert Wohlstetter,
"Spreading the Bomb without Quite Breaking the Rules," *Foreign Policy*, Winter 1976–
77, pp. 88–96, and Wohlstetter *et al.*, *Swords from Plowshares*, Chicago: University of
Chicago Press, 1979.

(3) But it is equally true and relevant that if a sensible political leader, contemplating a strike *in response* to aggression, expects that he and his entire political and social order will suffer a vastly greater disaster than if he does not respond, he is unlikely to decide in favor of responding. That follows from the same root assumption as the second-strike theory of deterrence. Where the harm he might suffer in responding is at the extreme, we can say he will not want to commit suicide. At any rate, he will not commit suicide in order to avoid death.

(4) If the aggressor can see that his victim has no response other than suicide, and that the victim is aware of that and says so all the time, then the aggressor may expect no response. If there is no response, he will suffer no harm. He may then find that his best way out of a palpable disaster, say, during a conventional invasion, is to launch a selective nuclear attack.

Some political leaders tend now to concede that a "deterrent" that promises no response is incoherent, but they cling nonetheless to the belief that it works and that it has worked for 40 years. But it has not. In the mid-1960s when Robert McNamara introduced the threat of Mutual Assured Destruction, he also made clear that if deterrence failed, the United States would respond with an attack designed to limit the damage, not to commit suicide. The drift toward not responding and the consequent erosion of the military balance and of deterrence is a quite recent phenomenon.

When the Soviets talk primarily for Westen ears, they indicate that if they ever attack they will do it massively and indiscriminately, even if it means the end of the world—either to frighten us into believing that it is futile to prepare to use nuclear weapons even in response to their use of nuclear weapons, or to lull us into believing that they would never use them. Or both. Such Soviet statements are in good part disinformation. They are a main support for the drift toward not responding, toward "Deterrence Only."

When Soviet military planners write primarily to inform each other, they may demonstrate an interest both in using force "massively," that is "decisively," to accomplish a key military purpose, and in using force selectively so as not to defeat that or any wider purpose. ("Size would reflect only the desire to achieve strategic results. [It] can be as few as several score weapons" to deliberately "reduce unwanted

and unnecessary damage."[21]) The development of their
military forces confirms this double interest. They are
increasingly capable of selecting some targets to be
immobilized or destroyed with important military effect
while leaving others essentially untouched. They have been
moving toward more precise, lower-yield weapons. This
ability to reduce unintended harm locally lessens also the
chance of bringing on a global disaster. Moreover, while the
Soviets show little interest in the purely symbolic, Western-
style use of nuclear weapons "to demonstrate resolve" and
"to send messages" in a process of "escalation control," their
force development shows a strong interest in keeping the battle under *their* control.

Any Soviet leadership which we could deter by
threatening disaster would also be deterred from an unlimited
strike by a prospect that the rebound from their own
weapons could, by itself, without our intervention, bring
disaster to the Politburo, Soviet military forces and Soviet
society. Soviet leaders would obviously prefer to extend their
control without having to fight at all. If they have to fight,
they would prefer to risk less and to win by conventional
means. If they do use nuclear weapons, they would prefer
to use them in a way that would not destroy their purpose
in attacking. But in any case they want to avoid suicide and
the end of life in the northern hemisphere. Members of the
Politburo do not believe in the hereafter. The Utopia the true
believers have sought—and the privileged rewards of the
nomenklatura—have to be realized here on earth. But
advocates of MAD, in their extremity, defy common sense.
In their zeal to show that the Soviets will always nullify any
defense we can construct, some scientists prophesy that if
the United States were to attempt any "serious" protection
of its cities, a "likely response" by the Soviet Union would
be "to target its missiles so as to maximize damage to the
U.S. population," even though that would "pose a serious
danger of triggering a climatic catastrophe (the nuclear
winter phenomenon)".[22]

Are the Soviets really possessed by so single-minded
and pure a passion to kill our harmless bystanders that they

---

[21] Joseph Douglass, Jr., *A Soviet Selective Targeting Strategy Towards Europe*,
Systems Planning Corporation Report, Arlington (Va.): SPC, August 1977, p. 1.
[22] Hans Bethe, Richard Garwin, Carl Sagan *et al.*, *Space-Based Missile Defense*,
Cambridge: Union of Concerned Scientists, 1984, p. 81.

would be willing to destroy themselves and any future for "communism" or for life itself in the Soviet Union? If so, they have an even better countermeasure to our ballistic missile defense. This one does not require them to penetrate our elaborate defenses at all: they could explode their warheads over their own cities in large enough numbers to bring on the death of the biosphere. Showing how hard it is for our advocates of MAD to beat Soviet efforts to make protection against Soviet attack seem hopeless, *Izvestia* recently printed a piece by Valentin Falin (former ambassador to West Germany) saying that the Soviets might very well counter our anti-ballistic missile defense in just that way: "No ABM options," Falin wrote ominously on December 14, 1984, "will change the fact that a precisely known quantity of nuclear devices detonated simultaneously on *one's own territory* would have irreversible global consequences [emphasis added]." If the Soviets were really that crazy, the prospects for arms control would be even dimmer than the skeptics believe.

Quite apart from the dangers of a nuclear winter, the Soviets have compelling incentives to use nuclear force selectively if at all. They have recognized this interest, as can be abundantly documented both from recently available materials of the Voroshilov General Staff Academy as well as from a fresh evaluation of Soviet military writings during the last 20 years.[23] Moreover, they are able to use nuclear force selectively and keep it under control, and have been greatly increasing this capability. I can only illustrate these points.

The most elementary concern the Soviets show for avoiding the indiscriminate use of nuclear weapons has to do, first, with local effects on their own military forces. They want to avoid "hindering the actions" of their "own troops,"[24] or having them "suffer heavy casualties" and "lose their combat capability," or having "their rear support

---

[23] Here I owe much to recent research of Dennis M. Gormley, Douglas M. Hart, John G. Hines, Phillip Petersen and especially Notra Trulock III, among others. My own citations merely illustrate these points rather than cumulate the evidence. But they suffice to refute the prevailing claim that the Soviets have shown no interest in keeping destruction under control.

[24] Colonel S.I. Krupnov, "The Dialectics of the Development of the Methods and Forms of Armed Combat," *Methodological Problems of Military Theory and Practice,* 2nd ed., Moscow: Voenizdat, 1969, pp. 340–361.

area . . . suffer heavy damages" and their "communications routes . . . destroyed."[25] And in particular they are concerned about "a break in the originally outlined plans for combat actions" and "an interruption in troop control."[26]

Second, the Soviets would prefer a Soviet Western Europe intact rather than in ruins. "The objective is not to turn the large economic and industrial region into a heap of ruins," but, among other things, "to sharply reduce the enemy capability to conduct strikes." Some "targets and regions should be left intact [to] strengthen the economic potential of our own country."[27] After World War II, the Soviets transferred whole factories from occupied lands and many German scientific and engineering cadres to the Soviet Union.

Third, Soviet military authorities have recognized the stake of both sides in exercising caution. "The accumulation of nuclear missiles," according to a contemporary statement, has "reached such extremes that their massive use could turn into catastrophic consequences for both sides."[28] This is not new; an earlier authority said that "the risk of destruction of one's own government" is so heavy that the belligerents will use other means to attain their objectives or, if not, will "limit themselves to inflicting some selective nuclear strikes on secondary objectives."[29]

Fourth, "in modern conditions, such [selective] nuclear attacks would primarily be the consequences of the expansion and development of a conventional war. . . ."[30] The conventional balance in the center of Europe is already very favorable to the Soviets. If they met unexpected reverses there, they could make up for them with a rather small number of low-yield nuclear weapons, precisely delivered and with quite confined damage. This sort of militarily

[25] Lecture materials from the Voroshilov General Staff Academy, "Strategic Operations in a Continental Theater of Military Operatons," (mid-1970s) cited in Notra Trulock's paper, "Weapons of Mass Destruction in Soviet Military Strategy," presented at the Conference on Soviet Military Strategy in Europe held in Oxfordshire, England, September 1984.

[26] Lieutenant General I.G. Zav'yalov, "The New Weapon and Military Art," *Krasnaya Zvezda (Red Star)*, October 30, 1970, pp. 2–3, reprinted in *Selected Soviet Military Writings, 1970–75*, U.S. Air Force, Washington, D.C.: GPO, 1977, pp. 206–213.

[27] Colonel M. Shirokov, "Military Geography at the Present Stage," *Military Thought (Voennaya Mysl')*, 1966, No. 11, pp. 59–61.

[28] Colonel General M.A. Gareyev, *M.V. Frunze—Voennyy Teoretik*, Moscow: Voenizdat, 1985, p. 240.

[29] General S.P. Ivanov, "Soviet Military Doctrine and Strategy," *Military Thought*, 1969, No. 5.

[30] Voroshilov lectures in Trulock, *op. cit.*

decisive contribution at the margin differs greatly from the "demonstrations of resolve" that figure in the Western strategic debate.

Fifth, the conventional war leading to the use of nuclear weapons may take place in a weakly armed but critical flank of NATO such as southeastern Turkey or its unstable neighbor Iran, and may be confined to that theater of military operations. That is not the canonical NATO scenario. But it is more likely to divide the allies and to give some the incentive and opportunity to opt out. The Soviets would risk less, and the autonomy of Europe would nonetheless be at stake. In World War II, they did not attack all their enemies at once but, successively, a weak Poland under attack also by Hitler, little Finland, the Baltic states, Bulgaria, then a Japan already beaten by the Allies. Hitler, a risk-taker, attacked the Soviets. Their military authorities do not exclude "the limited use of nuclear means in *one* or several theaters of military operations." Southeastern Turkey and the Persian Gulf are part of the Soviet southern theater.[31]

Sixth, even an intercontinental attack might be directed at disrupting the scheduled deployment from the United States of the military airlift tactical aircraft and ground forces most urgently needed for reinforcing NATO. The essential facilities involved are few, poorly protected and distant from any large population center; disrupting them would require only a modest number of air-burst weapons of moderate yield. Yet that could alter the "correlation of forces" decisively for a Soviet combined-arms invasion of Western Europe.[32] Such an attack could generate a thousand times less smoke than the baseline nuclear winter scenarios and essentially no stratospheric dust. The Soviets are greatly improving their ability to deliver weapons at long range precisely enough to employ low-yield nuclear weapons for such a purpose. (In fact, Marshal Nikolai Ogarkov has

---

[31] Marshal V.D. Sokolovsky and Major-General M.I. Cherednichenko, "Military Strategy and Its Problems," *Military Thought*, 1968, No. 10 (my emphasis). The U.S. Department of Defense, in its latest 1985 edition of *Soviet Military Power*, now recognizes that in the Soviet view "a nuclear exchange could occur in a limited or large-scale manner at the tactical, operational, strategic, or intercontinental level—or all simultaneously."

[32] Lieutenant General W.E. Odom, the new director of the National Security Agency, holds that the Soviets are much more likely to think of such an attack than the counter-silo exchanges that obsess Western analysts. "The Implications of Active Defense of NATO for Soviet Military Strategy," presented at the European American Institute for Security Workshop, November 1984.

stressed that the ongoing revolution in precision at very extended ranges will permit the use of *conventional* weapons deep in an adversary's homeland for some "strategic" purposes.[33])

The same incentives that impel the Soviets to be able to use nuclear weapons selectively impel them to *keep* the use of nuclear weapons under continuing control. In fact, the notion that Soviet political leaders would casually let nuclear weapons slip out of their hands is even less plausible than the notion that they might use them indiscriminately. For the Soviets have often been as brutal as they now are in Afghanistan; they might use nuclear weapons without much discrimination if it were a question only of compassion rather than their most elementary self-interest. Letting things get out of their political control, however, control that could decide the life or death of the party and their political order, is quite another matter. It has nothing whatsoever to recommend it in the Bolshevik canon.

The Politburo does not encourage spontaneity in the use of nuclear weapons. Nor is there any evidence that, after a few nuclear weapons were used, the Politburo would allow everyone in physical possession of them to fire at will. The Soviets will, of course, use *threats* of uncontrollability. We have seen some outstanding examples. But the threats were quickly followed by a demonstration that the Soviet political leaders had no intention of letting things get out of control.

During the Cuban missile crisis, for example, when confronted with the American threat to intercept, board and search a Russian freighter, Nikita Khrushchev asserted that this "would make talk useless" and bring into action the "forces and laws of war"; it would have "irretrievably fatal consequences."[34] However, when it became plain that President Kennedy was nonetheless proceeding to intercept Soviet freighters, Khrushchev changed his tune from ominous notes of uncontrollability to hasty reassurance that there was no occasion for the United States to act desperately. Khrushchev made clear he had no intention of deliberately responding in a massive way, of letting the laws of war take over, or of letting those romantic Cubans precipitate a nuclear

[33] Marshal N.V. Ogarkov, interview in *Krasnaya Zvezda*, May 9, 1984.
[34] Quoted by Roberta and Albert Wohlstetter, *Controlling the Risks in Cuba*, Adelphi Paper, London: International Institute for Strategic Studies (IISS), April 1965, p. 15.

conflict. Good, solid, stolid, sensible Russians were guarding the safety catches on the missiles in Cuba:

The means which are located on Cuba now, about which you are talking and which as you say concern you, are in the hands of Soviet officers. That is why any possibility of accidental usage of those means, which might cause harm to the United States, is excluded.[35]

After the crisis, Khrushchev made a good deal of the fact that he had "shown restraint" to save the world from imminent peril.

The Soviets clearly would want to maintain control. But could they? Arguments to the contrary proceed like arguments about collateral damage by assuming what they are supposed to be proving. In fact, the argument reduces to an unsupported or circular assertion about collateral damage and an equally circular assertion about "pressures for escalation."[36] Collateral damage from an initial attack, it is said would be essentially the same as from a direct attack on cities, now or in the future, no matter with what weapons or what targets. But evidence cited always seems to be based on calculations which assume the combatants do not try to reduce collateral damage.[37] They simply ignore attacks designed both to achieve a military purpose and to reduce unwanted harm. Much the same can be said of assertions about "escalation." These are usually spiced by statements that those in possession of a weapon would have to "use it or lose it." But using it could be a lot worse than losing it. On the nuclear winter theory, using a missile force indiscriminately might mean losing the hemisphere. All the

---

[35] *Ibid.*, p. 8. Cf. Nathan Leites' recent major study, *Soviet Style in War.*

[36] Raymond Aron, shortly before his recent death, observed that the formula "Better Red than Dead" is again becoming fashionable, and that once again ". . . the doctrinaires of capitulation . . . assume . . . escalation to extremes as inevitable. Once again, we find (an example of) begging the question: there is no limited nuclear war; or employment of a single nuclear weapon will suppress the taboo and open the floodgate: through the open breach will sweep in pure and unlimited violence, a homicidal and suicidal orgy. . . . why? Everyone agrees that a single nuclear weapon in Europe would spread terror: why will leaders on each side be led despite themselves to push further, to the limit?" "Suicide, Capitulation ou Riposte Limitée?" *Commentaire* (Paris), Spring 1984, p. 61.

[37] Desmond Ball, "Can Nuclear War Be Controlled?" Adelphi Paper No. 169, London: IISS, 1981, pp. 37–38. Ball refers for support to the oft-cited study by the Office of Technology Assessment for his conclusion that "even if cities were avoided, 100 nuclear detonations on key military or war-supporting facilities (such as refineries) would probably cause prompt fatalities in excess of a million people." But he is mistaken in assuming that the OTA example he refers to avoided cites. OTA explicitly assumed that no attempt was made to reduce collateral harm to population. Refineries in the heart of cities such as Los Angeles and Philadelphia were attacked.

enormous pressures to keep destruction within less than suicidal bounds are totally neglected.

Everything that we know about how the Soviets store and handle their nuclear weapons suggests that control is both extremely tight and well protected. For good reason. First, even more than the Western powers, the Soviets have to be concerned about the seizure of nuclear weapons by dissidents who might use them to help establish their independence from the Soviet government. The Soviets are in potentially hostile territory, not only in Eastern Europe, but in some parts of the Soviet Union. Second, the leadership is not unaware of the dangers of the "use it or lose it" syndrome. Marshal Ogarkov, to take one example, has rejected policies of "launch on warning," that is, launching one's own missiles on the basis of electromagnetic signals that enemy missiles are on their way to target.[38] Third, several Soviet military writers have made clear that not only is the decision to use nuclear weapons "the exclusive prerogative of the political leadership [but] it is the political leadership . . . not the military leadership . . . who select the primary targets and the moment of the infliction on these strike targets."[39]

Finally, the Soviets have spent tens of billions of dollars over many years to elaborate a mutually reinforcing network of measures for protecting political and military command and control that include deception, concealment, dispersal, mobility in the air, on the ground and below ground, deep underground structures and active defense.[40] Their formidable system is intended to survive in nuclear war, not just in peacetime. Those who speak easily of "decapitation" might consider the problem of destroying command in a deep underground structure whose location and actual use for command has been made uncertain by such measures. Take a hypothetical case where the command was located 1,000 feet deep in a spot unknown within a radius of, say, tens of miles. A blind barrage using many thousands of weapons could harm the environment without

[38] *The New York Times*, March 17, 1983, pp. 1, 6.
[39] Colonel M.P. Skirdo, *Narod, Armiya, Polkovodets (The People, the Army, the Commander)*, Moscow: Voenizdat, 1970, p. 121. Translated by the U.S. Air Force, Soviet Military Thought Series, No. 14. Washington, D.C.: GPO, 1978.
[40] U.S. Departments of Defense, *Soviet Military Power 1985*, pp. 17 ff.; and the Organization of the Joint Chiefs of Staff, *U.S. Military Posture FY 1985*, pp. 16–19; and Viktor Suvorov, *Inside the Soviet Army*, New York: Macmillan, 1982, pp. 153–155.

stopping command. In an era when precision endangers known fixed locations, making location uncertain is a powerful factor in assuring survival. The Soviets are exploiting such uncertainty not only in order to maintain command and control but, increasingly, to preserve the forces commanded. They are making their ICBMs, like their theater missiles, mobile.

In fact, many supporters of the doctrine of Mutual Assured Destruction are aware that the Soviets have made a huge investment in protecting wartime command and control; yet they oppose any major effort by the United States to improve its capability. They say that this would be a severe "provocation", to the Soviet Union.[41] No one suggests that the Soviet program has been excessively provocative.

Perhaps the most disturbing aspect of the dogma of Mutual Assured Destruction is that while it appears to be a description of a supposed fact, a state of affairs—the impossibility of discriminate attacks, the impossibility of maintaining control—it is really a policy which resists any *Western* improvements in precision and discriminateness and any *Western* attempts to keep destruction within less than suicidal bounds. Its proponents would force us to apocalyptic extremes.

Everyone sensible in the West assigns primacy to deterring nuclear war. This is clearly so even though scientists describing the effects of a global nuclear war often, as in the case of the Swedish Academy study, suggest in a now standard absurdity that U.S. decisions on defense are made in order to fight a nuclear war *rather* than to deter it.[42] The questions are how best to deter, whether that can be done without using apocalyptic threats, and whether we have to surrender freedom if deterrence fails. Nor should there be any issue about the West's need to rely less on nuclear weapons to deter a *non*-nuclear attack. Though Western

---

[41] See, for example, John Steinbruner, "Nuclear Decapitation," *Foreign Policy*, Winter 1981–82, p. 28. Desmond Ball's essay, "Can Nuclear War Be Controlled?" *op. cit.*, concludes that improvements in conventional force can better serve the purpose of improving control over our nuclear forces. But improved control of our nuclear forces has always been intended to deter or respond to Soviet selective *nuclear* attack and indeed at its abortive start in 1962 was part of a program that also called for reducing reliance on nuclear weapons and improving conventional forces. Both sorts of improvement are essential. Neither can replace the other. Both have lagged deplorably.

[42] Frank Barnaby, "The Effects of a Global Nuclear War: The Arsenals," *Ambio*, 1982, Vol. 11, No. 2–3 p. 78.

leaders—especially in Europe—have resisted it, that has seemed obvious for over 25 years.

Are we more likely to deter an attack by improving our ability to answer with the destruction of military targets rather than innocent bystanders, and by keeping the conflict under gross control? Or by making any nuclear war in which the West takes part as horrible as possible even if it means ending civilization and possibly the species? I have for many years advocated the first course. But that by no means implies that I think a war, even a non-nuclear war, is likely to be fought neatly, cleanly and, in Stanley Hoffmann's phrase, "without a smudge." Even if we could completely avoid the risk of killing bystanders—which we cannot—that would hardly make war and the slaughter of soldiers tempting.

The *live* issue is whether we should be trying to increase or to decrease our ability to discriminate between military and civilian targets, and to confine destruction to the military. There have already been revolutionary changes in precision, and therefore in the possibility of discrimination on both sides of the Iron Curtain. In spite of the enormous inertia of large military institutions and an ideology opposing precision that has dominated Western strategists for two decades, still greater improvements are under way. Nonetheless, even with these changes—past and future— some unintended harm would almost surely be done and there will always be the risk of losing control. Yet if we deliberately leave our own civilians defenseless and preclude the possibility of discrimination in responding to attack, we make a global nuclear disaster much more likely.

We should make clear that we will not respond to an attack in any way that would have a substantial chance of causing a nuclear winter. We should be prepared to use discriminating offense strategies, tactics and precise weapons with reduced yields and deliberately confined effects—such as weapons that penetrate and explode deep beneath rather than at the surface of the earth close to an underground military target; and to direct our weapons at the military rather than at bystanders—to select targets of a sort, number and location that will accomplish an important military purpose and yet contain the destruction. And we will benefit greatly if we can deploy a similarly discriminating *defense* that uses precise non-nuclear means to intercept

substantial numbers of enemy nuclear warheads on their
way to military targets located near our cities. We want
especially to emphasize the protection of the instruments
for exerising responsible control. The revolution in
microelectronics makes control more effective and easier to
defend since it permits less expensive, small packages of
reliable sensors, powerful data processors and communications that may be easily multiplied and moved. Our negotiations and agreements with the Soviets, moreover, should
be designed to further this policy of exercising discrimination and control, not to assure indiscriminate mutual
destruction.

Selective assaults—Soviet attacks that are clearly not
self-destroying—are the main threats the West must be
prepared to deter or counter. Yet the focus of attention among
our political and military leaders has been mainly on the
possibility of a massive and indiscriminate use of Soviet
nuclear force that would make nearly hopeless any Western
attempt to contain the conflict, and therefore any Western
response useless. Our elites vaguely hope against hope that
a useless, in fact improbably suicidal, Western response may
need to be only very slightly probable to deter an
indiscriminate uncontrolled Soviet attack. Now they grasp
at the possibility that a Soviet "all-out" attack—or any Soviet
attack—would destroy the attacker even without our
response.

The Western establishment only recently has begun
to face up to the possibility that the Soviets may use conventional force decisively. It continues to evade the military,
political and moral problems of responding in contingencies where the Soviets might use *nuclear* force decisively and
still leave both sides a large stake in avoiding suicide and
universal ruin. In such contingencies—the main ones worth
considering—any credible Western counter will itself have
to be well below the threshold of suicide, not to say universal ruin.

The West has limited options and needs more and
better ones in order to deter the plausible attacks. There is
no responsible *unlimited* option. This calls for greater clarity
in parts of our military as well as our anti-military establishment about what Soviet strategies will serve Soviet interests
in a variety of important and plausible contingencies, and
about what Western strategies in answer are responible ones.

When Western supporters of MAD say that MAD is a fact rather than a policy, they confuse prediction or description with prescription. Their expectations about future Soviet behavior are unqualified and more than dubious. Their statements about future U.S. behavior cannot be taken simply as predictions; they carelessly prescribe what we should do. They oppose improvements in offensive precision, discriminateness and control, and therefore implicitly support threats to destroy cities, and they oppose any defense.[43]

If MAD were simply a "fact," its proponents could hope to escape responsibility. But to rely on MAD threats and to try to restrict us to a capability solely to destroy civil society is to make a choice—a reckless choice, quite apart from any potential for disaster on a global scale. And the possibility of a nuclear winter makes the absurdity of MAD threats even clearer. That, however, is to draw nuclear winter's implications for policy in a way exactly opposed to that drawn by many theorists of nuclear winter most of the time.

Among the most revolutionary changes in precision that are in process, some will permit one or a few non-nuclear warheads effectively to destroy a variety of important military targets which previously had been thought of as susceptible only to nuclear attack or to huge non-nuclear raids. While such precisely delivered non-nuclear weapons are not likely to supplant nuclear weapons completely as a means of responding to nuclear attack, they have a large political importance—observed in the Soviet military literature, as well as in the West's—in reducing the pressures to resort to nuclear weapons. They would greatly increase the possibility of keeping a conflict under control. And they can reduce the one-square-mile area in which bystanders would be subject to unintended harm from even a small nuclear weapon to a thousandth of a square mile.

That should impress us. We tend to lose perspective. One square mile of destruction is still an enormous amount for a single weapon. We obscure these essential distinctions when we say, as do many who talk about "a spiralling race in weapons of mass destruction," that increasing precision implies that weapons are becoming more "destructive." For

---

[43] It was supporters of MAD during the ABM debate who revived the reckless idea that instead of defending ICBMs we should launch them on warning at Soviet cities. See, for example, R. Garwin, letter to The New York Times, October 22, 1967.

achieving a given military effect they are becoming *less* indiscriminately destructive.

There has been much misunderstanding on this subject. It has been said that the improved precision now feasible means that there is no important difference between nuclear and non-nuclear weapons. That is not the case at all. The key difference has to do with unintended harm. Non-nuclear weapons will not be as effective as nuclear weapons against military targets for some missions in response to nuclear attack. But the extreme precision required to make conventional weapons effective on some major military missions also makes them more discriminate than even small nuclear weapons. Furthermore, essentially the same technologies that make a discriminating offense possible will also make increasingly feasible a non-nuclear defense that can intercept nuclear or non-nuclear ballistic missiles on their way to targets in the United States and Western Europe. And they improve our ability to keep destruction under control.

Many things besides technology are relevant to the issues of how best to deter Soviet attack. The preoccupation of many scientists and strategists with the technologies of releasing nuclear energy has been obsessive. A technological determinism has led them to focus almost exclusively on nuclear brute force. The most characteristic and important technologies of our time concern information, sensing and the extension of discriminating and intelligent control. But the spectacular terrors of Hiroshima and the peculiar mixture of pride and guilt about nuclear energy felt by key figures in the Manhattan Project have encouraged us to think of our time as "The Nuclear Age," the age of the apocalypse, and even to take a certain comfort from the possible totality of the menace.

Let me summarize:

First, there is a substantial probability that if, in the course of a war, the opponents were to explode many thousands of high-yield nuclear weapons over targets in cities, they would directly kill or maim so many civilians and destroy so much of the substructure of civil society that little would be left of civilization on either side.

Second, while there are very large uncertainties that will not soon be resolved, there is also some finite chance that, aside from the enormous direct local destruction, such attacks might have global consequences endangering the species.

Third, this apocalyptic possibility underlines the necessity not only for relying less on nuclear weapons to counter conventional attack, but also for exercising restraint and discrimination in responding to nuclear attack. It does not mean that we have to ignore the long Western tradition that imposes constraints on conflict and calls for discrimination and proportionality. On the contrary, it makes that tradition more relevant than ever. It forms one more knockdown argument against preparing to respond to nuclear attack by destroying innocent bystanders in mass, and against eschewing any capability to respond by attacking military targets effectively with the least harm done to population that we can manage, including the least danger of initiating a nuclear winter.

Fourth, we do not have to subordinate all considerations of freedom in order to avoid the apocalypse. On the contrary, the chances of our avoiding catastrophe are much larger if Western leaders keep their heads and freedom of choice. Raymond Aron and Sidney Hook both pointed out that submission to a totalitarian power would not eliminate the risk of war. Nor, in a world that has known nuclear weapons, would it eliminate the possibility that the violence of such a war might climb to the nuclear level.

They were right. Communist Vietnam has attacked Communist Kampuchea. Communist China has fought Vietnam. And the only two nuclear-armed countries whose military forces have ever been locked in battle are Communist China and the Soviet Union. Even a nominally single totalitarian world is quite capable of dissolving into what would then have to be called civil wars rather than wars between nations. Nuclear weapons can easily be hidden, and also rather easily and quickly produced as a byproduct of nuclear electric power. They can be delivered by civil as well as ordinary military aircraft. In such a world, conventional conflicts could lead to the use of nuclear weapons and also to the mindless expansion of such use.

Fifth, escalation, of course, would not be inevitable even then. The People's Republic of China and the Soviet Union have used military force against each other warily. For the Chinese and Soviet communists, it is obviously "better to be red than dead." But then there is nothing inevitable about the escalation by a democraic government of the use of nuclear weapons to universal ruin, though it sometimes seems that ideologues in the West would like to make it so. They would like, at any rate, to foreclose any Western options for responding to nuclear attack other than the extremes of bringing on the apocalypse or giving up. Those who conjure up a vision of an imminent apocalyse to lend urgency to the potential surrender of Western autonomy would not eliminate that nightmare by subordinating the West to totalitarian power. In short, the alternatives are not whether to be red or dead. It is possible to be both red and dead. Or neither.

1985

MAINTAINING GLOBAL STABILITY

James R. Schlesinger

James R. Schlesinger currently serves as senior advisor at the Center of Strategic and International Studies at Georgetown University. He formerly served as Secretary of Defense and Secretary of Energy.

Though history can provide some guidance in the discharge of our international responsibilities, we must ever be aware that the position of the United States in this era is historically unique. Never before has a nation attempted to maintain stability essentially on a global basis. That task, immense as it is in itself, is made even more difficult in that the nation attempting to maintain stability is also a political democracy—and one with strong moral impulses. Therefore it is simply a fact of life, perhaps unwelcome to some, that foreign policy must take public sentiments into account and cannot simply be guided by calculations of *Realpolitik*. It should also be noted that in the United States there is little deference to a governing class. As a consequence any administration that persistently defies public sentiment on foreign policy is likely to be ousted.

In certain respects the task of fulfilling U.S. international responsibilities has become gradually more arduous since the end of the era that succeeded World War II. At the close of that war the United States was the preeminent

Reprinted with permission of James R. Schlesinger. Copyright © 1985 by James R. Schlesinger.

power in the world—economically, politically, and, within limits, militarily. Reasonable policy objectives were sustained with remarkable ease. For the American society it was a happy period—one to which many look with nostalgia. From an American perspective the only misfortune was that our preeminence was inherently transitory. As the war-torn powers of Europe and Asia recovered and as the Soviet Union gradually equipped itself to counter the military advantages of the United States, our position inevitably declined.

For an extended period it was easy for the United States to fulfill its commitments. And, it might be added, a national consensus backed those commitments. When the United States clearly defined its objectives, even in circumstances as inherently unfavorable as northern Iran or the Berlin airlift, the Soviet Union felt obliged to give way. Even as late as 1956, at the time of the Hungarian rising, the Soviet Union had to consider the possibility of direct American involvement. Clearly by 1968 in Czechoslovakia or by 1981 in Poland, the potential reach of U.S. power had been markedly reduced. In the 1950s Secretary Dulles could articulate the reality of U.S. strategic dominance in the doctrine of massive retaliation. Despite grave reservations in the intellectual community, for a while the doctrine worked quite well. But the era in which the United States could fulfill its commitments at relatively low risk could not long be sustained. Quite simply the United States was destined to lose its preeminence and, consequently, the doctrine of massive retaliation (which so eased the problem of meeting international commitments) would no longer be tenable.

As the United States lost its position of preeminence, its role inevitably changed. The decline of American power meant that the United States would be more regularly tested. Challenges of a sort previously unthinkable became inevitable. North Vietnam, Khomeini's Iran, and Sandinista Nicaragua are the outstanding examples of this changed environment. Perhaps one need do no more than contrast the ease and the success of the United States involvement in Lebanon in 1958 and in 1981-1982 to underscore the relative decline in American power and the increased difficulty for the United States in achieving its international objectives.

The upshot is that the United States can no longer have its way as readily as in the past. The United States will, as the saying goes, win some and lose some. When it does suffer a serious setback, as in Lebanon recently, that fact may not be fully borne home to the American public, whose chief reaction may be one of relief. Any defeat will, however, not go unnoticed by other audiences in the world. American loss not only damages our prestige, but it further reduces our capacity to fulfill our commitments. Yet, even under the best of circumstances, some losses are unavoidable. And, if we extricate ourselves with considerable dispatch and skill, the loss (as in Lebanon) may in some quarters be softened by admiration of our skill in extrication, perhaps in accordance with the ancient adage that he who fights and runs away lives to fight another day.

The decline of American power is made more serious by the simultaneous end of the national consensus on foreign policy, which was shattered by Vietnam. Associated with the end of national consensus has been the revival of conflict between the executive and legislative branches, a conflict inherent in the separation of powers, but which had been largely dormant in the period from Pearl Harbor to Tet.

There are, of course, ironies in these developments. At a time when our gross advantages in military power have declined, a national consensus is more necessary than heretofore to make our residual power more effective. Moreover, any domestic divisions weaken our capacity to make use of whatever power we have.

But pointing to ironies does not alter reality. A national consensus cannot be merely wished into being. It can be restored only gradually over time, if at all. It will come about only through the development of mutual trust, reasonable success and the sustained credibility of the executive branch. Conflict between the executive and the legislative branches also cannot be wished away. Legislative power may have been dormant in the 1950s and 1960s but it is now aroused. The deference earlier shown to the executive branch is not likely to be quickly restored. Whatever the longings of some past and present officials of the executive branch to "roll-back the legislative intrusion," the good old days (which means only the post-World War II days) will not return.

These changes on the international and domestic scenes create new dilemmas for American foreign policy. While the United States remains the leading nation on the international scene, its power, which earlier was scarcely disputable, is now very much disputable. Simultaneously—and by coincidence—national unity has been fractured—both in terms of the national consensus and in terms of the agreement between the executive and legislative branches. In short, these changes imply that the costs and risks of sustaining our international position have risen. Despite the relative decline of American power, not only in relation to the Soviet Union but even in relation to some Third World countries, the degree of American commitment worldwide has generally not altered. Indeed in some parts of the world, most notably in the Persian Gulf region, those commitments have risen.

The unchanged status of U.S. commitments accompanied by the relative decline of American power and the evaporation of national unity have led to two distinct gaps: the commitments-power and the consensus-policy gaps.

The reality that our commitments stretch thin our available resources has led to some hankering, especially during the Vietnam period, that we reduce our commitments to match our resources and thereby lower the risks the United States faces on the international scene. Generally speaking such expressions have been merely a longing. To the extent that such longings reflected a desire to significantly reduce military spending, they have rested on an illusion. The central foreign policy commitment of the United States since World War II has been to sustain a free Europe and it is to this commitment that the overall cost and structure of the U.S. military establishment has primarily been addressed. Senator McGovern is the only candidate in modern times who has directly challenged that commitment. His slogan of "come home, America" would have solved the power-commitments gaps, though in my judgment would have raised other and far greater difficulties. The Mansfield Amendment chipped away at that commitment to European defense, although it did not challenge it directly. If we are to sustain our obligations in Western Europe (which I believe we must) the hope for substantial reductions in our military posture is illusory.

From time to time attempts have been made to curb our involvement in other parts of the world, which appear less central to American foreign policy. The Nixon Doctrine, promulgated under the pressure of public opinion during

Vietnam, was one such attempt. It resulted in a thinning of our forces in several regions around the world. Perhaps its most distinctive feature was its attempt to establish the Shah of Iran as the principal guarantor of Western interests in the Persian Gulf. Even at the peak of his power, that concept imposed greater responsibility on the Shah's regime than the government could sustain. From the standpoint of the power-commitments gap, the irony lies in the major expansion of U.S. commitment in that region since the Shah's downfall—even in a period when our power relative to our commitments was still shrinking. Both the Carter Doctrine and the Reagan corollary imply a degree of U.S. commitment with which, to put it gently, our capabilities are not well matched.

President Carter also attempted to reduce our forces in Korea—a change in our overseas military posture that has intermittently been suggested since the close of the Korean War. The withdrawal of our ground forces was vigorously resisted on Capitol Hill—even by some individuals who previously had urged an adjustment of our commitments to our power.

I use these incidents to underscore a fundamental reality: it is far easier for individuals to call for reduced commitments in the abstract than it is for a great power to actually define those commitments that should be reduced or jettisoned. For any great power to back away from commitments is more easily said than done, especially the protecting superpower of the West. In practice, the loss in prestige may actually reduce our power more than the reduced claims on our militay resources enhance that power. In that may lie the supreme irony. Closing the power-commitments gap may not be possible through reduction of commitments. The United States, as a great power, has essentially taken on the task of sustaining the international order. Any abandonment of major commitments is difficult to reconcile with that imposing task.

The upshot is that our commitments will remain large and that our military power will remain more modest in relation to those commitments than it has in the past. That implies a degree of risk that we must acknowledge and accept. Try as we will, there is no acceptable way that we can escape from either these responsibilities or these risks.

It is of course the recognition of these costs and risks that has led to the so-called consensus-policy gap. Fulfilling our commitments was relatively simple in the past. When we had the visible power to smash our potential foes—as in the 1950s and 1960s—there was little difficulty in sustaining domestic agreement. Vietnam transformed domestic attitudes. The human and financial costs of conflict were brought home to the American public. Since then there has been a notable reluctance to see American forces become engaged notably in Third World areas. It has become potentially quite difficult to foster a national consensus in the event that U.S. troops become engaged abroad. No administration is eager to accept the domestic political penalties and the domestic divisions inherent in using U.S. forces to stabilize Third World areas.

In such places as Lebanon or Central America there is little question regarding the raw physical power of the United States to impose its will. There is no power-commitment gap, but rather a consensus-policy gap. Other nations have come to doubt, not the abstract power of the United States to achieve its goals, but rather its staying power in sustaining them. It is notable that this administration has shied away from engaging American forces in Central America—and also withdrew American forces from Lebanon despite some embarrassment, when the cost began to rise. Thus ultimately we are faced with a paradox. In dealing with what is the central strategic problem of the United States, the formidable capabilities of the Soviet Union in relation to finite American power, there is at base a domestic consensus with respect to both protection of the North American continent and our obligations in Europe. Yet, paradoxically it is here in this arena where the consensus is not seriously challenged that we may face a real gap between power and commitments. By contrast, in much of the Third World, in which our power is commensurate with our commitments, there is no domestic consensus regarding the prospective use of force. Thus, overall, in all parts of the world we are likely to have to contend with at least one of the two gaps. Such is the penalty for the loss of our postwar preeminence.

These perplexities lie behind the disputes between the Secretary of State and the Secretary of Defense. In effect, the Secretary of Defense has insisted upon domestic consensus before U.S. forces become employed. Given the circumstances, that is indeed a demanding requirement. Were it to be rigorously implemented, it would virtually assure other powers that they can count on not facing U.S. forces. Nonetheless, Secretary Weinberger has clearly and repeatedly indicated his willingness for the United States to face down the Soviet Union—a far more onerous commitment. It is for this reason that the Secretary has fretted about our military weaknesses (in respect to the Soviet Union) and has insisted on stronger military forces, which (in at least a superficial paradox) he argues should not be used in the most likely contingencies.

I cannot concur with the emerging belief that the United States must only fight popular, winnable wars. Such a self-denying ordinance is scarcely consistent with public support of the expanded defense spending of recent years. The likeliest physical challenges to the United States must come in the Third World—not in Europe or North America. If the more predatory states in the Third World are given assurance that they can employ, directly or indirectly, physical force against American interests with impunity, they will feel far less restraint in acting against our interests.

Much of American foreign policy inevitably is concerned with such problems. In a recent dispute Secretary Shultz may have somewhat overstated his case. I for one do not believe that there is a political base in this country for U.S. preemption against terrorist groups. Nonetheless, he is right with respect to his essential point: the United States must be prepared to retaliate against those who repeatedly employ physical force against our interests. It cannot allow an assured free ride. It ought not to give assurance to others that U.S. forces will never retaliate. It should not announce in advance what it will not do; that is unsound strategy. In the face of repeated provocations, the United States must be prepared to selectively retaliate.

All nations love "glorious little wars." Even World War II with its sequential victories was immensely popular in Germany, until 1942. The intelligentsia will, no doubt, have misgivings since public enthusiasm sweeps away serious legal and moral questions. But popular support is hardly weakened by such quibbles. Thus, it is useful to have a Grenada to trump a loser like Beirut. But from the national perspective such easy victories resolve remarkably little. If a conflict is sufficiently easy to be a glorious war, it is certain to be marginal to our interests.

Americans historically have embraced crusades (such as World War II) as well as glorious little wars. The difficulty is that the most likely conflicts of the future fall between crusades and such brief encounters as Grenada or Mayaguez. Yet, these inbetween conflicts have weak public support. Even in the best of times— with national unity and at the height of our power—public enthusiasm for Korea and Vietnam evaporated in just a year or two. Indeed, any war that is not a clearcut winner will not long enjoy public enthusiasm.

The problem is that virtually no opportunity exists for future crusades and those glorious little wars are likely to occur infrequently. The role of the United States in the world is such that it must be prepared for, be prepared to threaten, and be prepared to fight those intermediate conflicts that are likely to fare poorly on television.

Whether this nation, the leader of the free world, can measure up to such challenges will to a large extent define the future shape of international politics.

In the past twenty years, as our relative power has receded, our commitments have not receded commensurately. Indeed they have grown. Thus we unavoidably live with a higher level of risk. Such risks make it far more difficult, even in the best of times, to achieve domestic consensus regarding national policy.

Is there a path out of these perplexities? I wish I could suggest one. However, there is none. The United States is now obliged to live with the risks that have been the lot of all other nations less favored than we have been throughout much of our history. We shall have to bear continuously a degree of risk that is unwelcome.

In the aggregate, our international commitments exceed our capabilities to fulfill all of them simultaneously. Yet it is not easy for a great power to shed its commitments. Our commitments will continue to exceed our resources. Prudent planners will argue that we are running a bluff. Worriers will simply worry. But in fact it will represent the conscious acceptance of risk and a conviction that not everything will go wrong simultaneously.

None of the usual solutions is available to eliminate those perplexities. Despite all our longings we are not in a position to dramatically redefine our commitments. As a practical matter there is no way to unilaterally augment our forces to the extent necessary to reduce risk to a comfortable level. (Perhaps I should add that the president's Strategic Defense Initiative is not a panacea that could restore the United States' historic advantages. For any who embrace such a hope, it is illusory. Nor is it possible to engage our allies overseas to a degree that will eliminate either our responsibilities or our risks. No doubt, our allies should do more. Their real budget problems (as well as, in some cases, the desire for an essentially free ride) mean that we will not improve the Western position sufficiently so that we can cease to rely on nuclear deterrence.

Finally, although I am a strong proponent of arms control, it can never reduce the Soviet threat to a point at which we would be comfortable. Various measures may indeed limit certain risks, perhaps most notably the risk of instability. But the Soviet Union has achieved, and will continue to achieve, its international objectives by placing the United States in a position of risk that we find unwelcome. There is no conceivable set of arms control measures that could persuade the Soviet Union to ease the discomfort that the United States feels in bearing risk. For to do so means that the Soviets would be obliged to accept what would appear to them to be an intolerable level of risk. This condition of the international scene will continue until some distant date when there may be a change of heart with respect to basic ideological differences.